The Philosophy and Religion of Śrī Caitanya

(*The Philosophical Background of the Hare Krishna Movement*)

First Edition, 1977

PUBLISHED BY MUNSHIRAM MANOHARLAL PUBLISHERS PVT. LTD.
54 RANI JHANSI ROAD, NEW DELHI-110055. PRINTED IN INDIA
BY MODERN PRINTERS, K-30, NAVIN SHAHADRA, DELHI-110032.

Contents

Abbreviations vii
Preface ix
Chapter I *Pre-Caitanya Vaiṣṇavism* 1
Early History of Vaiṣṇavism 1
The Four Vaiṣṇava Saṁpradāyas (Sects) *7*
Pre-Caitanya Vaiṣṇavism in Bengal *13*
Chapter II *The life of Śrī Caitanya* 16
Birth and Divinity *16*
The Naughty Boy *17*
The Student *18*
The Householder *19*
Initiation and the Upsurge of Divine Love *20*
The Leader of Vaiṣṇavas *22*
Saṁkīrtana *23*
Saṁnyāsa *24*
Journey to Purī and the Conversion of Sārvabhauma *25*
Travel in South India and the Meeting with Rāmānanda *26*
The Conversion of Pratāparudra *28*
Pilgrimage to Vṛndāvana *29*
The Last Days in Purī and the Mysterious Passing Away *33*
Chapter III *The Saṁpradāya of Śrī Caitanya* 36
Affiliation with Mādhva *36*
Affiliation with Śaṁkara *46*
Chapter IV *Materials for the Philosophy of Śrī Caitanya* 53
The Works of the Six Gosvāmins *54*
The Biographies *57*
Chapter V *Sources of Knowledge* 63
Vaiduṣa Pratyakṣa (Mystical Cognition) *65*
Śabda (Revelation) *70*
Śrīmad-bhāgavata *72*
Chapter VI *Nature of the Absolute* 76
The Nirviśeṣa (Unqualified) Brahman *76*
The Absolute as both Saviśeṣa (Qualified) and Nirviśeṣa (Unqualified) *83*

The Inconceivable Power of Brahman to Reconcile the Irreconcilable *85*

Chapter VII *The Concept of the Absolute as Bhagavān* 90

Brahman, Paramātman and Bhagavān *91*

The Śaktis of Bhagavān *95*

Chapter VIII *Bhagavān Kṛṣṇa* 101

The Infinite Partial Manifestation of Kṛṣṇa *101*

The Dhāman (Celestial Abode) of Kṛṣṇa *107*

The Parikaras (Retinue) of Kṛṣṇa *113*

The Līlā (Beatific Sports) of Kṛṣṇa *115*

Kṛṣṇa as Rasa *117*

The Mādhurya (Sweetness) of Śrī Kṛṣṇa *123*

The Manner and Purpose of Kṛṣṇa's Appearance on Earth *126*

Chapter IX *Jīva—The Finite Self* 132

Mukti—Freedom from Bondage *136*

The Ultimate End *139*

Chapter X *The Phenomenal World* 142

The Doctrine of Māyā *142*

The Process of Creation *144*

Śakti-Pariṇāmavāda *145*

Chapter XI *The Doctrine of Acintya-bhedābheda* 150

Acintya-bhedābheda and the Advaita Vedānta of Śaṁkara *158*

Acintya-bhedābheda and Viśiṣṭādvaita of Rāmānuja *163*

Acintya-bhedābheda and Svābhāvika-bhedābheda of Nimbārka *166*

Acintya-bhedābheda and Bhedavāda of Mādhva *169*

Acintya-bhedābheda and Śuddhādvaita of Vallabhācārya *172*

Chapter XII *Bhakti, the Means* 176

Bhakti, Jnāna, Karman and Yoga *177*

The Nature (Svarūpa-lakṣaṇa) of Bhakti *180*

The Effects of Bhakti *184*

Sādhana-Bhakti *187*

Ritualistic (Vaidhī) and Spontaneous (Rāgānuga Bhakti) *194*

Chapter XIII *Priti, the End* 199

Stages in the Development of Prīti *201*

Higher Stages in Prīti *203*

Sthāyī Bhāva (Basic Emotions) *211*

Chapter XIV *Rasa or Transcendental Relish* 213

Madhura-rasa and Eroticism *216*

Parakīyā Rasa *221*

Select Bibliography 231

Index 237

Abbreviations

CC	*Caitanya-caritāmṛta by* Kṛṣṇa Dās Kavirāj*
C.Bh.	*Caitanya-bhāgavata by* Vṛndāvan Dās*
Bh.	*Bhāgavata-purāṇa*
Br.S.	*Brahma-sūtra.*
S.Bh.	*Śaṁkara-bhāṣya*
G.Bh.	*Govinda-bhāṣya by* Baladeva Vidyābhūṣaṇa
SR	*Siddhānta-ratna by* Baladeva Vidyābhūṣaṇa
TS	*Tattva-saṁdarbha by* Jīva Gosvāmin
Bh.S.	*Bhāgavat-saṁdarbha by* Jīva Gosvāmin
Par.S.	*Paramātma-saṁdarbha by* Jīva Gosvāmin
KS	*Kṛṣṇa-saṁdarbha by* Jīva Gosvāmin
BS	*Bhakti-saṁdarbha by* Jīva Gosvāmin
Pr.S.	*Prīti-saṁdarbha by* Jīva Gosvāmin
SS	*Sarva-saṁvādinī by* Jīva Gosvāmin
Br.Bh.	*Bṛhad-bhāgavatāmṛta by* Sanātana Gosvāmin

*References are to the edition by Radha Govinda Nath, in which the Sanskrit Slokas and the Bengali verses are separately numbered. Where reference is to a Sloka this is indicated by the letter 'Ś,' which precedes the number.

Preface

Whether we judge the intensity of a devotee's love for God by the frantic outbursts of emotion that reveal the inner working of his heart; whether we measure him by the range and depth of his spiritual realisation and the height of bliss perpetually experienced by him; or, whether we apply to him the test of shaping the minds and moulding the lives of his associates and followers by the magnetic influence of his personality, Śrī Caitanya stands out as the brightest luminary of divine love on the spiritual firmament of the world. His bountiful distribution of the nectar of divine love to the rich and the poor, the young and the old, the good and the wicked, regardless of any barriers of caste and creed; his congregational chantings of the ı ame of Lord, in which lakhs and lakhs of men joined at a time; his triumphs of love over his enemies; and the chastening effect of the mere touch and presence of his personality, which turned the kings and the chiefs into ascetics and the cruelest and the most hardened of sinners into saints, and made even the fiercest of animals dance with the joy of divine love, are all unparalleled in history.

The intensely devotional character of the personality of Śrī Caitanya, however, has eclipsed his philosophy. His place has been among the devotees and the mystics rather than among the philosophers. But the devotional side of his personality itself suggests a corresponding philosophical side of his nature—a definite and perfect sense of Reality, which must account for the particular way in which his heart and soul reacted to it. It is a mistake to suppose that the predominance of emotions in the life of a devotee renders him incapable of serious philosophical thinking. On the contrary, his understanding is so developed and purified that his grasp of things is more intuitive than ratiocinative and his knowledge of reality is more intimate and complete. His emotions are the natural outcome of his close apprehension of Reality.

It is not necessary for a devotee, who is in direct and intimate touch with reality, to supplement his knowledge by undergoing training in one of the accredited schools of learning. But Śrī Caitanya had the additional advantage of high scholarship, which enabled him to express his thoughts with the precision, accuracy and consistency that characterise a system of philosophy. It is true that he did not himself write any philosophical treatise, but he imparted philosophical teachings to his disciples, whose learned works are based on them.

It will be our endeavour in the present work to set forth in a systematic manner the philosophical and religious doctrine of Śrī Caitanya on the basis of his utterances, as contained in his biographies, some of which give an elaborate and authoritative account of his teachings to Rūpa, Sanātana and others, and some of the important works of his followers, which were written under his express command and according to the guide-lines provided by him.

The author is fully conscious of his responsibility in formulating the philosophy of Śrī Caitanya and the necessity of approaching the subject with an unbiased mind. The fact that he has sometimes argued as Śrī Caitanya himself would, in defence of his position, need not suggest that he has a sectarian outlook. He has only endeavoured by sympathetic understanding to enter deep into the spirit of his philosophy and represent it as accurately as possible. If he appears at times to own views, which are identical with those of Śrī Caitanya, it is only because of the non-sectarian and all-embracing character of his philosophy, which transcends all sectarian and mutually conflicting views and reconciles them in a higher synthesis.

The author is grateful to His Divine Grace A.C. Bhaktivedanta Swami Prabhupad, the Founder-Acarya of The International Society for Krishna Consciousness and the pioneer of what is popularly known as the 'Hare-Krishna-Movement,' for going through the type-script and promising, in token of his deep appreciation of the work, the participation of over hundred centres of ISKCON outside India in any scheme for its distribution abroad.

O.B.L. Kapoor

Vrindavan
October 5, 1976.

CHAPTER I

Pre-Caitanya Vaiṣṇavism

Early history of Vaiṣṇavism

It is easy to show that Vaiṣṇavism is at least as old as the *Ṛgveda*. The essential features of Vaiṣṇāvism are the recognition of Viṣṇu as the sole God and adoption of Bhakti or emotional service of love and devotion as a means of spiritual realization. There are clear indications of Viṣṇu worship in the *Ṛgveda*, but Viṣṇu, in the earlier Vedic period, is only one of the many gods to whom homage is paid. There are Indra, Varuṇa Agni, Mitra, and a list of others. They are regarded as deities underlying the different forces of nature, such as rain, wind, and fire, on which human life and prosperity depend. Each one of them is extolled as the greatest of all the gods when a hymn of praise is addressed to him. The largest number of hymns are, however, addressed to Indra, and there seems no doubt that he was universally acclaimed as the king of gods. But the philosophic spirit of the time was in search of a supreme, all pervading, and eternal Being. Indra did not answer the need, because he was never regarded as imperishable. So Viṣṇu, literally meaning the all-pervading one, naturally came to be regarded as the greatest of all the gods. He is well known for taking three strides, with which he crosses the universe.[1] The three strides undoubtedly represent Viṣṇu as the moving spirit behind the universe, which preserves it by maintaining fixed laws.[2] He is, therefore, called *ritasya garbham* or the germ of Rita, the basic law by which the whole world is regulated.[3] In course of time, Indra is completely eclipsed by Viṣṇu. The *Viṣṇusūktas* show how the greatness of Indra is transferred to Viṣṇu. Viṣṇu's abode is regarded as the highest place (*param pada*), in which men seeking after God delight.[4] In later Vedic literature, Viṣṇu is spoken of as the personification of sacrifice,[5] and the guardian of *dikṣā* or initiation.[6] Yamunācārya, in his *Mahāpuruṣanirṇaya*, proves that Viṣṇu is the Mahāpuruṣa of the *Puruśasūkta*, which is the 'essence of the Vedas.'

Scholars generally are of the opinon that in the later Vedic and Brahmanic period, Viṣṇu's supremacy over the gods was completely established,

[1] *Ṛgveda*, I, 22, 17. [2] ibid, I, 22, 18. [3] ibid, I, 154, 4.
[4] ibid, I, 155, 5.
[5] *Satapathabrāhmaṇa*, part I, 9, 3, 9.
[6] *Aitareya Brāhmaṇa*, I, 4.

but there are some who refuse to admit that this implies the prevalence of Vaiṣṇavism during this period. Thus, Dr. Hemchandra Raychaudhuri remarks, "Although Viṣṇu came to be looked upon by some as the most excellent of the gods, he was even now far from being regarded by any section of the Aryan people as the One God.... There is very little inner connection between Vedic and Brāhmaṇic Viṣṇu-worship and the Bhakti religion we call Vaiṣṇavism. The idea of a God of Grace, the doctrine of Bhakti—these are the fundamental tenets of the religion termed Vaiṣṇavism. But they are not very conspicuous in Vedic and Brāhmaṇic Viṣṇu-worship. Viṣṇu in the Brāhmaṇic texts is more intimately connected with *Yajana* (sacrifice) than with *Bhakti* or *Prasad*."[1] While it may be true that Vaiṣṇavism in its present form was not conspicuous in the Vedic age, there seems little doubt that the seeds of Vaiṣṇavism were sown at this time. Viṣṇu was not only regarded as the supreme God but as the one God. The Vedas unequivocally declare, "There is but one reality, whom the wise men call by different names: Agni, Yama, Mātariśvà."[2] Polytheism by this time had developed through henotheism to monotheism and the monotheism of the later Vedic period centred around Viṣṇu. Monotheism, or belief in one God, who is all powerful and endowed with all the auspicious qualities, who can grant all the prayers of the devotee, and upon whom they can fully depend, necessarily implied faith or *śraddhā*, which is the first step in *bhakti*. *Śraddhā* was recognized as the essence of the Vedic religion which mainly consisted in sacrifice.[3] It was the mother of the world of rites, while Manu was its father—*śraddhā mātā manuḥ pitā*.[4] The essence of the Vedic religion did not lie in rituals, though their importance was great. As Dr. B. K. G. Shastri remarks, "It lay in *Upāsanā* or *Bhajana* expressed in *namaskāra*, *vandanā*, *sevā*, *arcanā* and the like, all performed in course of or along with *stutis* or laudatory hymns. Fundamentally it was *śraddhā* which disclosed a genuine spirit of worship in the sacrifice. When the votary prostrated himself before the God, sang His greatness and glories, consecrated himself to his service, or adored the God with all the marks of respect due to him, he certainly breathed an air of religious purity. When, as the basis of all this, he put implicit faith in him and threw himself on his mercy, he could not but be on a high plane of Spirituality. Of course, in the Vedic religion, this *śraddhā bhakti* was in connection with the prescribed rituals. All the same they referred to the discharge of the worshipper's duties with a clear head and a clear heart. He placed his reliance upon his God and submissively prayed to him to come to his help in his difficulties."[5] Dr. Seal also remarks, "The Vedic hymns are replete

[1]Hemchandra Raychaudhuri, *The Early History of Vaiṣṇava Sect*, pp. 17-18.
[2]*Ṛgveda*, I, 164, 46.
[3]ibid, X, 151.
[4]*Sāmaveda*, I, 1, 9.
[5]B. K. G. Shastri, *The Bhakti Cult in Ancient India*, pp. 3-4.

with sentiments of piety and reverence (*bhakti* and *śraddhā*) in the worship of the gods .... The *Upāsanā Kāṅdās* of *Āraṇyakas* and *Upaniṣads* lay the foundations of the *Bhakti Mārga*, way of Devotion or faith."[1] The hymns addressed to Varuṇa are particularly replete with devotional sentiments. Referring to this deity Dr. Keith says, "The simple worship of that deity with its consciousness of sin and trust in the divine forgiveness is doubtless one of the first roots of *Bhakti*."[2]

Dr. Shastri thinks that it was under the wholesome influence of *śraddhā-bhakti* that the Vedic religion progressed from polytheism to monotheism, for *bhakti* essentially stands for a broad, comprehensive faith in one who is adored.[3] To our mind, belief in one God and Bhakti imply each other. To argue for the one is to argue for the other. Belief in one God automatically brings about the devotional attitude of respectful dependence upon Him, while Śraddhā or Bhakti necessarily enlarges our conception of Divinity. The more Śraddhā develops, the greater are the demands made upon the greatness and benevolence of the god of worship, who gradually comes to be regarded as the greatest. Exclusive devotion to a God gives rise to our belief in Him as the One God without a second. At the same time, belief in One God gives rise to the attitude of exclusive dependence upon Him. Prof. Garbe, in his translation of the *Bhagavadgītā*, remarks that a monotheistic religion in which the object of worship is looked upon as a kindly deity naturally begets the feeling of Bhakti in the hearts of devotees.[4]

The Bhakti religion, also called the Bhāgavata-sātvata, Ekāntika or Pañcarātra religion, first appears in a distinct form in the Nārāyanīya section of Śāntiparva and the Viṣṇopākhyāna of the Bhīṣmaparva of the *Mahābhārata*. It is declared to have been first taught by Kṛṣṇa-Vāsudeva to Arjuna before the commencement of the Kuru-Pāndava war. Its origin from Kṛṣṇa-Vāsudeva is further confirmed by the name Sātvata[5] religion applied to it, since Sātvata was another name of the Vṛṣṇi race to which Kṛṣṇa-Vāsudeva belonged.[6] The followers of this religion were, for the same reason, called Sātvatas.

Bhandarkar thinks that Vāsudeva and Kṛṣṇa were originally two distinct persons. Vāsudeva was the name of the Sātvata prince already referred to, while Kṛṣṇa was the name of an ancient holy seer, who, later on, came to be identified with Vāsudeva.[6] But Keith[7] and Raychaudhurī,[8] think that it is impossible to justify this view in the face of all the different available evidences, Hindu, Buddhist and Greek. In Pātāñjali's *Mahābhāṣya*

[1]Seal, *Comparative Studies in Vaiṣṇavism and Christianity*, p. 5.
[2]*Journal of Royal Asiatic Society*, 1915, p. 834.
[3]ibid, p. 9. [4]pp. 29 ff. [5]*Mahābhārata*, XII, 335, 19.
[6]Bhandarkar, *Vaiṣṇavism, Śaivism and Minor Religious Systems*, pp. 8-9.
[7]*Journal of Royal Asicatic Society of Great Britain*, p. 840.
[8]ibid, p. 36.

(commentary on the Sūtras of Pāṇinī), the slayer of Kaṅsa is referred to as Vāsudeva at one place and Kṛṣṇa at another. Bhandarkar argues that in Kielhorn's edition of the *Mahābhaṣya*, which is more accurate than the Benaras edition, "Vāsudeva is used four times and Kṛṣṇa only once."[1] Raychaudhuri replies to this: "From no manuscript is the name Kṛṣṇa entirely absent. The frequency of the name 'Vāsudeva' may be due to the fact, which he himself proved, that it was the proper name, while 'Kṛṣṇa' was the Gotra name."[2] Further, the name Kṛṣṇa, as the son of Devakī and the pupil of Ghora Angiras, occurs in the *Chāndogya Upaniṣad*, and, as Raychaudhuri points out, "here Kṛṣṇa learns the same doctrines—*tapodānamārjjanam ahiṁsā satyavacanam*—which Vāsudeva teaches in the Gītā.[3]"[4]

In his own time, Vāsudeva-Kṛṣṇa, the founder of the Bhāgavata religion, is identified with Bhāgavata Himself. Bhāgavata represents the Sātvatas as practising the devotional worship of the Supreme God Vāsudeva, and Vāsudeva is no other than Viṣṇu. It may here be noted that the process of Viṣṇu's gradual rise in divinity, which started in the Vedic period, continues till it is completed in every respect in the Paurāṇic period. The Paurāṇic literature is full of stories of Viṣṇu's ascendency as the supreme God. There are stories of Indra being defeated by Viṣṇu and deprived by him of all the good things he possessed. Prominent among these is the story of Viṣṇu's winning over Śrī or Lakṣmī, the goddess of fortune, from Indra. When the supremacy of Viṣṇu is thus fully established, He is identified with Vāsudeva-Kṛṣṇa, as is manifested from numerous evidences in the *Mahābhārata*.[5] The identification is philosophically justified, since 'Viṣṇu' and 'Vāsudeva' are very much similar in meaning. We have already noted that Viṣṇu means that which pervades the whole universe. The meaning of Vāsudeva is thus explained in the *Mahābhārata:*

Chādayāmi jagad viśvaṃ bhūtvā sūrya ivāṃśubhiḥ
Sarvabhūtādhivāsaśca Vāsudevāstatohyaham.[6]

"Assuming the form of the sun I cover the universe with my rays and, because I am the home of all creatures, I am called by the name Vāsudeva."

The date of *Mahābhārata*, however, is not certain. It can not, therefore, help us in assigning any date to the earliest existence of the Bhāgavata religion. The next dependable source is the epigraphic records. The inscriptions found at Ghosundi in Rajputana and at Besnagar[7] show that Bhāgavatas were the worshippers of Vāsudeva and that the Bhāgavata religion prevailed in the northern part of India and was adopted even by the Greeks[8] in the earlier part of the second century BC.

[1]*Vaiṣṇavism* etc. p., 10. [2]ibid, p. 37. [3]XVI, 1-2. [4]ibid, p. 39.
[5]Chapters 65 and 66 of the *Bhīṣmaparva* and Chapter 43 of *Śāntiparva*.
[6]*Mahābhārata*, XII, 348. 6-8.
[7]Bhandarkar, op. cit., p. 3.
[8]ibid.

A reference to Vāsudeva is found in Pāṇini, IV, 3, 98. Commenting upon this Sūtra, Pātāñjali states Vāsudeva is the name of the 'worshipful' or God. Böhtlingk, Macdonell,[1] Keith and many other western scholars place Pāṇinī in the fourth century BC. Bhandārkar thinks that Pāṇini must have flourished in the seventh century BC. or earlier still. Dr. Raychaudhuri considers at length the possible evidences that are available and concludes that Pāṇini "in all probability lived after the Persian conquest of Gandhāra in the later half of the sixth century BC. With a date in the fifth century BC all the evidence accomodates itself."[2] It is, therefore, certain that the Bhāgavata religion is at least older than the fifth century BC.

An important landmark in the development of the Bhāgavata religion is the emergence of the Pañcarātra system[3] with its doctrine of Vyūhas, which, according to Bhandarkar, must have taken place in about the third century BC,[4] and according to Raychaudhuri, in the first century BC.[5] The Pañcarātra literature was generally known as *Pañcarātra Āgama* and comprised 108 Saṁhitās.[6] Principal among these are *Pauśkāra, Vārāha, Brāhma, Sāttvata, Jaya, Ahirbudhanya, Parameśvara, Sanatkumāra, Parama, Padmodbhava, Mahendra, Kaṇva, Padma,* and *Īśvara Saṁhitas.* The Bhāgavatas came to regard them as superior to the Vedas in the sense that they were the teachings of Vāsudeva or Nārāyaṇa to Nara and a number of teachers such as Śāndilya, Prahlāda and Sugrīva. Like all other philosophical literature of India, the Bhakti philosophy contained in these works was, in course of time, reduced into *sūtra* forms in the well known *Bhakti Sutras* of Śāndilya and Nārada.

The development of the Bhāgavata literature, both in its general or Paurāṇika aspect and technical or Pañcarātrika aspect, is intimately connected with the Gupta period. The rulers of the Gupta period were great champions of the Bhāgavata religion. They called themselves Paramabhāgavatas and, due to their efforts, Bhāgavatism spread throughout the length and breadth of the Indian sub-continent.

An important feature of the Vaiṣṇavism of this period is that the doctrine of incarnation, which is already fully developed as a logical outcome of the doctrine of grace, is emphasised to the extent of eliminating the independent worship of the Vyūhas. Viṣṇu is again the supreme God.

[1] *Sanskrit Literature*, p. 17.

[2] Raychaudhuri, *The Early History of the Vaisnava Sect*, pp. 29-30.

[3] The Pañcarātra system is strongly denounced in some Purāṇas as non-Vedic, but some other Purāṇas, such as the *Mahābhārata,* the *Bhāgavata* and the *Viṣṇupurāṇa* are wholly in favour of it. This may be due to the distinction between Vedic and non-Vedic Pañcarātra, mentioned by Dr. Majumdar on the basis of *Viramitrodaya,* a work written in the 17th century *(Caitanya: His Life and Doctrine,* p. 27).

[4] Bhandārkar, op. cit., p. 39.

[5] Raychaudhuri, op. cit., p. 176.

[6] The number is at least 224 according to Dr. Otto Schrader. See his introduction to *Ahirbudhanya Saṁhitā.*

Though Kṛṣṇa is regarded as identical with Viṣṇu, the former is only the most perfect incarnation of the latter. Another important feature of the Guptan Vaiṣṇavism is that the influence of Yoga and Sāṁkhya, which is already apparent in the Gītā and the Nārāyaṇīya, becomes more pronounced. The influence of the Sāṁkhya doctrine of Puruṣa and Prakṛti is noticed in the installation of Lakṣmī beside Nārāyaṇa.

With the fall of the Guptas the Bhāgavata religion lost its supremacy in northern India. But the centre of gravity shifted to the South, where it flourished under the patronage of the Ālvāras, the great Tamil saints, who mainly preached Kṛṣṇa worship and Bhakti. Twelve Ālvāras are mainly mentioned:

1. Poygai or Poykai Ālvār
2. Bhūtattār Ālvār
3. Pey Ālvār
4. Tirumalisai Ālvār
5. Namm-Ālvār of Śaṭakopa
6. Madhurkavi Ālvār
7. Kulaśekhar Ālvār
8. Periy-Ālvār or Viṣṇucitta
9. Āṇḍāl
10. Toṇḍaraḍippoḍi Ālvār
11. Tiruppāṇa Ālvār
12. Tirumangai Ālvār

Krishnaswami places all the Ālvārs before the second half of the eighth century AD.[1] But according to Bhandarkar, Kulasekhar probably lived in the first half of the twelfth century, while the earliest of the Ālvārs may be placed about the fifth or the sixth century.[2] The Ālvārs composed the *Prabandham*, a collection of four thousand devotional songs in Tamil. They were regarded as very sacred and were worshipped as the Vaiṣṇava Veda. The special feature of the Bhāgavata religion as preached by the Ālvārs was its accessibility to people of high and low castes, men and women, rich and poor, wise and ignorant, pious and impious, alike. Among the Ālvārs themselves, Āṇḍāl was a woman, Tiruppāṇa belonged to the depressed class; Kulaśekhar was a king, and Toṇḍaraḍippoḍi was an abandoned sinner. The only thing necessary for realisation, according to the Ālvārs, was *prapatti* or self-surrender. Dhyāna and Yoga were neither necessary nor within easy reach of the common man.

The songs of the Ālvārs have been a great source of inspiration to Vaiṣṇavas throughout south India. They, may, according to some scholars, have influenced Vaiṣṇavism in the north as well, since the basic emotions of *dāsya* (servant's love for his master), *sakhya* (friendly love),

[1] *Indian Antiquary*, XXXV, p. 228.
[2] ibid, p. 30.

vātsalya (mother's love for her child) and *mādhurya* (woman's love for her beloved), which underlie them are also associated with the north Indian Vaiṣṇavism.

After the Ālvārs came the Ācāryas,[1] a group of teachers, who represented the intellectual side of Tamilian Vaiṣṇavism. They supplemented the doctrine of Bhakti, which alone was stressed by the Ālvārs, with Jnāna and Karma. They were called Ubhayavedāntins, because they reconciled the Tamil *Prabandha* with the *Prasthānatraya*, i.e. the Vedas, the Upaniṣads and the *Gītā*. The first Ācārya was Nāthamuni or Ranganāth Muni, who lived in Śrīrangam near Trichinopoly and died about 920 AD. He was an erudite scholar and a passionate lover of the songs of the Ālvārs. He rediscovered the *Prabandha* and popularised it. He also instituted a festival of which the special feature was the recitation of *Prabhandha* in the Śrīrangam temple for three weeks.[2] He wrote two important works, the *Yogarahasya* and the *Nyāyatattva*, of which the former is now lost. To him goes the credit of first giving a systematic shape to the doctrine of *prapatti*, which later became the central docrine of Śrī Vaiṣṇavism.

The four Vaiṣṇava Saṁpradāyas (*Sects*)

Śrī Vaiṣṇavism is the first of the four traditional Vaiṣṇava Saṁpradāyas, Śrī, Haṁsa, Brahma, and Rudra, which now rose into prominence, one after the other. Each one of these claims divine and the most ancient origin, but is associated with the name of an Ācārya, who at a much later time, re-established it by systematising its doctrine and re-interpreting the *Brahmasūtra* in the light of the same, and who, in this sense, is regarded as its founder. Śrī Sampradāya was established by Rāmānuja, Haṁsa by Nimbārka, Brahma by Madhva, and Rudra by Vallabha. We shall here give a brief, general account of each and discuss its philosophical position in detail, especially with regard to the problem of relation between Brahman, the individual self and the world, at a later stage, when we compare it with Śrī Caitanya's doctrine of Acintya Bhedā-bheda. An account of the Rudra Sampradāya may not appear to be justified in our discussion of Pre-Caitnaya Vaiṣṇavism, because Śrī Vallabhācārya was contemporaneous with Śrī Caitanya, but we have included it, because it is also linked with Viṣṇusvāmī, who lived much earlier.

Rāmānuja, the founder of Śrī Saṁpradāya, was born in 1017 AD and had a long span of life lasting upto 1137 AD. He was originally a pupil of Yādavaprakāśa, an Advita philosopher, whose teachings did not satisfy him and whom he had to leave. He came under the influence of Vaiṣṇava

[1]The importance given to the *Prabandha* in the temple festival and the consequent necessity of recognising an authority who could explain its obscure passages led to the origin of the system of Ācāryas. The function of the Ācārya was to interpret the *Prabandha* and to defend Vaiṣṇavism from critics.

[2]The Ācāryas, themselves, do not claim to be the founders.

thought wherein his main source of inspiration was the songs of the Ālvārs. He renounced the world and became the Ācārya at Śrīrnagam. The rest of his life was dedicated to the formulation and propagation of the Viśiṣṭādvaitic doctrine. In his *Vedārtha saṁgraha* he proved that the purpose of some of the principal Upaniṣads, upon which Śaṁkara had based his monistic philosophy, was not to teach Advaitism, and that the Upaniṣads did not uphold the impersonal Brahman, but the personal absolute who was none other than Nārāyaṇa. Though Nārāyaṇa is the most favoured deity of the school of Rāmānuja, Vāsudeva comes into prominence when the supreme soul and its Vyūhas are mentioned. The name of Gopālakṛṣṇa is not mentioned and Rāma, also, is not a favourite deity. The most important work of Rāmānuja is the *Śrī Bhāṣya* on the *Vedānta sūtras*, which, once again, securely laid the foundation of Vaiṣṇavism and made it safe from the onslaughts of Advaitism.

The philosophical position of Viśiṣṭādvaitavāda is styled as concrete monism. It is the non-duality of the Absolute, qualified by Jīva and Prakṛti as its body and modes or attributes. It accepts Pariṇāmavāda. Brahman is both the material and efficient cause of the world. Before creation, Jīva and Prakṛti exist in a subtle form, but when creation takes place, they develop in their present form. Thus, Brahman as the Absolute, including Jīva and Prakṛti as moments in its being, is the material cause of the world, while Brahman as the inward controlling spirit, which wills to create, is its efficient cause. Brahman is immanent as well as transcendent. In the immanent aspect, it is the cosmological principle expressing itself in the *līlā-vibhūti*; in the transcendent aspect it is Brahman-in-itself, expressing itself in Nityavibhūti. Jīva is Brahman in the sense that it has all the qualities of Brahman, except all-pervasiveness, and the power of controlling the world. It can attain salvation by devotion to Vāsudeva, which arises from *dhruva smṛtiḥ* or steady remembrance.

After the death of Rāmānuja the Śrī Vaiṣṇavas were divided into two sects, the Vaḍkalais and the Tenkalais. The Vaḍkalais think that salvation can be attained more easily through the Sanskrit holy works—the Vedas the Upaniṣads, and the Gītā, while the Tenkalais think that it can be attained more easily through the Tamil *Prabandha*. Both the schools recognize the necessity of *prapatti*. But the Vaḍkalais emphasise that *prapatti* is conditioned by Karma or self-effort: it is only when the soul makes efforts and these do not bring forth the desired result that the frame of mind necessary for *prapatti* is produced. The Tenkalais, on the other hand, insist that God's grace is spontaneous and not conditioned by any effort on the part of the devotee.

While Vaiṣṇavism was thus developing in the south there was a great upheaval against Advaitism and its doctrine of Māyā or Illusion pioneered by Nimbārka in the north. The exact date of Nimbārka's birth is not known but it is believed that he lived some time after Rāmānuja. He was a

Tailanga Brāhmaṇa by birth but lived in Vṛndāvana near Mathurā. He wrote a commentary on the *Brahma sūtras* which is known as *Vedāntapārijātasaurabha* and a small treatise called *Dasaślokī* (also *Siddhāntaratna*), because it consists of ten Ślokas describing the essentials of his system. There is a commentary on *Vedāntapārijātasaurabha* by Nimbārk's immediate successor, Śrīnivāsa, and a commentary on *Dasaślokī* by Harivyāsadeva, who is the thirty-second in the disciplic line from Nimbārka.

Nimbārka's philosophical position is known as *Dvaita-advaita* or *Bhedābheda*. The categories of existence, according to him, are three, i.e., *Cit*, *Acit* and *Īśvara*. Cit and Acit are different from Īśvara, in the sense that they have attributes and capacities, which are different from those of Īśvara. Īśvara is independent and exists by Himself, while Cit and Acit have an existence dependent upon Him. At the same time Cit and Acit are not different from Īśvara, because they cannot exist independently of Him. Difference means a kind of existence which is separate but dependent, while non-difference means impossibility of independent existence. Thus Nimbārka equally emphasises both difference and non-difference, as against Rāmānuja, who makes difference subordinate to non-difference, in as much as, for him, Cit and Acit do not exist separately from Brahman, but as its body or attributes. Nimbārka accepts Rāmanuja's Pariṇāmavāda theory of creation, but not in exactly the same sense. For Rāmānuja, the animate and the inanimate worlds are the result of the development of subtle forms of these, which constitute the body of Brahman. For Nimbārka, the rudiments from which the two worlds develop do not form the body of Brahman, but exist in a subtle form in the various capacities which belong to Brahman in its natural condition. Brahman is the material cause of the universe in the sense that Brahman brings the subtle rudiments into the gross form by realizing these capacities. The most important point of difference between Rāmānuja and Nimbārka is that, while the former advocates the worship of Nārāyaṇa with His consorts (Lakṣmī, Bhū and Līlā), for Nimbārka, the highest object of worship is Kṛṣṇa and his consort Rādhā, attended by thousands of Gopīs, or cowherdesses, of the celestial Vṛndāvana. Devotion, according to Nimbārka, consists in *prapatti*, or self-surrender, rather than in *upāsanā* or meditation in the Upaniṣadic sense prescribed by Rāmānuja.

We have for the first time alluded to the worship of the cowherd Kṛṣṇa and Rādhā, which may, therefore, appear to be a comparatively new element in the Bhāgavata religion. Bhandarkar thus expresses himself on the point:

"The inscriptions, the work of Pātañjali and even the Nārāyaṇīya itself indicate no knowledge of the existence of such a god. In the last the Avatāra of Vāsudeva is mentioned as having been assumed for the destruction of Kaṁsa, but of none of the demons whom the cowherd Kṛṣṇa killed in the cow-settlement (Gokula). The contrast between this and the statements in the Harivaṁśa, (vv. 5876-5878), *Vāyupurāṇa*, chapter 98, vv. 100-102, and *Bhāgavatapurāṇa*, II, 7, of Kṛṣṇa Avatāra having been assumed for destroying all the demons that appeared in the cow-settlement as well as of Kaṁsa is significant. When these works were written, the legend about the cowherd Kṛṣṇa must have already become current and his identification with Vāsudeva-Kṛṣṇa been effected. And the story of the Vṛṣṇi prince Vāsudeva having been brought up in a cow-settlement is incongruous with his later career as depicted in the *Mahābhārata* . . ."

"In the Śabhāparva (Chapter 41), however, Śiśupāla introducing Kṛṣṇa alludes to his various deeds, such as the killing of Pūtanā and others, which were done in the cow-settlement, and speaks of Bhīṣma's having praised them. But the praise bestowed on Kṛṣṇa by Bhīṣma (Chapter 38) does not contain a mention of these deeds. This passage, therefore, is interpolated."[1]

Since *Harivaṁsa*, which is the chief authority for the story of Kṛṣṇa's boyhood in the Gokula, contains the word *dināra*, corresponding to the Latin word *denarius*, Bhandarkar thinks that the work must have been written about the third century of the Christian era, and the story could not have been known before the beginning of the Christian era.[2] He further concludes that the worship of the boy-god, the story of his birth, his father's knowledge that he was not his son, and the massacre of the innocents suggest Christian influences, which were brought to India by a tribe of Ābhiras in the course of their wanderings eastward from Syria and became engrafted on the story of Vāsudeva-Kṛṣṇa of India.[3]

Weber[4] thinks there is a gap between the Kṛṣṇa of *Mahābhārata* and the Kṛṣṇa of Gokula, which can be explained only with reference to some external influence. He also suggests that the influence is Christian, since there is much similarity between the legends of Kṛṣṇa's birth, the solemn celebration of his birthday and his life as a herdsman and the Christian legends. In support of this, he alludes to the legend of Śveta-dvīpa (White Island) in the Śāntiparva of the *Mahābhārata*, which, according to him, refers to some Christian settlement. Ekata, Dvita and Trita go to the White Island to see Hari or Nārāyaṇa. They perform austerities for a long time, but are told that they cannot see Nārāyaṇa, because they are not Bhaktas. They give a description of the White Island and its inhabitants, who are so different from Indians.

Dr. Raychaudhuri effectively counters all suggestions of a Christian influence with regard to this element in the Bhāgavata cult: "With regard to the birth-day festival of Kṛṣṇa, the representation of him as a suckling at his mother's breast, and the homage paid to the mother," he observes

[1]Bhandarkar, op. cit., pp. 35-36.
[2]ibid.
[3]ibid, pp. 37-38; also *Indian Antiquary*, 1912, p. 15.
[4]*Indian Antiquary*, 1871, Weber on the Kṛṣṇa Janmāṣṭamī.

that it does not suggest any Christian influence, because, "the association of Kṛṣṇa with Devaki, his mother, is as well known and is as old as the *Chāndogya-upaniṣad*," and "Recent discoveries at Mohenjodaro in Sind prove that the worship of the Mother Goddess can claim a hoary antiquity." The Śveta-dvīpa cannot refer to a Christian settlement because geography does not know of any quarter of the earth which lies to the north of the Ocean of Milk, and to the north-west of Mount Meru, and above it by 32,000 *yojanas*, where the island is said to be situated.[1] "As regards the pastoral associations of Kṛṣṇa," says Raychaudhuri, "Viṣṇu the Vedic deity, with whom Kṛṣṇa is identified in the pre-Christian *Taittirīya Āraṇyaka*, is called in the *Ṛgveda*, *Gopa*,[2] which means 'protector of cows' according to Macdonell and Keith[3] and 'herdsman' according to Hopkins."[4]

Bhandarkar's theory is incorrect, because, "we learn from *Periplus* of the *Erythraean Sea* that the Ābhiras were already settled in western India (Abiria), in the first century AD. They are also mentioned by Pātañjali.[5] How could they bring with them traditions of the birth of Christ in a stable, of the massacre of the innocents and so on?"[6]

There was a stronger current of the Bhakti movement in the north of which Rāmānanda was the fountainhead. He was the pupil of Rāghavānanda, a teacher of the Rāmānuja school, and lived probably from 1300 to 1400 AD. He preached the Viśiṣṭādvaitic doctrine, but he substituted the worship of Rāma and Sītā in the place of the worship of Nārāyaṇa and Lakṣmī, and succeeded in making it popular. One of the reasons for his success was that he used the vernaculars in the propagation of his creed, but a more important reason was the abolition of caste within the Vaiṣṇavas. It is true that the Vaiṣṇavas had always taken a more liberal attitude towards the lower castes. Rāmānuja had gone to the extent of allowing the lower castes to imitate the customs and habits of the Vaiṣṇavas and to study the *Prabandhas*. But the lower castes were never taken into the inner fold and treated on terms of equality. They were not allowed to read the Vedas and wear the sacred thread. Rāmānanda brought about a radical reform, making no distinction whatsoever between the Brāhmaṇas and the lower castes. Many of his noted followers, such as Kabīr and Raidās, came from the depressed classes usually regarded as untouchables.

The most important teacher of Vaiṣṇavism was Madhvācārya or

[1] *Mahābhārata*, XII, 335, 8, 9.

[2] Viṣṇu is also called *yuva akumārah* (*Ṛgveda*, I, 155, 6), which means ever young, like Kṛṣṇa.

[3] *The Vedic Index*, I, p. 238.

[4] *The Religions of India*, p. 57.

[5] *Indian Antiquary*, 1918, p. 36.

[6] Raychaudhuri, op. cit., p. 151.

Ānanda Tīrtha. He was born near Udipi in 1199 AD and is said to have lived for 79 years. The mission of his life was to refute the pure monism of Śaṁkara as well as the qualified monism of Rāmānuja and to promulgate the Dvaita school of Vedānta. He wrote commentaries on Bādrāyana's *sūtras*, *Ṛgveda*, the *Upaniṣads* and the *Gītā*.

Madhva's philosophy is purely dualistic in character. He holds that there are five kinds of eternal and absolute difference between Brahman, Jīva and Jaṇa, namely, the difference between Brahman and Jīva, Brahman and Jaṇa, Jīva and Jīva, Jīva and Jaṇa, and Jaṇa and Jaṇa. He rejects the Pariṇāmavāda doctrine, as it does violence to the independent majesty of Brahman. Brahman exists independently, and does not undergo any change at the time of creation. He creates the world by disturbing the equilibrium of Prakṛti and, like an absolute ruler, directs it by His will. He is the ground of *cit* and *acit*, which depend upon Him for their form and function.

To avoid pluralism, which is the logical outcome of his doctrine of fivefold difference (*pañcabheda*), Madhva introduces the principle of Viśeṣa (specific particulars). Being, with its manifoldness, is an integral being, exclusive of differences, but differences, are perceived in it on account of Viśeṣa. It is undivided though not unqualified. The undivided being admits of qualitative differences on account of Viśeṣa.

Madhvaites recognize the authority of the Pañcarātra Saṁhitās but do not give any place in their system to Vyūhas. They identify Brahman with Viṣṇu and adore Rāma and Kṛṣṇa as His incarnations, but do not show any inclination for the worship of Gopāla-Kṛṣṇa and Rādhā. The means of realization adopted are physical, moral and spiritual disciplines comprised in Aṣṭāṅga Yoga. These have Bhakti as their fruition and Bhakti is completed in divine grace.

In 1479, about six years before the advent of Śrī Caitanya, was born Vallabha, the founder of the Śuddhādvaita school. He was the son of a Telugu Brahmin, and derived his Vedantic theory from Viṣṇusvāmī, who is said to have lived about the middle of the thirteenth century. He was the last of the four successors of Viṣṇusvāmī mentioned by Nābhāji in his *Bhaktamāla*, the first three being Jnānadeva, Nāmadeva and Trilocana. He lived for some time in Mathura and for some time in Vṛndāvana.

Śuddhādvaita means pure unity of Brahman, which is free from Māyā. Brahman is all and all is Brahman (*Sarvaṁ-khaluidam-brahman*). Brahman is *sat-cit-ānanda* and Jīva and the world are not different from Him. Only Jīva is Brahman with the quality of Ānanda obscured and the world is Brahman with the qualities of *cit* and *ānanda* obscured. All the objects in the world are Brahman in those forms. The relation between Brahman, Jīva and the world is that of pure identity (Advaita). Non-difference alone is real. Difference is only for the sake or sport of Līlā.

Kṛṣṇa of Gokula is the highest Brahman. Viṣṇu, Brahmā and Śiva are the manifestations of his qualities of Sattva, Rajas and Tamas, and discharge respectively the functions of protection, creation and destruction.

Bhakti is either *Maryādā bhakti* or *Puṣṭi bhakti*. The former consists in practising Sādhanā, or spiritual discipline as laid down in the Śastras and leads to Mukti (Sāyujya). The latter consists in pure and simple love of God and leads to the soul's participation in the divine sports in the celestial Gokula.

Pre-Caitanya Vaiṣṇavism in Bengal

There is epigraphic evidence to show that the roots of Vaiṣṇavism in Bengal go as far back as the fourth century AD. The first literary evidence is the *Gīta govinda* of Jayadeva, who flourished in the twelfth century and enjoyed the patronage of the Vaiṣṇavite Sena kings. It has been suggested that the twenty-four songs of *Gīta govinda* are the Sanskrit renderings by Jayadeva of the originals in *Aprabhaṁśa* or old Bengali, representing a tradition much earlier than Jayadeva. This theory has not been convincingly proved, but it is thought, "there is fair ground for believing that the sensuous verses depicting the love of Rādhā and Kṛṣṇa were parts of a popular mass literature now lost."[1]

Besides Jayadeva, the lyrics of Vidyāpati,[2] who lived sometime between 1370-1460, and Candīdāsa[3] had considerable influence in Bengal. The direct influence on Śrī Caitanya of the songs of Jayadeva, Vidyāpati, and Candīdāsa is evident from the fact that he is depicted by his biographers as having great fondness for them. The fact that the followers of Śrī Caitanya draw profusely from the *Gīta govinda* and the songs of Vidyāpati to illustrate their Bhakti-rasa-śastra also shows how the emotional tendencies depicted in the former resemble the emotionale of the school.[4]

While, thus, the influence of Jayadeva, Vidyāpati and Candīdās on Śrī Caitanya is obvious, it is not easy to determine the source from which

[1]A. K. Majumdar, op. cit., p. 77.

[2]Dr. S. K. De thinks that Vidyāpati was a Smārta Pañcopāsaka and not a Viṣṇava, because he composed verses on Śiva and Gaurī as well as on Rādhā and Kṛṣṇa. The ground for the belief is rather flimsy, because many Vaiṣṇavas, who recognize Kṛṣṇa as the highest deity, also adore Śiva (see S. K. De, op. cit., p. 1, f.n.)

[3]There are several poets who bear this name. Some scholars think that Candīdāsa, whose lyrics Śrī Caitanya loved to hear was Dvija Candīdāsa, while others think that he was Ananta Badu Candīdāsa, who wrote *Śrī Kṛṣṇa-kīrtana* (Majumdar, op. cit., p. 78).

[4]Dr. S. K. De regards it as a tendency on the part of the Caitanyite to read his Bhaktirasa-śāstra in *Gīta govinda*, composed three hundred years before, which, he says, is not historically correct (op. cit., pp. 7-8). The criticism is hardly justified, for the canons of Rasa-śāstra are universal in application, like the rules of grammar, and there is nothing to prevent their application to compositions made prior to their formulation.

they themselves have drawn. Dr. De considers the possibility of Jayadeva's drawing directly from the *Brahmavaivarta-purāṇa*, in view of the fact that both *Gīta govinda* and the *Brahmavaivarta-purāṇa* present Rādhā in the most vivid background of sensuous imagery and in both the Mādhurya aspect of Kṛṣṇa-worship as the beloved and its Aiśvarya aspect as the supreme deity are equally emphasised, as also in view of the fact that there is no other Purāṇa in which Rādhā is given the same prominence as in *Brahmavaivarta*. But he finds "no direct proof of Jayadeva's indebtedness to the *Brahmavaivarta purāṇa*, and it is difficult to explain why Jayadeva should prefer its authority to that of the almost exclusively paramount Vaiṣṇava scripture, the *Śrīmad-bhāgavata*."[1]

Some writers seem to countenance the theory of Śrī Caitanya having been influenced by the songs of the Ālvārs through Mādhvendra Purī, his *paramaguru*. Dr. Majumdar says, "Not only he (Mādhvendra) had visited South India (for all we know he might have been a southerner), but unlike a Madhva ascetic, which he is said to have been, he was a devotee of great capacity. Thus it is possible that the seed of emotional devotion was transplanted by Mādhvendra from South to Bengal, and the sapling was nourished to maturity during Caitanya's long tour of south India."[2] The possibility is strengthened, at least theoretically, by the prevalence of the Mādhurya form of Bhakti amongst the Ālvārs and the mention, by Aṇḍāl, of one Nappinnāi, who seems to be an early prototype of Rādhā.[3]

But with sources like the songs of Jayadeva, Vidyāpati and Candīdās so near at hand, geographically, culturally and linguistically, it is most unlikely that Śrī Caitanya should have drawn from so remote a source as the songs of the Ālvārs. There is also no direct evidence that Jayadeva, Vidyāpati and Candīdās were influenced by them.

In preceptorial succession Śrī Caitanya is linked with the Madhva Saṁpradāya, through his *guru*, Īśvara Purī, who was a disciple of Mādhvendra Purī. The chances of his being influenced by the Madhva Sampradāya should, therefore, be great. But in doctrinal matters Śrī Caitanya differs from Madhva, who even despises the Mādhurya form of devotion, which is an essential part of the teachings of Śrī Caitanya.[4]

There is no other source from which Śrī Caitanya could have drawn. There are, of course, two other Saṁpradāyas in which Rādhā is worshipped with Kṛṣṇa, namely the Saṁpradāyas of Nimbārka and Vallabha. But there is no evidence that Caitanya ever came under the influence of the Nimbārkites. There is also no evidence of Jayadeva coming under the influence of Nimbārka, though he is supposed to have been contemporaneous

[1]op. cit., p. 9. [2]op. cit., p. 50. [3]ibid.

[4]The question of the exact nature of relationship between Śrī Caitanya and Madhva is very complicated and controversial. We have, therefore, discussed it in chapter III 'The Saṁpradāya of Śrī Caitanya.'

with him. Vallabha is a contemporary of Caitanya, and we shall speak later of the evidence in *Caitanya caritāmṛta* of his himself coming under the influence of Caitanya.[1]

The only single source form which Śrī Caitanya has undisputedly drawn is the *Śrīmad bhāgavata*, which he holds in such high esteem that it is identified with Kṛṣṇa Himself.[2] It is, it seems, the common source of inspiration to Jayadeva, Nimbārka and the writers of such late Purāṇas as the *Brahmavaivarta*.

[1]*See* Chapter II.

[2]We have discussed in detail the importance of *Śrīmad Bhāgavata* for Caitanyism in the chapter on 'Sources of Knowledge.'

CHAPTER II

The Life of Śrī Caitanya

Birth and divinity

Śrī Caitanya was born at Navadvīp, situated on the bank of the holy Ganges in Bengal in February 1486 (Phālguna Paurṇamāsī) just before an eclipse of the full moon, amidst loud chantings of the Name of Lord, usual amongst the Vaiṣṇavas on such occasions. His father was Jagannātha Misra and mother Śacī. The ancestors of Jagannātha Misra had migrated from Jājpur in Orissa and settled in Śrīhaṭṭa (Sylhet). Jagannātha had gone to Navadvīp for study and settled there before his marriage with Śacī. He was a devout and scholarly Brāhmaṇa of moderate means. Śacī was the daughter of Nīlāmbara Cakravartī, a pious and scholarly Brāhmaṇa, who had also migrated to Navadvīp from Sylhet. Before the birth of Śrī Caitanya Jagannātha had lost eight children. The ninth, a boy named Viśvarūpa, left home to become a Saṁnyāsin and died at a young age. Śrī Caitanya was, thus, the only child of his parents to survive. They gave him the name Viśvambhara. But the people generally called him Gaura or Gaurāṅga. After his Saṁnyāsa he was named Śrī Kṛṣṇa Caitanya.

The biographers of Śrī Caitanya depict him as Lord Śrī Kṛṣṇa Himself, who appeared on earth to show to the fallen Jīvas the path of Bhakti by His own example and precept, and to proclaim the chanting of Divine Name (*nāma-saṁkīrtana*) as the special dispensation for this age (*yuga-dharma*), to realise the depth and bliss of Radha's love for Himself by adopting her devotional attitude (*bhāva*), which is the highest form of divine love (*mahā-bhāva*), and to experience the sweetness and charm of His own Personality, as it appears to her.[1] It is believed that the personality of Śrī Caitanya is a mysterious combination of the divine forms of Śrī Kṛṣṇa and Rādhā. His inner self is that of Kṛṣṇa and the molten gold complexion of his body on account of which he is called Gaura or Gaurāṅga, and his attitude of devotion to Kṛṣṇa, which he had adopted for the purpose already stated, are the manifestations of Rādhā, the

[1] *śrīrādhāyāḥ praṇaya mahimā kīdṛśo vānayaivā—*
svādyo yenādbhutamadhurimā kīdṛśo vā madīyaḥ
saukhyaṁcāsyā madanubhavataḥ kīdṛśaṁ veti lobhā—
tadbhāvāḍhyaḥ samajani śacīgarbhasindhau harīndūḥ.
(Cited in *CC*, Ādi, I, 6 from Svarūpa Gosvāmin's Kaḍacā)

principle of divine love personified.[1] Numerous texts from the Śāstras are cited to prove that he is the incarnation having yellow or golden complexion (*pīta-varṇa*) referred to in Śrīmad Bhāgavata[2] who appeared as a Saṁnyāsin in the age of Kali to preach Nāma-saṁkīrtana as the only means of deliverance for the people of this age.[3]

Śrī Caitanya's divinity cannot be made a subject of scientific investigation. But it is a fact that millions worshipped him as the Divine Lord in his own life time,[4] and amongst his worshippers were men of the highest learning and intelligence. Śrī Caitanya is represented by his biographers as giving out the secret of his divinity and revealing his Divine form to several of his associates.[5] The devout followers of Śrī Caitanya find it difficult to believe that he or his biographers, who upheld in their lives the highest standard of morality, would do so to dupe the world.

The naughty boy

Śrī Caitanya showed great fondness for Name of Lord from the very moment of his birth. He would often weep and cry and would not be consoled until the people round him began to chant the Name. His favourite game was to sing *Hari Bola, Hari Bola* and dance. His dances were the

[1]*antaḥ kṛṣṇaṁ bahirgauraṁ darśitāṅgādivaibhavam/*
kalau saṁkīrtanādyaiḥ smaḥ kṛṣṇacaitanyamāśritāḥ// (*Tattva saṁdarbha*, 2)

[2]*Bh.*, 10,8,3.

[3]*kṛṣṇavarṇaṁ tviṣākṛṣṇah sāṅgopāṅgāstra-pārṣadam/*
yajnaiḥ saṁkīrtana prāryeryajanti hi sumedhasaḥ// (*Bh.*, 11, 5, 32.)
suvarṇavarṇo hemāṅgo varāugaścandanāṅgadī/
saṁnyāsakṛchamaḥ śānto niṣṭhā-śāntiparāyaṇaḥ// (*Mahābhārata, Dānadharma*, I, 49)
ahameva dvijaśrestha nityaṁ pracchannavigrahaḥ/
bhagavadbhaktarūpeṇa lokān rakṣāmi sarvadā// (*Ādipurāṇa*)

[4]Images of Śrī Caitanya are worshipped all over Orissa and Bengal. Some of these were installed in his life time. For example, the famous image of Śrī Caitanya, which is enshrined in a beautiful temple at Nadiā was worshipped by his wife Viṣṇupriyā Devī after his Saṁnyāsa; the image in the temple at Katavā was made and worshipped by Gadādhara; the image of Kālanā was made and worshipped by Gaurī Pandit.

[5]Once when Śrīvāsa Pandit was worshipping the deity inside the temple in his house, Śrī Caitanya knocked at his door and said, "Whom are you meditating upon? He whom you are worshipping is standing before you." Srīvāsa then saw Śrī Caitanya in the form of Viṣṇu (*Caitanya Bhāgavata*, II, ii, 256-258). Similarly Śrī Caitanya appeared in the form of Barāha Avatāra to Murārī Gupta (*C. Bh.*, II, iii), in the form of Kṛṣṇa to Advaita (*C. Bh.*, II, vi), Srīdhara (*C. Bh.*, II, ix), and Śacī (*C. Bh.*, II, viii), in the form of Rāma to Murārī Gupta (*C. Bh.*, II, x), and in the form of Śiva to a devotee (*C. Bh.*, II, viii). He appeared as Saṇbhuja (six-armed) to Nityānanda (*C. Bh.*, II, v), Sārvabhauma Bhattācārya (*CC.* II, vi) and Rājā Pratāparudra (Kaḍacā of Murārī Gupta, III, xvi, 13). The Ṣaṇbhuja-rūpa was a combination of Rāma, Kṛṣṇa and Gaurāṅga, holding the bow and arrow in two of his arms, playing the flute with two others, and keeping the remaining two up in a dancing posture. He also showed his Viśva-rūpa form to Advaita (*C. Bh.*, II, xxiv).

spontaneous expression of an inward bliss, which seemed to reign in his heart and control the movements of his body. With hands uplifted and eyes upturned he seemed to dance in a fit of divine madness, which enraptured all and sundry and made them dance as by a spell.

The boyish frolics of Śrī Caitanya or Nimāi, as he was fondly nicknamed by his parents, bear close resemblance to those of Śrī Kṛṣṇa. Once he saw a cobra passing by and caught hold of it. The cobra coiled round his body but he lay smiling on it. When Śacī saw this she shreiked aloud with fear and the cobra quickly made off.

Nimāi was easily induced to dance when people promised to give him sweets. He played on the bank of the Ganges and teased the people who went there to bathe. He would run away with the articles they brought for worship and eat the offerings intended for the deities; he would interrupt someone in meditation and say, "Worship me, for I am the God you are meditating upon." He would climb the shoulder of another and proclaim, 'I am Lord Śiva' and then jump into the Ganges, using his shoulder as diving board. He would dive into the river and pull the legs of persons bathing. He would interchange the clothes of the males and females as they would be bathing. Frequently, therefore, the people would go to his parents and complain.

The student

Jagannātha Miśra and Śacī did not send their Nimāi to school, because they were afraid that studies would have the same baneful effect upon him as they had upon his elder brother and he would become an ascetic. But since he was growing wild they were obliged to put him under the tution of pandits Sudarśana and Viṣṇu.

Later he was sent for higher education to the school of Pandit Gangā Dāsa, the most learned pandit of Navadvīpa. There were about a thousand students in the school. Most of these were much older than Nimāi, who was only fourteen. Kamalākānta, who was famous for his knowledge of rhetoric, Kṛṣṇānanda, the author of *Tantrasāra*, and Murārī were his classmates. But this lad of fourteen eclipsed them all by his extraordinary intelligence. They found him far superior to them in academic discussions. It was his favourite pastime to challenge the pupils of different schools for intellectual fight with him on the bank of the Ganges. He would offer his own explanation of certain Sūtras and ask others to criticise it. On their failing to find any flaw, he would himself point a number of flaws and offer another explanation which he would again criticise to re-establish his original explanation with extraordinary skill and felicity.

Nimāi's only passion at this time was study, to which he applied himself with single-minded devotion. An intellectual giant that he was, he acquired mastery over the different branches of Sanskrit learning at a very early age. Some scholars, however, believe that he confined himself to the study of Grammar.[1] The reasons stated for the belief are that Gangādāsa, his teacher was a reputed scholar of Grammar,[2] that Vṛndāvana Dāsa admits he had no knowledge of Nyāya (as he makes people wish that he had studied Nyāya),[3] and that Kṛṣṇa Dāsa makes him admit he never studied rhetoric.[4] It may be admitted that Nimāi's teacher was famous only as a grammarian and that Nimāi, himself was mainly a teacher of Grammar. But this cannot be advanced as an argument against his proficiency in other branches of learning. Nimāi's saying that he did not study rhetoric cannot be regarded as of much significance, as it was not unusual with him to conceal things that would give him prominence, and he actually vanquished in disputation Keśava Bhatta, a well known scholar, by pointing rhetorical flaws in a verse composed by him, and humbled the pride of Mukunda, another scholar of rhetoric, in a similar rhetorical fight with him. Similarly the wish casually expressed by some one at sometime, that Nimāi studied Nyāya, cannot be regarded as a valid ground for the belief that he never studied Nyāya, specially in view of the fact that the same author, who discribes the wish, also narrates how he defeated Pandit Gadādhara in a discussion pertining to Nyāya[5] and vanquished in disputation Vāsudeva Sārvabhauma Bhattācārya, the greatest authority of the time on Nyāya, and earned from him the certificate that he was well versed in all branches of learning.[6] Mukunda, who had challenged Nimāi to a rhetorical fight, to which reference has already been made, under the impression that he was only a grammarian, was also compelled to recognize him as a prodigy, who was well versed in all the Śāstras.[7] Jayānanda expressly states that he studied all the different branches of Sanskrit learning one by one.[8]

The householder

Nimāi was still a student when Jagannātha Miśra died, and the responsibility of managing the household fell on him. He married Lakṣmī,

[1]S. K. De, *Early History of the Vaiṣṇava Faith and Movement in Bengal*, pp. 53-54.

[2]*vyākaraṇa śāstrera ekānta tattvavid*/ *C. Bh.*, I, vii.

[3]*keha bale e brāhmaṇa nyāya jadi paṇe*/
bhattācārya haya tabe kabhu nā naṇe// ibid, I, xiii, 202; cited by S. K. De.

[4]*nāhi paṇi alaṅkāra kariyāchi sravaṇa*/ *CC*, I, xvi, 49.

[5]*hena jana nāhika je prabhu sane bale*/
gadādhara bhāve āji bāci palāile// *C. Bh.*, I, viii, 26.

[6]*sārvabhauma bale—tumi sakala vidyāya*/
parama pravīna āmi jāni sarvathāya// *C. Bh.*, III, iii, 77.

[7]*manuṣyera emata pāṅditya āche kothā*/
hena śāstra nāhika abhyāsa nāhika jathā// *C. Bh.*, I, viii, 18.

[8]*smṛti, tarka, sāhitya paṇilā eke eke*/ *Caitanya Maṅgala*, p. 18.

daughter of Vallabha Ācārya and set up a school where he taught grammar. He was at this time imbued with the scholastic spirit and indulged in dialectical bouts with the scholars of Nadiyā. In one such bout he defeated a Digvijayī Pandit[1] (world conquerer), whom the blessings of goddess Saraśvatī had made invincible (*C. Bh.*, I, xiii, 21-22). The goddess told the Pandit in a dream that the man who had vanquished him was the Lord Himself.

As a result of his victory over the Digvijayī Pandit Śrī Caitanya soon rose to great eminence as a scholar. But he did not show any marked tendency towards religion till now. He seemed on the other hand to be averse to it, and Vaiṣṇavas, inspite of his personal charm and scholarship, avoided his company on account of his scholastic arrogance (*C. Bh.*, I, vii, 172).

When Nimāi was about twenty-two years old he visited East Bengal. His biographers give scanty account of this tour. Only *Preman Vilāsa* mentions some of the places he visited. He is said to have visited Faridpur, Bikramapur in the district of Dacca, Bhitadia, which was then a great seat of Sanskrit learning, and Dacca Dakṣin, in the district of Sylhet, where his grandfather Upendra Miśra and his uncles lived. Probably one of the objects of his tour was to meet these people. At Bhitadia he met Puruśottama, who later became one of his close associates and was known as Svarūpa Dāmodara.

During this tour his wife Lakṣmī died. After her death he married Viṣṇupriyā, daughter of Pandit Sanātana Miśra of Navadvīpa.

Initiation and the upsurge of divine love

In the year 1508, about a year after his tour of Bengal, Nimāi went on a pilgrimage to Gayā with the professed object of performing the Śrādha ceremony of his father. He was accompanied by Candraśekhara Ācārya[2] and a large number of his pupils. After performing the Śrādha he went to Cakrabeṇa to see the footprints of Lord Kṛṣṇa in the temple of Gadādhara. As his gaze was fixed on the footprints, the Brāhmaṇas were singing in praise of the Divine Feet. The songs aroused spiritual emotions in Nimāi. He stood for sometime like a statue oblivious of his surroundings. Then his hair stood on ends, tears flowed from his eyes in continuous stream, and his whole body trembled. This was the first distinct manifestation of spiritual emotions in him.

Īśvara Purī, a disciple of Mādhvendra Purī of the Mādhva sect also happened to arrive here at this time. Nimāi's meeting with Īśvara Purī

[1]Some think that this Digvijayī was the same as Keśava Bhatta of Nimbārka Sampradāya. The name of the Digvijayī, however, is not mentioned in any of the biographies of Śrī Caitanya.

[2]His wife's sister's husband.

proved a turning point in his life. He became his disciple and obtained the Daśākṣara Kṛṣṇa-mantra from him. This may as well have been the real object of his visit to Gayā, for Gayā was a Mādhva centre at this time[1] and a meeting with Īśvara Purī there, was probable. This is also indicated by Śrī Caitanya's saying to Īśvara Purī "Now that I have seen your holy feet I regard my pilgrimage to Gayā as successful . . . . . No holy place on earth is holier than your holy feet, the sight of which brings immediate relief to one's ancestors from all kinds of bondage" (*C. Bh.*, I, xii, 49). This was, however, not the first meeting of Nimāi with Īśvara Purī. They had met once before at Nadiyā. At that time Īśvara Purī's religious advice to him did not prove effective. But even so he was so much impressed by his personality that he regarded him as an incarnation of God.[2] Nimāi also must have been highly impressed by the devotional qualities of Īśvara Purī and secretly harboured a desire to be initiated by him ever since his mind turned to religion, which must, of course, have been long after his first meeting with him.

On his return journey from Gayā, Nimāi was blessed with the vision of Kṛṣṇa in a village called Kanāira Nātaśālā. Ever since then Kṛṣṇa took complete possession of his personality and he was a completely changed man when he returned to Navadvīpa. His pride of learning and his aggressive spirit were gone. His fondness for dress and care for personal appearence had disappeared. He was the meekest and the simplest man on earth. He hardly paid any attention to anything of this world, and was always lost in the thought of Kṛṣṇa. Tears incessantly flowed from his eyes at the very name of Kṛṣṇa or anything associated with him sent him into trance. It was impossible for him to teach his pupils. The only meaning he knew of the Sūtras of grammar which he was accustomed to teach, or, in fact, of any word or letter, was Kṛṣṇa (*C. Bh.*, II, i, 144, 171). So he always discoursed on Kṛṣṇa, and in the midst of the discourses laughed and wept and raved and lost himself in trance. The Pandit, who was so far given only to scholastic pursuits, was now completely mad with the love for Kṛṣṇa (*C. Bh.*, II, i, 242). His pupils did not know what to do. It was not possible for them to leave him and take their lessons from someone else. They went and reported every thing to Gaṅgādāsa, their preceptor's preceptor, who gave some good counsel to Nimāi. Nimāi promised earnestly to follow his advice, but he could not. In utter helplessness he had to tell his pupils one day, "I always see a dark complexioned Boy of excusite beauty standing before me and playing on his flute. I cannot always, but speak of Him and Him alone. I must, therefore, stop teaching from today. You are

[1]See A. K. Majumdar, *Caitanya His : Life and Movement*, p. 137. fn. 1.

[2]*balena īśvara purī—sunaha paṅdita/*
tumi je īśvara aṁsa jāninū niścita// C. Bh., I, xii, 55.

free to go and take your lessons anywhere you like (*C. Bh.*, II, i, 367, 369)." And so saying he closed the book and burst into tears. The pupils also closed their books saying "No more education for us Master! Only bless us that we may remember life after life what we have learnt at thy feet." The Master was visibly moved. He took them one by one in his lap and kissed and wept. Then he performed Saṁkīrtana with them. He stood in the middle singing:

haraye namaḥ kṛṣṇa-yādavāya namaḥ|
gopāla govinda rāma srī-madhusūdana||

and keeping time with his hands, while the pupils went round and round repeating the song. As the song and the dance went on their hearts were filled with the presence of the divine and tears of joy flowed from their eyes. Many people from the neighbourhood were attracted to the scene. But every one, who came as a spectator was caught in the current of devotion and began to sing and dance. This marked the end of the academic career of Nimāi and the beginning of Saṁkīrtana, which was the professed mission of his life.

The leader of Vaiṣṇavas

The news of this change in Nimāi spread all over Navadvīpa. People thought that it was a fit of lunacy. But the Vaiṣṇavas of the town knew that Nimāi had become a Vaiṣṇava—a change though seemingly impossible, they had long wished and prayed for, and so there was no end to their rejoicings. Nimāi was soon acknowledged as the leader of the Vaiṣṇavas of the town and became the nucleus of their devotional activities, which now began to grow in intensity with great rapidity. People in large numbers began to be drawn to him. His influence was so contageous that the very touch or presence of his body converted sinners into saints. He was like a live wire charged with the current of divine love and anyone, who came into his contact, was similarly charged.

Principal among those, who joined the group of Vaiṣṇavas, Nimāi was now heading, were Nityānanda, Advaitācārya, Śrīvāsa, Gadādhara and Haridāsa. Nityānanda was an Avadhūta Saṁnyāsin, whom tradition regards as the elder brother of Kṛṣṇa, and who plays the second important role in the cult of Śrī Caitanya.[1] He was born at Ekcākā, in the

[1]R. G. Bhandarkar, *Vaiṣṇavism*, p. 83, identifies Nityānanda with Nimāi's elder brother Viśvarūpa. In Aufrecht's *Catalogus Catalogorum* also Nityānanda is mentioned as the elder brother of Śrī Caitanya. Dr. S. K. De, op. cit., p. 59 f.n., thinks that the source of the mistake is the fact that Śrī Caitanya used to address him as an elder brother. But the source actually is the theological belief that both Nityānanda and Viśvarūpa are the manifestations of the spiritual principle known as Mahā-Saṁkrṣaṇa, on account of which they are actually regarded as identical. Vṛndāvana Dāsa describes Viśvarūpa as *Nityānanda-svarūpera abheda śarīra* (*C. Bh.*, I, v, 93; also I, v, 118).

district of Bīrbhum and was about eight years older than Nimāi. His parents Haṇāi Pandit and Padmāvatī are said to have made a gift of him to a Saṁnyāsin, who had come to beg for him. He travelled all over the country for about twenty years and was at Navadvīpa, when, providentially, he met Nimāi. According to another account he went to Navadvīpa from Vṛndāvana at the bidding of Īśvara Purī, who told him that Śrī Kṛṣṇa, whom he was looking for at Vṛndāvana had appeared as Nimāi Pandit at Navadvīpa.

Advaitācārya was an inhabitant of Lāur, in Sylhet. He was born in 1434 AD, that is, fifty-two years before Nimāi. His father Nāvā was a courtier of Kṛṣṇa Dāsa, the Raja of Lāur. He came to Navadvīpa for higher education. His scholarship was well recognized and it won him the title of Advaitācārya. He was a pious man and was regarded as the holiest of Vaiṣṇavas (*C. Bh.*, I, ii, 74). His heart broke to see that the people had lost faith in God. He was accustomed to sit on the bank of Ganges and pray to Lord Kṛṣṇa that he might appear on earth again and restore the faith of the people. He is even said to have taken a vow to make Kṛṣṇa come down on earth and, as Vṛndāvana Dāsa says, Śrī Caitanya often referred to him as the cause of his advent (*C. Bh.*, I, ii, 91).

Śrīvāsa[1] was another Brāhmaṇa scholar, who had gone to Navadvīpa from Sylhet with Advaitācārya for study and settled there. He must have been quite old when Nimāi was born, for he and his wife Mālinī, who was a friend of Śacī, were present at the time of his birth. He was a constant companion of Advaita. He had a musical voice and was a good singer.

Gadādhara was a student of Nyāya and was young and handsome. He was intensly devoted to Nimāi and ranked as the highest in the inner circle of his followers.

Haridāsa[2] was a Mohamedan convert to Vaiśṇavism. He was born at Būḍan in the district of Jessore in 1464 AD. His father Malāi Kāzī was a magistrate. He came to Navadvīpa when he was young and was considerably influenced by Advaitācārya, who admitted him into the Vaiṣṇava faith in spite of great opposition from the Vaiṣṇavas. The Vaiṣṇavas later reconciled themselves to him on account of his inimitable qualities of piety and devotion and his strength of conviction, which enabled him to withstand severe persecution at the hands of the Mohamedans.

Saṁkīrtana

The court-yard of the house of Śrīvāsa became a regular meeting place

[1]Also called Saīnivāsa.
[2]His Mohamedan name is not known.

for the Vaiṣṇavas. Here Nimāi had his nightly Saṁkīrtanas in which only his close associates were allowed to participate. The doors of the house of Srīvāsa were closed when the Saṁkīrtana started and no outsider was allowed to enter. It was at these meetings that Nimāi is said to have revealed his divine form to his followers. These nocturnal and private gatherings continued for some time. But as already indicated the professed mission of Nimāi's life was to preach Saṁkīrtana as the only means of deliverance in the age of Kali. He could not, therefore, confine his devotional activities to the limited circle of his friends, and it did not take him long to organize Saṁkīrtana parties and processions in which thousands and thousands of people participated and which paraded the streets of Navadvīpa, singing and dancing and surcharging the whole atmosphere of the city with unique devotional fervour.

The movement had a universal appeal, but a small and influential section of people, who were proud of their learning and social status, did not like the tumultuous scenes it released, which threatened to wipe off the age old distinctions of caste and creed and high and low in society. They, therefore, complained to Cānda Kāzī,[1] the Mohamedan governer of the town. The Kāzī tried to crush the movement,[2] but fell a helpless prey to the tremendous spiritual influence of Nimāi's personality and became a Vaiaṣṇava.

Saṁnyāsa

The conversion of the Kāzī broke the bone of the opposition Nimāi had to encounter, but the pedantic scholars and the godless persons persisted in their attitude of scornful indifference. He, therefore, resolved to renounce the world and become a Saṁnyāsin. Thus he thought everybody would be compelled to revere him and he would be able to work exclusively for the redemption of all (*C. Bh.*, II, XXV, 224-26). He persuaded Keśava Bhāratī, a Saṁnyāsin of the Bhāratī order, who lived at Katavā, near Navadvīpa to initiate him into Saṁnyāsa. The initiation ceremony took place at Katavā, on the Purṇimā of Māgha in Śaka 1431, that is, January 1510 AD, when Nimāi was twenty-four years old. On initiation he was given the name Śrī Kṛṣṇa Caitanya. There is nothing to suggest that Śrī Caitanya was considerably influended by Keśava Bhāratī either before or after the initiation. As Keśava Bhāratī lived at Katavā and Śrī Caitanya lived at Navadvīpa, there was very little chance of personal contacts between them. According to the account given by Vṛndāvana-dāsa the initiation itself was a formal affair. Śrī Caitanya first whispered the Mantra into the ears of Keśava Bhāratī

[1]K Sirāzuddina Khān.

[2]He broke the *mṛdangas* or *Khols* (drums) of a Saṁkīrtana party and the place in Navadvīpa, where this happened is to this day called *Khola Bhāngāra Dāngā.*

and enquired if that was the Mantra he wanted to give. Keśava Bhāratī confirmed the Mantra and then formally whispered it into the ears of Śrī Caitanya (*C. Bh.*, II, xxvi, 197-201). The fact that Keśava Bhāratī did not add 'Bhāratī,' the name of the order to which he belonged, after the name of Śrī Caitanya also indicates that the initiation was formal. Probably he did not like one, whose spiritual greatness he had recognized and whom he regarded as the spiritual master of all, to be marked out as his disciple by name.[1]

Journey to Purī and the conversion of Sārvabhauma

Not more than a month after his initiation Śrī Caitanya took leave of his heart-broken mother and the Vaiṣṇavas of Navadvīpa to go and live at Purī in Orissa. Four of his disciples, Nityānanda, Dāmodara Pandit, Jagadānanda and Mukunda accompanied him to Purī. An important event in the life of Śrī Caitanya, after his arrival at Purī and in the history of the great religious movement he was heading, was the conversion of Vāsudeva Sārvabhauma Bhattāchārya, a veteran scholar of Nyāya and Vedānta.[2] Vāsudeva had founded the dialectical school of Navya Nyāya at Navadvīpa, to which scholars were drawn from all over India and which had eclipsed the Mithila school, the most important centre of learning in Northern India at that time.[3] He was driven from Navadvīpa by the persecution of Husen Śāha, the Mohamedan ruler of Bengal and was now living at Purī under the patronage of Pratāparudra, the king of Orissa, who held him in high esteem. He was about eighty years old, when Śrī Caitanya arrived at Purī. Vāsudeva saw him lying unconscious in a fit of emotion before the holy image in the temple of Jagannātha and brought him home. When he came to know that the charming young man was a grandson of Nīlāmbara Cakravartin, who was a friend of his father Viśārada, he became anxious about his future and tried to initiate him into Vedānta. He gave him religious discourses for seven days, but these did not have the desired effect. Śrī Caitanya said, "The meaning of the Upaniṣads is quite clear to me. But your explanations seem to cloud their real meaning by adopting Saṁkara's indirect method of explanation and avoiding the direct method." The young Saṁnyāsin thus threw out a challenge to Vāsudeva and a long discussion followed. The arguments of Śrī Caitanya and his simple and direct explanations of the Sūtras combined with the depth of feeling and conviction,

[1] *tumi se jagadguru jānilā niścaya|*
tomāra gurura jogya keha kabbu naya||—*C. Bh.*, II, xvi, 170.

[2] The author of the Sanskrit work *Sārvabhauma-Nirukti*, and the teacher of Raghunatha Śiromaṇi, whose name tops the list of those, who founded the Bengal school of logic.

[3] See D. C. Sen, *Caitanya and His Companions*, pp. 76-81.

from which they came, won over the old scholar from the path of Advaita Vedānta to that of pure devotion. He not only accepted Śrī Caitanya as his saviour, but became so passionately attached to him that he could bear anything in the world but not his separation (*CC*, II, ix).[1]

Travel in south India and the meeting with Rāmānanda

Soon after his arrival at Purī Śrī Caitanya started on a long pilgrimage in south India, which lasted for about a couple of years. His visit to the South created a deep and lasting impression on the minds of the people. The stream of devotion which had flown freely in that part of the country in the days of the Tāmil Ālvārs, but which had dried up through passage of time was revived. This was visible in the form of a sudden outburst of devotional songs in Kanarese and Marāthī. The Marāthā saint Tukārāma, and the author of numerous devotional songs acknowledged the debt of the teachers of the order of Śrī Caitanya even a hundred years later.[2]

In the earlier part of his journey Śrī Caitanya met Rāmānanda Rāya, governor of Rājmundrī, under Prataparudra, king of Orissa, near Rājmundrī on the bank of Godāvarī. Rāmānanda Rāya was a devout Vaiṣṇava and Vāsudeva Sārvabhauma had already spoken of him to Śrī Caitanya. He became one of his closest associates and was his constant companion during his long stay at Purī towards the end of his life. He stayed at Rājmundrī for several days to have the pleasure of his company. During this period he had important theological discussions with him of which an elaborate account is given by Kṛṣṇadāsa Kavirāja in *Caitanya Caritāmṛta*, and which have an important place in the development of the Vaiṣṇava theological doctrine, attributed to Śrī Caitanya. Doubt is sometimes expressed about the authenticity of these discussions on the ground that in the description given by Kṛṣṇadāsa Kavirāja texts are freely quoted from the works of Rūpa, Sanātana and Jīva, which were not yet written, along with those from Bhāgavata and Gītā.[3] But it is obvious that this is done to enrich the author's own account of the discussion and to make it more effective rather than "to depict Caitanya as a scholar," for otherwise the wise scholar would not quote from the works, which were written later and least of all from his own *Govindalilāmṛta*. The poetic and somewhat pedantic exposition of the principles and stages of devotion does not render the discussion as purely imaginative. On the other hand it may be suggested that the author quotes from the works of the Gośvāmins, who were the contemporaries

[1]Vasudeva is reported to have been blessed at this time by the vision of God in His Ṣaṇ-bhuja form, in Śrī Caitanya, *C. Bh.*, III, iii, 94.

[2]G. Nelson Fraser, *The Poems of Tukārām*, I, No. 80.

[3]S. K. De, op. cit., pp. 70-71.

of Śrī Caitanya precisely with the object of showing that the description of the doctrine of devotion, as elaborated in the discussion, accords with the descriptions given by the learned disciples of Śrī Caitanya, whom he had commissioned with the task of propagating the doctrine, and is, therefore, authentic.

From Rājmundrī Śrī Caitanya proceeded further south. He visited Sidhaut, Veṅkatagirī, Śivakānci or Conjeevaram, Viṣnaukāncī, Pakṣtīrtha, and Vriddhācalam. From Vriddhācalam he went to Cidambaram, Vedavana, Kumbakonam and Śrīrangam. At Śrīrangam he stayed for four months at the house of Veṅkata Bhatta and his brother Tirumalla and Prabodhānanda. Veṅkata Bhatta was the father of Gopāla Bhatta, one of the six Gosvāmins, who propogated the teachings of Śrī Caitanya and Prabodhānanda was the author of *Caitanya Candrodaya* and an exponent of Śrī Caitanya's doctrine and divinity. From Śrīrangam he proceeded to Riśaba Parvata in the Madurā district, where he met Paramānanda Purī, who was also one of his closest associates during his stay at Purī. From Madurā he went to Rāmesvaram, Dhanuṣkodi Setubandha, Śrī vaikuntha and Cape-Comorin.

Then he turned northward and, travelling along the bank of Truvattaur river in the Travencore state, reached the temple of Ādikeśava in Trivandrum district, where he acquired a copy of *Brahmasaṁhitā* (V. chapter). He visited the Śṛṅgerī monastery in Mysore, founded by Śaṁkarācārya and Udipi, in South Kanada district, the home of Madhva and discoursed with the followers of Madhva. Proceeding further north he reached Pandharpur, where he worshipped Viṭṭhala Deva, the famous deity of the Marhaṭṭās. Then, passing through the land between the rivers Krishnā and Venva (Bhīmā) to the west of Sholāpur, from where he obtained a copy of Vilvamaṅgal's *Kṛṣṇakarṇāmṛta*, which he cherished throughout, as a precious treasure of his life, and the bank of Tāptī, he arrived on the banks of river Narmadā. Then, taking a south-easterly course, he went to Dhanuṣtīrtha, Nāsika and Kusāvarta, the source of the river Godāvarī. From here he turned to the east and, proceeding along the bank of Godāvarī, reached Rājmundrī, where Rāya Rāmānaṅda had been anxiously waiting for his return, and from Rājmundrī he went back to Purī.

According to Govinda Karmakāra Śrī Caitanya had gone farther north on his return from the south and visited Somanātha, Dvārakā and Prabhāsa. It may be noted that there is considerable difference in the accounts of Śrī Caitanya's travels in the south, given by his different biographers, and it is difficult to determine the exact itinerary. Even Kṛṣṇadāsa Kavirāja starts his description by admitting that it is not in strict chronological order.

Kṛṣṇadāsa Kavirāja's account, however, seems to be more correct as he got it from Gopāla Bhatta and the diaries of Svarūpa Dāmodara and

Raghunātha Dāsa (*CC*, II, viii, 263), who were the closest disciples of Śrī Caitanya and had lived long with him. It is also certain that Śrī Caitanya travelled widely in the south and left a deep impression upon the minds of the people. Kavikarṇapūra says that Śrī Caitanya's Vaiṣṇavism was accepted as the state religion of the Karnāta country (*Caitanya Candrodaya Nātaka*, Act, vii).

Shortly after Śrī Caitanya's return to Purī, Rāmānanda Rāya came to stay there with him for the rest of his life. Pratāparudra not only permitted him to do so but was pleased to order that he would continue to draw his salary. Paramānanda Purī, who had met him in the south and Govinda, an attendant of Īśvara Purī, who was commanded by him to serve Śrī Caitanya as his personal attendant, Rāmabhadra Ācārya, Bhagavān Ācarya and Kāśiśvara also came. Bhavānanda Rāya, the father of Rāmānanda Rāya, who was feudatory chief to Pratāparudra and had become a fervent disciple of Śrī Caitanya along with his three other sons, also dedicated his son Bānīnātha to the personal service of Śrī Caitanya. Of the other disciples of Śrī Caitanya Nityānanda, Gopīnātha Ācārya, Jagadānanda and Svarūpa Dāmodara (known as Puruśottama Ācārya before his Saṁnyāsa), were already staying at Purī and had gone to Ālālanatha along with Sārvabhauma to receive him before the conclusion of his return journey to Purī.

The conversion of Pratāparudra

The most important event which took place at this time and which firmly planted Caitanyism in Orissa was the conversion of Gajapati Pratāparudra himself.[1] It is the triumph of Śrī Caitanya over Sārvabhauma Bhattācārya and the latter's acceptance of him as his saviour that must have first drawn the attention of the scholarly and religious king of Orissa towards him. The king begged an interview with him through Sārvabhauma, but he refused to meet him on the ground that it was not proper for a Saṁnyāsin to have familiarity with a king. When the king's efforts through the other companions of Śrī Caitanya also failed, he one day stole into the court-yard of Kāśī Miśra, where he was lying unconscious in a trance, in the lap of Nityānanda, whilst his other companions were performing Kīrtana round him, and fell on his feet. On regaining consciousness Śrī Caitanya expressed deep regret for having come in contact with one, who was devoted to power and pelf. When the king heard this there was no end to his grief. He offered to surrender all his wealth and power at the feet of Śrī Caitanya and prayed to him to be

[1]S. K. De, says that, "there is no satisfactory evidence to show that Pratāparudra was actually converted into the new faith," but Jīvadeva Ācārya, the family priest and court poet of Pratāparudra clearly alludes to his conversion in his *Bhakti Bhāgavata Mahākāvya*. See Sambidānanda Dās, *Śri Caitanya Mahāprabhu*, p. 120.

accepted as the lowliest of his servants. Śrī Caitanya was moved by these words and clasped the king in a loving embrace, which brought tears of joy into his eyes. Rāmānanda Rāya, describing this incident, in his famous Sanskrit drama *Jagannātha Vallabha*, marvels that the Rājā, who was a terror to the Pathāns and whose physical strength and iron contact was dreaded by wrestlers, melted at his touch.

Soon after his return from the south, about two hundred Bengali disciples of Srī Cairanya, led by Advaitācārya, arrived at Purī to celeberate the occasion, and to participate in the car festival of Srī Jagannātha. A huge Kīrtana procession, the first of its kind in Purī, was organized, in which Śrī Caitanya and his followers sang and danced in groups in front of the car carrying the image of Lord Jagannātha, as it moved from the Jagannātha temple to Guṅḍīcā. The Bengal disciples stayed for four months at Purī, passing their time in daily *kīrtans* and theological discussions in the company of Śrī Caitanya, after which they were sent back to Bengal. This was the first of a series of pilgrimages to Purī, which were performed every year by the Bengal devotees during the life time of Śrī Caitanya. Śrī Caitanya, however, persuaded Nityānanda, after the second pilgrimage, not to visit Purī every year as it interfered with the propogation of Bhakti in Bengal, a task with which he and Advaita had been specially comissioned.

Pilgrimage to Vṛndāvana

In the year 1514 Śrī Caitanya started on a pilgrimage to Vṛndāvana. About five years before at the time of his Saṁnyāsa, he had dispatched Lokanātha Ācārya, one of his principal disciples with the object of reclaiming the holy city, which had long been neglected and lost (Premavilāsa). Lokanātha had succeeded in his mission, and this was a landmark in the revival of Vaiṣṇavism in northern India. Śrī Caitanya was naturally anxious to visit the newly restored Vṛndāvana. He, therefore started for Bengal enroute to Vṛndāvana, with Svarūpa Dāmodara, Paramānanda Purī, Jagadānanda, Kāśīśvara, Haridāsa, Gopīnātha Ācārya and others. As he was now virtually recognized as the state-god of Orissa elaborate arrangements regarding his journey through the territory were made. Passing through Bhavānīpur, Bhuvaneśvara and Cuttack he reached the border of Orissa, where he halted for a few days, so that necessary arrangements regarding his safe conduct through the adjoining territory of a ferocious Mohamedan chief could be made. At this time the Mohamedan chief, whose curiosity was greatly aroused on hearing about Śrī Caitanya, himself came to meet him. He was so much overpowered by the personality of Śrī Caitanya that he fell on his feet and prayed to be accepted as one of his humble servants. Having received his grace he made adequate arrangements for his journey through his territory to Pānihātī (*CC*, II, xvi). He stayed at Pānihātī for a night and then went to Kumārahatta, where Śrīnivāsa lived, to Kāncrāpāra where Śivānanda Sena and Vāsudeva Datta lived and to Jasdā, where the images of Jagannātha and Śrī Caitanya, installed by Jagadīśa Pandit still exist. From Jasdā he went to the house of Vidyāvācaspati, brother of Vāsudeva Sārvabhauma, at Vidyānagar. A large number of people, including even those, who, five years before, had been hostile to Śrī Caitanya, came to pay homage to him at Vidyānagar from distant places and the rush was so great that he had to leave the place stealthily and go to Kuliā, the present town of Navadvīpa, where he delivered a famous discourse on Bhāgavata.

Then he went to Rāmakeli, where lived two Brāhmaṇa brothers, who were ministers in the court of Mohamedan king Hussain Shah of Bengal and were known by their Mohamedan names or titles of Sāker Malik and Dabīr Khās. They were won over by Śrī Caitanya and became his disciples. He called them Sanātana and Rūpa, by which names they are now known. The conversion of these brothers was a great event in the history of the development of Caitanya Vaiṣṇavism. For they and their nephew Jīva turned out to be the three great pillars of the faith, upon whose writings rest its theological and philosophical foundations. It is said that Śrī Caitanya was advised by Sanātana and Rūpa not to go on pilgrimage to Vṛndāvana in the company of a large number of people, who were following him, and so he returned to Purī. Dr. Das concludes from sources in Assamese literature that before returning to Purī Śrī Caitanya paid a visit to Assam, where at the foot of the Manikuta hill, he met his beloved disciple Dāmodara and lived for some time in a cave now known as Caitanya Guphā.[1]

He started for Vṛndāvana again in the autumn of 1515. This time he took with him only Balabhadra Bhattācārya and one other attendant, followed a different route through the forests of Jhārikhaṅda to avoid being noticed by people. Arriving at Vārāṇasī he met Raghunātha, afterwards known as Raghunātha Bhatta Gosvāmin, besides his old followers Tapana Miśra and Candraśekhara. He stayed at Vārāṇasī for ten days and then proceeded to Allahabad. From Allahabad he went to Mathura and Vṛndāvana along the bank of river Jamunā. At Vṛndāvana the intensity of his love for Kṛṣṇa increased a thousand-fold. He wandered through the forests of Vṛndāvana, seeing all the places connected with Kṛṣṇa Līlā, and himself located the sites of Rādhākuṅda and Śyāmakuṅda.

Kṛṣṇadāsa has given a vivid description of Śrī Caitanya's state of mind during his journey to Vṛndāvana and his wanderings in the holy forests, where he found every creeper and blade of grass vibrating with the spiritual associations of Kṛṣṇa Līlā. He chanted the Name of Kṛṣṇa, danced

[1]Dr. Sambidānanda Dās, *Śri Caitanya Mahāprabhu*, p. 145 f.

and wept and occasionally fell senseless on the ground, exhibiting in unprecedented form all the *aṣṭasāttvika bhāvas* or the bodily manifestations of divine love. His personality was so charged with the current of divine love that his very sight generated the feeling of devotion and compelled people to chant the name of Kṛṣṇa.[1] Even the Mohamedans, who came in contact with him could not escape the magic influence of his personality. Caitanya Caritāmṛta narrates the incident of a Muslim divine (Pīra), afterwards known as Kṛṣṇadāsa, a Muslim prince Bijulī Khān and his attendants, who were later known as Pathāna Vaiṣṇavas,[2] becoming his disciples at their very first meeting with him, on his way to Mahāvana. The Pīr, with whom Śrī Caitanya discoursed on the Muslim scriptures acknowledged that the Name of Kṛṣṇa spontaneously came on his lips to see him (*CC*, II, xviii).

On his return from Vṛndāvana Śrī Caitanya stayed at Allahabad for some time during Kumbha Melā. Here he met a Vaidika Brāhmaṇa named Vallabha Bhatta, who, according to most scholars, is Śrī Vallabhācārya, the founder of the Vaiṣṇava sect of that name.[3] Here he also met Rūpa

[1] *jei jei jana pāilā prabhur daraśana|*
śei preme matta kare ucca saṁkīrtana||
—*CC*, II, xviii, 209.

[2] *pathān vaiṣṇava bali haila tār khyāti|*
sarvatra gāiyā bule mahāprabhu kirti||
—*CC*, II, xviii, 210.

[3] *See* D. C. Sen, *Caitanya and His Age*, p. 239; *Caitanya and His Companions*, pp. 200f.

Also *see* M. T. Kennedy, *The Caitanya Movement*, p. 49.

The reason why Kṛṣṇadāsa Kavirāja refers to Vallabhācārya as simply Vallabha Bhatta, without making any mention of his position as the founder of an important Vaiṣṇava sect, may, it is suggested, have been that his followers forcibly took possession of the Gaudīya Vaiṣṇava temple of Srīnātha at Gokula and Kṛṣṇadāsa was a witness to it (*see* A. K. Majumdar, op. cit., p. 236).

There is, however, no doubt that Vallabhācārya met Śrī Caitanya at Purī, as mentioned in *Caitanya Caritāmṛta* and some of the texts of Vallabha Sampradāya. *Caitanya Caritāmṛta* also narrates how Śrī Caitanya refused to listen to Vallabhācārya's commentary on Bhāgavata Purāṇa, which he was writing at this time, and took him to task for his interpretaion of Bhāgavata, which was opposed to that of Śrīdhara Svāmin (*CC*, III, vii, 115-120). It is significant in this connection that Vallabhācārya's commentary was never completed.

Caitanya Caritāmṛta also records how Vallabha, who had introduced the worship of Bāla-Gopāla in his sect, was influenced by the *Madhura Rasa Upāsanā* of Śrī Caitanya and was led in the end to obtain Kiśore-Gopāla Mantra-dīksā from Gadādhara Pandit (*CC*, III, vii, 155). The importance attached to the worship of Rādhā in the Sampradāya of Vallabhācārya, as evidenced particularly by the works of Vitthalanātha, son of Vallabhācārya, therefore, is most probably due to the influence of Śrī Caitanya (A. K. Majumdar, op. cit., p. 236). An important factor in this connection must have been the fact that Viṭṭhalanātha lived for some time in Navadvīpa for the study of Nyāya, and he must have come in close contact with the followers of Śrī Caitanya (M. C. Parekh, *Śri Vallabhācārya*, pp. 160-61).

and his younger brother Anupama, who had renounced the world for his sake and come all the way from Bengal to receive his instructions. He gave them detailed instructions on Bhakti for ten days and sent them to Vṛndāvana commissioning Rūpa to devote himself to the preparation of foundational literature for the propogation of Bhakti. Proceeding to Vārāṇasī he met Sanātana, the elder brother of Rūpa. Sanātana had been imprisoned by the king, because his meeting with Śrī Caitanya had brought a complete change in his state of mind, and he was not able to attend to the duties of his ministerial office. He managed, however, to escape from the prison and go in disguise to Vārāṇasī to surrender himself completely at the feet of his master. Śrī Caitanya gave him elaborate discourses on Bhakti and commissioned him as well with the task of laying securer foundations of Vaiṣṇavism by rediscovering the holy places in Vṛndāvana, building temples and producing canonical literature.

An important event at Vārāṇasī this time was his triumph in theological discussions over the Māyāvādin Samnyāsins, who followed the path of Jnāna and deprecated Bhakti as pure sentimentalism. The result was the conversion of Prakāśānanda Sarasvatī, the head of the Māyāvādin Samnyāsins of Vārānasī, along with his many followers, which was a great step in the revival of Vaiṣṇavism in northern India.[1]

[1]S. K. De, however, remarks "With the exception of the so called conversion of a leading Vedāntist, Prakāśānanda, Caitanya's presence at Benares does not appear to have been very fruitful, and made little impression in that great centre of Śiva worship and Advaita Vedānta (op. cit., p. 75)." He refers in this connection to Śrī Caitanya's own regret, recorded in *Caitanya Caritamṛta*, that his sentimental wares did not sell in Kāśī (*CC.*, II, xxv, 161-62). But he has obviously missed the lines, which follow immediately and in which he states that since his followers did not like that he should carry the burden of the wares back, he distributed them at Vārāṇasī free of cost, as also the lines in which his followers express their satisfaction on his having ultimately redeemed Vārāṇasī, the centre of religion in northern India, which was so far deprived of his blessings, though he had blessed the east, the west and the south (*CC*, II, xxv. 124-25).

Some scholars doubt even the story of Prakāśānanda on the ground that Murārī Gupta, Kavikarṇapūra and Vṛndāvana Dāsa are silent on the point. It is obvious that this negative evidence by itself does not prove that the story is false and fabricated. But it has no meaning at all, at least in so far as Vṛndāvana Dāsa and Kavikarṇapūra are concerned, since they do not give an account of Śrī Caitanya's journey to the west to which the story relates. As regards Murārī Gupta it would not be fair to say that he is completely silent on the point. On the other hand he says that Mahāprabhu blessed with Kṛṣṇa-bhakti 'all the inhabitants of Vārānaṣi' (Kadcā, 413, 20), which cannot be interpreted to mean 'all the inhabitants of Vārāṇasī except Prakāśananda.' Besides, there is no reason to disbelieve the account of Kṛṣṇadāsa Kạvirāja, whose informants are Sanātana and Raghunātha Bhatta, the eye-witnesses of the whole episode at Vārāṇasī.

Particularly important in this connection is the evidence of Prakāśānand's *Vedanta-siddhāntamuktāvali*, which clearly shows the influence of Śrī Caitanya. The author rejects *Vivartavāda* and admits that Brahman's Śakti is the material cause of the world. *See* A. K. Majumdar, op. cit., p. 221.

The last days in Purī and the mysterious passing away

Śrī Caitanya returned to Purī probably in April 1516. Thus for six years after his Saṁnyāsa he travelled all over the country, broadcasting the seeds of Bhakti. The seeds having sprouted and taken root in the soil, he could now leave the plants to the care of his able leiutenants, and pass the remaining eighteen years of his life in monastic seclusion at Purī. So he settled there permanently in the garden-house of Kāśī Miśra. All his days were passed in deep communion with the Lord, interrupted only by occasional conversation with a few of his chosen disciples, who lived near him or came from distant places to receive instructions from him.

The biographers of Śrī Caitanya are agreed that he passed away in Śaka 1455.[1] But according to Dr. D. C. Sen he passed away in the month of Asāḍha (July, 1533 AD), which cannot be correct. For, Kṛṣṇadāsa says that Srī Caitanya lived for forty-eight years, twenty-four years as householder and twenty-four years as Saṁnyāsin;[2] which means that he could not have passed away before February 1534 AD. This is confirmed by an account given by Narahari Cakravartin[3] in his *Bhakti-ratnākara,*[4] which states that Śrīnivāsācārya started for Purī on the fifth lunar day in the month of Māgha and learnt about the passing away of Śrī Caitanya on the way. This suggests that Śrī Caitanya passed away in the month of Māgha (February). If he had passed away in Asāḍha (July) the tragic news must have reached Bengal before Śrinivāsācārya started, as there was regular communication between Purī and Navadvīpa since Śrī Caitanya took Saṁnyāsa and settled at Purī and the devotees from Bengal went to Purī every year before Rathayātrā in July and returned in October. Further Kṛṣṇadāsa says that Śrī Caitanya sent the presents he had received on the occasion of the performence of Gopa-Līlā (*CC*, III, xix, 11) to his mother at Navadvīpa through Jagadānanda, and Jagadānanda returned from Navadvīpa after staying there for about a month, with a message from Advaitācārya to Śrī Caitanya suggesting that their mission was over, which served to highten Śrī Caitanya's feeling of seperation from Kṛṣṇa and ultimately brought his end (*CC*, III, xix, 26, 28, 30). Gopa-līlā was performed by Śrī Caitanya on the Nandotsava day in August or September. Jagadānanda must have gone to

[1]*cauddaśata sāta śake janmera pramāṇa|*
cauddaśata pañcānne hailā antardhāna|| *CC*, I, viii, 8.

[2]*cabbis batsara prabhu kāilā gṛhabāsa|*
niraṅtara kaila tāhe kīrtana-bilāsa||
cabbīsa batsara śeṣe kariyā saṃnyāsa|
cabbisa batsara kaila nīlācale bāsa|| *CC*, I, xiii, 9-10.

[3]Son of Jagannātha, who was a disciple of Visvanātha Cakravartin.

[4]The work, though it must have been written in the eighteenth century, is regarded as authentic by historians. *See* B. B. Majumdar, *Caitanya caritera upādāna,* pp. 485-86.

Navadīpa in October with the devotees from Bengal after their usual four months stay at Purī and returned in December. This also suggests that Śrī Caitanya could not have passed away in July as held by Dr. Sen. The source of Dr. Sen's information is an account given in the *Caitanya-maṅgala* of Jayānaṅda, which is neither recognized by the Vaiṣṇavas nor regarded as authoritative enough by the scholars.[1] Its description of the life of Śri Caitanya is based on hearsay and runs in many respects counter to the accounts given by other biographers, which are generally accepted as authentic.[2]

As Śrī Caitanya passed away at Purī, where he also spent the last twenty-four years of his life, the accounts given by his disciples of Orissa in regard to the latter part of his life may generally be regarded as more trustworthy than those of his Bengal disciples. Turning to these we find that Acyutānaṅda, a contemporary of Śrī Caitanya says in his *Śūnya Saṁhitā* that after the passing away of Śrī Caitanya king Pratāparudra organized a one month festival in his honour, beginning from Vaiśākhi Pūrṇimā. Īśvaradāsa, a later writer says in his *Caitanya-bhāgavata* (Chap. LXXV) that Śrī Caitanya passed away on the third lunar day of Vaiśākha. It may be difficult from these accounts to determine the exact date of the passing away of Śrī Caitanya, but combining these with the accounts given in the more authoritative biographies of his Bengal disciples we can safely conclude that he could not have passed away before February 1534 AD.

The manner in which Śrī Caitanya passed away is veiled with mystery. The general belief is that he disappeared physically and merged with the deity of the temple of Jagannātha, as Acyutānanda, Īśvaradāsa and Locanadāsa say, or in the deity of the temple of Ṭoṭā Gopīnātha in Purī, as mentioned in *Bhakti-ratnākara*. Dr. Sen, however, thinks that he died of septic fever, caused by injury to his left foot from a brick while dancing on the Rathayātrā day. He says that he was in the Guñdicā temple of Jagannātha, when he suffered from high fever. "When the priests apprehended his end to be near they shut the gate against all visitors. This they did to take time for burying him and repairing the floor after burial. The priests opened the gate at 11 PM and gave out that Śrī Caitanya was incorporated with the image of Jagannātha."[3]

[1]There is no doubt that Locanadāsa's *Caitanya-maṅgla* also mentions that Srī Caitanya passed away on the seventh lunar day of Asāḍha. But scholars do not attach any historical importance to this work (*see* B. B. Majumdar, op. cit., p. 274) and it is likely that Locanadāsa derives his information from Jayānaṅda himself, as it was written in 1575 (D. C. Sen, *Baṅga Bhāṣā o Sāhitya*, V, 314), soon after Jayānaṅda's *Caitanya-mañgala*, which was written sometime between 1560 and 1570 (B B. Majumdar, op. cit., p. 230).

[2]B. B. Majumdar, op. cit., pp. 223-36. and S.K. De, op. cit., p. 77.

[3]D. C. Sen, *Caitanya and his age*, p. 264.

Dr. Sen seems to have constructed the story partly from Jayānand's account, according to which Śrī Caitanya was hurt in the foot, while dancing on the Rathayātrā day and partly from Locanadāsa's *Caitanya-maṅgala*, which states that when Śrī Caitanya entered the Guṅdīcā temple of Jagannātha, its doors automatically closed and Sanātana, Haridāsa and others remained crying outside. We have already said that Jayānanda is not reliable, his account being based on hearsay. The statement in Locanadasa's *Caitanya-maṅgala* is said to occur in spurious pages contained only in one of the editions of the work.[1] But apart from the nature of the sources from which the story has been inferred it is not believeable for several other reasons. We have seen that Jayānand's account of Śrī Caitanya's death on the seventh lunar day of Asādha does not conform to the more authoritative accounts, relating to the time of his disappearence. The story, therefore, of his dieing of septic fever, caused by injury to his foot on the Rathayātrā day cannot be true. His secret burial by the priests in the temple of Ṭoṭā Gopīnātha can at best be a wild conjecture. How could Svarūpa, Rāmānaṅda Rāya, Raghunātha Dāsa and Govinda, who took care of him day and night, and Śaṁkara, who was specially deputed to serve him at this time and slept with him in the same room at night, allow him to walk alone to the temple of Ṭoṭā Gopīnātha from the house of Kāśī Miśra in the state of fever to die in isolation and uncared for? How could the temple priests, who were not closely associated with Śrī Caitanya and whom Kṛṣṇadāsa despises as worldly-minded,[2] suddenly aquire the authority of burying the body of Śrī Caitanya, without any reference to Svarūpa Dāmodara, Rāmānanda Rāya and Kāśī Miśra, the Guru of Pratāparudra, whose authority over the temple was supreme, and even Pratāparudra himself, who loved and worshipped Śrī Caitanya as his God?

That the whole story is fabricated is evident from the fact that Haridāsa and Sanātana are said by Locanadāsa to have been shut out of the temple while the burial was going on inside. But Haridāsa had already died and his burial was performed by Śrī Caitanya himself, while Sanātana had left Purī for Vṛndāvana much earlier and never returned.

Whatever the truth about the manner of the passing away of Śrī Caitanya, one thing, which lends support to the general belief of his merging with the deity, and which may also be the most important cause of the belief, is that no trace of his body was ever found. If the body were actually buried in the temple it is unbelieveable that king Pratāparudra would not have raised a memorial on it befitting the personality of Śrī Caitanya and the dignity of his empire.

[1]Sambidānanda Dās, *Srị Çaitanya Mahāprabhu*, p. 208.
[2]ibid, Chapter XV.

CHAPTER III

The Saṁpradāya of Śrī Caitanya

Affiliation with Mādhva

The question regarding the Saṁpradāya or the religious sect to which Śrī Caitanya belonged is controversial. Most of his followers link him with Mādhvācārya. Others think that he started a new sect of his own. We may state at the outset that so far as doctrinal matters are concerned there is no affiliation between Śrī Caitanya and Mādhva. In some respects Mādhva is even opposed to Śrī Caitanya. The following are some of the important points of difference:

(*a*) Mādhva is an advocate of Dvaita or dualism, while Śrī Caitanya is an advocate of Acintya Bhedābheda or inconceivable identity-in-difference.

(*b*) According to Mādhva the ultimate object of worship is Nārāyaṇa, while according to Śrī Caitanya the ultimate object of worship is Śrī Kṛṣṇa, Nārāyaṇa being only a partial manifestation of Kṛṣṇa.

(*c*) According to Mādhva, devotion consists in dedication to Kṛṣṇa of actions performed in accordance with Varṇāśrama Dharma, while according to Śrī Caitanya it consists in renunciation of Varṇāśrama Dharma for the sake of Śuddha Bhakti.

(*d*) The end, according to Mādhva, is the attainment of five kinds of Mukti in Vaikuṇṭha. According to Śrī Caitanya it is the loving service of Śrī Kṛṣṇa.

(*e*) According to Śrī Caitanya the Gopikās of Vraja are not ordinary Jīvas but the manifestations of the Svarūpa Śakti of Kṛṣṇa, eternally engaged in His service which is selfless and lustless. According to Mādhva, they are maidens of Svarga (*apsaraḥ strī*), who worship Kṛṣṇa with the object of satisfying their lust.

(*f*) According to Mādhva the highest in the order of devotees of Kṛṣṇa is Brahmā, while according to Śrī Caitanya the Gopikās of Vraja rank the highest, and even Brahmā covets the dust of their holy feet. Mādhva's description of the Gopikās as *Apsaraḥ Strī* has been strongly criticised by Śrī Sanātana and Śrī Jīva.

Śrī Caitanya himself regarded his doctrine as distinct from that of Mādhva. This is evident from his dialogue with the Ācārya of Mādhva Saṁpradāya in *Caitanya-caritāmṛta*, in which he calls the Saṁpradāya of

Mādhva as 'your Saṁpradāya.'[1] In *Caitanya-candrodaya* he calls the Vaiṣṇavas of the Mādhva school as "The Tattvavādin[2] Vaiṣṇavas of the South—the worshippers of Nārāyaṇa" and describes their doctrine as defective, while he describes the doctrine of Rāmānanda as *rucitama.*[3] Sārvabhauma says in reply to this: "No, my Lord! Rāmānanda Rāya has accepted your doctrine. He does not have any doctrine of his own. Our own doctrine, which has been accepted by many people and is supported by all the Śāstras is the best."[4] This proves not only that Śrī Caitanya's doctrine is distinct but that he is himself its founder.

This view finds frequent support in the writings of Śrī Jīva. In his commentary on *BP*, X, xii, I, he refers to the Saṁpradāya of Mādhva as 'his (Mādhva's) Saṁpradāya' and to those, who, like Śrī Caitanya but unlike Mādhva, do not regard Chaps. X-XIV of the tenth Skandha of the Bhāgavatam as interpolation, as belonging to 'other' Saṁpradāyas.[5] In *Sarvasaṁvādinī* he distinguishes his doctrine from that of Mādhva by calling his doctrine as his own (*svamata*) and that of Mādhva as the doctrine of Mādhva (*Mādhvācāryamata*). He also describes Śrī Caitanya as the presiding deity of his Saṁpradāya (*sva-saṁpradāya-sahasrādhidaivam*).[6]

Śrī Rūpa Gosvāmin describes Śrī Caitanya as the bestower of Bhakti of the highest order, which had remained unbestowed for so long.[7] Śrī Prabodhānanda Sarasvatī says in a similar strain, "Before the advent of Śrī Caitanya, who had ever heard of Prema as the highest end? Who was aware of the glory and greatness of the Holy Name? Who had experienced the beauty and sweetness of the celestial garden of Vṛndāvana? Who knew of Śrī Rādhā, the highest and the most wonderful manifestation of sweetness, beauty, and Rasa?"[8] It is, thus, obvious that Śrī Caitanya was regarded by his followers as the giver of the highest order of pure and Rasa-oriented Vraja bhakti, which is the distinguishing feature of his school of Vaiṣṇavism.

There is also historical evidence to prove that in doctrinal matters the followers of Śrī Caitanya were recognised as belonging to a school quite

[1] *karmī Jnānī dui bhakti hīna /*
tomārasampradāye dekhi sei duī cinha //
tabe ek guna dekhi tomāra saṁpradāye /
śrī vigraha īśvare karaha nirṇaye // *CC*, II, ix, 249-50.

[2] Mādhvācārya himself called his doctrine *Tattvavāda.*

[3] *niravadyaṁ na bhavati teṣāṁ mataṁ . . . rāmānandamatameva me rucitama. Caitanya-candrodaya,* VIII, 1.

[4] ibid. [5] *SS*, 149. [6] ibid, p. 1.

[7] *anarpitacariṁ cirāt karuṇayāvatīrṇah kalau*
samarpayitumunnatojjvalarasāṁ svabhaktiśiriyaṁ. Vidagdha-Mādhava, 1, 3.

[8] *premānāmādbhutārthaḥ kasya sravaṇapathagataḥ nāmnāṁ mahinmāḥ ko vetto vrndāvanavipinamādhurīṣu kasya praveśaḥ; ko va Jānāti rādhāṁ paramarasacamatkāra mādhuryasīmāmekaścaitanyacandraḥ paramakaruṇayā sarvamāviścakāra. Caitanya-candrāmṛta*

distinct from the traditional four schools of Vaiṣṇavism. There is a tradition that the question regarding the position of the school of Śrī Caitanya in relation to the recognised four schools of Vaiṣṇavism came into prominence when there was a dispute regarding rituals in the temple of Govinda Jī at Jaipur, during the time of Viśvanātha Cakravartī and Baladeva Vidyābhūṣaṇa, both of whom then lived in Vṛndāvana. The Gauḍīya, Vaiṣṇavas, who were in-charge of the temple, gave precedence to Govinda Jī over Nārāyaṇa in their service of the deities to which the other Vaiṣṇavas, who regarded Nārāyana as superior, raised serious objection. The ruler of Jaipur called a conference of pandits to resolve the dispute. Śrī Viśvanātha Cakravartī sent Baladeva Vidyābhūṣaṇa to the conference to represent the Gauḍīya Vaiṣṇavas. Baladeva was required first to prove that the Gauḍīya Vaiṣṇavas were a recognised Vaiṣṇava community, duly authorised to speak on matters pertaining to Vaiṣṇava religion and rituals. Baladeva started by showing the affiliation of Gauḍīya Vaiṣṇavism with Mādhva. But in the discussion that followed the doctrinal approach of Gauḍīya Vaiṣṇavism appeared to be distinct from that of Mādhva and the three other schools of Vaiṣṇavism. Nobody was prepared to recognise it as an independent sect unless it was supported by an independent commentary on *Brahmasūtra*. Baladeva, therefore, wrote a commentary on *Brahmasūtra*, which he called *Govinda-bhāṣya*, because, as described in the gloss written by himself, he wrote it under the command of Govinda. The learned commentary, which is really an improvement in many respects on the previous commentaries, was accepted and Gauḍīya Vaiṣṇavism was duly recognised as an independent doctrine.

It cannot, however, be said, exclusively on the basis of Śrī Caitanya's doctrinal approach, that he had no affiliation with Mādhva or any other śaṁpradāya. The question relating to Guru-paraṁparā or apostolic succession is of primary importance according to the Vaiṣṇava tradition in determining the Saṁpradāya of a person. It is possible, in the case of a specially gifted and powerful Ācarya, that he may belong to a particular Saṁpradāya and preach a different doctrine. Dr. S. K. De, points to the case of Mādhvācārya himself, who was initiated into the Advaita Saṁpradāya of Śaṁkara but promulgated the Dvaita doctrine, which was directly opposed to Advaitism. Śrī Jīva also makes a mention of this in his *Tattva-saṁdarbha*.[1]

Indian tradition makes formal initiation into one of the recognised Saṁpradāyas necessary even if one wants to start a Saṁpradāya of his own. Rādhā-mohana Gosvāmin stresses this point in his commentary on *Tattva-saṁdarbha*. Even Śaṁkara says, in his commentary on the Gītā, that "a man who does not belong to a sect must be ignored as if he was

[1] *ṣaṁkara śiṣyatāṁ labdhvāpi śrī-bhāgavat-pakṣapātena tato-vicchidya* (*Tattva-saṁdarbha*, p. 70)—cited by S. K. De, in *Vaiṣṇava Faith and Movement in Bengal*, p. 12.

a fool."[1] It cannot, therefore, be imagined that Śrī Caitanya was not duly initiated into some Saṁpradāya.

The earliest authoritative statement regarding the initiation of Śrī Caitanya is by Kavikarṇapūra. In his *Gaura-gaṇoddeśa-dīpikā* he states, on the authority of *Padma-purāṇa*, that there are only four recognised Saṁpradāyas in this age of Kali—Śrī, Brahma, Rudra, and Sanaka, and links Śrī Caitanya with Brahma-saṁpradāya, the Saṁpradāya of Mādhva, through Īśvara Purī, his Dikṣā Guru, and Mādhavendra Purī, his Parama Guru. Baladeva makes a similar reference to the four recognised Vaiṣṇava-saṁpradāyas in his gloss on *Govinda-bhāṣya*, called *Sukṣmā-ṭīkā*, and records, both in this and *Prameya-ratnāvali* the Guru Paraṁparā of Śrī Caitanya, linking him with Mādhva.

Dr. B. B. Majumdar mentions, besides the above, the following works in support of the view that Śrī Caitanya belonged to the Mādhva Saṁpradāya:[2]

1. Narahari Cakravartin's *Bhakti-ratnākara*
2. Devaki-nandana's *Vṛhadvaiṣṇava-bandanā*
3. Viśvanātha Cakravartin's *Śrī Gauragaṇasvarūpa-tattva-candrikā*
4. Manohara Dāsa's *Anurāgavallī*
5. Gopāla Guru's *Padya*
6. Lāla Dāsa's *Bhakta-māla*
7. Īśāna Nāgara's *Advaita-prakāśa*, and
8. *Muralī-vilāsa*.

This makes quite an impressive list of works that can be cited in support of Śrī Caitanya's affiliation with Mādhva. But scholars have raised several objections against this, which we may state as follows:

1. There are three important reasons for regarding the Ślokas relating to the Guru-paraṁparā of Śrī Caitanya as interpolated:

(*a*) The author of *Gaura-gaṇoddeśa-dīpikā* himself contradicts the view of Śrī Caitanya's affiliation with Mādhva in *Caitanya-candrodaya.* He makes Sārvabhauma Bhattācārya enquire from Gopīnātha, "Who is the *Mahā-vākyaupadeṣṭā* of Śrī Caitanya?"[3] Since the practice of imparting *Mahā-vākya* at the time of initiation obtains only in Śaṁkara-saṁpradāya, it is obvious that Sārvabhauma regarded Śrī Caitanya as a Samnyāsin of Śaṁkara-saṁpradāya. This is confirmed by Gopīnātha, who replies, "Śrī Caitanya is a Saṁnyāsin of the Bhāratī order."

(*b*) The *Padma-purāṇa* Śloka relating to the four Saṁpradāyas of Kali is not found in any of the editions of the Purāṇa now available.

(*c*) *Gaura-gaṇoddeśa-dīpikā* mentions Mādhavendra Purī as the disciple

[1] Gita Press edition, p. 310. Cited by A.K. Majumdar in *Caitanya : His Life and Doctrine*, p. 266.

[2] B. B. Majumdar, *Caitanya-caritera upādāna*, p. 582.

[3] *Caitanya-candrodaya*, 2, 6, 70-72.

of Lakṣmīpati of the Mādhva-saṁpradāya, which is doubtful, because the Saṁnyāsa title of Mādhvendra is 'Purī' while the Saṁnyāsa title of the Mādhva-saṁpradāya is 'Tīrtha.' Besides, the object of worship in the Mādhva-saṁpradāya is Lakṣmī-Nārāyaṇa, while Mādhvendra was a worshipper of Rādhā-Kṛṣṇa, and the end to be achieved according to Mādhva is Mukti, while the end for Mādhvendra Purī was the loving service of Kṛṣṇa. Sundarānanda Vidyāvinoda says that Mādhvendra Purī is not mentioned as a disciple of Lakṣmipati in any of the lists of apostolic succession maintained in the Mathas of the Mādhva-saṁpradāya.

2. The *Sūkṣmā-ṭīkā* of *Govinda-bhāṣya* does not give the name of the commentator. But the commentator writes: "Lord Govinda under whose command Vidyābhūṣaṇa (Baladeva) composed this commentary, may He help me in this my undertaking also." Dr. Rādhā Govinda Nāth concludes from this that the commentator is not Baladeva but some follower of Mādhva, who at the commencement of the commentary, gives the *paraṁparā* of the Mādhva-saṁpradāya as '*sva-guru paraṁparā*.' What further lends support to this view, according to him, is the commentator's statement: "Baladeva the wise, composed this commentary (*bhāṣyameta-dviracitam baladevena dhīmatā*) under the command of Śrī Govinda," since it is most unlikely that Baladeva would thus call himself 'wise.'[1]

3. The evidence of *Prameya-ratnāvali* is regarded as unauthentic on the assumption that the work was compiled by Baladeva, when he was a follower of Mādhva and had not even thought of his initiation into the Gauḍīya-saṁpradāya. It is pointed out, in this connection, that a Śloka of *Prameya-ratnāvali*, which lists nine important points of similarity between the doctrine of Mādhva and the doctrine of Śrī Caitanya, with a view to link Śrī Caitanya with Mādhva, is an interpolation.[2]

4. The other works to which reference is made by Dr. B. B. Majumdar are not considered to be of any importance either because they are not properly edited,[3] or because their authorship is disputed.[4]

5. The works of Śrī Rūpa, Śrī Sanātana, Śri Jīva and others, whose importance is universally recognised, do not make any mention of Śrī Caitanya's affiliation with Mādhva.

6. The end, according to the Gauḍīya-saṁpradāya of Śrī Caitanya, is the loving service of Śrī Kṛṣṇa in Vraja, while according to the Mādhva-saṁpradāya it is the attainment of Mukti in Vaikuntha. If it is accepted that Śrī Caitanya is connected through Guru-paraṁparā with Mādhva, it becomes difficult to explain how the devotees initiated into the Gauḍīya-saṁpradāya can realise the end as conceived by them, since they are

[1] *Gauḍīya Vaiṣṇava-darśana*, Introduction, p. 189.
[2] ibid, I, p. 1871.
[3] Sunderānanda Vidyā-vinoda, *Acintya-bhedābheda*, pp. 207-13.
[4] A. K. Majumdar, *Caitanya: His Life and Doctrine*, pp. 260-61.

connected in apostolic succession with Gurus, who are not themselves initiated into the kind of service of Kṛṣṇa, which they seek. The contradiction is highlighted by the special emphasis laid in the Gauḍīya-saṁpradāya on the need of seeking initiation from a Guru, who is qualified by his own attainment to lead to the kind of devotional service one seeks.

Dr. Rādhā Govinda Nāth aptly points out in this connection that although we find different types of devotees amongst the direct disciples of Śrī Caitanya, the Ādi Gurus of the different sects in the Gauḍīya-saṁpradāya are only those who are devoted to Kṛṣṇa in Vraja. There is, for instance, no line of apostolic succession commencing from Śrīvāsa Paṅdita, who is a devotee of Lakṣmī-Nārāyaṇa and Murārī Gupta, who is a devotee of Rāma Candra.[1]

7. If we recognise Śrī Caitanya's affiliation with Mādhva, then only the Vaiṣṇavas belonging to the line of apostelic succession commencing from Śrī Nityānanda and Śrī Advaita can be regarded as Gauḍīya Vaiṣṇavas, since both of them were initiated into the Mādhva Saṁpradāya. All others, including those belonging to the lines of Śrī Gadādhara Pandit and Śrī Narottama, must be regarded as non-Gauḍīyās, for Gadādhara and Narottama were not initiated into the Mādhva-saṁpradāya and there is no evidence of their having been initiated by Śrī Caitanya. Yet the disciples of both Gadādhara Pandit and Narottama are universally recognised as Gauḍīya Vaiṣṇavas.[2]

The above objections must be carefully examined. The most important of them relates to the fact that none of the six Gosvāmins makes any mention in his works of Śrī Caitanya's affiliation with Mādhva, nor does any of them make obeisance to him in the customary Vandanā at the commencement of his works. It is mainly for this reason that the Ślokas concerning the Guru-paraṁparā of Śrī Caitanya in *Gaura-gaṇoddeśa-dīpikā* and *Prameya-ratnāvali* etc. are regarded as spurious. But if we take into consideration the fact that the Gosvāmins regard the philosophy of Mādhva as not only different but opposed to that of Śrī Caitanya on some of the most fundamental points, the objection loses much of its importance. It is not unnatural from this point of view that, inspite of Śrī Caitanya's formal affiliation with Mādhva, they should omit reference to him in their writings. The works of Śrī Vallabhācārya provide a suitable illustration. Śrī Vallabhācārya belongs to the Viṣṇusvāmin-saṁpradāya. Yet he does not make any reference to Viṣṇusvāmin in his works, because he reshaped the Śuddhādvaita doctrine of which Viṣṇusvāmin is the founder and departed in several ways from the orthodox approach of the school as defined by him.[3]

[1]*Gauḍīya Vaiṣṇava-darśana*, III, pp. 1876-77.
[2]ibid, V, p. 3790.
[3]A.K. Majumdar, op. cit., p. 269, f. 24.

Another important reason for the omission in the works of the Gosvāmins of any reference to Mādhva may be that the traditional belief in the existence of only four recognised Vaiṣṇava-saṁpradāyas in the age of Kali which made it obligatory for every new faith to have a link with one of them, was not so strong and prevalent during their time. But in the time of Baladeva Vidyābhuṣaṇa the belief acquired such great importance that he was led to emphasise the link of the Gauḍīya-saṁpradāya with Mādhva through Guru-paraṁparā inspite of his explicit recognition of the doctrinal difference between Śrī Caitanya and Mādhva, which earned for the Gauḍīya-saṁpradāya universal recognition as the fifth school of Vaiṣṇavism at the historic conference of pandits at Jaipur. If he had not done so he would perhaps have been dubbed *asaṁpradāyi* (not duly initiated into a recognised Saṁpradāya) and not given a hearing at the conference at all.

It would, therefore, not be proper to deny Śrī Caitanya's affiliation with Mādhva merely on the basis of absence of any mention of it in the works of the Gosvāmins. What is important, that they do not say anything regarding the initiation of Śrī Caitanya into this or that Saṁpradāya, while there is much that they say regarding the necessity of initiation in the path of Bhakti and regarding Śrī Caitanya's role as a teacher of Bhakti to imply that he must have been initiated into some Saṁpradāya. To find out the particular Saṁpradāya into which he was initiated we must turn to such other evidence as is available and examine it with an unbiased mind.

There is no evidence whatsoever of Śrī Caitanya's initiation into any Vaiṣṇava-saṁpradāya except Mādhva. It is against this background that the evidence, listed above in favour of his affiliation with Mādhva, should be examined. We apprehend that it has not been examined in this light and the tendency to regard it as spurious because it is not supported by the works of the six Gosvāmins has persisted throughout.

This is particularly clear from the way in which the evidence of *Prameya-ratnāvali* is dismissed as fabricated by Dr. Rādhā Govind Nāth. He does not give any reason for presuming that the work was written before Baladeva Vidyābhūṣaṇa was initiated into the Gauḍīya-saṁpradāya, except that it shows his Mādhva leanings, a characteristic from which his other works cannot be said to be altogether free. Also, he does not mention how the presumption detracts from the value of the work as an evidence in favour of Śrī Caitanya's affiliation with Mādhva. Equally unwarranted is his presumption that the Śloka mentioning nine points of similarity between the doctrine of Śrī Caitanya and the doctrine of Mādhva is an interpolation. He seems to think that the parallels drawn in the Śloka are not well founded and therefore they cannot be attributed to a scholar of the stature of Śrī Baladeva. But a careful study of the parallels will reveal that the belief in their inadequacy springs more from a conscious or unconscious desire to underrate the evidence in favour of Śrī Caitanya's affiliation with Mādhva than from any genuine defects in them. We have already pointed out the important points of difference between the doctrines of Śrī Caitanya and Mādhva, but these do not preclude the possibility of points of agreement, which Baladeva has emphasised.

Similarly, the fact that Kavikarṇapūra represents the doctrine of Śrī Caitanya as different from that of Mādhva in *Caitanya-candrodaya* is not a sufficient justification for regarding the Ślokas relating to the Guru-paraṁparā of Śrī Caitanya in *Gaura-gaṇoddeśa-dīpikā* as interpolated, as some writers seem to think.[1] We have made it clear at the outset that though ordinarily a disciple adheres to the doctrine of the Saṁpradāya into which he is initiated, the Ācāryas, who have regenerated a Saṁpradāya or founded a new sect, have been notable exceptions to the rule. The fact, therefore, that Śrī Caitanya's doctrine is different from that of Mādhva does not necessarily imply that he must have been initiated into a different Saṁpradāya. Conversly, the fact that Śrī Caitanya was initiated into the Mādhva-saṁpradāya does not imply that his doctrine must have been exactly the same as Mādhva's. It is, perhaps, to remove the impression that Śrī Caitanya's doctrine was the same as the doctrine of the Saṁpradāya to which he belonged by Guru-paraṁparā that, having linked Śrī Caitanya with Mādhva by stating his Guru-paraṁparā in the *Gaura-gaṇoddeśa-dīpikā,* Kavikarṇapūra takes care to declare, unequivocally, in *Caitanya-candrodaya* that his doctrine was not the same as Mādhva's.

As regards the 'Sukṣmā' commentary on *Govinda-bhāṣya,* even if the traditional belief that it was written by Baladeva himself is set aside, the evidence of the commentary itself, whosoever may have been its author, remains. We have no reason to regard the Guru-paraṁparā given in it as spurious unless we presume that anything not directly supported by the writings of the six Gosvāmins must be so regarded. Dr. Rādhā Govind Nāth's statement, that the author of the commentary must be the same enthusiast of the Mādhva-saṁpradāya who has interpolated the Ślokas concerning the Guru-paraṁparā in *Gaura-gaṇoddeśa-dīpikā,*[2] does not bear scrutiny, since the Guru-paraṁparā given in both is not exactly the same.[3]

The importance attached to the 'Purī' title of Mādhvendra in determining the Saṁpradāya to which he belonged is not justified. The title, though suggestive of his link with the Śaṁkara-saṁpradāya, can by no means be regarded as a sure indication of it. It is true that 'Purī' is one of the ten orders into which Śaṁkara divided his disciples, others being *Tīrtha, Āśrama, Girī, Paravata, Sāgara, Sarasvatī, Bhāratī, Vana,* and *Araṇya.* It

[1] Suderānanda Vidyāvinod, *Acintya-bhedābheda,* p. 205.
[2] Radha Govind Nath, op. cit., I, Introduction, p. 189.
[3] Sunderananda, op. cit., pp. 237-38.

may also be true that none of the Vaiṣṇava-saṁpradāyas assigned these titles to their Saṁnyāsins. But the tradition was obviously broken with Mādhvācārya, who adopted the title 'Tīrtha.' It is said that he was originally initiated into the Tīrtha order of Śaṁkara-saṁpradāya by his Guru Puruśottama Tīrtha. But he continued to designate himself as Tīrtha even after he promulgated his Dvaita doctrine under his Saṁnyāṣa name of Ānanda Tīrtha, and the Gurus who succeeded him, also continued to be designated as 'Tīrthas.'[1] It would not be far-fetched to presume that the tradition was further broken at a later date, when Mādhvendra was designated 'Puri' by his Guru Lakṣmīpati. Farquhar admits that, in the later history of the Mādhva-saṁpradāya, the ascetics of the Mādhva sect called themselves Purīs and Bhāratīs.[2] In our own time we find that the Saṁnyāsins of the Gauḍīya Maṭha freely adopt any of the ten titles, supposed at one time to have been associated with the Śaṁkara-saṁpradāya alone.

It is also not unlikely that Mādhvendra himself was a Saṁnyāsin of the Purī order of Saṁkara-saṁpradāya before he was initiated by Lakṣmīpati into the Mādhva-sampradāya and that he adhered to his 'Purī' designation even after his conversion into Vaiṣṇavism, like Mādhvācarya and the distinguised Prakāśānanda Sarasvatī of the Śaṁkara-saṁpradāya, who also carried his 'Sarasvatī' designation with him when he was converted into Gauḍīya Vaiṣṇavism and renamed Prabodhānanda Sarasvatī.[3] Even if he was given the 'Tīrtha' designation of the Mādhva-saṁpradāya after his new initiation it was soon forgotten, since he had already become so famous as Mādhvendra Purī and the people had become so accustomed to his 'Purī' designation. The fact that his name does not appear in the lists maintained in the Mādhva Maths does not prove anything more than that he was never in-charge of any of them. It cannot be regarded as a proof that he was not initiated into the Mādhva-saṁpradāya.

There is no doubt that Mādhvendra Purī's doctrine is not exactly the same as Mādhva's. In *Caitanya-caritāmṛta* he is described as the seed of Prema-bhakti of Vraja, which was later reared into a huge tree by Śrī Caitanya.[4] But his doctrine is wholly different from that of Śaṁkara, who regards the God of Bhakti as illusory. It is impossible for the seed of Bhakti to sprout in the ground of Advaitism as preached by him. It is not unlikely that Mādhvendra was drawn into the Mādhva-saṁpradāya by the very fact of its extreme opposition of Śaṁkara and its firm faith in the personal form of God.

Dr. Rādhā Govind Nāth's argument relating to the possibility of realisation of the end as conceived by Śrī Caitanya, if his affiliation with Mādhva

[1]S. K. De, op. cit., p. 12.

[2]Farquhar, *An Outline of the Religious Literature of India*, p. 304.

[3]It is mentioned in the *Bhaktamāla* of Lāla Dāsa that he was named Prabodhānanda Sarasvati by Śrī Caitanya himself.

[4]*CC*, I, ix, 10-12.

is accepted, is to some extent valid. But the objection on this basis against Śrī Caitanya's affiliation with Mādhva would hold only if the affiliation is not purely formal. We have already made it clear that from the doctrinal point of view there is a fundamental difference between Śrī Caitanya and Mādhva, and that Śrī Caitanya accepted Īśvara Purī as his Guru only to abide by the injunction of the Śastras relating to the formal necessity of initiation. But even if we agree with Dr. Rādhā Govind Nāth that neither Īśvara Purī nor Keśava Bhāratī belonged to the Mādhva sect, the objection raised by him will be equally valid against any other sect to which they are supposed to belong, since, according to him, the loving service of Kṛṣṇa as His Kāntā or beloved in Vraja is not regarded as the end by any other Saṁpradāya to which Śrī Caitanya may be said to be affiliated, least of all by the Śaṁkara-saṁpradāya to which they may be said to belong on account of their 'Purī' and 'Bhāratī' titles.

The argument that Śrī Caitanya's affiliation with Mādhva would make Gadādhara Pandit and Narottama Thakura *a-saṁpradāyī*, because they were neither initiated by a Mādhva Guru nor by Śrī Caitanya, also does not have any force. Here, again, Śrī Caitanya's affiliation with any other Saṁpradāya would not make any difference to Gadādhara Pandit and Narottama Thākura and the line of Gurus descending from them. They would still remain *a-saṁpradāyī* according to Dr. Rādhā Govind Nāth.

What the above arguments seem to imply is that Śrī Caitanya, as the incarnation of Kṛṣṇa and the founder of his Saṁpradāya, is also the Guru of all the Ādi-guru's of the different orders of the Saṁpradāya, who, whether directly initiated by him or not, derive their authority from him. His position in the Gauḍīya-saṁpradāya is unique. He is both the worshipper and the worshipped. He is the object (Viṣaya) of Bhakti as well as its subject (Āsrya). The Object (Bhagavān) becomes the subject (Bhakta) to show to the Jīvas of Kali the path of Bhakti and, thus, to pave the way for their redemption.

Sunderānanda goes a step farther. He says that just as the Avatārī, or the source of the Avatāras, includes all other Avatāras, the Saṁpradāya founded by the Avatārī Puruṣa Śrī Caitanya includes all other Saṁpradāyas. It cannot be regarded as the branch of any Saṁpradāya.[1]

We have no intention of questioning the faith of the Saṁpradāya regarding the divinity of Śrī Caitanya or disregarding the uniqueness of the position of Śrī Caitanya in it. What we must urge is that there is also a historical aspect of his personality, which cannot be ignored. It is a fact that he took Mantra-dīkṣā from his Guru, Īśvara Purī, and he must, from that point of view, be regarded as formally affiliated with the Saṁpradāya to which Īśvara Purī belonged. Even the uniqueness of his position as Bhakta-

[1]op. cit., pp. 240-41.

Bhagavā n involves this aspect, since as a Bhakta, who must seek initiation before he can start his Sādhanā he must be linked with some Saṁpradāya. It is neither in conformity with his doctrine, nor in conformity with his personality to think that his prestige as the founder of his Saṁpradāya or as incarnation of Kṛṣṇa is compromised if he is linked with some other Saṁpradāya, as some people are inclined to think.[1] For, as Bhagavān, he takes pride in following his devotees and taking the dust of their holy feet,[2] while as Bhakta he considers himself humbler than even a blade of grass (*tṛṇādapi-sunīcena*). How can his prestige be compromised by accepting a Saṁnyāsin of some other Saṁpradāya as his Guru, if it is not compromised by accepting Jagannātha Miśra and Śaci as his parents?

The above examination of the arguments against Śrī Caitanya's affiliation with Mādhva shows that they are, neither wholly unbiased nor conclusive. If along with this we take into consideration the fact that there is no evidence whatsoever of his affiliation with any other Vaiṣṇava-saṁpradāya, we are compelled to accept the view of his affiliation with Mādhva, though we must recognise, in view of the doctrinal differences between Śrī Caitanya and Mādhva, that this affiliation cannot be more than formal. It would, therefore, be proper to describe the relation between the Gauḍīya-saṁpradāya and the Mādhva-saṁpradāya as that of identity-in-difference (*bhedābheda*)—identity in respect of their Guru-paraṁparā and difference in respect of their doctrines.

Affiliation with Śaṁkara

Before, however, we take this conclusion as final, we must also consider the view of Śrī Caitanya's affiliation with Śaṁkara-saṁpradāya, which though scoffed by the supporters as well as the critics of Śrī Caitanya's affiliation with Mādhva, is forcefully argued by Dr. S.K. De. He says:

"The indications are strong that Caitanya formally belonged to the Dasanāmī order of Śaṁkara-saṁnyāsins, even though the ultimate form which he gave to Vaiṣṇava-bhakti had nothing to do with Śaṁkara's extreme Advaitavāda. Barring the two passages referred to above, there is no evidence anywhere in the *early* standard works of Bengal Vaiṣṇavism that Mādhavendra Purī or his disciple, Īśvara Purī, who influenced the early religious inclinations of Caitanya, was in fact a Mādhva ascetic. There is no evidence to show that either they or their alleged disciple Advaita were Mādhvas in outlook. Tradition records that Mādhva himself was initiated into the 'Tīrtha' order of Śaṁkara by Acyutaprakāśa or Puruśottama Tīrtha; and even after he promulgated his Dvaita doctrine in opposition to Śaṁkara's teaching of Advaita, he adhered to his 'Tīrtha' designation under his Saṁnyāsa name of Ānanda Tīrtha. Ever since his

[1]op. cit., pp. 240-41.
[2]*Bh.*, XI, xiv, 16.

time and up to the present day, all the Gurus of his order called themselves 'Tirthas,' and not 'Purīs' or 'Bharatīs.' Mādhavendra and Īśvara were both 'Purīs' and not 'Tīrthas'; while Mādhavendra's other alleged disciple Keśava Bhāratī was apparently also a Saṁnyāsin of the 'Bhāratī' order of Śaṁkara. To Vāsudeva Sārvabhauma at Purī, Caitanya is introduced (*CC*, Mādhya, vi) as a Saṁnyāsin belonging to the Bhāratī-sampradāya. There are, also, other facts recorded in his authoritative biographies which militate against the assumption of Caitanya's Mādhva leanings. His calling himself a Māyāvadin ascetic on several occasions, Kavikarṇapūra's distinct statement that he belonged to the Advaita monastic order and did not approve of the 'Tattva-vàdins'; the raillery of Prakāśānanda, an Advaita-saṁnyāsin, on Caitanya's avoidance of his fellow Māyāvadin ascetics and on his improper indulgence in singing and dancing; his direct disapproval of Mādhva doctrines—all these and other indications raise a legitimate doubt regarding the historical accuracy of Caitanya's alleged connection with Mādhvism... The roots therefore of the Bhakti movement, which Mādhavendra Purī is said to have started in Bengal and which Caitanya carried forward and definitely shaped, must be sought in such traditions as originated from Srīdhar's great commentary on *Srīmad-bhāgavata*, which was accepted with much veneration by the Bengal school. Caitanya himself is said to have possessed the highest admiration for Srīdhara Svāmin, and, on one occasion, he is said to have repudiated a commentary on the *Srīmad-bhāgavata* by one Vallabha Bhatta on the ground that it departs from Srīdhar Svāmin's interpretations."[1]

We have already discussed how far it is justifiable, merely on the basis of the 'Purī' title of Mādhvendra Purī and Īśvara Purī, to conclude that they belonged to the Śaṁkara-saṁpradāya, when the reasons for regarding the recorded evidence in favour of their belonging to the Mādhva saṁpradāya as spurious are not fairly strong and conclusive. As regards Keśava Bhāratī, Kavirāja Gosvāmin says that he was a disciple of Mādhvendra Purī.[2] But since *Caitanya-candrodaya* regards Śrī Caitanya as a Saṁnyāsin of the Bhāratī order of Dasanāmī Saṁnyāsin, presumably on the basis of his being a disciple of Keśava Bhāratī, and since in *Caitanya-caritāmṛta*, he says that he is a Māyāvādī-saṁnyāsin, it would not be unreasonable to conclude that Keśava Bhāratī was a Māyāvādī-saṁnyāsin initiated into Māyāvāda by Mādhvendra Purī before the latter joined the Mādhva-saṁpradāya. The case of Rāmacandra Purī, another disciple of Mādhvendra also lends support to this view. His attitude towards Bhakti was opposed to that of Mādhvendra and similar to that of a Māyāvādī-saṁnyāsin, on account of which he was severely scolded by Mādhvendra.[3] This proves that Mādhvendra must have initiated him while he was him-

[1] op. cit., pp. 12-16. [2] *CC*, I, ix, 13. [3] op. cit., III, viii, 19-22.

self a Māyāvādī-saṁnyāsin and that he must have changed his creed later.

The fact of Śrī Caitanya's taking his Saṁnyāsa Dīkṣā from a Saṁnyāsin of the Śaṁkara-saṁpradāya cannot be totally denied. But if we reflect on its propriety and consider carefully the evidence on which the belief is based, it is possible that the Dīkṣā may turn out to be more apparent than real.

The question anyone would ask is whether, considering Śrī Caitanya's most uncompromising attitude against the Śaṁkara-saṁpradāya, there could be any possibility of his taking Saṁnyāsa Dīkṣā from a Saṁnyāsin of that Saṁpradāya. The end as conceived by Śrī Caitanya was the loving service of Śrī Kṛṣṇa, while, according to Śaṁkara it was Mukti. Śrī Caitanya considered even the company of a person aspiring after Mukti as the greatest obstacle (*kaitava pradhāna*) for a Bhakta. Reference has already been made to Prakāśānanda's resentment against him for his avoidance of Māyāvādī-saṁnyāsins. Would it not, therefore, have been like commiting spritual suicide for him to accept a Māyāvādī-saṁnyāsin as his Guru?

It cannot be argued that Śrī Caitanya's Kṛṣṇa Prema was a later development. It is very well known that it germinated during his visit to Gayā and came to fruition at the time of Saṁnyāsa. The very motive behind his Saṁnyāsa was the distribution of the fruit of divine-love (*prema-phala*) and not the attainment of Mukti.[1] His abhorrence of Mukti and the Māyāvādī-saṁnyāsins, who advocated it, is evident even from his conversation with Sārvabhauma Bhattācārya soon after Saṁnyāsa.

It may, however, be argued that on the basis of doctrinal differences one may also question the possibility of Śrī Caitanya's initiation into the Mādhva-saṁpradāya. But the doctrinal differences between Śrī Caitanya and Mādhva are not as fundamental as those between Śrī Caitanya and Śaṁkara. Since Śrī Kṛṣṇa Prema is the highest end for Śrī Caitanya, the point of utmost importance for him is the reality of Śrī Kṛṣṇa, which is denied by Śaṁkara but accepted by Mādhva. On account of this, Śrī Caitanya eulogises the Mādhva-saṁpradāya in the following terms:

tabe eka guṇa dekhī tomāra saṁpradāye|
satya vigraha īśvara karaha nirṇaye|| CC, II, ix, 250.

"Even so, there is one good quality in your Saṁpradāya—you regard the body form of God as real."

As against this he says of Prakāśānanda Sarasvatī, the head of the Māyāvādī-saṁnyāsins of Vārāṇasī, in a state of trance, in which not he but Kṛṣṇa speaks through him:

kāśī te paṇāya betā Prakāśānanda|
seī betā kare mora aṅga khaṅda khaṅda|| *C. Bh.*, II, iii, 37.

[1] *CC*, I, ix, 27.

"Prakāśānanda, the rascal, teaches in Kāśī. He has the audacity to destroy My Body (by saying that it is illusory)."

There are, besides, other important points of resemblance between Śrī Caitanya and Mādhva, which Baladeva Vidyābhūṣaṇa sums up in a Śloka of Prameya-ratnāvali, referred to above. They are as follows:

1. Viṣṇu is the ultimate Reality.
2. All the Vedas speak only of Viṣṇu.
3. The world is real.
4. There is difference between Viṣṇu and the world.
5. Jīvas are the eternal servants of Viṣṇu.
6. Jīvas are of different grades.
7. Mukti is the attainment of the Lotus Feet of Viṣṇu.
8. Worship of Viṣṇu is the only means of attaining Mukti.
9. Pratyakṣa etc. are the three kind of Pramāṇa.[1]

Dr. Rādhā Govind Nāth has twice referred to this Śloka and said that it is an interpolation, presumably because he thinks that some of the comparisons drawn are not valid.[2] He has, however, failed to point out the particular respects in which the comparisons are faulty. We do not think that the comparisons are wrong or even superficial. Only in respect of the relation between Viṣṇu and the world the comparison may not appear to be correct. According to Śrī Caitanya the relation is that of inconceivable unity-in-difference while Baladeva seems to suggest that the relation is that of difference according to both Śrī Caitanya and Mādhva. But it is not conceivable that Baladeva would commit such a blunder. It should be obvious that he does not, here, describe the exact nature of the relation between God and the world according to Śrī Caitanya and Mādhva. He only states that according to both there is difference between God and the world, that is, they are not one, as the Advaitins hold.

Thākura Vṛndāvana Dāsa clears the mist surrounding Śrī Caitanya's Saṁnyāsa Dīkṣā by disclosing that it was not, strictly speaking, Śrī Caitanya who received Dīkṣā from Keśava Bhāratī, but vice-versa. Before Śrī Caitanya actually received the Saṁnyāsa Mantra from Keśava Bhāratī, he said to him, "I have received this Mantra from a saint in my dream. See if this is correct," and forthwith he whishpered the Mantra into his ear. Thus, pretending to receive Saṁnyāsa Dīkṣā from him, he actually imparted Dīkṣā to him and made him his disciple:

chale prabhu kṛpā kari tāre śiṣya kaila| C. *Bh.*, II, xxviii, 157.

Exactly the same thing is said by Murārī Gupta in his *Kaḍacā*:

vyājena dīkṣāṁ gurave sa datvā lokaikanātho gururavyayātmān|
gurodadasvādya manīṣitaṁ me saṁnyāsamityāha
putaṁjalih prabhuḥ|| *Kaḍacā*, III, ii, 9.

[1] *Prameya-ratnāvali*, I, 5.
[2] op. cit., I, Introduction, p. 190; III, pp. 1870-71.

The *Kaḍacā* also says that the Mantra, which Śrī Caitanya received in his dream, was '*Tattvamasi*,' which is a Mahāvākya of the Śaṁkara-saṁpradāya and means 'You are the same (*brahman*).' Śrī Caitanya was very unhappy to receive the Mantra, because he could not tolerate its monistic interpretation. Narrating the dream to Murārī Gupta he said, "Ever since I have seen this dream I have been weeping." Murārī Gupta advised him to interpret the word '*tattvaṁ*' according to *ṣaṣthītatpuruṣa samāsa*, according to which it means 'You are His.'[1] Śrī Caitanya could then reconcile himself to it and was happy, as we are also told by Kavikarṇapūra in his *Mahākāvya.*[2]

It is apparent from the *Kaḍacā* of Murārī Gupta that the Dīkṣā of the Śaṁkara-saṁpradāya was not acceptable to Śrī Caitanya even in dream. He, therefore, converted Keśava Bhāratī himself into Vaiṣṇavism before acting, as it were, as the recipient of Dīkṣā from him. On receiving from Śrī Caitanya the Saṁnyāsa Mantra, reinterpreted and charged with the dynamism of Bhakti, Keśava Bhāratī himself was charged with *Kṛṣṇa-prema* and all the external signs of Prema began to appear on his body (*Caitanyama-ṅgala*, II, p. 159):

Mantra suni nyāsivara haila premamaya|
Kampa pulakādi aṅge Rādhā-kṛṣṇa kaya||

That Mahāprabhu's Saṁnyāsa Dīkṣā by Keśava Bhāratī was only apparent is also proved by the fact that Keśava Bhāratī did not give him the title 'Bhāratī' but only the name 'Śrī Kṛṣṇa Caitanya,' which was against the usual practice of his Saṁpradāya. Keśava Bhāratī knew that Śrī Caitanya was the Lord Himself and that he had only formally taken Dīkṣā from him so that he might set an example for others. He had said to Śrī Caitanya even before initiating him (*C. Bh.*, II, xxviii, 127-29):

Je bhakti tomāra āmi dekhilā nayane|
E śākti anyera nahe īśvara bine||
Tumi se jagadguru jānilā niścaya|
Tomāra gurūra yogya Keha kabhu naya||
Tabe tumi loka-śikṣā nimitta-kārane|
Karibā āmāre guru hena mane laya||

"The Bhakti which I notice in you, cannot exist anywhere except in God. I know it for certain that You are That, the Guru of the whole world. Nobody can ever be fit to be Your Guru. But, I think, You would accept me as Your Guru only to set an example for the world."

To this Śrī Caitanya had replied (ibid, 130):

Māyā more na kara prakāśa|
Hena dikṣā deha jena haun Kṛṣṇa-dāsa||

"Pray do not deceive me thus. Give me such Dīkṣā as would make me

[1]*Kaḍacā*, II, xviii, 3.
[2]*Mahākāvya*, XI, 41-42.

a servant of Kṛṣṇa."

Thus Śrī Caitanya was very specific in his request. He did not want the usual Dikṣā of the Śaṁkara-saṁpradāya, which led to Mukti, but Vaiṣṇava Dikṣā. Since he knew that Keśava Bhārati was not competent for it, he gave him the Vaiṣṇava Dīkṣā himself before pretending to receive it from him.

It is significant that Śri Caitanya did not behave like this towards his Mantra Guru Īśvara Purī. It is clear, also, from the relative positions assigned by Kṛṣṇa Dāsa Kavirāja to Īśvara Puri, Śri Caitanya and Keśava Bhāratī in the wishing tree of Bhakti (*bhakti-kalpataru*) that Īśvara Purī was his real Guru, while Keśava Bhārati was, truly speaking, his disciple, and a Guru only in name. Īśvara Puri is described as the seedling of the tree, Śri Caitanya as the trunk, which grew out of it, and Keśava Bhāratī as only one of the nine branches that sprang from the trunk. Even Paramānanda Purī, who is described as the central branch, is ranked higher than Keśava Bhārati.[1]

This is also confirmed by Sanātana Gośvāmin in his commentary on the third Śloka of the first chapter of *Bṛhadvhāgavatāmṛta*, in which he emphasises the difference between *rūpa* (intrinsic form) and *veśa* (external garb) of Śri Caitanya. In his intrinsic self he is a Bhakta, while his external form is that of a *yati* or Saṁnyāsin.[2]

In the light of the above, Śrī Caitanya's statement to Rāya Rāmānanda, that he was a Māyāvādi Saṁnyāsin cannot be taken as anything more than an expression of his characteristic humility. He had stated:

māyāvādī āmi ta saṁnyāsin|
bhakti tattva nāhi jāni māyāvāde bhāsī||

"I am a Māyāvādī Saṁnyāsin, who keeps always floating in Māyāvāda. What do I know of Bhakti?" If we take Śrī Caitanya's statement by the letter we shall also have to believe that he knew nothing about Bhakti.

The reason why Śrī Caitanya decided to be initiated into Saṁnyāsa by a Saṁnyāsin of the Śaṁkara-saṁpradāya probably was that the purpose of his Saṁnyāsa which was to attract to the path of Bhakti even those who kept away from it on account of ignorance or self-conceit, as we are told by Kṛṣṇa Dāsa Kavirāja,[3] was thus served better. The examples of Sārvabhauma Bhattācārya and Prakāśānanda Sarasvati show how, on account of his being known as a Māyāvādi Saṁnyāsin, he was successful in attracting their attention and converting them to Bhakti.

It may not be inappropriate to suggest that Śrī Caitanya's Saṁnyāsa Dikṣā is the practical side of his synthetic approach in philosophy. Just

[1] *CC*, I, ix, 10-13.

[2] *tatasca prasaṁgasāmarthyād yativeṣa ityādi viṣeṣaṇavaśāt bhaktarūpa evavatīrṇa itī bodhavyam.*

[3] *CC*, I, xvii, 264-67.

as in his philosophical doctrine he gives a place to formless Brahman, even though he does not recognise it as the Ultimate Reality, in his religious life he establishes an outward and artificial relation with the Śaṁkara-sampradāya even though, in the strict sense he does not have even such formal relation with it, as he has with the Mādhva-saṁpradāya. Again, just as according to him qualified Brahman (Kṛṣṇa with the Flute) is the Ultimate Reality, while formless Brahman only appears as such to those who approach Him through the path of Jnāna, his Dīkṣā in Dasākṣara Kṛṣṇa-mantra by Īśvara Puri, is his real Dīkṣā, while his Dīkṣā by Keśava Bhāratī is only a show for the followers of Jnāna Mārga, so that he may win their confidence and lead them to Bhakti.

CHAPTER IV

Materials for the Philosophy of Śrī Caitanya

Doubt is sometimes entertained regarding the scholarship of Śri Caitanya on the ground that he did not, like the other Ācāryas, write a commentary on the Vedas or produce any work of his own. But the fact that he flourished in Navadvīpa at a time when it had reached the highest pitch of its cultural glory, and scholars from all over India flocked to its numerous schools to complete their education, shows that the people whom he had to address were men of highest intelligence and learning; and by the tremendous success he achieved in carrying the conviction of his philosophy into their hearts and converting them to his creed, we are persuaded to believe that he must have been a great scholar himself. We have already referred to the various evidences in support of the view that he had thorough knowledge of Indian philosophy and was a veteran scholar of logic, Sanskrit, grammar and rhetoric. Thākura Vṛndāvana Dāsa represents him as being constantly engaged in scholastic pursuits in his early days and challenging eminent scholars for discussion on any subject in the above branches of learning (*C. Bh.*, Ādi, x). His scholastic triumphs over Murāri Gupta, an aged scholar of Sanskrit grammar, Gadādhara, a great scholar of logic, and the Digvijayī Pandit of Kāshmir, who had vanquished all the reputed scholars of India, Vāsudeva Sārvabhauma Bhattācārya,[1] the greatest Naiyāyika of the time and the most erudite scholar of the Vedānta philosophy, and Prakāśānanda Sarasvatī, the learned leader of the Māyāvādin Saṁnyāsins of Vārāṇasī, and his dialectic exploits of the period during which, like most educated Brāhmaṇas of the time, he set up a Tol (school), leave no doubt about his philosophical insight and scholarship.

Śrī Caitanya, it is true, did not write any book of his own. Advaita Prakāśa ascribes to him a commentary on Nyāya, which he is alleged to have thrown into the Ganges out of sympathetic consideration for a Brāhmaṇa, who also had written a commentary on Nyāya, but who apprehended that its importance might be minimised by the more learned commentary of Śri Caitanya. Certain other works are also sometimes ascribed to him, including a commentary on Vilvamangala's *Kṛṣṇa-karṇāmṛta*, mentioned in R. G. Bhandārkar's report 1884-87 (Bombay, 1894), p. 48, no.

[1]The author of the well-known commentary on Lakṣmī dhara's *Advaita-Mārkaṅda.*

326, but these have not been mentioned in the orthodox biographies of Śrī Caitanya. The only work that we can ascribe to him is the *Śikṣāṣṭaka*, consisting of eight verses attributed to him in Rūpa Gosvamin's *Padyāvali* and represented in *Caitanya-caritāmṛta* as having been uttered and explained by him to his disciples (*CC*, Antya, xx, 64). We might also, with certainty, ascribe to him a few other Ślokas, which he is said to recite in *Caitanya-caritāmṛta*, e.g. Ādi, xvi, 82; Madhya, i, 211; Madhya, ii, 45; and Antya, vi, 285.

But though Śri Caitanya does not present himself to us as the author of any work giving a systematic and elaborate account of his religious philosophy, he is the recognised founder of the Gauḍīya Vaiṣṇava Community, and it seems quite natural that he should have formulated the philosophical tenets of his school, which his learned disciples were commissioned to broadcast all over the country.

The works of the six Gosvāmins

Śrī Caitanya is represented in *Caitanya-caritāmṛta* as communicating to his disciples the details of his system and commanding them to write books on the lines suggested by him.[1] The works of the learned disciples of Śrī Caitanya, mainly Śri Rūpa, Śrī Sanātana, Śrī Jīva, Śrī Gopāla Bhaṭṭa, Śrī Raghunātha Dāsa, and Śrī Raghunātha Bhaṭṭa,[2] commonly known as the "Six Gosvāmins" of Vṛndāvana, who were directly inspired, instructed, and commissioned by him to write, may be regarded as truly representing the doctrine and dogma of his faith. The most important of these are the *Bhāgavata-saṁdarbha* and *Sarva-saṁvādinī. Bhāgavata-saṁdarbha* consists of six Saṁdarbhas, namely *Tattva-saṁdarbha*, *Bhagavat-saṁdarbha*, *Paramātma-saṁdarbha*, *Kṛṣṇa-saṁdarbha*, *Bhakti-saṁdarbha*, and *Prīti-saṁdarbha. Sarva-saṁvādinī* is a supplement to the *Bhāgavata-saṁdarbha.* These contain an elaborate and systematic exposition of the philosophical tenets of the school of Śrī Caitanya.

But since "Caitanya's life of continuous and absorbing devotional ecstasies . . . throws considerable doubt upon his personal responsibility in such scholastic pursuits," some scholars do not feel confident that "these tenets of a later time actually represent Caitanya's own views,"[3] particularly because Jīva was the youngest of the Gosvāmins, who never came in contact with Śrī Caitanya.[4] The title *Bhāgavata-saṁdarbha* and the general plan of the work, which consists in a direct exposition of important

[1]Note the outline supplied to Sanātana by Śrī Caitanya in *CC*, Madhya, xxiv, 242-260.

[2]Only Raghunātha Bhatta of the six Gosvāmins is not known to have written anything.

[3]S. K. De, *Early History of the Vaiṣṇava Faith and Movement in Bengal*, p. 85.

[4]ibid, p. 86.

texts, carefully selected and arranged, from *Śrimad-bhāgavata,* are also taken by them to suggest that they were designed to be a commentary on a considerable portion of *Śrīmad-bhāgavata* rather than treatises expounding the philosophy of Śrī Caitanya.

The belief that the practise of excessive emotionalism by a devotee renders him incapable of philosophical thinking is based on a faulty psychology. Therefore, any doubt in the personal responsibility of Śrī Caitanya in the formulation of the philosophical tenets of his school, which stems from his devotional ecstasies, must be regarded as baseless.[1]

The fact of Śrī Jīva's not coming in direct contact with Śrī Caitanya need not cast any reflection on the authority of the Saṁdarbhas, as representing the views of Śrī Caitanya, since they are not the original creation of Jīva, but works based on the instructions directly received by Rūpa and Sanātana from Śrī Caitanya. Śrī Jīva repeats at the beginning of each Saṁdarbha that he is only systematising and giving final shape to a work originally compiled by Gopāla Bhaṭṭa for the satisfaction of Rūpa and Sanātana. This clearly indicates that the Saṁdarbhas were written by Gopāla Bhaṭṭa at the behest of Rūpa and Sanātana. Since Rūpa and Sanātana were specially commissioned by Śrī Caitanya to propagate his doctrine, they must have taken care to see that it was faithfully delineated in the Saṁdarbhas. Gopāla Bhaṭṭa must himself have taken care that he did not depart in any manner from the essential teachings of Śrī Caitanya, not only because he was as devout a follower of Śrī Caitanya as Rūpa and Sanātana, but because he would have otherwise failed in his effort to please Rūpa and Sanātana, which was his professed aim in compiling the Saṁdarbhas. In the case of Jīva, the question of his deviating from the teachings of Śrī Caitanya did not arise, because he was only to systematise the Saṁdarbhas, for which ground-work had already been prepared, and also because Rūpa and Sanātana, who were his uncles as well as preceptors, must have given him the necessary training and instrctions. Regarding Jīva's association with Rūpa and Sanātana, and his general role in the preparation of Vaiṣṇava Śāstras, Dr. De himself suggests that Śrī Jīva "must have been carefully instructed by them (Rūpa and Sanātana) in the *bhakti-śāstra*, and afterwards taken in as a worthy collaborator in their literary efforts for the cause of Caitanyism."[2]

It should, therefore, be clear that the Saṁdarbhas were a joint venture. They were prepared by Gopāla Bhaṭṭa and Jīva, with the possible collaboration of Rūpa and Sanātana, or, at least, under their general guidance.

The possibility of collaboration is strengthened in view of the fact that some other works were also produced in a similar manner. It is difficult, for instance, to say whether the *Haribhaktivilāsa* is the work of Gopāla

[1]For a detailed discussion of the subject, *see* the chapter on 'Sources of Knowledge.'
[2]op. cit., p. 112.

Bhaṭṭa or Sanātana. Both Jīva and Kṛṣṇadāsa Kavirāja attribute it to Sanātana, while Manohara Dāsa says in his *Anurāgavallī* that Sanātana wrote the work and Gopāla Bhaṭṭa supplied the illustrative passages from the Śāstras.

Collaboration among the Gosvāmins was natural, not only because they lived together in Vṛndāvana, but also because they had a common source of inspiration in Śrī Caitanya and were selflessly dedicated to the common task of popularising his teachings.

Narottama Dāsa, one of the immediate successors of Śrī Caitanya, eulogizes Śrī Rūpa in his Namaskriya in *Premabhakti-candrikā,* as one, whose only purpose in life was to fulfil the mission of Śrī Caitanya.[1] This can be said with equal emphasis of each one of the other Gosvāmins. They were not ordinary persons, or merely 'leisured recluses,' as Dr. S. K. De calls them, who "could devote their keenly trained minds to the construction of elaborate systems," suggesting thereby that they indulged in scholarly pursuits, because they had nothing else to do, and their works represent their own thoughts rather than the philosophical views of Śrī Caitanya. On the contrary, they were great men, who combined the gift of learning with important positions in life and became ascetics so that they might devote all their time and energy to the propagation of the teachings of Śrī Caitanya with single-minded devotion. They did not renounce power and pelf to become leisured recluses and to earn a name for themselves as propounders of a new doctrine, but to serve Śrī Caitanya and his cause. Dr. De himself admits this elsewhere. Speaking of Rūpa, Sanātana and Jīva, he says, "Their authoritative position as fit and chosen disciples especially instructed and commissioned for the exacting task, their austere and saintly character, their self-less devotion to the cause, and their laborious and life-long scholarship, gave them a unique influence as the three authoritative Gosvāmins or teachers of the cult."[2]

The title, *Bhāgavata-saṁdarbha* given to the Saṁdarbhas by the author and the general plan of the work, no doubt, suggest that it was designed to be a commentary on *Śrīmad-bhāgavata*. But this, instead of detracting from the value of the work as representing the philosophy of Śrī Caitanya, adds greatly to it. For Śrī Caitanya not only regards *Śrīmad-bhāgavata* as Vyāsa Deva's own commentary on *Brahma-sūtra*, but declares that it fully represents his own doctrine (*CC*, Madhya, xxi, 17).[3] It is, therefore, natural that Jīva should base his exposition of the doctrine of Śrī Caitanya on *Śrīmad-bhāgavata.*

It is, in fact, because Śrī Caitanya gave due importance to *Śrīmad Bhāgavata* as Vyāsa Deva's own commentary on *Brahma-sūtra* that he did

[1]*Śrī Caitanya-mano' abhīstaṁ sthāpitaṁ yena bhūtale|*

[2]op. cit., p. 87.

[3]*Bhāgavate kahe mora tattva abhimata.*

not consider it necessary to write an independent commentary on *Brahma-sūtra* like Śaṁkara, Nimbārka, Vallabha, Mādhva and Rāmānuja, or any other philosophical or theological work of his own.

Next in importance to the Saṁdarbhas are the works of Rūpa and Sanātana themselves, principally, *Bhakti-rasāmṛta-sindhu* and *Ujjvala-nīlamaṇi* of Rūpa and *Vṛhad-bhāgavatāmṛta* and *Vaiṣṇavatoṣnī*, commentary on the tenth Skandha of *Śrīmad-bhāgavata* by Sanātana. There are, besides, a number of other works from which a systematic philosophy of Śrī Caitanya may be built.[1]

But these works, it is sometimes held, though important for our present purpose, cannot, in strict conformity with principles of scientific research, be regarded as basic to any formulation of the philosophy of Śrī Caitanya, since they do not formally acknowledge their debt to him or make a direct reference to his teachings.

To meet this formal objection, we shall lay the foundation of the philosophy of Śrī Caitanya on the authoritative biographical literature, in which his direct utterances are contained. While, however, these will constitute the foundation of the philosophy of Śrī Caitanya, its superstructure will be built with the help of material drawn from the more elaborate works of the Gosvāmins, mainly Jīva, Sanātana and Rūpa. For, even though these works do not directly refer to Śrī Caitanya, there is no doubt that they represent his views, since they are the works of persons specially entrusted by him with the task of propagating his teachings, which they follow closely in their general presentation and outlook.

Śrī Caitanya is, in this respect, compared to Socrates amongst the ancient Greek philosophers. "Just as we know of Socrates and his teachings not from his own writings, but through the writings of his disciples like Plato, so also we know of Śrī Caitanya's philosophy principally through the writings of his spiritual disciples."[2]

The biographies

There are four important biographies of Śrī Caitanya in the Bengali language: (1) *Caitanya-bhāgavata* by Thakura Vṛndāvana Dāsa, (2) *Caitanya-caritāmṛta* by Kṛṣṇadāsa Kavirāja, (3) *Caitanya-mangala*, by Jayānanda, and (4) *Caitanya-mangala* by Locana Dāsa.[3] Besides these, three *kaḍcās* or notes were written on his life by his most intimate disciples,

[1]*See* the bibliography at the end.

[2]S. K. Maitra, *Studies in Philosophy and Religion*, p. 275.

[3]The *Caitanya-maṅgala* by Jayānanda mentions the following biographical works on Śrī Caitanya of which no trace is found at present: (1) poems on Caitanya by Gaurī Dāsa, (2) poems on Caitanya by Gopāla Vasu, (3) poems on Caitanya by Paramānanda Gupta. *Caitanya-caritāmṛta* also indicates that many other biographies of Śrī Caitanya were written by his contemporaries, but unfortunately, none of them is now available (*CC*, Antya, xiv, 7).

Murārī Gupta, Svarūpa Dāmodara, and Raghunātha Dāsa. The *Kaḍcās* of Svarūpa Dāmodara and Raghunātha Dāsa have not yet been recovered, while the one written by Murārī Gupta, being purely a narrative of events, is of little philosophical importance. There is yet another *Kaḍcā* alleged to have been written by Govinda Dāsa Karmakāra, a contemporary of Śrī Caitanya, which is held in high esteem by Dr. D. C. Sen,[1] but which, on account of the modern Bengali language in which it is presented, and serious mistakes in its description of the personality, conduct and teachings of Śrī Caitanya, does not deserve to be treated without suspicion.[2]

Of the biographies mentioned above, *Caitanya-bhāgavata* and *Caitanya-caritāmṛta* are the most authoritative. They are huge works, containing exhaustive philosophical discourses given by Śrī Caitanya to Sārvabhauma Bhattācārya at Purī, Rāya Rāmānanda at Vidyānagar, Vainkata Bhaṭṭa in the Deccan, Rūpa, Raghupati and Vallabha Bhaṭṭa at Prayāga, Sanātana and Prakāśānanda Sarasvatī at Vārāṇasī, and to his other disciples and followers in different places during the course of his tours and pilgrimages. Their importance as sources of the philosophy of Śrī Caitanya is, therefore, great and they are held in high esteem by the Vaiṣṇava community. *Caitanya-maṅgala* by Jayānanda, which was written about the year 1574, shortly after Vṛndāvana Dāsa wrote his *Caitanya-bhāgavata*, does not seem to have been written under the guidance of the six Vṛndāvana Gosvāmins, all of whom, except Śrī Jīva, were the contemporaries of Śrī Caitanya and were regarded as living sources of information regarding his life and teachings. The information given by it regarding certain events in the life of Śrī Caitanya does not agree with the other authoritative accounts. It is, therefore, treated with indifference by the followers of Śrī Caitanya and suspected of interpolation by scholars. The *Caitanya-maṅgala* by Locana Dāsa is a lyrical poem rather than a historical work, and it also does not seem to be free from interpolation, particularly by the followers of the Ṣahajiyā cult.[3] Moreover, neither the *Caitanya-maṅgala* by Locana Dāsa nor the *Caitanya-maṅgala* by Jayānanda possess the philosophical accuracy and completeness of the *Caitanya-bhāgavata* and the *Caitanya-caritāmṛta,* which we shall now proceed to examine more closely.

Thākura Vṛndāvana Dāsa, the author of *Caitanya-bhāgavata*, was the son of Śrīvāsa Pandit's niece, Nārāyaṇī. The exact date of his birth is not known, but it is known that Nārāyaṇī was only four years old in Śaka 1430, when Śrī Caitanya returned from Gayā. It can, therefore, be concluded that he was not born before Śaka 1440, that is, 1518 AD.

The date when *Caitanya-bhāgavata* was compiled also cannot be

[1]Dr. D. C. Sen, *History of Bengali Language and Literature*, p. 443.
[2]cf., Kennedy, *Caitanya Movement*, pp. 129-30.
[3]Dr. D. C. Sen, *The Vaiṣṇava Literature of Mediaeval Bengal*, pp. 81-82.

determined with certainty. Dr. D. C. Sen puts it at 1573 AD, while Dr. B. B. Majumdar thinks it must have been written about the year 1548, since the author says, it was written at the behest of Nityānanda, his master. It consists of 25,000 lines in verse and is divided into three parts, called the Ādi Khaṅda, the Madhya Khaṅda, and the Antya Khaṅda The Ādi Khaṅda contains twelve chapters, the Madhya Khaṅda twenty-six, and the Antya Khaṅda eleven. The author describes the earlier part of the life of Śrī Caitanya in great detail, and deals somewhat summarily with the latter, probably because he finds that the work has already grown big, or because he is carried away by the desire to give a detailed description of the activities of his master, Nityānand, which keeps him largely occupied towards the end (*CC*, Ādi, viii, 44). This deficiency was made up by Kṛṣṇa Dāsa Kavirāja, who wrote *Caitanya caritāmṛta*, partly with a view to supplement the work of Thākura Vṛndāvana Dāsa (*CC*, Antya, xx, 73-78). As historical accounts of the life of Śrī Caitanya, therefore, the two works cannot be isolated from each other.

Kṛṣṇa Dāsa Kavirāja pays high tribute to Thākura Vṛndāvana Dāsa for his masterly exposition of the life and teachings of Śrī Caitanya, and, recognizing his absolute authotity in the matter, calls him the "Sage Vyāsa of the Līlā of Śrī Caitanya" (*CC*, Adi, xi, 52). Thākura Vṛndāvana Dāsa derives his authority from first-hand sources like (1) Nityānanda, (2) his mother, Nārāyaṇī, (3) the Kaḍcā of Murārī Gupta (4) the six Gosvāmins of Vṛndāvana, (5) Advaitācārya, and (6) Gadādhara Pandit.

Nityānanda was the most beloved disciple of Śrī Caitanya, and his personality was so closely associated with that of the latter in the theological dogma of the sect that homage to him was regarded as a necessary condition of winning the favour of Śrī Caitanya. Vṛndāvana Dāsa had the privilege of sitting at the feet of Nityānanda, and hearing directly from him the teachings of Śrī Caitanya. The supreme authoritativeness of *Caitanya-bhāgavata* is mainly due to the fact of its author's deriving most of the material for his work from this most reliable source (*C. Bh.*, Madhya, xx, 153). The author also derived some material from his mother, Nārāyaṇī, who was the niece of Śrīvāsa Pandit, and was living at the time when Śrī Caitanya used to perform Saṁkīrtana with his party in the historic courtyard of her uncle. The *Kaḍcā* of Murārī Gupta was also made use of by him. On its completion, the work was brought to the six Gosvāmins for their approval. They examined it closely and were so much satisfied that they changed its original name *Caitanya-mangala*, and gave it the name it now bears, in order to publicise the view that it had the same authority regarding the life and teachings of Śrī Caitanya as *Śrīmad-bhāgavata* had regarding the divine Līlā of Śrī Kṛṣṇa. This fact by itself is of supreme importance in adding to the value of the great work of Thākura Vṛnādvana Dāsa. While the above are, thus, the main sources of the work, Vṛndāvana Dāsa also derived some material from persons like Advaitācārya (*C. Bh.*, Madhya, xxiv, 68) and Gadādhara Pandit (*C. Bh.*, Antya, xi, 84).

The writing of *Caitanya-caritāmṛta*, it is clear, was taken up by Kṛṣṇa Dāsa Kavirāja some time after the *Caitanya-bhāgavata* was written, but a common misunderstanding seems to prevail regarding the exact date of its completion. Most writers, like Dr. D.C. Sen, assign it to 1582 AD, relying on the note that appears at the end of some of the manuscripts. But this, as Paramahaṅsa Bhakti Siddhānta Sarasvatī Gosvāmin points out, in his preface to the Gauḍīyā Maṭha edition of *Caitanya-caritāmṛta*, is apparently the note of the copyist. *Caitanya-caritāmṛta* quotes from some works like the *Gopāla-campū*, which were written after 1582 AD. If the authority of Dr. Sen himself is accepted, *Gopāla-campū* was written some time after the year 1599. *Caitanya-caritāmṛta*, therefore, could not have been written earlier than 1601. The author says that he wrote it at an extreme old age, when he was weak and infirm and could neither walk nor move (*CC*, Antya, xx, 84-86). He was, according to our estimate, born about the year 1531, and if he wrote it when he was about 80 years old, it must have been completed about the year 1611. According to Dr. Sen, however, he was born in the year 1496.[1] If this be correct, he must have been about thirty-eight years old when he came to Vṛndāvana, where the six Gosvāmins, including Raghunātha Dāsa, had settled, after the passing away of Śrī Caitanya in the year 1534. But Dr. Sen writes elsewhere that he was, at that time, merely a lad, whom the Vṛndāvana Gosvāmins had to give proper education and spiritual training.[2] Moreover, if Kṛṣṇa Dāsa was actually born in the year 1496, he would have been a contemporary of Śrī Caitanya for thirty-eight years and should have, in that case, at least given an indication of this somewhere in his writings.

Kṛṣṇa Dāsa Kavirāja was born of poor parents, and was orphaned when he was only six years old. At the early age of sixteen he decided to lead a saintly life. Just at that time, according to his own account, Nityānanda appeared to him in a dream and commanded him to go to Vṛndāvana (*CC*, Ādi, v, 177-87). When he came to Vṛndāvana, the six Gosvāmins were highly impressed by his purity of heart and earnestness of purpose and they readily admitted him into their disciplic order. They initiated him into the spirit of the teachings of Śrī Caitanya and helped him in his spiritual career in every way they could (*CC*, Ādi, v, 177-82). Each of the Gosvāmins bequeathed to him his own treasure of spiritual knowledge received from Śrī Caitanya, so that when, in his old age, he was requested by the Vaiṣṇava devotees of Vṛndāvana to write a more exhaustive biography of Śrī Caitanya than that of Thākura Vṛndāvana Dāsa, he already possessed a fund of first-hand information regarding the

[1]op. cit., p. 62.

[2]*History of Bengali Language and Literature*, p. 478

life and teachings of Śrī Caitanya, derived from the most authentic sources. He was specially favoured in this respect by Śrī Raghunātha Dāsa Gosvāmin, who had been a close associate of Śrī Caitanya at Purī during the last sixteen years of his life, and possessed more intimate knowledge of the teachings imparted by him during this period. Raghunātna Dāsa and Svarūpa Dāmodara were the only two biographers (Kaḍca-kartās) of Caitanya who lived so close to him (*CC*, Antya, xiv, 6-7). All other contemporary biographers stayed far away and could not note the details of his life so accurately. Svarūpa took notes in brief but Raghunātha Dāsa in a more amplified form (*CC*, Antya, xiv, 10-11). Kṛṣṇa Dāsa often repeats that his own biography is nothing but a still more amplified form of the Kaḍcā of Raghunātha Dāsa (*CC*, Madhya, ii, 73). He had the privilege of hearing the Kaḍcā read and explained by the author himself, as he lived with him at Rādhākuṅda, while he was compiling *Caitanya-caritāmṛta.*

Svarūpa Dāmodara's Kaḍcā was also made available to Kṛṣṇa Dāsa by Śrī Raghunātha Dāsa Gosvāmin. The importance of Svarūpa Dāmodar's Kaḍcā is due to the fact that it was written by one whose association with Śrī Caitanya was the closest and the longest. Svarūpa Dāmodara, or Puruśottama Ācārya, which was his name before he took Saṁnyasa, hailed from Navadvīpa. He had, therefore, direct knowledge of Śrī Caitanya's life and activities before the latter took Saṁnyāsa. Immediately after Śrī Caitanya's initiation into Saṁnyāsa, he also took Saṁnyāsa and went to Purī, where he stayed with him, from the time of his return from the South to the end. He was not with him only during his journeys from Bengal to Purī, from Purī to the South, and from Purī to the West, but he was able to gather the information about this period from Mukunda Dutta, Sārvabhauma Bhattācārya, Rāya Rāmānaṅda, and Balabhadra Bhattācārya, besides Śrī Caitanya himself.

Besides the information which Kṛṣṇa Dāsa obtained from Raghunātha Dāsa and the other Gosvāmins, he also had the advantage of consulting the *Caitanya-bhāgavata* and the *Caitanya-candrodaya Nātaka* of Kavi Karṇapūra. It is for these reasons that it is regarded as the most authoritative work on Śrī Caitanya.

What further adds to the importance of the work and makes it of special significance for our present purpose is its philosophical presentation. The author exhibits thorough knowledge of Indian philosophy in all its branches and gives an elaborate exposition of the doctrine of Śrī Çaitanya, quoting profusely from a huge list of Sanskrit and Bengali works, some of which are mentioned in the footnote below.[1] This makes the work difficult to understand by the lay Vaiṣṇavas, who are not fully acquainted with the six systems of Indian philosophy. The language of the work, also, is by no means easy. It is a strange mixture of Hindi, Sanskrit and Bengali. In length it exceeds even the *Caitanya-bhāgavata* and runs into as many as 15,050 Ślokas. Like the *Caitanya-bhāgavata* it is also divided into three Khaṅdas, the Ādi, the Madhya, and the Antya. But, in spite of its language and size, it is regarded as a work of rare merit, which has no parallel in the whole of Bengali literature.[2] In point of sanctity it is given the same place as the Bhāgavata and is read with reverence in the meetings of Vaiṣṇavas. The fact that it quotes as many as 380 times from the Bhāgavata, with which, according to Śrī Caitanya himself, his views are identical, shows how it breathes the essential spirit of his philosophy from beginning to end.

[1]1. *Abhijnāna-śakuntalā Nātaka*, 2. *Amarakoṣa*, 3. *Alankāra-śāstra*, 4. *Ādi Purāṇa*, 5. *Āryaśataka*, 6. *Itihāsa Samuccaya*, 7. *Ujjvala-nīlamaṇi*, 8. *Uttara-rāmacarita*, 9. *Udvāhatattva*, 10. *Upa-purāṇa*, 11. *Ekādaśī-tattva*, 12. *Kātyāyana saṁhitā*, 13. *Kāvya-prakāśa*, 14. *Kūrma-purāṇa*, 15. *Kṛṣṇa-saṁdarbha*, 16. *Garura-purāṇa*, 17. *Gītagovinda*, 18. *Govindalīlāmṛta*, 19. *Gautamīya-tantra*, 20. *Caitanya-candrodaya Nātaka*, 21. *Jagannātha-vallabha Nātaka*, 22. *Tattva-saṁdarbha*, 23. *Dānakeli-kaumudī*, 24. *Nātaka-candrikā*, 25. *Nāmakaumudī*, 26. *Nāradapañcarātra*, 27. *Nṛsiṁha-purāṇa*, 28. *Naiṣadhīya*, 29. *Padma-purāṇa*, 30. *Padyāvalī*, 31. *Pāṇini*, 32. *Vidagdhamādhava*, 33. *Viśvaprakāśa*, 34. *Viṣṇudharmottara*, 35. *Viṣṇu-purāṇa*, 36. *Vṛhat-gautamīya-tantra*. 37. *Vṛhannāradīya-purāṇa*, 38. *Vaiṣṇava-tantra*, 39. *Vaiṣṇavatoṣanī*, 40. *Brahma-saṁhitā*, 41. *Brahmānda-purāṇa*, 42. *Bhakti-rasāmṛta-sindhu*, 43. *Bhāgavat-saṁdarbha*, 44. *Bhagavad-gītā*, 45. *Bhāgavata*, 46. *Bhāgavatāmṛta*, 47. *Bhāvārthadīpikā*, 48. *Bhāravī*, 49. *Malamāsatattva*, 50. *Mahābhārata*, 51. *Raghuvaṁśa*, 52. *Rāmāyaṇa* (*Vālmīkikṛta*), 53. *Laghubhāgavatāmṛta*, 54. *Lalita-mādhava*, 55. *Svetāsvatara-upaniṣad*, 56. *Sarvajnyasūkta*, 57. *Sātvata-tantra*, 58. *Samudraka*, 59. *Sāḥitya-darpaṇa*, 60. *Skandha-purāṇa*, 61. *Stavamālā*, 62. *Stavāvalī*, 63. *Stotraratna*, 64. *Kaḍcā* (*Svarūpa Gosvamīkṛta*), 65. *Hayaśirṣa-pañcarātra*, 66. *Haribhakti-vilāsa*, 67. *Haribhakti-sudhodaya*.

[2]Dr. D. C. Sen, *The Vaiṣṇava Literature of Mediaeval Bengal*, p. 62.

CHAPTER V

Sources of Knowledge

An elaborate account of the sources of knowledge is nowhere to be found in the biographies of Śrī Caitanya. Reference is occasionally made to Pratyakṣa or perception, Anumāna or inference, and Śabda or revelation (*CC*, Madhya, vi, 81; Ādi, v, 18, 101). But Śabda is clearly recognised as the only proper source of knowledge. Śrī Caitanya is represented, in *Caitanya-caritāmṛta,* as saying to Sanātana that the only way to right knowlege is through scriptures: *amā saba jīvera haya śāstra dvārā jnāna* (*CC*, Madhya, xx, 293).

But Śrī Jīva Gosvāmin gives a detailed account of all the traditional sources of knowlege in his *Sarva-saṁvādinī.* Besides Pratyakṣa, Anumāna and Śabda, he mentions Upamā or analogy, Arthāpatti or implication, Saṁbhava or equivalence, Aitihya or tradition, Ārṣa or the words of Ṛṣis, Anupalabdhi or non-recognition, and Ceṣṭā or knowledge derived by physical effort, e.g., by lifting a weight. Of these, he says, Arthāpatti and Saṁbhava may be included under Anumāna, Anupalabdhi, Aitihya and Ceṣṭā under Pratyakṣa, and Ārṣa under Śabda. Further, he says that Pratyakṣa and Anumāna must function as subordinate to Śabda and not as independent sources of knowledge. Thus, Śabda alone is left, which he also recognises as the only independent and proper source of knowledge. He supports his view by referring to the following *Brahma-sūtras*:

srutis tu śabdamūlatvāt (i. I. 27)
tarkapratiṣthānāt (ii. I. 2)
śāstrayonitvāt (ii. I. 27)

Most philosophers, however, limit themselves to perception and inference as the only sources of knowledge. According to Śrī Caitanya, perception and inference, as based on our sense organs, are defective and unreliable (*CC*, Ādi, V, 17-18; Madhya, VI, 81). They are vitiated by four defects, namely: Bhrama or wrong perception of one thing for another, Pramāda or negligence, Vipralipsā or proneness to deceive, and Karaṇāpātava or incapacity of the various sense organs, which are natural to the ordinary man under the spell of Māyā or Prakṛti (*CC*, Ādi, vii, 101-102).

The insufficiency of these sources of knowledge is borne out by the history of philosophy. Empiricism, the philosophy based on sense perception, resulted, in India, in the despicable philosophy of Cārvāka, while it came to its logical conclusion, in Europe, in the scepticism of Hume. Rationalism, which is based exclusively on inference, came to its natural end in the Monadism of Leibnitz, which is little different from solipcism.

Herbert Spencer, Kant, Hamilton, and Mansel have shown the limits of human reason. According to them, our thought necessarily implies conditions. It cannot, therefore, apprehend the Absolute Truth, which is beyond all limits and conditions. Mansel forcefully argues from this in his Bampton Lectures, entitled 'Limits of Religious Thought,' that a demonstrable theology is impossible. As an agnostic, he goes even farther than Kant in maintaining that neither human logic nor human ethics are applicable to the Divine Being. Spencer goes farther still, and objects to Mansel's calling the Absolute or 'the Inscrutable Power manifested to us through all phenomena' even as personal. He regards every attempt to conceive the Absolute as equivalent to reducing Him to the human level. 'Have we not seen,' he asks, 'how utterly incompetent our minds are to form even an approach to a conception of that which underlies all phenomena? It is not proved that this incompetency is the incompetency of the conditioned to grasp the unconditioned? Does it not follow that the Ultimate Cause cannot in any respect be conceived by us, because it is in every respect greater than can be conceived? May we not refrain from assigning it any attributes whatever because such attributes, derived as they must be from our own nature, are not elevations but degradations?'

The Hegelian criticism of relativity of human knowledge, that the very consciousness of the limits of our knowledge implies the consciousness of that which falls beyond the supposed limits, does not go very far, according to Mansel. It only proves that the consciousness of the limits of our thought implies, though it does not directly reveal, the existence of something, which refuses to submit to the laws of our thought. 'When we lift up our eyes to that blue vault of heaven, which is itself but the limit of our own power of sight, we are compelled to suppose, though we cannot perceive the existence of space beyond, as well as within it; we regard the boundary of vision as parting the visible from the invisible. And when in contemplation we are conscious of relation and difference, as the limits of our power of thought, we regard them in like manner, as the boundary between the conceivable and the inconceivable, though we are unable to penetrate, in thought, beyond the nether sphere to the unrevealed and unlimited which it hides from us."[1]

While, however, in the opinion of the relativists, perception and inference, must by their very nature, be always denied access to Reality, according to Śrī Caitanya they can be treated as valid sources of knowledge when purified by Bhakti. Thus, the devoted souls can see the divine personality of Kṛṣṇa, which the ordinary persons may see, and yet see not (*C.*

[1]Mansel, *Selections from the Literature of Theism*, pp. 361-62.

Bh., Madhya, x, 243).[1] The washerman of Kaṁsa saw Kṛṣṇa and yet was not blessed with a vision of His divine form, because he lacked the essential quality of devotion (*C. Bh.*, Madhya, X, 248-51). An owl cannot see the rays of the sun, even though it has eyes (*CC*, Ādi, III, 169); so, also, it is not given to a soul averse to God to perceive Him (*C. Bh.*, Madhya, x, 252-53). But God can never hide Himself from His devotees (*CC*, Ādi, iii, 70).[2]

Vaiduṣa Pratyakṣa (*mystical cognition*)

Śrī Jīva Gosvāmin mentions two kinds of perception: Vaiduṣa, which belongs to the learned or the wise, who are purified by Bhakti, and Avaiduṣa, which belongs to those who are not so purified. Vaiduṣa Pratyakṣa is the basis of Śabda itself, being free from all kinds of error. Avaiduṣa Pratyakṣa is liable to error.

Vaiduṣa Pratyakṣa or the vision of the pure soul is the mystic[3] element in religion on which so much has been written in recent years. The arguments used against it as a proper source of knowledge are also familiar. It is not only regarded as something purely subjective but as indicative of an unhealthy and abnormal attitude of mind. This misconception is due to the vicious use of psychology in religion, a characteristic instance of which is found in Leuba's treatment of the relation between theology and psychology.[4] Starting with the assumption that 'the gods of religion are inductions from experience,' Leuba goes on to make an arbitrary distinction between metaphysical and empirical theology. He then rejects the metaphysical theology, because, in his view, it gives us a God-idea, which is essentially foreign to the true nature of religion. He regards empirical theology as simply a matter of psychological analysis and banishes from it all the transcendental or supernatural factors. Theologians, in his view, have made a hopeless muddle of the problem, and the only persons who can successfully deal with it are the scientific psychologists.

But the psychologist tends to obliterate the distinction between the exoteric and esoteric, the temporal and the permanent, the accidental and the essential elements in the life of a mystic. Psychology can give us only a succession of states in the mind of the mystic. It cannot give us what Herman calls, "The Divine Activity initiating, sustaining and unifying the human." It cannot do more than describe certain reactions which take place in the mind in response to stimuli which may or may not have

[1] *bhakti binā āmā dekhileū kichu naya/*

[2] *āpanā lukāite kṛṣṇa nānā jatna kare/*
tathāpi tāhāra bhakta jānaya tāhāre//

[3] The word "mysticism" has been used in a great variety of senses. We shall use it to denote religion in its most acute, and living stage.

[4] *See* Leuba's *A psychological study of religion*, Chapter XI.

objective value. But that which gives meaning to religious experience is precisely that transcendental and objective element concerning which psychology has nothing to say.

Mystic experience is a thing *per se*. It differs from ordinary experience in having a trans-subjective reference. William James says, "It is as if there were in human consciousness a sense of Reality, a feeling of Objective Presence, a perception of what we may call 'something there,' more deep and more general than any of the special and particular senses by which the current psychology supposes existing realities to be originally revealed."[1] T. M. Watt says, "It is one thing to exclude the transcendental from among the valid working causes recognized by psychology and an entirely different matter to deny the reference of religious experience to a Transcendental Object, whose reality is therefore affirmed."[2]

William James insists that religious experience has a 'noetic' quality, which gives the experient the assurance of its objective validity. Otto coins the word 'numinous' to describe the distinctive quality of religious experience. 'I shall speak then,' he says, 'of an unique numinous category of value and of a definitely numinous state of mind which is always found where the category is implied.' The numinous, for him, is felt as objective and outside the self.

The following Śloka of *Mundaka-upaniṣad* also lays stress on the numinous quality of mystic experience:

bhidyate hṛdaya-granthiśchidyante sarvasaṁśayaḥ|
ksīyante cāsya karmāṇi yasmin dṛṣṭe parāvare|| *Mundaka*, 2, 2, 8.

According to Śrī Caitanya, the numinous quality of mystic experience is due to the ingress of Śuddha-sattva in the devotee's consciousness. Śuddha-sattva is the essence of Saṁdhinī-śakti, or the potency of God, which is the ground cause of all kinds of transcendental existence, including the existence of God Himself:

saṁdhinīra sāra aṁśa śuddha sattva nāma|
bhagavānera sattā haya jahāte viśrāma|| *CC*, Ādi, iv, 59.

It may be argued that the distinctive character of mystic experience is no proof of its objectivity. Its trans-subjective reference does not establish the real existence of the object of reference; and the feeling of certitude by which it is characterised does not prove that its truth value is beyond question. We have no hesitation in admitting that the validity of mystic experience is not capable of strict logical proof, because mystic experience does not, by its very nature, submit itself to examination by reasoning. As speculative philosophers we can neither affirm nor deny its validity. But strong and convincing arguments may be adduced to elicit our belief in its validity, and to remove any doubts regarding its wholesomeness

[1]James, *Varieties of Religious Experience*, p. 58.
[2]T. M. Watt, *The Intuition of God*, p. 48.

We cannot judge a mystic experience by its content. But we can judge it by its antecedent spiritual conditions, and the effect it has on the life of the mystic as a whole. With regard to the former, it is important to note that mystic experiences are not like hypnotic trances into which anyone can go. They demand vigorous spiritual discipline on the part of the subject. Purgation or purification is a necessary stage in the life of the mystic. "Blessed are the pure in heart for they shall see God," says the Gospel. A man whose heart is tainted with the least propensity for worldly enjoyments, and whose thought and actions do not flow in a single current of loving devotion to the Lord, cannot hope to attain the mystic experience (*CC*, Ādi, III, 169-516). This fact, by itself, marks out the mystic experience from any thing derogatory or unwholesome.

Greater in importance is the general bearing of the spiritual realisation of the mystic on his life and character. Herman lays stress on the 'life-enhancing quality' of the mystic experiences, and says that they are of value to us in as much as we can trace in them "the genesis of great illuminating, fructifying forces which we see wrought into the life and teaching of the mystic." The mystic is also the embodiment of an ideal character. An account of the qualities of a Vaiṣṇava mystic is given by Śrī Caitanya in his teachings to Sanātana Gosvāmin. He is described as merciful, harmless, truthful, just, guileless, generous, polite, pure, lowly, beneficient, peaceful, dependent wholly on Kṛṣṇa, free from desires, quiet, steady, sane, humble, respectful towards others, solemn, friendly, wise, skilful and silent (*CC*, Madhya, xxii, 45-48). Indeed, a true Vaiṣṇava is like God Himself (*C. Bh.*, Madhya, xxiii, 413; xxiv, 102).

The transcendental character of the mystic experience is also indicated by its passivity. It is said that God is not discovered but makes himself known to his devotees, the latter contributing nothing directly to this result. Mystical cognition is to the soul precisely what sensation is to the body. This dependence of the soul on some power outside or "The Wholly Other," as Otto calls it, protects mysticism from the charge of auto-suggestion, which reduces mystic experience to the product of the suggestive activity of mind.

Rightly understood, however, even auto-suggestion is a different way of stating the true nature of mystic experience, since it implies a self to which something is suggested and a self that suggests. What can be the larger suggesting self, if not that to which the mystic totally surrenders? Auto-suggestion is only another way of saying that God and man are conjunct and that in the interior of the soul divine suggestions come to human consciousness in a manner, which it is not possible for us to comprehend. We may call this auto-suggestion or we may say, like St. Paul, 'It is I, yet not I,' but it is obvious that it is a mystery, which psychology cannot explain.

The misunderstanding regarding the essential nature of mysticism is also due to its immediacy, which is often confounded with the immediacy of sensuous experience. But the immediacy of mystic experience is higher than the immediacy of sense experience. It is an immediacy, which is qualified by the mediacy of thought. The immediate and intutive character of mystic experience, no doubt, signifies that the realisation of truth cannot come through any conceptual system, however logically articulated, but this does not mean that the mystic experience is of the nature of sensuous experience, or that it is irrational. Intuition gives the soul a new immediacy, whereby the abstract terms of philosophical and theosophical insight are incorporated in a direct apprehension of God. The mystic thus completes the work of the philosopher or the theologian, and goes a step beyond. His philosophical or religious doctrine is no longer a doctrine but a life.

This is fully demonstrated by the lives of saints. They live a life of which a mere philosopher has no experience, but which is not lacking in a philosophical background. It is true that feelings and emotions, which, by their very nature, fall outside the scope of an abstract philosophy, form a prominent part of their nature, but it is also true that their feelings and emotions have a philosophical background from which they spring. The philosophical side of their nature may be concealed by the very simplicity and innocence of their lives, but it is never absent. Speaking of Christ, Herman says "The cross and all it meant and the ministry of which it was the culminating point did not grow immediately out of the homely, simple life of Nazareth, but issued out of a long and patient brooding on the facts of life.... Just as a fact is not truly and wholly a fact, if it does not include an interpretative theory, so the new life of Christ to be *life indeed* and not merely a set of moods, impressions and sensations, must include its reasoned interpretation."

Śrī Caitanya's insistence on the rational character of mystical experience is apparent from his distinction between lower and higher understanding. The lower understanding pertains to ordinary persons and the higher to the sages (*CC*, Madhya, xxiv, 121-22).[1] The former, which is impure, does not help in spiritual realisation, but the latter, which is free from the influence of Prakṛti, leads to the realisation of God (*CC*, Madhya, xxiv, 123-24). Indeed, devotional service to Kṛṣṇa, the study of Bhāgavata, the recitation of Holy Name, the company of holy persons, and residing in Vṛndāvana, the five most important means of God-realisation, are fruitful only in the case of persons who possess *Subuddhi*, or the higher understanding (*CC*, Madhya, xxiv, 128-29). In the case of persons not possessing the higher understanding, no amount of spiritual exercise will

[1] *ātmā śabde "buddhi" kahe buddhi viśeṣa|*
sāmānya buddhiyukta jata jīva aśeṣa||

be of any avail. But those having the higher understanding will march steadily on the path of God-realisation, unobstructed by anything (*CC*, Madhya, xxiv, 131).[1]

Thus, mystic experience is not something purely subjective or emotional. Based as it is on the unerring vision of the released soul, and the pure light of higher understanding, it is free from all subjective prejudices and preconceived notions that usually vitiate the mind of the ordinary philosopher, and may claim, in this sense, even higher objectivity than knowledge based on thought and sense.[2] The mere logical intricacy of a system of thought is no proof of its objective validity. Even a very cleverly argued, highly articulated, and profoundly reasoned philosophy may be nothing more than the philosopher's own web, artfully spun out of his preconceived ideas, if it is not based on a reflection of Reality on the mirror of his soul, purified from all taints of worldly desires, or predilections. The importance, in this connection, of Fichte's remark, that "The kind of philosophy that a man chooses depends on the kind of man that he is," cannot be exaggerated. Muirhead compares philosophies to "the creation of the poet or the artist, embodying his idea, expressing his feeling" rather than to "scientific discoveries or technical inventions, which are not only impersonal but depersonalised and thus in a sense self-explanatory products of intelligence."[3]

The subjectivity of mystic experience is not Subjectivism. It is the kind of subjectivity upon which the Existentialists insist, "the self-penetration of the individual in himself and his God-relationship," the the basing of life on the immediate consciousness of "the deepest root of my existence, something through which I am linked with the divine." It is the turning of mind from vain intellectualism, which teaches that essence is prior to existence and has no application to concrete particulars of life, to the centre of all existence. It is turning from the so called objective criterion of truth to Truth as realised in man's inner existence. Truth, according to Kierkegaard, has no meaning except as 'appropriated' by the subject or realised in his life.

Caitanyism resolves the conflict between subjective experience and objective knowledge through its belief in the ingress of Śuddha-sattva, the principle of transcendental existence to which we have already referred. The ingress of Śuddha-sattva in the consciousness of the devotee, whose heart is purified and whose surrender to the divine is complete, results in such interpenetration of the subject by the transcendental existence that his thought, feeling and will are wholly transformed and sublimated and

[1]*subuddhi janera haya kṛṣṇa premodaya//*
[2]*udāra mahiti jāra sarvottmā buddhi/*
nānā kāme bhaje tabu pāya bhakti siddhi//
[3]*Contemporary British Philosophy*, p. 7.

he comes face to face with Truth. The Truth is no more an external object of contemplation for him. He not only knows it, but lives it.

In the present state of the Jīva, however, when its vision is eclipsed and it cannot have a first hand experience of Reality, the only source of knowledge is revelation or *Śabdā* (*CC*, Madhya, xx, 107).[1] This does not mean that reason is to be completely discarded, but that it can be of help only when subordinated to revelation. 'Reason,' as Flint says, "sends forth a true light which is to be trusted and followed so far as it extends, but which is much more limited than the wants of human nature. The deepest discoveries and the highest achievements of the unaided intellect need to be supplemented by truths which can only come to us through special revelation."[2]

The doctrine of revelation finds its rational justification in the nature of the Absolute Himself. Because the Absolute is unconditioned, He implies the negation of the conditions under which alone the processes of our thought and perception are possible. But because He is all-merciful, He is eternally revealing Himself to those who, adopting the path of Bhakti, submit to Him wholly and unconditionally, and listen to His transcendental Voice, the Vedas and the Purāṇas, with faith and devotion.

Śābdā (*Revelation*)

In three ways, the Absolute communicates His knowledge to the finite souls. He sits in their hearts and directs their understanding (*CC*, Madhya, xxii, 30); He takes the form of the Guru or the spiritual preceptor, and helps them through initiation to realise the Truth; He descends to the level of the finite in the form of the Amnāya or the *heard transcendental word* (*Śruti*), received through the channel of preceptorial succession from Brahmā, the creator of this world, and embodied in the scriptures (*CC*, Madhya, xx, 108).[3]

The Guru is the manifest form of the Supreme Being and an embodiment of His quality of Mercy (*CC*, Ādi, i, 27). He is known as Caitya or Mahānta, according as He manifests Himself in our hearts in the form of a spiritual principle (*antaryāmin*), guiding and controlling our activities from within, or in the form of a principal devotee, inspiring and imparting instructions from without (*CC*, Ādi, i, 29).[4]

Revelation or *Śabda*, however, primarily means the word of the Āmnāya, which is taken to include the four Vedas, the eighteen principal

[1] *Māyāmugdha jīvera nahi kṛṣṇa smṛti jnāna/*
jīvera kṛpāya kela kṛṣṇa veda purāṇa//

[2] Flint, *Theism*, p. 302.

[3] *Śāstra-guru-ātma-rūpe āpanāre jānāna/*

[4] *jīve sākṣātā nahi tāte guru caitya rūpa/*
śikṣā guru haya kṛṣṇa mahānta svarūpa//

Purāṇas, the eighteen Upa-purāṇas (secondary Purāṇas), the eleven Upaniṣads, and the Sūtras or the aphorisms, made by the great spiritual teachers. These are the only proper source of knowledge. Being the word of God, they do not suffer from any of the four defects from which perception and inference are known to suffer (*CC*, Ādi, VII, 101-2).[1]

The Āmnāya is self-evident, the other sources of knowledge are not. They depend on the Āmnāya and are useful only so long as they are consistent with it. But the Āmnāya loses its self-evident character, if its meaning is distorted (*CC*, Ādi, vii, 125).[2] It is the Abhidhā Vṛtti, or the way of interpretation that relies on the primary or direct meaning of words and not the Lakṣaṇā Vṛtti or the way of interpretation that relies on their secondary or indirect meaning that should be adopted in our study of the scriptures (*CC*, Ādi, vii, 103-4). The secondary meaning should be adopted only where the primary meaning does not make any sense. For example, it is not necessary to call in the aid of Lakṣaṇā Vṛtti if we want to understand the expression *ayaṁ śacinandanaḥ sākṣāt nandanandana eva.* As soon as these words are heard the direct impression created is that "the son of Śaci (Śrī Kṛṣṇa Caitanya) is the son of Nanda (Śrī Kṛṣṇa) Himself." But the expression *gangāyāṁ ghośaḥ,* when directly interpreted, means "the village of cowherds *in* the Ganges," which does not carry any sense. It becomes necessary to adopt Lakṣṇā in order to obtain the real meaning, which is "the village of the cowherds is situated on the bank of the Ganges (and not in the stream)."

Madhvācārya, however, thinks that in the case of the Vedas, the Lakṣṇā Vṛtti has no place at all. He argues that, "If in interpreting the transcendental words of the Vedas the Abhidhā Vṛtti is useless, what purpose can be served by Lakṣṇā, which is only subsidiary to it? Where there is no village, the question of its boundary does not arise. There can be no son without the parents" (Madhvācārya, *Tatvamuktāvali,* 22).

But the Vedas are so extensive that it is not possible to master them all in this age of Kali, when the span of life is short. They are also so terse and obscure that it is not always easy to grasp their real meaning. They are so differently interpreted by the sages that one is puzzled by the diversity of their meaning. The only scriptures, which can make the obscure sense of the Vedas clear, are the Itihāsa and the Purāṇa, which were compiled for this purpose. Many things which are vaguely described or briefly indicated in the Vedas are thoroughly explained and amplified in the Itihāsa and the Purāṇa.

The Itihāsa and the Purāṇa are, in this sense, complementary parts of the Veda. This is indicated by the word *purāṇa* itself. As complementary

[1]*See* also *TS*, 10.
[2]*svataḥ pramāṇa veda pramāṇa śiromaṇi|*
lakṣṇā karile svataḥ pramāṇatā hāni||

parts, the Purāṇas cannot be distinguished from the Veda (*TS*, 12). Śrī Jīva Gosvāmin discusses at length the inseparability of the Purāṇa and the Itihāsa from the Veda and quotes from various texts to prove that the Purāṇa and the Itihāha together constitute the fifth Veda and deal in an elaborate manner with Ākhyāna, Upākhyāna, Gāthā and Kalpa-śuddhi, topics which are not exhaustively treated in the four Vedas (*TS*, 13, 14). The Purāṇa and the Itihāsa are even regarded as superior to the Veda, not only because they complete the sense of the Veda, but because, unlike the Veda, they are easily understood and are accessible to all, the Brāhmaṇas and the Śūdras, the men and the women, and the young and the old. Therefore, a man, who has studied the Veda but not the Itihāsa and Purāṇa, cannot be regarded as truly learned (*TS*, 15).

Of the Itihāsa and the Purāṇa, greater importance is attached to the latter because the Itihāsa is primarily narrative in character. But the Purāṇas, in the present age, do not seem to fulfil their specific purpose of unfolding the real meaning of the Veda, because they are neither extant in their completeness, nor they cherish the same gods, or propound the same views. They were written at different times to suit different religions and persons of different tastes and capacities. It is stated in the *Matsya-purāṇa* that in different ages the Purāṇas uphold different gods. In the *Sāttvika-kalpa*,* they glorify Hari, in the *Rājasika-kalpa* Brahmā, and in the *Tāmasika-kalpa* Śiva and Agni. Thus, according to the different Kalpas in which they were written, they are classified into *Sāttvika Rājasika*, and *Tāmasika* (*TS*, 17). The Sāttvika Purāṇas are the most authoritative and they should be given preference over others, because the quality of Sattva is the seat of knowledge and it leads to the realisation of Brahman. But even the *Sāttvika-purāṇas* do not always express the same views. They sometimes describe Brahman as personal and sometimes as impersonal, sometimes as intelligent and sometimes as non-intelligent. How then are we to determine the real sense of the Purāṇas?

Śrīmad-bhāgavata

Brahma-sūtra, which was apparently written by Srī Vyāsadeva to determine the sense of the Vedas and the Purāṇas is not helpful, because it is aphoristic and has been differently interpreted by the commentators of different schools. If among the Purāṇās themselves we find a Purāṇa that contains the essence of the *Veda*, the *Itihāsa* and the *Purāṇa*, and is also easily comprehensible, our problem may be solved.

Such a Purāṇa we find in *Śrīmad-bhāgavata*. It is the quintessence of the Veda, the Itihāsa and the Purāṇa (*Bh.*, 1, 3, 42)[1] and was extracted

*A day and night of Brahmā, a period of 432 million solar years of mortals.

[1]*sarva vedetihāsānāṁ sāraṁ sāraṁ samuddhṛtaṁ*/

from them as butter is skimmed out of curd (*C. Bh.*, Madhya, xxi, 16).[1] It is the ripened fruit of the Veda. the supreme tree of plenty that fulfils all desires (*CC*, Madhya. xxv, 541).[2] One who drinks of the nectar of its divine teachings has neither the desire nor the need for reading any other scripture. It is, indeed, the crest-jewel of the whole body of scriptures, as proved by an account of its origin in the mind of sage Vyāsa.

It is stated that after Vedavyāsa had composed the *Vedānta-sūtras* and the other seventeen Purāṇas, he was still restless in mind (*C. Bh.*, Antya, iii, 507). He engaged himself in deep meditation in order to have a fuller realisation of Truth. He was then blessed with a divine vision, through which the contents of *Śrīmad-bhāgavata* were revealed and with that revelation came the joy and peace he had sought (*C. Bh.*, Antya, iii, 508).

Therefore, *Śrīmad-bhāgavata* is regarded by the Bengal school of Vaiṣṇavas as containing the highest revealed truth and as being Vyāsa-deva's own commentary on his *Brahma-sūtra* (*CC*, Madhya, xxv, 108).[3] The supreme authoritativeness and excellence of *Śrīmad-bhāgavata* is described by Śrī Caitanya thus: "The *Vedānta-sūtra* of Vyāsa is not intelligible to ordinary mortals. Therefore, the benign sage has expounded the meaning of his own Sūtras in *Śrīmad-bhāgavata.* The *Bhāgavata* is, really speaking, an exposition of *Praṇava* or *Om,* the transcendental word of eternal harmony. *Praṇava* and *Gāyatri* are identical in meaning. This meaning was expanded by Īśvara in the four Ślokas which He communicated to Brahmā. Brahmā in his turn related them to Nārada and Nārada to Vyāsa. The *Brahma-stūras* of Vyāsa only elucidate these Ślokas and the *Bhāgavata* is nothing but a Bhāṣyā on the Sūtras" (*CC*, Madhya, xxv, 76-81).

Śrīmad-bhāgavata is thus, the most authoritative of all the *Sāttvika-purāṇas* (*TS*, 20). It is complete in itself (*TS*, 21), because it is in essence identical with Kṛṣṇa, the most perfect of all beings (*C. Bh.*, Madhya, xxi, 14).[3] Being essentially divine in character, it is not the creation of any individual. Like the Matsya, Kūrma and other incarnations of God, it appears or disappears of its own accord (*C. Bh.*, Antya, iii, 500-1). It is said in *Śrīmad-bhāgavata* that, "when Kṛṣṇa retired to His spiritual realm along with Dharma and Jnāna, the sun of *Bhāgavata* appeared on the horizon of the world in the age of Kali to dispel the gloom surrounding the Jīvas, who had lost their spiritual sight" (*Bh.*, 1, 3, 43).

Śrī Jīva proves the importance and authority of *Śrīmad-bhāgavata* by pointing to its great popularity and referring to some of the excellent commentaries on it by the ancient and the modern scholars, such as

[1]*cāri veda dadhi bhāgavata navanīta|*
mathilena śuke khāilena parīkṣita||
[2]*ataeva bhāgavata sūtrera artharūpa*
nijakṛta sūtrera nija bhāṣya svarūpa||
[3]*grantha rūpe bhāgavata kṛṣṇa avatāra|*

Hanumad-bhāṣya, Vasnā-bhāṣya, Sambandhokti, Vṛhat-kāmadhenu, Tattva-dīpikā, Bhāvārtha-dīpikā, Paramahaṁsa-priya and *Śuka-hṛdaya*. He also refers to *Tantra-bhāgavata*, which is mentioned as a commentary on *Śrimad-bhāgavata* in *Hayaśirṣa-pancarātra* and mentions several other works on the *Bhāgavata* such as *Muktā-phala, Hari-līlā*, and *Bhakti-ratnāvali*.

The question is sometimes asked why Śaṁkara did not accept *Bāhga-vata* as Vyāsadeva's own commentary on *Brahma-sūtrā*. In reply to this *Caitanya-caritāmṛta* quotes a sloka from the *Padma-purāṇa*, according to which Śaṁkara was an incarnation of Śiva, the prince of devotees, who was himself devotionally inclined at heart, but whose special mission in coming down to this world in the role of an Ācārya was to misguide the people at the behest of God by wrongly interpreting Śastras with the help of Lakṣṇā-vṛtti of words (*CC*, Madhya, vi, Ś13).[1] He did not explicitly accept *Śrīmad-bhāgavata*, because he knew it contained teachings which were decidedly above his own, and he did not want to misinterpret it as he did in the case of the other *Śāstras*, because he considered it to be the most sacred to God. But his real love for *Bhāgavata* is evinced by his occasional references to the pastimes of Kṛṣṇa in his *Govindā śataka* and other similar works, as also by some of his hymns which echo the ideas contained in the *Bhāgavata* (*TS*, 23).

The fact that the *Bhāgavata* was recognised as Śrī Vyāsadeva's own commentary on *Brahma-sūtra* is the reason why Śrī Caitanya or any of the six Gosvāmins did not, like the other Ācāryas, try to base their philosophy on an original commentary on *Bhrama-sūtra*.

Śrīmad-bhāgavata is thus the foundation stone of the philosophy of Śrī Caitanya. He clearly states this while reprimanding Devānanda, a scholar of Nadiyā, for his careless study of the *Bhāgavata* (*C. Bh.*, Madhya, xxi, 17).[2] The writings of Śrī Rūpa, Śanātana, Jīva, Vṛndāvana Dāsa and Kavirāja Gosvāmin are also characterised by a faithful dependence on this great Purāṇa and are replete with references from it. Some of these, such as the *Bhāgavatāmṛta* of Sanātana and *Saṁkṣepa-bhāgava-tāmṛta* of Rūpa are apparently works on *Śrimad-bhāgavata* itself. The *Saṁdarbhas* of Jīva Goswamin were designed to be a commentary on selected portions of *Srīmad-bhāgavata*, as the name *Bhāgavata-saṁdarbha*, origianally given to them by the author, indicates. Srī Jīva also wrote a running commentary on the *Bhāgavata* which was called the *Krama-saṁ-darbha*.

The contents of *Śrīmad-bhāgavata* are classified by Śrī Caitanya under three heads: *saṁbandha, abhidheya* and *prayojana* (*CC*, Madhya, xxv,

[1] *svāgamaiḥ kalpitaistvañca janān madvimukhān kuru|*
mānca gopaya yena syāt sṛṣtiresottarottarā|| (cited from *Padma-purāṅa*, Uttara Khanda, Chapter XXV, I).

[2] *mora priya śuka śe jānena bhāgavata|*
bhāgavate kahe mora tattva abhimata||

105).[1] *Saṁbandha*, which means relation, treats of the relationship between Jīva, world and Īśvara. But since Jīva and the world are the manifestations of the *cit* and the *acit* potencies of Īśvara, *saṁbandha-jnāna* primarily means knowledge of the complete personality of Īśvara, and *saṁbandha-prāpti* the realisation of our true relationship with Him. *Abhidheya* means the way that leads to the attainment of this relationship, and *prayojana* the purpose for which the relationship is sought. Īśvara, conceived in all His perfection, is *saṁbandha*; Bhakti is *abhidheya*; and Prema is *prayojana* (*CC*, Madhya, xxv, 86-87). This classification is extended by Śrī Caitanya to the other scriptures as well (*CC*, Madhya, xx, 109-10).

[1] *ataeba bhāgavate eī tin kaya|*
sambandha-abhidheya-prayojana-maya||

CHAPTER VI

Nature of the Absolute

The philosophical position of the Vaiṣṇava schools is a kind of concrete monism, in which a Personal Absolute embraces the totality of existence. But Śrī Caitanya recommends a concrete monism, which goes even farther in its comprehensiveness. The Personal Absolute, or Para-brahman, according to him, enfolds even the *nirviśeṣa* or formless and attributeless Brahman. This is possible on account of His inconceivable power of reconciling the irreconcilable, which enables Him to rise above our imperfect and contradictory notions of qualified and unqualified Brahman and reconcile them in a higher synthesis.

The Nirviśeṣa (unqualified) Brahman

The Nirviśeṣa Brahman, according to Śrī Caitanya, is but an aspect of the Absolute, which by its very nature is endlessly qualified and perfect. But the concept of the Absolute as merely *nirviṣeṣa*, which is beyond thought and speech, is dismissed by him as meaningless. Such an Absolute cannot be made the subject of an intelligible proposition. Any intelligible proposition about it would cancel the concept itself. For, even to say that Brahman is inexpressible or unthinkable is to say or think something about it (*SS*, p. 96).[1]

The Advaitins themselves refer to Brahman by such words as *svaprakāśa* (self-luminous) and *paramārtha-sat* (transcendental reality), which proves that it is not altogether inexpressible. It cannot be maintained that these words do not directly imply, but indirectly point to it, because they do not have any other meaning and cannot signify anything except Brahman.[2] There are, no doubt, some Upaniṣadic texts which seem to teach that Brahman is unknowable by mind and inexpressible by words, as for example:

yato vāco nivartante aprāpya manasā saha (*Tait. Up.*, II, 4. 1).

"From whom speech and mind turn away, because they are unable to reach Him."

[1]*brahmacedavacanīyaṁ bhavati tarhyavacanīyapadenocyate iti vācyatvamevāyāti* (*SS*, p. 96).

[2]*evaṁ nirviśeṣasvaprakāśaparamārthasadityādi śabdaiḥ brahmocyate cedvācyatvasiddhiḥ/na ca tairapi lakṣyate-tattacchabdamukhyārthasyānyasyābhāvāt//* ibid, p. 97.

yadvācānbhyuditam yena vagabhyudyate|
tadeva brahmatvaṁ viddhi nedaṁ yadidamupāsate|| *Kena. Up.*, 1.5.
"He Who is not expressed by speech and by Whom speech is expressed, That alone know as Brahman, not that whom people here adore."

But there are also passages which support the opposite view. In the Śruti texts, *atha kasmāducyate brahman*, and *tasmāducyate paraṁ-brahman*, it has been clearly indicated that Brahman is the subject of thought and speech. The *Gītā* says, it is *called* Brahman, and even describes it as the highest subject of speech.[1] The *ikṣternāśabdam* Sūtra of Bādarāyaṇa also supports the same view. For, it means, according to Baladeva, Brahman is not inexpressible by words, because we see that it is expressly taught in the Vedas.[2] Baladeva further points out that in the *Vṛhadāranyaka-upaniṣad*, Brahman is designated as *aupaniṣad*,[3] which means that it is known through the words of the *Upaniṣad*, and in the *Kathā-upaniṣad* it is described as one 'Whom all the Vedas declare,'[4] etc.

Thus, it will appear that when Brahman is said to be *Aśabdam* or ineffable, it does not mean that it cannot be expressed at all. This word is here used in a restricted sense, in the same manner in which the word invisible is used in a restricted sense when applied to the mountain Meru. It does not mean that the Meru is absolutely invisible, but that we cannot see all its parts. Similarly, the word 'ineffable' with reference to Brahman does not mean that it cannot be expressed at all, but that it cannot be completely expressed by words. If Brahman were completely beyond thought and speech, the *Kena-upaniṣad* saying, "*Know* Him to be Brahman," will have no meaning. Being infinite and unbounded, Brahman cannot be circumscribed by words. This is the real meaning of the text, *Yato vāco nivartante* etc.[5]

It may be urged that Brahman, truly speaking, is neither expressible nor inexpressible. But to say this, again, is to make it unintelligible and to reduce the ground and source of all existence to nothingness.[6]

The objection that if Brahman were expressible by words, it would not be described as self-manifest, does not hold good, because the Vedas being the body of Brahman are, in a way, identical with it and the idea of Brahman being expressed through them does not come into conflict with the idea of Brahman as self-revealed.[7]

[1] *SS*, p. 97.
[2] *C. Bh.*, I.I.5.
[3] *tvantvaupaniṣadaṁ puruṣaṁ pṛcchāmi|* *Br.* III. 9. 26.
[4] *sarve vedā yat padamāmananti|* *Kaṭha*, II, 15.
[5] *SS*, p. 41; also p. 54.
[6] *vacanīyatvāvacanīyatvābhāve tu anirvacanīyatvāpātah.* ibid, p. 96.
[7] *GB.*, I. I. 5.

According to the Advaitins, Brahman is a pure identity. It is above the application of all kinds of difference, whether *svajātīya* (which appears between things of the same category), *vijātīya* (which appears between things of different categories), or *svagata* (which manifests itself in one and the same thing, either between its essence and form or between its component parts). It is the absolute denial of the last of these three kinds of difference that makes the Brahman of the Advaitins devoid of all forms and attributes. Śrī Caitanya and his followers also recognise the importance of identity as a fundamental characteristic of reality, and deny all kinds of difference in Brahman. But, while their denial of the first two kinds of difference is absolute, their denial of the last is not. They are adverse to the conception of the Absolute as a pure and undifferentiated being and their criticism of Nirviśeṣa Brahman bears a close resemblance to that of Rāmānuja, to whom Jīva Gosvamin frequently refers in his Saṁdarbhas.

Having accepted the undifferentiated Brahman as the sole category of existence, the *advaitins* fail to give a satisfactory explanation of the world of appearance, which necessarily implies *viśeṣa* or qualification in Brahman. They regard the world as a superimposition (*adhyāsa*), like the superimposition of silver in the conch-shell. But there must be some *adhiṣṭhāna*, or object, upon which the superimposition rests. Since nothing exists besides Brahman, the *adhiṣṭhāna* must be Brahman. This implies some kind of *viśeṣa*, or qualification, in Brahman.[1] For if Brahman did not have this quality, it would not be possible to explain its tendency (*pravṛtti*) towards superimposition.[2] If, however, this is not accepted, we may ask, "Has Brahman anything to do with the superimposition?" If not, then *ajnāna* alone explains the superimposition and the existence of Brahman is ruled out as a gratuitous hypothesis. If Brahman has something to do with the superimposition, its *śakti* naturally follows.[3] The very etymological meaning of the term 'Brahman,' as explained by Śruti, shows that the Śruti accepts the Śakti of Brahman. For, according to Śruti, the term 'Brahman' implies 'greatness' as well as 'expansive activity' and Brahman, in respect of its expansive activity, is dynamic and saviśeṣa.[4]

[1]*vivarte'pi rajatādi-sphūrttāvadhiṣṭhānaṁ śuktyādikamevāṅgīkriyate, na cāṅgārādi; prastute'pi brahmaṇa eva jagadadhiṣṭhānatvaṁ, na tvanyasyeti, tathaiva svarūpa-śaktitvaṁ viditam. SS*, p. 29.

[2]ibid, pp. 52-53, 247.

[3]ibid, p. 29.

[4]*atha kasmāducyate 'brahman vṛṁhati vṛṁhayati' iti śrutiśca, 'vṛhattvadvṛṁhanatvāc-ca yadbrahman paramaṁ viduḥ' iti viṣṇupurāṇam ca vṛhatvena śaktimatvaṁ darśayati. tatsannidhāna-balenaiva tathātathābhāve 'nyeṣāmaṅgīkṛte'pi śaktireva paryyavasyatīti,* ibid, p. 30.

Śaṁkara has explained the advaitic position with regard to the creation of the world in his commentary on *Pravṛtteśca-sūtra.*'[1] He maintains that Brahman brings about changes in other things without losing its integrity as the changeless One, even as the lodestone attracts iron or a beautiful object stimulates the eye without causing any change to itself. But this again proves the Śakti of Brahman. For, how can the lodestone attract iron or a beautiful object attract the eye, unless it has the power to do so?[2]

It is urged that the world is the effect of *ajnāna* and is, therefore, false like *ajnāna*. The Sūtra *neh na nāsti kiṅcana* is cited in support of this and explained to mean that nothing exists besides Brahman. But, if the world is declared as false, what, says Jīva, remains to show the existence of Brahman? Brahman and its Śakti, which causes the world, are organically related. We cannot affirm the one and deny the other. Any attempt to do so would be like cutting a hen into two so as to give one half to the Brāhmaṇa and keep the other to lay eggs.[3] Besides, if Brahman be the negation of everything else, one may ask, 'What is the subject of this knowledge of negation of everything?' Adhyāsa or superimposition cannot be the subject, because it is included in everything that is negated.[4] Brahman cannot be the subject, because if it be so, the question arises whether in the knowledge "nothing exists besides Brahman" the knowledge activity of Brahman is superimposed or intrinsic. If superimposed, then the superimposition as well as its cause, which is *ajnāna*, must presuppose the knowledge which cancels it, and the cancelling knowledge, being itself a superimposition, must in turn presuppose another cancelling knowledge, thus leading to an infinite regress. If, on the other hand, the knowledge activity be the intrinsic quality of Brahman, *śakti* is granted.[5]

Further, Nirviśeaṣa Brahman connot be proved, firstly because the object of proof is always *saviśeṣa* and, secondly, because all objects of proof, according to the Advaitins, are perishable. In the absence of proof, the Nirviśeṣa is unreal like the horns of a hare.[6] Nor can it be accepted on the authority of the scriptures, because the scriptures depend on the various forms of speech, which do not apply to it.[7]

The inherent weakness of the *advaita* philosophy also appears in the state of *kaivalya*, which is set-up as the supreme end (*parama puruśārtha*). It is described as pure consciousness, which is devoid of the consciousness of self and the not-self, the subject and the object. But, there can be no knowledge without a subject. Also there

[1]*SB*, II, 2. 2.
[2]*SS*, p. 30.
[3]ibid, p. 31.
[4]ibid.
[5]ibid, p. 32.
[6]ibid.
[7]ibid.

can be no knowledge without an object, just as there can be no sensation without a stimulus. The sense organ, when not stimulated, is like any other unconscious object. So also the state of *kaivalya*, without any knowledge activity, is like the unconscious matter or pure non-being.[1] Since, however, such an end is uninspiring, the *advaitins* are constrained to describe it as self-realisation (*svarūpāvasthāna*). But, they warn us against any impression that self-realisation implies *śakti*. It is stated that the self, by its very nature, is self-luminousness. Self-luminousness is not its quality. It is its very nature as independent existence, and it implies that Brahman is self-proved (*anapekṣasiddhi*).[2] This, however, gives rise to the paradoxical position of accepting Brahman as something positive while at the same time denying that it has any attributes. If self-luminousness means the nature of Brahman as independent existence and self-provedness, how can it be denied that this is its intrinsic quality (*svarūpa-śakti*).[3]

Even if it be admitted that pure consciousness is different from ordinary consciousness and that it has the capacity to shine by itself, without involving the subject-object relationship, it stands contradicted by this very capacity, which implies *viśeṣa*. Similarly, it is contradicted by the attribute of eternity (*nityatva*), usually attributed to it by the *advaitins*.[4] If it be argued that eternity and self-luminousness do not imply any positive attributes but the negation of transitoriness and unconsciousness then *viśeṣa* reasserts itself in the form of the nature of the self to exclude these qualities, for unless negation of transitoriness and unconsciousness be a distinct quality of the self, negation is useless and without meaning.[5]

In *advaitism* the knowledge activity is illusory and the subject and object of knowledge are superimpositions. With the disappearance of the superimposition, as in dreamless sleep, the knowledge activity also disappears and what remains is pure consciousness. But Jīva and Baladeva contend that knowledge is eternal, being the natural quality of the soul.[6] Just as the sun which has light as its essence, also gives light, the soul which has knowledge as its essence also acts as the substrate of knowing.[7] It is not pure consciousness. The subject or the knower persists even in the state of deep sleep. For, on rising from sleep he does not represent that state to himself as one of pure consciousness but says, "I slept soundly. I was not aware of anything at all." This implies,

[1] *SS*, p. 31. [2] ibid. [3] ibid, p. 33.

[4] ibid; also *see Siddhānta-ratna*, VII, p. 5.

[5] *Siddhānta-ratna*, VII, 4.

[6] "*jñānaguṇāśrayatvameva jñātṛtvaṁ. jñānaṁ tu nityasyāpyautpattikadharmatvānnityaṁ*" (*Siddhānta-ratna*, VII, 3); also *see Tattva-saṁdarbha*, 51.

[7] "*jñānarūpasya jñānāśrayatvaṁ tu prakāśarūpasya raveḥ prakāśakatvavadaviruddhamiti bhāvaḥ . . . tasmājjñānādiśaktimadeva brahaman na tvanubhūtisaṁvitparyāyaṁ jñānamātram*" (*SR*, VII, 3); also *see SS*, pp. 52-53.

besides the absence of the object of knowledge, the presence of a subject who can realise the comfort of deep sleep. If we are not distinctly aware of it, it is because of the influence of *tamas* by which the self is over-powered in sleep.[1] Śaṁkara, also, in a way admits this, when he says that the self exists in deep sleep as the witness (*ākṣin*) of the general nescience. The term *sākṣin*, as used by Pāṇinī, implies the quality of witnessing directly. That which is not a knower cannot be a witness.[2]

The self-luminousness of knowledge rests upon the character of the self as knower. It is the self-conscious subject, the subject which says, "I am," which is self-luminous. That which is not self-conscious is not self-luminous and not different from the not-self or matter. Such is the Advaitin's pure consciousness. His attempt to put the subject, which is thus established, in the category of the object or the not-self is contradictory like the statement, 'My mother is barren.'[3]

Baladeva asks whether pure consciousness is proved or not. If it is proved it implies the property of being proved, if not proved it is non-existent like the sky-flower.[4] If pure consciousness is regarded as the consciousness of proof, then either the proof does or does not relate itself to some object. If it does not relate itself to any object it is not proof; if it does the consciousness cannot be pure. If consciousness be its own proof, the difference between proof and consciousness will, in any case, have to be admitted and proof will appear as an attribute of consciousness.[5]

Bṛhadāraṇyaka-upaniṣad describes Brahman as both consciousness and bliss. Jīva asks whether these two terms have the same meaning or not. If they have the same meaning, the description is tautologous. If they have different meanings, intrinsic difference in the nature of the absolute is accepted.[6] It is argued that both refer to the same undifferentiated being, but each is a negation of a different quality. 'Consciousness' is the negation of 'unconsciousness' and 'bliss' the negation of 'unhappiness.' The primary question, however, is whether they refer to some kind of being or not. If they do not, we are led to the *śūnyavāda* of the Bauddhas. If they do, then, in as much as they both refer to it, they are both established[7]. Still, if one of these alone is accepted as ultimately real, we have to explain, besides finding a reason for denying the other, how it can be the negation of both unconsciousness and unhappiness.[8] It may be held that bliss is actually the negation of both. In that case 'bliss' will also include consciousness and the description of Brahman as 'bliss

[1] *SR*, VII, 9.
[2] *SR*, VII, 2; also *see SS*, p. 52.
[3] *SR*, VII, 7.
[4] Cp. *RB*, I, 1, 1. and II, 3, 18.
[5] *SR*, VII, 6.
[6] *SS*, p. 38.
[7] ibid, p. 39.
[8] *SS*, p. 39.

and consciousness' would be tautogolous.[1]

Again 'bliss' and 'consciousness' may be taken to refer to *vidyā* as the negation of both unconsciousness and unhappiness, *vidyā* in the aspect of negation of unconsciousness being consciousness, and *vidyā* in the aspect of negation of unhappiness being bliss, and what remains after the cancelling activity of *vidya* may be regarded as the undifferentiated Brahman. But *vidya* is not independent of Brahman. It is an integral part of Brahman-consciousness. And if *vidya* can perform the dual function of cancelling unconsciousness and unhappiness, it must be due to the nature of Brahman as having intrinsic difference.[2]

Finally, it may be suggested that Brahman, being beyond the reach of thought and language, the terms '*vijnāna*' and '*ānanda*' do not really apply to it. Knowledge as well as bliss are the functions of mind (*antaḥkaraṇa*) energised by its relation to Brahman; so they refer to it only in an indirect way. Brahman is not characterised by them but they are due to it, as the texts *yena cetyed viśvam* and *eṣa hyevānandayati* also imply. But the very relation of these functions to Brahman shows that Brahman is qualified by them. The moon causes radiance and whiteness in the yard, because it is so qualified; otherwise the moon's causing these qualities will have no meaning.[3]

In order, therefore, to be intelligible or to be assigned any real existence the Absolute must be a positive concept, and, since nothing positive is without attributes, the Absolute must be *saviśeṣa*.[4] Not only must it be determined by certain qualities or attributes, but just because it is infinite, it must be determined or qualified in endless ways (*CC*, Madhya VIII, 116).[5] There should be nothing in which it may be wanting, nothing that may not be predictable of it in its proper context. If there is anything which in some form does not belong to it, then in so far as it is lacking in that, it is imperfect and cannot, properly speaking, be called Absolute. The Absolute by its very nature must be perfect in all possible ways (*CC*, Madhya, VI, 132).[6] It is, thus, not personification or attribution of character or qualities to the infinite that puts limitation upon it, but determination not carried to the fullest extent. The notion of personality is not only consistent with the infinite but essential to it. 'The infinite' in mathematics, as Pringle Pattison points out, means something different than in theology. In mathematics it 'means having no limits at all.' But if it meant exactly the same thing in theology, no character or qualities could be attributed to God. He would be merely an undiffer-

[1] *SS*, p 39. [2] ibid.
[3] ibid, pp. 38-39.
[4] *SS*, pp. 52-53.
[5] "*Kṛṣṇera ananta śakti tāte tin pradhāna*" ; *CC*, Madhya, 50; "*ekai bigraha tāra ananta svarūpa.*" *CC*, Madhya, XX, 137. Also *see Gītā*, X, 40.
[6] "*sarvaiśvarya paripūrṇa svayaṁ bhagavān,*"

entiated substance or a *tabula rasa*. But God is certainly not an empty concept of this sort. He is not something vague or indefinite, which the mathematical notion of infinitude implies. He has character, which implies something *definite*, and in this sense He is limited. But He is unlimited in the sense that 'He is immeasurable and there is nothing outside Him, whereby He may be limited.'

The Absolute as both Saviśeṣa (qualified) and Nirviśeṣa (unqualified)

The scriptures describe the Absolute as both qualified and unqualified. *Chāndogya-upaniṣad* describes Brahman as *sarvakarmā sarvakāmaḥ sarvagandhaḥ sarvarasaḥ*,[1] which indicates that Brahman is not only qualified, but qualified in endless ways. The Śrutis frequently describe Brahman as *vijnāna-ghana* and *ānanda-ghana* as in *Gopāla Tāpanī*: '*vijnānaghana ānadaghanaḥ saccidānandaikarase bhaktiyoge tiṣṭhati.*'[2] The word '*ghana*' implies that Brahman is knowledge (*vijnāna*) and bliss (*ānanda*) personified. *Brahma-saṁhitā* also describes Brahman as having a concrete form, made of *Sat*, *Cit* and *Ānanda*. Many scriptural texts, as for example, '*yatrāvatīrṇaṁ kṛṣṇākhyaṁ paraṁ brahman narākṛti*,'[3] '*gopaveśamabhrāmaṁ taruṇaṁ kalpadramāśritam*,'[4] '*gūḍhaṁ paraṁ brahman manuṣyalingam*' clearly describe the name, form and dress, etc. of Brahman. All the texts which relate to the creation and destruction of the universe also describe the qualified Brahman, because the unqualified Brahman is without any activity.

Similarly, there are many texts which describe Brahman as unqualified. *Kaṭha-upaniṣad* describes Brahman as '*aśabdam, asparśam, arūpam*,'[5] which means 'that which has neither sound, nor touch, nor form,' *Bṛhadāraṇyaka* describes Brahman as '*acakṣuṣkam, aśrotram*,' *avāk, amanaḥ . . . . aprāṇam, amukham . . . anantaram, avāhyam*, which means, 'that which has neither eyes nor ears, nor speech, nor mouth, nor mind, nor life, and that which has neither inside nor outside.' The texts '*sarvaṁ khalu idaṁ brahman*,'[6] '*ahaṁ brahmāsmi*,'[7] '*ātma eva idaṁ sarvaṁ*,'[8] are also taken by the Advaitins to imply that the unqalified, formless Brahman alone pervades the universe.

The apparently contradictory statements of the Śāstras regarding the nature of Brahman are sometimes reconciled by saying that they are not all of equal importance. Those, who believe that Brahman is qualified,

[1] *Chānd.*, 7. 14. 4.
[2] *Gopāla Tāpanī*, 79
[3] *Viśṇu-purāṇa*, 5.
[4] *Gopāla Pūrvatāpanī*, 12.
[5] *Katha*, I. 3. 15.
[6] *Chānd.*, 6. 2. 1.
[7] *Bṛhad.*, I. 4. 10.
[8] *Chānd.*, 7. 25. 22.

minimise the importance of the texts describing it as unqualified, while those, who believe that it is unqualified, minimise the importance of the texts describing it as qualified. But Śaṁkarācārya thinks this undermines the authority of the Vedas, since the words of the Vedas are all equally authoritative.[1]

Sometimes the contradiction is sought to be removed by taking the direct meaning of some of the texts and the indirect meaning of others. According to Śrī Caitanya, Śaṁkara's view of Unqualified Brahman is based mainly on indirect meaning. His exclusive emphasis on unqualified Brahman makes him conceal the real and direct meaning of the Sūtras, which describe Brahman as *saviśeṣa* or qualified (*CC*, Madhya, XXV, 36, 53).[2] The indirect meaning of words (*lakṣṇā vṛtti*) is justified only where the direct meaning (*mukhyā vṛtti*) does not make any sense. At many places the Śrutis clearly describe Brahman as both qualified and unqualified in the same breath. In such cases the application of *lakṣṇā* to support one aspect of Brahman and exclude the other would amount to wilful distortion of meaning.

Śrī Jīva Gosvāmin's attempt to resolve the contradiction is more realistic. He relies upon the Śāstras for the real meaning of the words *saviśeṣa* and *nirviśeṣa* by which Brahman is described as both qualified and unqualified. He quotes a Śloka[3] from the *Padma-purāṇa* to show that the word *nirviśeṣa* is used to deny all *prākṛta* or worldly qualities of Brahman and not to deny qualities as such.[4] If it were used to deny qualities as such it would not be possible to attribute to Brahman the qualities of *nityatva* (eternity) and *vibhutva* (all-pervasiveness), which are accepted by the Advaitins themselves.[5] He also quotes from the *Viṣṇu-purāṇa* to prove that although Brahman does not have any ordinary or worldly qualities, it has infinite transcendental qualities.[6]

This view is also supported by the first sentence of *Gopāla Pūrvatāpanī Śruti*, which describes Brahman as *saviśeṣatayojjvalam* and *pratiyogī-vinirmuktaṁ*. The first of these epithets means that which shines by its attributes, or which has transcendental attributes, because only the transcendental attributes are self luminous. The second means that which is free from all that is contrary to its nature as *sat-cit-ānanda*, or all that is material.

[1] *Ś. Bh.*, 3. 2. 15.

[2] *vyāsasūtrera artha ācārya kariyāche acchādana/*
ei haya satya srī kṛṣṇa-caitanya bacana//
ācāryera āgraha advaitavāda sthāpite/
tāte sūtrera vyākhyā kare anya rīte /

[3] *yo'sau nirguṇa ityuktaḥ śāstreṣu jagadīśvaraḥ/*
prakṛtairheya saṁyuktairguṇairhinatvamu ytaę iti//

[4] *Br. S*, p. 229.

[5] *SS*, pp. 53-54.

[6] ibid.

Śrī Jīva describes the unqualified Brahman as merely the subject of predication apart from its predicates, or the substance apart from its attributes. Since the complete (*samyak*) form of an object includes both its substance and attributes, the unqualified Brahman is incomplete (*asamyak*) manifestation of the Absolute. The Advaitins ignore the attributes of Brahman and concentrate on its unqualified form as pure existence. In the state of complete concentration they have direct experience of *Nirviśeṣa* Brahman. Śrī Jīva emphasises that their experience, though incomplete, is not unreal.

According to Śrī Caitanya, the difference between the qualified and unqualified forms of Brahman is due to the difference between its *svarūpa lakṣaṇa* (intrinsic nature) and *taṭastha lakṣaṇa* (extrinsic nature). While *svarūpa lakṣaṇa* is the intrinsic nature of a thing, *taṭastha lakṣaṇa* is the way it functions (*CC*, Madhya, xx, 296). The *svarūpa lakṣaṇa* of Brahman is indicated by the Śrutis *satyaṁ jnānaṁ anantaṁ brahman*, and *vijnānamānandaṁ brahman*, which describe Brahman as *sat-cit-ānanda*. The *taṭastha lakṣaṇa* is indicated by the texts, which describe its functions, such as the creation and destruction of the universe.

The inconceivable power of Brahman to reconcile the irreconcilable

Our thought at first revolts against such an idea of Brahman. We say that Brahman, who is infinitely qualified and claims to possess all that exists, must be a huge nest of fallacies and contradictions. But this misconception is based on the assumption that the infinite is subject to the same laws of thought as the finite. We have to bear in mind that there is an essential difference between the finite and the infinite and we cannot fetter the infinite with our human thought and terms. When dealing with any problem relating to the infinite, we have to use the laws of our understanding with reservation and with the necessary precaution that they do not impair the perfection of the infinite or impoverish our notion of Divinity.

It is the application of the law of contradiction that is mainly responsible for our crippled notion of the infinite. But the infinite, by virtue of its inconceivable potency (*acintya śakti*), in a sense, transcends even the law of contradiction (*CC*, Ādi, IV, 110).[1] The very infinitude of the infinite consists in its transcendence of this law and harmonious blending within itself of contradictory notions or qualities, while the very finitude of the finite consists in its subjection to it. The finite is finite because it is what it is and not its contrary. But the infinite is infinite because there is

[1]*āmi jeche paraspara viruddha dharmāśraya/*
rādhā-dharma teche sadā viruddha dharmamaya//
See also *SS*, p. 65.

nothing that does not fall within it.[1] This meaning of the infinite is supported by the *Chāndogya-upaniṣad*, which says, "That other than which we may not see, hear or know is infinite." The infinite logically excludes the possibility of the existence of anything other than itself.[2] The Śruti text, *neha na nāsti kincana*, should also be interpreted in a similar way. It is taken by the *advaitins* to imply that nothing exists besides Brahman, conceived as pure identity. But it really means that whatever exists is a manifestation of Brahman and is internally related to it. Nothing exists apart from it and independent of it.[3] The text denies difference but not difference in identity. Otherwise how shall we explain the text, 'I shall be many'? This text clearly recognises functional differences in the Absolute, which naturally follow from its inconceivable potency (*acintya śakti*).[4]

If, therefore, the infinite is to retain its infinitude or perfection it must as necessarily transcend the law of contradiction as the finite must conform to it. It would be a contradiction in terms to say that, because a particular quality or thing is included in the infinite, its contrary must be excluded from it. For it would mean that the Absolute is not the absolute. Anything that we can speak or think of must in some way be a manifested part of the infinite (*CC*, Madhya, XXIV, 56).[5] And to say in an unqualified manner that the infinite excludes 'this' or 'that' would be equivalent to saying that the whole excludes the part, and to violate the law of contradiction in the very attempt to conform to it. Thus, although the infinite, in one sense, transcends the law of contradiction, in another sense, and in a higher sense, it most truly conforms to it; and paradoxical as it may seem, it would not be inconsistent with its nature to say that in the very act of its transcendence or repudiation of the law of contradiction it also conforms to it.

For, it must be emphasised that the repudiation of the law of contradiction in the case of the infinite is not arbitrary; it is due to a necessity inherent in the nature of thought itself. "The attempt to construct

Thakur Bhaktivinod in his Srīman Mahāprabhūra Śikṣā quotes the following Kārikā to prove that one of the potencies of the Absolute is to reconcile the irreconcilable:
virodha-bhañjikā śaktiyuktarūpa saccidātmanaḥ|
vartante yugapaddharmaḥ paraspara virodhinaḥ|
svarūpatvamarūpatvaṁ vibhutvaṁ mūrtireva ca|
nirlepatvaṁ kṛpāvatvamajatvaṁ jayamānatā||
sarvārādhyatvaṁ gopatvaṁ sarvajnaṁ narabhāvatā|
saviśeṣatvasampattistathāca nirviśeṣatā|
sīmāvadyuktiyuktānāmasīmatatvavastuni|
tarko hi viphalastasmācchṛdhāmnāye phalapradā|

[1] *SS*, p. 54.
[2] ibid.
[3] ibid.
[4] ibid.
[5] *ātma-śabde kahe kṛṣṇa vṛhat-svarūpa|*
sarvavyāpaka sarvasākṣī paramasvarūpa||

in thought an object answering to our notion of the Absolute," says Mansel, "necessarily results in a contradiction—a contradiction, however, which we have ourselves produced by the attempt to think, which exists in the act of thought and not beyond it, which destroys the conception as such, but indicates nothing concerning the existence or non-existence of that which we try to conceive. It proves our own impotence and it proves nothing more. Or rather, it indirectly leads us to believe in the existence of that infinite which we cannot conceive, for the denial of its existence involves a contradiction no less than the assertion of its inconceivability."[1]

We are thus constrained to believe that the concepts of infinity and personality are both essential to the real nature of the Absolute. Mansel expresses the same necessity thus:

"It is our duty, then, to think of God as personal; and it is our duty to believe that He is infinite. It is true that we cannot reconcile these two representations with each other, as our conception of personality involves attributes apparently contradictory to the notion of infinity. But it does not follow that this contradiction exists any where but in our own minds, it does not follow that it implies any impossibility in the absolute nature of God. The apparent contradiction, in this case, as in those previously noticed, is the necessary consequence of an attempt on the part of the human thinker to transcend the boundaries of his own consciousness. It proves that there are limits to man's power of thought, and it proves no more."[2]

To describe the Absolute as merely *nirviśeṣa* or without quality and attributes is to make Him imperfect (*CC*, Madhya, xxv, 30)[3] by amputating, as it were, the auspicious limbs of His divine personality (*CC*, Madhya, III, 36-37).[4] Once the absolute perfection or *Bhagavattā* of the Divine Being is recognised, the advaitic philosophy of Śaṁkara cannot consistently be maintained (*CC*, Madhya, xxv, 40).[5]

The real purpose to the Śruti is to describe the absolute as both *saviśeṣa* and *nirviśeṣa*, or rather as possessing infinite attributes and forms (*CC*, Madhya VI, 141).[6] When this is understood, the conflicting statements of

[1]Cadecott and Mockintosh, *Selections from the Literature of Theism*, p. 362.
[2]ibid, p. 363.
[3]*brahmanśabda kahe ṣadaiśvaryapūrṇa bhagavān/*
tāre nirviśeṣa sthāpi pūrṇatā haya hāni//
[4]*hasta pada mukha mora nāhika locana/*
eī mate vede mora kare viḍambana//
kāśī te paṇāya betā prakāśānanda/
śeī betā kare mora aṅga khaṅda khaṅda//
[5]*bhagavattā mānile advaita na jāya sṭhāpana/*
ataeba saba śāstra karaye khaṅdana//
[6]*ataeba śruti kahe brahman saviśeṣa/*
mukhya chāṇi lakṣṇā te māne nirviśeṣa//

the Vedas and the Purāṇas can easily be reconciled. But according to the primary and the general sense of the scriptures the Absolute is essentially *saviśeṣa*, because only in a *saviśeṣa* Absolute, possessing infinite and inconceivable potencies, can the infinite forms of Godhead, including the *nirviśeṣa* Brahman inhere. This is supported by the *Gītā* text, *brahmaṇo hi pratiṣṭhāhaṁ*, in which the Personal Absolute describes Himself as the *substratum* of Brahman.

There are numerous Śruti texts, which testify the inconceivable power of Brahman to reconcile the irreconcilable. *Śvetāśvatara* describes Brahman as greater than the greatest and smaller than the smallest (*aṇoraṇīyāna mahato mahīyana*).[1] *Kaṭha* says that He can travel long distances while sitting and wander here, there and everywhere while sleeping (*āsīno dūraṁ brajati sayāno yāti sarvatra*).[2] *Kaivalyopaniṣad* clearly describes Him as *acintyaśaktiḥ*, or the Possessor of inconceivable power.[3] Śrī Jīva has also tried to prove the inconceivable power of Brahman by referring to the *Brahma-sūtra* '*ātmani ca evaṁ vicitrāśca hi*' and other texts. Even Śaṁkara has recognised the inconceivable power of Brahman in his commentary on *Br. S.*, 2. I. 24.

The Acintya Śakti of Brahman is also proved by the miraculous performances of Śrī Kṛṣṇa as mentioned in the *Bhāgavata*. Mother Yaśodā once failed to tie the tiny hands of the child Kṛṣṇa with all the strings she could collect, while at the same time his waist, bigger in circumference than his hand, was circumscribed by the much smaller ornamental string he was wearing round it. On another occasion, she saw the infinite universes in his mouth. In the *Rāsa-līla*, Kṛṣṇa assumed many forms and danced simultaneously with each one of the milk-maids of Vraja present at the dance. Similarly when Brahmā stole away the cows and companions of Kṛṣṇa and kept them in concealment for a year, that did not make any difference to anyone in Vraja, for Kṛṣṇa had assumed their forms and played their role without anyone ever coming to know that any such thing had happened.

The inconceivable in modern science

Curiously enough, the concept of inconceivable potency of Brahman seems to find powerful support in science, which, only a few years back, was the bitterest enemy of anything that was supernatural and of which it was not possible to make a mechanical image. The ultimate stuff, according to modern science, of which the reality is made, is the electron. The exact nature of the electron is not known, but it is known that it is most unlike a material object and is completely free in its behaviour.

[1] *Śvetāsvatara*, 3, 2, 20.
[2] *Kathaka-śruti*, 1, 2, 21.
[3] *Kaivalya*, 1, 21.

The mechanical laws of science do not apply to it, and, like Brahman, who moves without moving, it goes from one point to another without crossing the intermediate points!

The modern science of mathematics demonstrates the inconceivable power of the Infinite by referring to the mathematics of what are known as trans-infinite numbers. It is said of trans-infinite numbers that you may divide, multiply, or perform any mathematical operation with them, they would change correspondingly, yet remain equal. You raise infinity to the power infinity. This magnitude is an infinite number of times greater than infinity, and yet the two are equal This violates the fundamental laws of mathematics accepted for finite numbers and is remarkably similar to the Īśāvāsya saying, 'If you subtract the perfect from the perfect, what remains is the perfect (*pūrṇasya pūrṇamādāya pūrṇamevāvaśiṣyate*).

The concept of the inconceivable implies that there are stages of being and intelligence higher than our own. Mr. Hinton has made this clear with the help of a number of examples in his book entitled *Scientific Romances.* In one of the examples, he gives, a microbe, who is supposed to be a two-dimensional creature—a creature who is so constituied that it can be aware of only length and breadth—travels along the surface of a card-board placed horizontally on a table. Another piece of card-board is made to stand vertically on it. As soon as the microbe reaches the second card board, its movement is suddenly stopped. You pick it up and place it on the other side of the vertical card-board; it again begins to move. The whole thing is a miracle to it. It is not able to understand how its movement was stopped and how it began to move again, since both the events relate to the third dimension of height, which is beyond its ken. What is inconceivable in the world of two dimensions becomes quite natural and feasible in the world of three dimensions. If the difference of only one dimension can make all the difference between the conceivable and the inconceivable, it is but natural that the power of Brahman, whose dimensions are unlimited, should appear as inconceivable to our finite minds.

CHAPTER VII

The Concept of the Absolute as Bhagavān

Śrī Caitanya's idea of the Absolute is based on the following verse of *Śrīmad-bhāgavata*, which is believed to contain in a nutshell the entire philosophy designated by the term *Saṁbandha* (*CC*, Madhya, xxv, 927):

vadanti tattaivavidastatva yajjnānamadvayaṁ|
brahmeti paramātmeti bhagavāniti śabdyate||

Śrī Jīva Gosvāmin makes some of his principal Saṁdarbhas rest mainly on this. A thorough analysis of the first line of the verse is given by him in his *Tattva-saṁdarbha*, which reveals some of the most important characteristics of the Absolute. The word '*advaya*' signifies 'that which has no second,' which again implies 'that like which there is no other reality'; the word Jnāna is explained as 'that of which consciousness is the only form' (*cideka-rūpaṁ*) or pure consciousness, which shines by itself; and the word '*tattva*' is taken to signify 'the eternal principle, which is also the highest good (*paraṁ puruśārtha*), and the highest bliss (*paraṁ sukha*) (*TS*, 51).'

The verse establishes the essential unity of the Supreme Being and places it above the application of categorical difference, which may manifest itself in three ways. It may manifest itself (1) between things of the same category (*svajātīya-bheda*), (2) between things of different categories (*vijātīya-bheda*) or (3) in one and the same thing, either between its essence and form or its component parts (*svagata-bheda*). The first type of difference is not applicable to the Absolute, because there is no other being possessing precisely the same nature. It is stated that the Absolute is one and the same but different religions call Him by different names (*C. Bh.*, Ādi, xvi, 73-74). An unbaised study of the *Kurān* of the Muhammedans and the *Purāṇas* of the Hindus will reveal that both, in the end, aim at the same eternal, indivisible, immutable and perfect Being, which is immanent in the hearts of all, but describe it differently in respect of its name, form and attributes (*C. Bh.*, Ādi, xvi, 75-76). The second type of difference cannot be applied to the Absolute because the phenomenal world, though categorically different from it, is not self-existent. It depends for its existence on the Absolute, Who is the cause of His own existence and everything else (*CC*, Madhya, viii, 106).[1] The third type of difference

[1]*parama īsvara kṛṣṇa svayaṁ bhagavān|*
sarva avatārī sarva kāraṇa pradhāna||

also does not apply to the Asolute, because in Him the body and its owner are not two different principles. Whereas, in the case of the bound Jīvas the soul is in essence different from the material body, in which it is encased, in the case of the Absolute the body and its owner are made of the same ingredients of consciousness and bliss (*cidānanda*) (*CC*, Madhya, xvii, 128-29; Antya, v, 118). In the case of the Absolute His Name, Attributes, Sports and Dwelling are all the manifestations of the same Eternal Spiritual Principle (*CC*, Madhya, xvii, 130).[1]

Brahman, Paramātman and Bhagavān

According to both Śaṁkara and Śrī Caitanya, the Absolute is devoid of all kinds of difference whether external or internal. But while, according to Śaṁkara, the Absolute is incapable of manifesting Himself in different forms without losing His oneness, the Absolute, according to Śrī Caitanya, possesses the inconceivable power of doing so. Although He is one and indivisible, He has innumerable forms and manifests Himself in infinite ways to the devotees, according to their different capacities and the different means of realisation adopted by them, (*CC*, Madhya, ix, 141).[2] Still, He manifests Himself in three definite grades as Brahman, Paramātman and Bhagavān, according as He is approached by the paths of Jnāna, Yoga and Bhakti (*CC*, Madhya, xxiv, 57-58).[3] This threefold aspect of the Absolute is described in the verse quoted from *Srīmad Bhāgavata* above. Of these three forms, each succeeding one supersedes and includes the preceding, and Bhagavān, who is the highest in the hierarchy of manifestations, supersedes and includes both Brahman and Paramātman. Thus, unlike Saṁkara, and unlike the other teachers of Vaiṣṇavism, Śrì Caitanya does not adhere exclusively to any one grade of realisation of the Absolute, but is responsive, in the spirit of the *Gītā* text *ye yathā māṁ prapadyante tāṁstathaiva bhajāmyahaṁ* to all the different grades, from undifferentiated homogenity to concrete unity.

Bhagavān is indentified with the supreme personality of Kṛṣṇa, Who is the source of all incarnations, the ultimate ground of all that exists, and in Whom are centred infinite grandeur, infinite powers and infinite rasas or modes of Divine Bliss (*CC*, Madhya, VIII, 106-8). All the scriptures, explicitly or implicitly, speak of Kṛṣṇa as the Ultimate Reality (*C. Bh.*, Madhya, I, 145-56). The Supreme authority in this connection is

[1]*kṛṣṇa-nāma kṛṣṇa-guṇa kṛṣṇa-līlāvṛnda|*
kṛṣṇera svarūpa sama saba cidānanda||
[2]*eka īśvara bhaktera dhyāna anurūpe|*
ekai vigraha kare nānākara rūpe||
[3]*seī kṛṣṇa prāpti hetu trividha sādhana|*
jnāna yoga bhakti tinera pṛthak lakṣaṇa||
tin sādhane bhagavān tin svarūpe bhāse|
brahman paramātmān bhagavattā trividha prakāśe||

the *Bhāgavata* text:

ete cāṁśakalā puṁsaḥ kṛṣṇastu bhagavān svayaṁ/ *Bh.*, 1, 3, 28.

It establishes the identity of Kṛṣṇa with Bhagavān in the most emphatic and unambiguous terms (*CC*, Madhya, IX, 133). *caitanya-caritāmṛta* quotes Kṛṣṇa's own testimony on this:

ahamevāsamevāgre nānyadyat sadasat param/
paścādahaṁ yadetacca yoavaśiṣyate so'asmyahaṁ// *Bh.*, 2,9,32.

The verse implies that before the beginning and after the end of creation, as also during its continuance, He is the only Reality that subsists without any change (*CC*, Madhya, XXIV, 55).[1]

Bhagavān is the highest being (*pūrṇa āvirbhāva*), in whom all the auspicious qualities are most perfectly manifested. Brahman is the incomplete form (*asamyak·āvirbhāva*) of Bhagavān, in whom all the divine attributes and potencies lie in a dormant state. It is primordial sameness, but not a barren stillness; it is indeterminateness, but not an indeterminateness that totally denies distinctions and definiteness; it has distinctions but the distinctions are not clearly brought out; it is a creative potentiality, but a potentiality that is eternally actualised in its most perfect state as Bhagavān. The attributes of Bhagavān and His potencies inhere in Him essentially and eternally and are not unreal or superimposed, as are the attributes of the Nirviśeṣa Brahman of the Advaitavādins. The relation between Bhagavān and His attributes or energies is that of *Samavāya* (inseparable) and not *saṁyoga* (separable), (*Bh.* S., 3).[2]

Bhagavān is essentially *Līlāmaya.* It is His nature to indulge eternally in spiritual pastimes (*CC*, Ādi, v. 21).[3] He has therefore a spiritual body, an eternal dwelling place, and eternal companions (*CC*, Ādi, vii). His body is not made of gross matter (*CC*, Ādi, VII, 110).[4] It is not the outcome of Sattva-guṇa (*CC*, Madhya, vi, 150-1); nor is it Māyika or false (*CC*, Madhya, XXV, 32), but it is real and consists of the three attributes of *Sat*, *Cit*, and *Ānanda* (*saccidānanda-ākara*). When the Śrutis describe the Absolute as *Nirviśeṣa* or unqualified, they do not deny its form and attributes. But they warn us against anthropomorphism, and state that the body of Bhagavān and everything that pertains

[1]*sei advaya tattva kṛṣṇa—svayaṁ bhagavān*/
tin kāle satya tihoñ—śāstra pramāna//

[2]Later philosophers of the school (Rādhādāmodara and Baladeva Vidyābhūśana) introduce the category of Viśeṣa to describe the relation between Bhagavān and His Śaktis. They describe Viśeṣa as the power of Bhagavān to produce the consciousness of difference where there is no difference. Śrī Jīva also mentions the concept of Viśeṣa (*Bh. S.*, 3), but he does not define it so clearly.

[3]*ei tin loke kṛṣṇa kevala līlāmaya*/
nija jana laiyā khele ananta samaya//

[4]*prākṛta kariyā māne viśṇu kalevara*/
viṣṇu nindā āra nāhi ihāra ūpara//

to Him is essentially transcendental or Aprākṛta (*CC*, Madhya, VI, 133).[1] The familiar Śruti text *apāṇipādo javano gṛhītā* etc. is, in fact, intended to make this clear. The Absolute Being is described as devoid of hands, feet, eyes and ears and yet it is said to perform the functions of all of these. The apparent meaning is that it does not possess a physical body like our own, but has a supersensuous (*aprākṛta*) frame consisting solely of bliss and consciousness (*CC*, Madhya, VI, 140-51). Similarly the Śruti, which says that when Bhagavān desired to be many He glanced at His Prākṛta-śakti, credits Him with *aprākṛta* mind and eyes, since at that time He did not have *prākṛta* mind and senses (*CC*, Madhya, vi, 137-37).[2]

The existence of Bhagavān rests on *Śuddha-sattva*, which is the essence of His Saṁdhnī-śakti or the Divine Energy of pure existence (*CC*, Ādi, IV, 59).[3] Everything in the transcendental abode of Bhagavān is the manifestation of *Śuddha-sattva*, which is qualified by Cit-śakti (*CC*, Ādi, IV, 60).[4] Everything in the phenomenal world is the manifestation of *Misra-sattva* which is qualified by Māyā-śakti. The principle of Śuddha-sattva combined with the principle of *Cit* or consciousness is called Vāsudeva (*Bh.* 4, 3, 23). Vāsudeva is described as Adhokṣaja, because he is essentially beyond Prakṛti and cannot be realised through our senses.

Bhagavān in His highest and most perfect form as described above can be realised only by means of devotion (*CC*, Madhya, XX, 137)[5] Those who try to realise Him by Jnāna perceive Him in His incomplete aspect as Brahman, which is but the outward glow or divine lustre of His spiritual body (*añgakānti*) (*CC*, Ādi, II, 8, Ś 5, Ś 9). Even as the sun perceived from a distance by our physical eyes appears as Nirviśeṣa or a plain mass of light (and not as the real sun-god, riding the chariot), Bhagavān, when approached by the path of Jnāna, appears in His homogeneity as Brahman (*CC*, Ādi, II, 9; V, 28-30). The etymological meaning of the word, 'Brahman' is 'that which is great.' Since greatness is the quality of Īśvara, Bhagavān in mere magnitudinal reference is called Brahman (*CC*, Madhya, VI, 131).[6]

Bhagavān is said to have sixfold magnificence or lordliness (*CC*, Madhya,

[1]*nirviśeṣa tāre kahe jei sruti gaṇa/*
prākṛta niśedha kare aprākṛta sthāpana//
[2]*bhagavān aneka hete jabe kela mana/*
prākṛta śakti te takhana kela vilokana//
se kāle nāhi janme prākṛta mana nayana/
ataeba aprākṛta brahmera netra mana//
[3]*saṁdhinīra sāra aṁsa śuddha satva nāma/*
bhagavānera sattā haya jahāte bisrāma//
[4]*mātā pitā sthāna gṛha ṣayyāsana āra/*
esaba kṛṣṇera śuddha satvera vikāra//
[5]*bhaktye bhagavānera anubhava pūrṇa-rūpa/*
[6]*sei brahman bṛhadvastu īśvara lakṣṇa/*

xxv, 91). Śrī Jīva Gosvāmin, referring to the etymological meaning of the word '*bhagavān*' shows how each letter in it implies one or more of the six majestic qualities, accounting for the perfection or the *bhagavattā* of Bhagavān. The letter '*Bha*' indicates the power of supporting and protecting the universe and unfolding and sustaining the natural function of devotion in His devotees; the letter '*ga*' signifies the idea of His leading the devotees to the attainment of His transcendental realm; '*va*' implies that all beings lie within Him and He lies within them. In a verse of *Viṣṇu-purāṇa*, cited by Jīva Gosvāmin in *Bhagavat-saṁdarbha*, the six majestic qualities are distinctly named as *Aīṣvarya*, *Vīrya*, *Yaśas*, *Śrī*, *Jnāna*, and *Vairāgya* (*Bh. S.*, 3). *Aiśvarya* is interpreted to mean power to influence all; *Vīrya* means potency like that of precious stones or spells; *Yaśas* means fame due to the qualities of the body (*Śrī Vigraha*), mind and speech; *Śrī* means prosperity of all kinds; *Jnāna* means omniscience and, *Vairāgya* means non-attachment to phenomenal things (*Bh. S*, 3). Two of these qualities—*Aiśvarya* and *Vīrya* are attributed to Bhagavān in the aspect of *Paramātman*.

Paramātman is a step higher than Brahman in the hierarchy of manifestations of the Absolute Personality of Bhagavān. Brahman is the basic reality underlying all concrete formations; Paramātman is the basic principle controlling and regulating concrete formations. Brahman implies an absolutely undifferenciated and unqualified state of Bhagavān, but Paramātman implies a differenciated and qualified state. Paramātman is, however, qualified in a limited sense and is but a partial manifestation of Bhagavān, Who is qualified in endless ways (*CC*, Madhya, xx, 136).[2] Paramātman is the principle of consciousness conditioned by Jīva-śakti and Māyā-śakti, from which emanate the finite souls and the phenomenal world. He is immanent in the Jīvas and the *Prakṛti* and is the conscious regulative principle of all beings (*antaryāmin*) (*CC*, Ādi, II, 12).

Paramātman is thus Bhagavān in relation to Jīva and *Prakṛti*. Bhagavān creates the world and enters into it in the form of His partial manifest Viṣṇu. Paramātman is, therefore, no other than Viṣṇu in his perfection, pervading and sustaining the entire universe. He has threefold function, corresponding to His threefold manifestation as Kāraṇārṇavaśāyi Saṁkarṣaṇa, Garbhodakaṣāyī Puruṣa and Kṣīrodasāyī Puruśa (*CC*, Ādi I, 7). As Kāraṇārṇavaśāyī, He rests in Kāraṇa Samudra or Virajā, which divides the spiritual (*cit*) from the phenomenal (*acit*) world, and by His glance at Prakṛti initiates the entire process of creation. He is the immanent regulator of all the finite souls and the phenomenal worlds (*brahmānda*) treated as a whole. After *Mahāpralaya* or the total dissolution, all the Jīvas rest in Him. He is also known as Mahāviṣṇu or

[1]*paramātmān jeho teho kṛṣnera eka aṁśa*/

Kāraṇārṇavaśāyī Nārāyaṇa. As Garbhodakaśāyī He is the regulator of the totality of individual souls (*samaṣṭijīvāntaryāmī*). As Kṣīrodaśāyī He is the immanent regulator of each individual soul (*vyaṣṭi jīvāntaryāmī*).

The śaktis of Bhagavān

The full significance of the concept of the Absolute as Bhagavān and the doctrine of Trinity, which it implies, will be understood more clearly if we examine the theory of Śakti or Divine energy in the philosophy of Śrī Cāitanya. Bhagavān, as already stated, has infinite Śaktis, but the most important of these are Cit-śakti, Māyā-ṣakti, and Jīva-śakti (*CC*, Madhya, VIII, 116).[1] They are not adventitious but inherent in the nature of Bhagavān (*CC*, Madhya, VIII, 118). According to their relationship with Him they are successively styled as Antaraṇgā, Bahiraṅgā and Taṭasthā (*CC*, Madhya, VI, 146).[2]

The Antaraṅgā or Svarūpa-śakti, as the name indicates, constitute the very essence or the intrinsic self of Bhagavān and is the substratum of the entire Cit-jagat or the transcendental world in which are displayed the transcendental activities (*līlā*) of Bhagavān (*Gītā*, IV, 6).

The Bahiraṅgā or Māyā-śākti, which is externally related to Bhagavān, is the cause of the Acit Jagat or the material world. It is related to Bhagavān in the sense that all Śaktis must ultimately inhere in Him. But Bhagavān in His intrinsic and perfect selfhood necessarily transcends it, and is absolutely free from its evil influence. Śrī Jīva brings out the exact nature of the relation between Bhagavān and the Bahiraṅgā-śakti by referring to the *Bhāgavata* text 2.9.33, which he explains thus:

"That is Māyā, which does not appear, where I (*Bhagavān*) am, but appears, where, I am not; in other words, which appears out of me but not without me, like the reflection of the sun, which appears in the pond on the earth, away from the sun, but not without the sun, which is its cause (*āśraya*) (*Bh. S.*, 17). Just as the reflection of the sun does not touch the sun, even though it cannot exist without it, Māyā does not touch Bhagavān, even though it cannot exist without Him."

There is also another reason why Māyā is called the śakti of Bhagavān even though it does not exist in Him. Bhagavān regulates and controls Māyā from outside. Māyā, being unconscious, cannot function by itself. The three Guṇas, Sattva, Rajaḥ and Tamaḥ, are in a state of equilibrium before creation. Bhagavān starts the process of creation by casting His glance at Prakṛti (Māyā), which disturbs its equilibrium and energizes

[1] *kṛṣṇera ananta śakti tāte tin pradhāna|*
cicchakti, māyāśakti, jīva-śakti nāma||
[2] *antaraṅgā—cicchakti, taṭasthā—jīva-śakti|*
bahiraṅgā—māyā, tine kare prema bhakti||

it (*CC*, Ādi, v, 28). It has the function of deluding the Jīvas who are averse to the service of Bhagavān; but it has no power over the Jīvas devoted to Bhagavān, Who, on account of His power to subjugate it is called Māyādhiśa or the Lord of Māyā, as against the Jīvas, who, on account of their inherent weakness to be overcome by it, are called Māyadāsa or the servants of Māyā (*CC*, Madhya. VI, 148).

The product of the Māyā-śakti is neither eternal nor unreal. This Śakti must, therefore be distinguished, on the one hand, from Yoga-māyā, which is but another name of Svarūpa-śakti (*Bh.*, 10, 29, I), and which manifests the negion of the Lord, and, on the other hand, from the Māyā of Advaitins, which gives rise to the appearance of an imaginary world. The material world created by it is real, but unlike the transcendental realm of Bhagavān, it is subject to change and annihilation.

Māyā is a material manifestation of Yoga-māyā; hence it also serves Bhagavān. But while Yoga-māya serves Him in the antaraṅgalīlā on the transcendental plane, Māyā serves Him in the Bahiraṅga-līlā, on the mundane plane. Like Yoga-māyā, it has the power to delight and charm. But, while Yoga-māyā charms the Jīvas who are devoted to Bhagavān, Māyā charms the Jīvas, who are averse to Him. Even though Māyā is a part of Yoga-māya, it does not touch the latter, just as the cast skin of the snake does not touch the snake. Again, though it is a part of Yoga-māyā, it is unconscious, just as the cast skin of the snake is unconscious.

The Taṭasthā or Jīva-śakti is neither a constituent of the intrinsic self of Bhagavān, nor it pertains to His Bahiraṅgā-śakti or the external potency. It is included neither in the Cit-jagat nor in the Acit-jagat; but manifesting itself, as it does, on the borderline between the two, it is related to them both. It is due to the peculiar position occupied by it that the Jīvas, who emanate from it, have the choice of either serving Bhagavān and dwelling with Him in the transcendental world or enjoying Prakṛti and dwelling in the material world, dominated by *Māyā*.

It must, however, be noted that since in the Advaya-Jnāna-Tattva Bhagavān there can be no distinctions of the inner, outer and marginal positions of His body, the distinctions of Aṅtaraṅgā, Bahiraṅgā and Taṭasthā in the Divine energies are due to the different realisations of the Jīvas in their different capacities. The authority on which the distinctions are recognised is the verse of the *Viṣṇu-purāṇa*, which calls the Antaraṅgā, Bahiraṅgā and Taṭasthā śaktis as Parā, Kṣetrajnya and Avidyā (*CC*, Madhya, XX, Ś 9).[1]

Since the Antaraṅgā-śakti pertains to Bhagavān in His intrinstic and perfect selfhood, it is ranked highest in the hierarchy of manifestations

[1]*viṣṇuśaktiḥ parāproktā kṣetrajnyākhyā tathāparā/*
avidyā karma saṁjnyānyā tṛtīyā śaktirīṣyate/ cited from *Viṣṇu-purāṇa*, 6, 7, 60.

of the divine energies and is called Parā-śakti (*CC*, Madhya, VIII, 117).[1] It has a threefold aspect as *Saṁdhinī*, *Saṁvit* and *Hlādinī*, corresponding to the three essential ingredients of the spiritual body of Bhagavān—*Sat*, *Cit* and *Ānanda* (*CC*, Madhya, VIII, 118).[2] The Saṁdhinī-śakti corresponds to *Sat*, *Saṁvit* to *Cit* and *Hlādinī* to *Ānanda* (*CC*, Madhya, VIII, 119).[3] Just as the elements of *Sat*, *Cit*, and *Ānanda* do not exist separately in the spiritual body of Bhagavān, the Saṁdhinī, Saṁvit and Hlādinī Śaktis do not exist separately from each other. Yet they are called by these different names, because in the different manifestations of Bhagavān the elements of *Sat*, *Cit* and *Ānanda* are present in different proportions. When in any manifestation the element of *Sat* predominates, it is regarded as the manifestation of Saṁdhinī-śakti; when the element of *Cit* predominates, it is regarded as the manifestation of Saṁvit-śakti; and when the element of Ānanda predominates, it is regarded as the manifestation of Hlādinī-śakti.

By the Saṁdhinī-śakti Bhagavān maintains His own existence as well as the existence of other beings. It is by virtue of this Śakti that He exists as an independent substance and forms the ground or support of all other things, which derive their existence from Him. The Saṁvit-śakti is the power of knowledge that makes Bhagavān omniscient and enables Him to impart knowledge to others. The Hlādinī-śakti is the energy of bliss. On account of this Śakti Bhagavān enjoys bliss and infuses bliss into the hearts of His devotees (*CC*, Ādi, IV, 53).[4]

The essence of the Saṁdhinī-śakti is the Śuddha-sattva of which mention has already been made (*CC*, Ādi, IV, 57). The essence of the Saṁvit-śakti is the knowledge that Srī Kṛṣṇa is identical with Bhagavān. The knowledge of Brahman, Paramātman and other things is included in the knowledge of Kṛṣṇa (*CC*, Ādi, IV, 58).[5] The essence of Hlādinī-śakti is *Prema* or Divine Love. *Prema* in its intensified from is Bhāva. Bhāva in its perfect state is called *Mahābhāva* (*CC*, Ādi, IV 59).[6] *Mahābhāva* finds its fullest manifestation in Śrī Rādhā, the divine consort or the counter-whole of the personal absolute Śrī Kṛṣṇa (*CC*, Ādi, IV, 60).

[1] *antaraṅgā bahiraṅgā taṭasthā kahi jāre|*
antaraṅgā—svarūpa-śakti sabāra ūpare||

[2] *sacchidānandamaya kṛṣnera svarūpa|*
ataeva svarūpa-śakti haya tin rūpa||

[3] *ānandāṁśe hlādinī, sadāṁśe saṁdhinī|*
cidāṁśe saṁvit jāre jnāna kari māni||

[4] *hlādinī karāya kṛṣne|ānandāsvādana|*
hlādinīra dvārā kare bhaktera poṣaṇa||

[5] *kṛṣne bhagavattā jnāna saṁvitera sāra|*
brahmajnānādika saba tāra|parivāra||

[6] *hlādinīra sāra prema, premasāra bhāva|*
bhāvera parākāṣṭhā nāma mahā-bhāva||

Just as Śrī Kṛṣṇa is the possessor of infinite divine energies displayed in their highest perfection (*Pūrṇa-śaktimān*), Śrī Rādhā is the embodiment of these divine energies in their most developed form (*Pūrṇa-śakti*) (*CC*, Ādi, IV, 83).[1] Śrī Kṛṣṇa is the ultimate source of the infinite partial manifestations of the divine personality, and Rādhā is the ultimate source of the endless divine energies of Śrī Kṛṣṇa. The relationship between Kṛṣṇa and Rādhā is that of inconceivable identity in difference. They are, in essence, one and the same entity, which assumes two different forms to enjoy the bliss of divine sports (*CC*, Ādi, IV, 85).[2] Rādhā is one with Kṛṣṇa, as she is identical with the highest development of the Hlādinī-śakti of Kṛṣṇa. But she is different from him, because she is the predominated moiety, while Śri Kṛṣṇa is the predominating moiety of the absolute. It is on account of this distinction that Śrī Kṛṣṇa in his intrinsic selfhood appears in the form of a male, while Rādhā appears in the form of a female. The relationship between them must not, however, be likened to the physical relationship between a male and a female on the mundane plane. The body of Rādhā, like that of Kṛṣṇa, is made of bliss and consciousness and the love between the two is spiritual. The difference between spiritual love and sensuality will be more clearly brought out at a later stage. We may here state that while spiritual love is pure and blissful and the highest end to be achieved by the soul, sensuality is the most odious feature of the soul in bondage.

The function of Rādhā as the divine consort of Kṛṣṇa is to please him by fulfilling all his desires and administering to all his needs (*CC*, Madhya, VIII, 125). This purpose is eternally fulfilled by her in the company of her innumerable partial manifestations in the form of Gopīs or the milk-maids of Vraja, who also join in the spiritual pastimes of Kṛṣṇa (*CC*, Madhya, VIII, 82). The services rendered to Kṛṣṇa by the Gopīs are the associated aspects of the service of Rādhā. The association of numberless consorts in the amorous pastimes (*Rāsa*) of Kṛṣṇa is necessary to enhance the bliss enjoyed by him (*CC*, Ādi, IV, 69);[3] hence, the emanation of numberless divine consorts from Rādhā.

It is important to note that in the philosophy of Śrī Caitanya the Hlādinī-śakti, is placed above all others and is identified with the intrinsic and perfect self of Bhagavān. The other Śaktis are regarded as subservient to it and are associated with the partial aspects of Bhagavān. The Saṁvit-śakti is identified with Paramātman and Saṁdhinī with Brahman.

[1]*rādhā pūrṇa-śakti kṛṣṇa pūrṇa śaktimān|*
dui vastu bheda nāhi śāstra pramāṇa||

[2]*rādhā-kṛṣṇaāche sadā ekai svarūpa|*
līlā-rasa āsvādite dhare dui rūpa||

[3]*bahu kāntā binā nahe rasera ullāsa|*
līlāra sahāya lāgi bahuta prakāśa||

The gradation of the Śaktis closely corresponds with the gradation of the three aspects of the personality of the Absolute. Just as Bhagavān is the highest manifestation of the Absolute and includes Paramātman, and Paramātman includes Brahman, the Hlādinī-śakti, which is the highest and the most perfect Śakti, includes the Saṁvit-śakti and the Saṁvit-śakti, in its turn, includes the Saṁdhinī-śakti. This also explains the relative positions of the different aspects of the personality of the absolute in terms of the qualities of *Sat*, *Cit* and *Ānanda*. Brahman is merely *Sat*; Paramātman is *Sat-cit*; and Bhagavān is *Sat-cit-ānanda*.

The identification of the Hlādinī-śakti with Bhagavān and its exclusion from Brahman and Paramātman is significant. Bliss in the real sense belongs only to Bhagavān. Bliss, which is sometimes associated with Brahman, is only an infinitesimal part of the bliss of Bhagavān. Real bliss is, therefore, experienced only by those who realise the Absolute as Bhagavān. The supreme bliss of the divine sports of Srī Kṛṣṇa attracts even the liberated souls, who, having freed themselves from the influence of Māyā, are established in Brahman (*CC*, Madhya, XVII, 132-33).[1] But the highest form of bliss known as *Madhura-rasa* is enjoyed only by the maids of Vraja, who are eagaged in the most confidential and loving service of Kṛṣṇa. Indeed *Madhura-rasa* is the very essence of Kṛṣṇa. We shall have occasion to read of it in detail at a later stage.

Western thinkers like Bergson often characterise Hindu religion as static,[2] because they are generally familiar with one particular strand of Hinduism, which has been influenced by the Advaitic philosophy of Saṁkara, and are ignorant of the main currents of Hindu thought and religion, which emanate from Vaiṣṇavism. The Vaiṣṇava religions are based on a dynamic conception of reality. But the concept of Śakti in Bengal Vaiṣṇavism introduces a new and more deep-rooted dynamism. Since the Śaktis, according to Bengal Vaiṣṇavism, are related either externally or internally to Bhagavān, Bhagavān is essentially creative, His creative activity relating itself to two different planes—the cosmic reality and the supra-cosmic reality, the order of nature and values and the order of spirits. The former is the stirring of the external or Bahiraṅgā, Śakti, which gives rise to the cyclic order of creation and destruction. The latter is the stirring of the internal or Antaraṅgā-śakti, which manifests the eternal Līlā of Bhagvān. The eternal Līlā is the movement of the absolute spirit within itself. It supersedes the order of values in transcendent beauty and sublimity of spiritual life, in beatitude and in the ease and grace of movement.

[1]*brahmānanda haite pūrnānanda kṛṣṇa guna|*
ataeva ākarṣaya ātmārāmera mana||
ātmārāmāśca munayo nigranthā apyurukrame|
kurvantyahaitukiṁ bhaktimitthambhūtaguṇo hariḥ||

[2]*See* Bergson's two essays on Religion and Morality.

Since there is no movement, which is not related directly or indirectly to the integrating centre, this introduction of dynamism in the absolute calls for a reorientation of the entire view of life. It leads to an aesthetico-teleological conception of reality, which makes our knowledge and experience concrete and meaningful at every stage.

CHAPTER VIII

Bhagavān Kṛṣṇa

Para-brahman has infinite forms (*CC*, Madhya, xx, 137). Each is related to it as part is related to the whole. But since *Para-brahman* has no internal difference, the part is not like a piece of stone chopped off from the whole. The part is actually the whole—the same all-powerful, all-knowing and all-pervading being. Still, it is called a part, because the Svarūpa-śakti of *Para-brahman* is not fully manifested in it, and the whole is called the whole, because the Svarūpa-śakti is fully manifested in it.

The infinite partial manifestations of Kṛṣṇa

We have already indicated that Nirviśeṣa Brahman is the lowest manifestation of Svarūpa-śakti and Kṛṣṇa is its highest manifestation. Kṛṣṇa is, therefore, indentical with Bhagavān—*Kṛṣṇastu bhagavān svayaṁ* (*Bh.*, I, 3, 28). Between Kṛṣṇa and the Nirviśeṣa Brahman there is an infinite hierarchy of partial manifestations, each of which has a different form. The differences in form are due to the difference in extent to which the might (*aiśvarya*) and sweetness (*mādhurya*) of Bhagavān are manifested in different forms. The differences in form, however, do not imply any difference in the identity of Bhagavān. All the different forms inhere in Kṛṣṇa as Svayaṁ Bhagavān. Therefore He is called *Bahūmūrtyeka mūrtikaṁ* (*Bh.*, 10, 40, 7).

Srī Jīva argues at length in *Kṛṣṇa-saṁdarbha* to establish the indentity of Kṛṣṇa with Bhagavān on the basis of numerous Śruti-texts. We shall, however, not dwell on this point at length. It will be our purpose in the present chapter to describe the supreme personality of Śrī Kṛṣṇa in its various aspects by giving a somewhat complicated account of the divine forms in which He manifests himself in the transcendental world and the different Avatāras or divine forms in which He descends on the mundane plane.

An elaborate account of the different manifestations of Śrī Kṛṣṇa is given by Śrī Caitanya in his teachings to Sanātana Gosvāmin. All the divine forms of Kṛṣṇa are broadly grouped by him under three main heads: Svayaṁ-rūpa, Tadekātma-rūpa and Āveśa-rūpa (*CC*, Madhya, xx, 132). Jīva Gosvāmin defines the three forms thus: *Svayaṁ-rūpa* form is that which is self-manifest, that which does not depend upon any other form for manifesting itself; *Tadekātma-rūpa* is that which although undifferentiable from the *Svayaṁ-rūpa* in essence, appears as distinct from it in form; *Āveśa-rūpa* is that in which Kṛṣṇa manifests Himself by transfusing His power in some favoured Jīva (*SS*, p. 346).

The *Svayaṁ* form is again divisible into *Svayaṁ-rūpa* and *Svayaṁ-prakāśa*. In the *Svayaṁ-rūpa* form, which is his intrinsic form, Kṛṣṇa is the cow-herd boy in Vraja. Being in every sense identical with Bhagavān, He is the possessor of infinite potencies, infinite attributes and all the divine excellences that are attributed to Bhagavān. He is the ultimate source of everything, the prime cause of all causes.[1] He has a spiritual body, the beauty of which is beyond description. His divine figure tinged with the hue of blue clouds resembles that of an adolescent boy in size and form; his blooming eyes are like a full-blown lotus; his head is bedecked with peacock feathers; he is adept in playing on his flute; his loveliness is unique and he is much more charming than even millions of cupids. But his body, which is thus described in human terms, should not be supposed to bear more than an outward resemblance to the human form. One of its peculiar characteristics is that, composed as it is of the elements of *Sat*, *Cit* and *Ānanda*, it is full of the most dazzling splendour. Each of its organs is capable of discharging the functions of all other organs, and each manifests and maintains within itself infinite universes, both spiritual and mundane.[2]

Kṛṣṇa sometimes manifests himself simultaneously in many places and there is no qualitative difference between these manifested forms and the original form. The manifested forms are called the *Svayaṁ-prakāśa* forms. They have a two-fold aspect as *Prābhava-prakāśa* and *Vaibhava-prakāśa*. An example of the *Prābhava-prakāśa* form is Kṛṣṇa's simultaneous appearance in many similar forms, each dancing separately in the company of one of the innumerable Gopīs in the Rāsa pastime (*CC*, Madhya, xx, 140). In the *Vaibhava-prakāśa* form Kṛṣṇa manifests himself as Balarāma, who is different from Kṛṣṇa only in colour (*Varṇa-mātra-bheda*), while in every other respect he is the same as Kṛṣṇa. The *Vaibhava-prakāśa* forms sometimes manifest themselves as two-armed, as in the case of Vāsudeva, son of Devakī in Mathurā, and sometimes as four-armed, as in the case of Vāsudeva, son of Devakī in Dvārakā, and are respectively known as *Vaibhava-prakāśa* and *Prābhava-Vilāsa* forms. There is a difference of conceit between Kṛṣṇa as *Svayaṁ-rūpa* and his *Vaibhava-prakāśa* forms. *Svayaṁ-rūpa* Śrī Kṛṣṇa has the guise and conceit of a Gopa, while Vāsudeva has the guise and conceit of a Kṣtriya. *Svayaṁ-rūpa* Śrī Kṛṣṇa excels Vāsudeva in beauty (*saundarya*),

[1]*īśvaraḥ paramaḥ kṛṣṇaḥ saccidānanda vigrahaḥ/ anādirādigovindaḥ sarvakāraṇa kāraṇaṁ//* cited in *CC*, Madhya, viii, from *Brahma-saṁhitā*, V, 1.

[2]*aṅgāni yasya sakalendriyavṛttimanti paśyanti pānti kalayanti ciraṁ jaganti/ ānanda cinmaya sadujjvalavigrahasya govindaṁmādipuruṣaṁ tamahaṁ bhajāmi// Brahma-saṁhitā*, V, 32.

majesty (*aiśvarya*), sweetness (*mādhurya*), and humour (*vaidagdha-vilāsa*) (*CC*, Madhya, xx, 148-50).

The *Tadekātma-rūpas* are classified into (1) *Vilāsa* (forms for expanded activity) and (2) *Svāṁśa* (constituent fractional forms) (*CC*, Madhya, xx, 153). Those manifested forms of Kṛṣṇa, which are nearly equal to him in power are called *Vilāsa*-forms, for example, Baladeva and Vaikuntha-Nārāyaṇa; less powerful forms as Matsya and Varāha are called Svāṁśa forms. The *Vilāsa* forms are again divisible into *Prābhava* and *Vaibhava*. The principal deities of the *Prābhava-vilāsa* form are Vāsudeva, Saṁkarṣaṇa, Pradyumna and Aniruddha (*CC*, Madhya, xx, 155). They are together known as the *Ādi-caturvyūha*, which is the origin of the infinite lower *caturvyūhas*. Their eternal dwelling places are Dvārakā and Mathurā (*CC*, Madhya, xx, 189-90). From this original *caturvyūha* emanate twenty-four deities who are known by different names according to the different weapons owned by them (*CC*, Madhya, xx, 160). These twenty-four are the *Vaibhava-vilāsa* forms and their appearance is affected by Kṛṣṇa in the following manner:

Kṛṣṇa appears in the form of Nārāyaṇa in Paravyoma with his second Caturvyūha consisting of Vāsudeva, Saṁkarṣaṇa, Pradyumna and Aniruddha, who are the extensions in Vaikuṇṭha of the *Ādi-caturvyūha* in Dvārakā and Mathurā (*CC*, Madhya, xx, 192). Each of the deities constituting the second Caturvyūha manifests in his turn three more deities, who are called the *Prakāśa-vigrahas*. Thus Vāsudeva manifests Keśava, Nārāyaṇa, and Mādhava; Saṁkarṣaṇa manifests Govinda (distinct from the Govinda of Vraja), Viṣṇu and Śrī Madhusūdana; Pradyumna manifests Trivikrama, Vāmana and Śrīdhara; and Aniruddha manifests Hṛṣīkeśa, Padmanābha and Dāmodara (*CC*, Madhya, xx, 164-66). Each of these twelve deities is the presiding deity of one of the twelve months of the year: Keśava is the presiding deity of the month of Mārga·śīrṣa, Nāṛayaṇa of the month of Pauṣa, Mādhava of the month fo Māgha, Govinda of the month of Phālguna, Viṣṇu of the month of Caitra, Madhusūdana of the month of Vaiśākha, Trivikrama of the month of Jyeṣṭha, Vāmana of the month of Āṣāḍha, Śrīdhara of the month of Srāvaṇa, Hṛṣīkeśa of the month of Bhādra, Padmanābha of the month of Āśvina, and Dāmodara of the month of Kārtika (*CC*, Madhya, xx, 163-70). Further there are two *Vilāsa-mūrtis* of each of the deities of the second Caturvyūha. The *Vilāsa-mūrtis* of Vāsudeva are Adhokṣaja and Puruṣottama; of Saṁkarṣaṇa, Upendra and Acyuta, of Pradyumna Nṛsinha and Janārdana; and of Aniruddha, Hari and Kṛṣṇa (who is distinct from the Kṛṣṇa of Vraja) (*CC*, Madhya, xx, 174-75). All these forms reside eternally in Paravyoma, but they also manifest themselves in some particular places in the mundane world (*CC*, Madhya, xx, 212). For example, Keśava dwells in Mathurā; Puruṣottama in Nīlācala, where he is known by the name Jagannātha; Mādhava in Prayāga; Madhusūdana in Purī; Viṣṇu in

Viṣṇu-kāncī; Hari in Māyāpur; and Vāsudeva, Padmanābha and Janārdana in Ānandāraṇya (*CC*, Madhya, xx, 184-86). They manifest themselves in the mundane world for the purpose of destroying sin, establishing virtue and imparting happiness to their devotees (*CC*, Madhya, xx, 188). Some of these deities, like Viṣṇu, Trivikrama, Nṛsinha and Vāmana, also appear as Avatāras (*CC*, Madhya, xx, 189).

In the *Svāṁśa* form, Kṛṣṇa is the source of infinite *Avatāras*, which are mainly grouped under six heads: Puruṣāvatāra, Līlāvatāra, Guṇāvatāra, Manvantarāvatāra, Yugāvatāra and Śaktyāveśāvatara (*CC*, Madhya, xx, 211-14). It should be noted that the English word incarnation is not the correct translation of *avatāra*. Avatāra literally means the descent of a deity. Accordingly, when a particular deity residing in the Paravyoma descends into the phenomenal world, he is known as an Avatāra. The Avatāras are beyond the influence of Prakṛti; as such they do not get encased in physical body at the time of their descent, as the word incarnation suggests, but retain their essentially transcendental character (*CC*, Madhya, xx, 227-28).

The first in order is the Puruṣāvatāra, which has a three-fold aspect as Kāraṇārṅavaśāyī, Garbhodaśāyī and Kṣīrodaśāyī, known as the First Puruṣa, the Second Puruṣa and the Third Puruṣa. The creative function of the Puruṣāvatāra in its different aspects has been already stated in the foregoing chapter.

The next in order is the Līlāvatāra. There are countless Līlāvatāras of Kṛṣṇa. Some of the important ones are Matsya, Kūrma, Varāha, Nṛsinha, Vāmana, Rāmacandra, Kalki and Buddha.

The Guṇāvatāras are Brahmā, Viṣṇu and Rudra, the presiding deities of the three Guṇas: *Sattva*, *Rajas* and *Tamas*. They emanate from the Garbhodaśāyī Puruṣa. Brahmā is the cause of creation of the world, Viṣṇu is the cause of its sustenance and Rudra is the cause of its dissolution (*CC*, Madhya, xx, 246-48). Viṣṇu is reckoned both as Guṇāvatāra and the Third Puruṣa of Puruṣāvatāra (*CC*, Madhya, xx, 252). The role of Brahmā is usually performed by a highly advanced and devoted Jīva, whose mind is conditioned by *Rajoguṇa* and who is provided with the power of creation by the Garbhodaśāyī Puruṣa. But when such a Jīva is not available, Kṛṣṇa manifests a part of his own self as Brahmā (*CC*, Madhya, xx, 259-260). Similarly, the role of Rudra is sometimes assigned to a Jīva and sometimes it is performed by a partial manifestation of Kṛṣṇa. The Jīvas to whom the roles of Brahmā and Rudra are assigned are respectively called Jīva-koti Brahmā and Jīva-koti Rudra. The role of Viṣṇu is never assigned to a Jīva. When Kṛṣṇa assumes the form of Rudra he has to do so by associating himself with *Māyā* and appropriating *Tamoguṇa* for causing the destruction of the world. Rudra loses his purely transcendental character because of his association with *Māyā*, just as milk when mixed with acid loses its character as milk and forms into curd. Therefore, Rudra, instead of being regarded as a manifestation of Kṛṣṇa, is properly regarded as Jīva-tattva (*CC*, Madhya, xx, 262-64).

Both Brahmā and Rudra are Bhakta-avatāras, or Avatāras belonging to the category of devotees of Kṛṣṇa and they carry out his orders (*CC*, Madhya, xx, 268); but Viṣṇu, who is conditioned by Śuddha-sattva, is the manifestation of Kṛṣṇa's intrinsic self (*Svarūpa-ākara*). Although a Guṇāvatāra, he is uncontaminated by *Māyā* on account of his being conditioned by Śuddha-sattva, and, therefore, to a great extent, he resembles Kṛṣṇa in his glory and power (*CC*, Madhya, xx, 266-69).

The *Manvantarāvatāra*[1] is so called because it appears once in each-Manvantara. There are fourteen Manvantaras in a single day of Brahmā; therefore, there are fourteen *Manvantaraavatāras* in a day, four hundred twenty *Manvantarāvatāras* in one month, five thousand forty *Manvantarāvatāras* in a year and five lac four thousand *Manvantarāvatāras* in one hundred years of Brahmā, which is the total period of his life (*CC*, Madhya, xx, 270-72). The fourteen Avatāras, corresponding to the fourteen Manvantaras in a day of Brahmā, are Yajna, Vibhu, Sattyasena, Hari, Vaikuṇṭha, Ajita, Vāmana, Sārvabhauma, Ṛṣabha, Viśvaksena, Dharmasetu, Sudhāman, Yogeśvara, and Vṛhad-bhānu (*CC*, Madhya, xx, 270-80). There are four Yugāvtaras corresponding to the four Yugas: *Satya*, *Tretā*, *Dvāpara* and *Kali*. They appear in four different colours to initiate the finite souls into their proper spiritual function in a particular *Yuga*. The Avatāra of *Satya-yuga* is white and he teaches meditation on Kṛṣṇa; the Avatāra of *Tretā* is red and he teaches *Yajna* or sacrifice; the Avatāra of *Dvāpara* is of a dark complexion and he teaches ritualistic worship of Kṛṣṇa; the Avatāra of *Kali* is yellow and he teaches Saṁkīrtana or congregational chanting of the Name of Kṛṣṇa and the doctrine of unalloyed devotion or Prema (*CC*, Madhya, xx, 280-84).

The *Pīta* or yellow Avatāra of *Kali* is Śrī Kṛṣṇa Caitanya himself. This is indirectly acknowledged by Śrī Caitanya in his conversation with Sanātana Gosvamī, on the latter's persuading him to disclose the identity of the *Pītaavatāra* (*CC*, Madhya, xx, 289-91). But it is clearly acknowledged by him on several other occasions. For example, he is depicted by Thākura Vṛndāvanadāsa as saying to a Brāhmin guest of his father, "I have appeared on earth to inaugurate *Saṁkīrtana*. I shall preach *Ṣaṁkīrtana* all over, and at every door I shall knock to initiate the people in the religion of divine love" (*C. Bh.*, Ādi, III, 293-94).[2]

[1]Manvantara consists of seventy-one *Divya-yugas* and each *Divya-yuga* consists of the four Yugas known as *Satya-yuga*, *Tretā-yuga*, *Dvāpara-yuga* and *Kali-yuga*.

[2]*saṁkīrtana ārambhe āmāra avatāra|*
karāimu sarvadeśe kīrtana pracāra||
brahmādi je premabhakti yoga vāñchā kare|
tāhā bilāimū sarva prati ghare ghare||

For his unbounded mercy towards the Jīvas, Śrī Caitanya is known as the Mahāvadānya, or the most merciful Avatāra. In no other Avatāra of Bhagavān was such mercy shown towards the fallen souls. This special feature of the Caitanya Avatāra was explained by Śrī Caitanya to some of his followers at Rāmakeli, to whom he said, "Verily, I shall deliver all the fallen souls. The demons and the atheists, who never had faith in me, will weep at the mere mention of my name out of love for me. The sinful, the untouchables, the lowly and the women folk will all be favoured by me in this *yuga* with the gift of divine love, which even the gods, the sages and the freed souls aspire after" (*C. Bh.*, Antya, iv, 120-23). This promise was fulfilled by Śrī Caitanya even beyond the limits of human expectation and belief. Not only he made all sorts of people, without any distinction of caste or creed, sex or age, drink deep of the nectar of divine love, but he made even the animals and the trees of the forests of Jhārakhaṅda and Vṛndāvana dance with joy, chanting the name of Kṛṣṇa and reciting *Ślokas* in his praise (*CC*, Madhya, xvii, 190-99).

Many texts are quoted from the Śāstras to prove the divinity of Śrī Caitanya. *Caitanya-caritāmṛta* refers to a *Śloka* from *Śrīmad-bhāgavata* (10. 8. 9) describing the golden yellow complexion of the *Pīta Avatāra*, which is also the complexion of the body of Śrī Caitanya (*CC*, Madhya, vi, Ś 3). It goes on to cite the following *Śloka* from *Viṣṇusahasranāma* which, besides speaking of the golden complexion of the body of Bhagavān, refers to Him as Saṁnyāsakṛta, implying thereby that in some particular Avatāra He embraces Saṁnyāsa:

Suvarṇa-varṇo hemāṅgo varāṅgaścandanāṅgādī saṁnyasakṛcch-amaḥ śānti niṣṭhā parāyaṇāḥ (*Sahasranāma*, 75; cited in *CC*, Madhya, vi, Ś 5).

The name Saṁnyāsakṛta is said to refer to Śrī Caitanya, because in no other Avatāra has Bhagavān adopted Saṁnyāsa. *Caitanya-caritāmṛta* also cites the following *Śloka* from *Śrīmad-bhāgavata* to prove that Śrī Caitanya is the Avatara of Śrī Kṛṣṇa Himself, who appeared in this age to inaugurate Saṁkīrtana:

kṛṣṇvarṇaṁ-tviṣākṛṣṇaṁ sāṅgopāṅgāstrapārṣadaṁ|
Yajnaiḥ saṁkīrtanaprāyairyajanti hi sumedhasaḥ|| (*Bh*, 11, 5, 32; cited in *CC*, Madhya, vi, Ś 4).

The belief in the divinity of Śrī Caitanya was wide spread in his own time and continues to this day to be shared by a large number of his devoted followers, now spread all over the world.

Next come the Śaktyāveśa Avatāras, or the divine appearances in the form of inspiration. Divine inspiration is of two kinds: that which comes from Bhagavān himself or that which comes from some Śakti of Bhagavān. The Avatāras belonging to the former category regard themselves as Divinity, and are properly included under the class of Avatāras described as Aveśa-rūpa; those belonging to the latter category regard themselves as devotees or the servants of God. Vyāsadeva and Ṛṣabhadeva are the Avatāras that proceed from Bhagavān. The Avatāras that proceed from the different Śaktis of Bhagavān are (*1*) Catuḥsan (from Jnāna-śakti), (*2*) Nārada (from Bhakti-śakti), (*3*) Pṛthu (from Pālana-śakti), (*4*) Paraśurāma (from Duṣṭanāśana śakit), (*5*) Jīva-brahmā (from creative-śakti) (*6*) Śeṣa (from Śva-sevana-śakti), and (7) Ananta (from Bhūdhāraṇa-śakti) (*CC*, Madhya, xx, 305-10).

The Avatāras, being the manifestations of Kṛṣṇa, are all perfect. But different degrees of perfection are manifested in different Avatāras. They are, therefore, graded into *Pūrṇa* (perfect), *Pūrṇatara* (more perfect) and *Pūrṇatama* (most perfect). The Avatāras in whom only a few of the divine qualities are manifested are *Pūrṇa* (perfect), those in whom all the divine qualities are partially manifested are *Pūrṇatara* (more perfect), and Bhagavān Kṛṣṇa, who is the source of all the Avatāras and in whom all the divine qualities are fully manifested, is *Pūrṇatama* (most perfect).[1] In Vraja, Kṛṣṇa manifests himself as *Pūrṇatama,* in Mathurā as *Pūrṇatara* and in Dvārakā as *Pūrṇa* (*CC*, Madhya, xx, 332-33).[2]

Thus Kṛṣṇa, according to Śrī Caitanya, is the supreme reality. He is not the incarnation of Viṣṇu as Śaṁkara and Rāmānuja think, but the hypostasis of Viṣṇu and all other gods. The historical Kṛṣṇa is the decent of the eternal Kṛṣṇa, in whom are embodied supreme puissance, supreme love, and supreme bliss. He is both concrete and expansive. By his infinite nature he encircles the whole universe, but his infinitude is centred in a concrete form. He is all-embracing in the organic unity of his being. His concrete form does not make him limited or restricted in freedom, because the modulations of his being spread everywhere in the infinite expanse of existence. He combines wideness of spirit with intensity of modulations, the eternal peace and calm of perfection with the dynamism of eternally self-revealing and self-fulfilling creative activity, and quickness of movement with intensive harmony and gracefulness. His flute wakes up such modulations in our being that our demands for love, knowledge and peace are all satisfied in an integrative synthesis. It provides freedom, elasticity, harmony and everything that makes for the richest and the most complete spiritual life.

The dhāman (*celestial abode*) *of Kṛṣṇa*

Vṛndāvana is the transcendental dwelling place (*dhāman*) of Kṛṣṇa.

[1] *kṛṣṇasya pūrnatamatā vyaktābhuta gokulāntare|*
pūrnatā pūrnataratā dvārakāmathurādiṣu|| cited from *Bhaktirasāmṛtasindhu* in *CC*, Madhya, xx, Ś 66.

[2] *vraje Kṛṣṇa sarvaiśvarya prakāśe pūrnatamā|*
purī dvaye paravyome pūrṇatara pūrna||

Being a manifestation of his Svarūpa-śakti or Intrinsic Energy,[1] it is a part of himself. It consists like him of the attributes of existence (*sat*), intelligence (*cit*) and bliss (*ānanda*), and is different from the phenomenal world, which is a manifestation of his Māyā-śakti or Extrinsic Energy. Also, being a manifestation of his Svarūpa-śakti, it is inseparably related to him. We can neither think of Kṛṣṇa without Vṛndāvana, nor of Vṛndāvana without Kṛṣṇa. Kṛṣṇa eternally stays in Vṛndāvana and does not move even a step out of it:

vṛndāvanaṁ parityajya sa kvacit naiva gacchati/ (Cited in *Laghu-bhāgavatāmṛta* from *Yāmala*).

Just as there are infinite manifestations of Kṛṣṇa, there are infinite manifestations of his *dhāman*. For each manifestation of Kṛṣṇa there is a corresponding manifestation of his *dhāman*. Since Kṛṣṇa is the highest manifestation of Bhagavān, his *dhāman* Vṛndāvana is the highest *dhāman*. Just as Kṛṣṇa is Bhagavān himself (*svayaṁ bhagavān*), and all other manifestations of Bhagavān are the manifestations of Kṛṣṇa, Vṛndāvana is the *dhāman* itself (*svayaṁ dhāman*), and all other dhāmans are the manifestations of Vṛndāvana.[2] Vṛndāvana manifests itself partly or fully according as Kṛṣṇa manifests Himself partly or fully. Just as each partial manifestation of Kṛṣṇa is transcendental and all-pervading (*vibhu*) even though it appears to be phenomenal and limited, each partial manifestation of *dhāman* is transcendental and all-pervading, even though it appears to be phenomenal and limited. Even the different kinds of objects in the *dhāman*, which look so much like the phenomenal objects are transcendental (*cinmaya*) (*CC*, Ādi, V, 45).[3] Sanātana Gosvāmin states that each one of them is concentrated Brahman (*brahman-ghana*) and therefore inconceivable.[4]

Even though each *dhāman* is infinite and all-pervading, the *dhāman* are said to be situated one above the other. Above the mundane sphere, which is graded into fourteen worlds—the seven *Lokas* and seven *Pātālas*, and beyond the river Virajā, is situated the Brahman-loka or the Siddha-loka, which is the residing place of all the freed (*mukta*) souls (*CC*, Madhya, XIX, 153). Above the Brahman-loka is the Paravyoma, where reside the infinite Avatāras or partial manifestations of Kṛṣṇa, and which is the support of infinite spiritual regions called Vaikunṭhas (*CC*, Ādi, V,

[1]More specifically it is the concentrated (*mūrta*) form of that aspect of Svarūpa-śakti, in which the Saṁdhinī-śakti, which is the ground and source of all existence predominates.

[2]*vaikunṭhādi tadāṁśāṁśaṁ svayaṁ vṛndāvanaṁ bhūvi*. —*Padma-purāṇa, Pātāla-khanda*, 38, 39.

[3]*vaikunṭhera pṛthivyādi śakala cinmaya*/
māyika bhūtera tathi janma nahi haya// —*CC*, Ādi, V, 45.

[4]*teṣāṁ rūpaṁ tattvaṁ manasāpi grahitaṁ na śakyate brahmanghanatvāt*. —*Br. Bh.*, 2, 4, 50, *Tikā*.

15). Above all these *dhāmans* is situated Kṛṣṇa-loka, which, according to the difference in the Līla and the Parikaras or the retinue of Kṛṣṇa, appears in three different forms as Dvārakā, Mathurā and Gokula (*CC*, Ādi, V, 13). Gokula, which is the highest of the three, is also called Vṛndāvana, because Vṛndāvana is the central portion of Gokula.

The situation of the *dhāmans* above or below each other should not, however, be taken in its literal sense. It actually implies their gradation according to their excellence (*mahimā*). The excellence of a *Dhāman* depends on the degree of manifestation in it of the highest *Dhāman* Vṛndāvana. Thus the excellence of the Siddha-loka is greater than the excellence of the phenomenal world, the excellence of Paravyoma is greater than the excellence of Siddha-loka, the excellence of Kṛṣṇa loka is greater than the excellence of Paravyoma, the excellence of Gokula is greater than the excellence of the rest of the Kṛṣṇa-loka and the excellence of Vṛndāvana is the greatest of all.

In *Ṛgveda* Vṛndāvana is described as the highest *Dhāman* (*paramaṁ padaṁ*) of Viṣṇu.[1] In the Bhāgavata also it is described as the highest *Dhāman*. In *Gītā* Kṛṣṇa himself describes it as "My highest *Dhāman*."[2] It is so described because it surpasses all other *Dhāmans* in its granduer (*aiśvarya*) and sweetness (*mādhurya*). But its peculiarity is that its Aiśvarya is completely eclipsed by its Mādhurya, so that everything here assumes a form that is sweet beyond expression. Kṛṣṇa does not appear here as God or even as a king, but as a cow-herd boy with the crest of a peacock feather on his crown and a flute in his hand, eternally engaged in amorous pastimes with his consorts on the bank of the river Jamunā, underneath the Kadaṁba trees and in the green groves, laden with sweet smelling flowers, all of which breathe an atmosphere of freedom and sweetness, most congenial to him and his consorts.[3]

It is, therefore, not possible to think of Kṛṣṇa's presence anywhere else. Kṛṣṇa in Mathurā and Dvārakā is not really the Kṛṣṇa of Vṛndāvana, but his partial manifest called Vāsudeva. When Kṛṣṇa is said to go out of Vṛndāvana, as for example, when he goes to Mathurā at the invitation of Kaṅsa, it is really his partial manifest Vāsudeva, who goes there and not Kṛṣṇa. who remains unmanifest during that period in his manifest Līlā (*prakaṭa-līlā*) in Vṛndāvana.

That Kṛṣṇa, in his highest aspect, in which his Mādhurya is fully displayed, is inseparably connected with Vṛndāvana, is testified by the fact that Rādhā, to whom even a moment's separation from Kṛṣṇa is unbearable, is not satisfied to find him in Kurukṣetra, where he appears as a

[1] *Ṛgveda*, 1, 154, 6.

[2] *yaṁ prāpya na nivartanti taddhāma paramaṁ mama|* —*Gītā*, 8, 21.

[3] *nityaṁ vṛndāvanaṁ nāma nityarāsarasotsavaṁ|*
adṛśyaṁ paramaṁ guhyaṁ pūrnapremarasotsavaṁ|| —*Padma-purāṇa*, *Pātāla-khanda*, 51.

king with his entourage and not as a cowherd with his flute (*CC*, Madhya, I, 72-73). She is also not satisfied to find him in Nava-Vṛndāvana, a replica of Vṛndāvana, specially prepared for her in Dvārakā, because it lacks in the atmosphere of freedom and the charm and grace so natural to Vṛndavana and is not, therefore, conducive to the highest kind of bliss she is accustomed to experience in the company of Kṛṣṇa in Vṛndāvana.

It is not surprising, therefore, that Uddhava, the wisest of the assosiates of Kṛṣṇa wishes to be a blade of grass or a creeper in Vṛndāvana so that he may be consecrated by the dust of the holy feet of the Gopīs:

āsāmahocaraṇareṇu juṣāmahaṁ syāṁ vṛndāvane kimapi gulmalatauṣadhīnāṁ/ *Bh.*, 10, 47, 61.

Even the great Śaṁkarācārya, who regards the personal form, the *Dhāman* and the Līlā of Kṛṣṇa as creations of Māyā, reveals a secret desire to be in Vṛndāvana, so that he may sit on the bank of the Jamunā and pass each long day of his life in the twinkling of an eye, meditating on Kṛṣṇa:

kadā vṛndāraṇye taraṇi tanayā puṇya puline,
smaran srīgopālaṁ nimiṣamiva neṣyāmi divasān/ *Abhilāṣāṣṭaka.*

The celestial Dvārakā, Mathurā and Gokula or Vṛṅdāvana have their replica on earth in the form of the geographical Dvārakā, Mathurā and Vṛndāvana, which are known as their Prakaṭa-prakāśa or manifest forms. These appear as parts of the phenomenal world on account of our clouded vision, but are in essence identical with their celestial counterparts. Here also Kṛṣṇa is eternally present with Nanda, Yaśodā and the other Parikaras and performs His Līlā with them as in the celestial Dvārakā, Mathurā, and Vṛndāvana. If we could see them with spiritual eyes, they would, without doubt, appear in their true form (*CC*, Ādi, V, 20-21). The devotees, who attain accomplishment (*siddhāvasthā*) in dovotion are even today blessed with the vision of the divine Līlā of Kṛṣṇa with his Parikaras while staying in these Dhāmans in their present bodies, without being transported to any other Dhāman or any other level of existence. When, however, Kṛṣṇa descends on these Dhāmans at the time of his manifest Līlā (*Prakaṭa-prakāśa*), even those, who are not devoted, can see him and his Parikaras in their true form. Such is the effect of the divine touch of Kṛṣṇa with these Dhāmans, which otherwise appear to be phenomenal.

Besides this Prakaṭa-prakāśa of Kṛṣṇa-loka there is also an Aprakaṭa-prakāśa of it on earth, which has the peculiar power of always remaining invisible and which remains on earth without touching it. There are, thus, two Aprakaṭa-prakāśas of Kṛṣṇa-loka. One is the Kṛṣṇa-loka situated above Paravyoma, which is called by various names: Goloka, Gokula, Śvetadvīpa, Vraja-loka or Vṛndāvana. The other is the invisible Kṛṣṇa-loka situated on earth, which is different from the Prāpañcika or phenomenal Kṛṣṇa-loka, visible to our material eyes but which actually touches the earth. It is also called Gokula or Vraja.

Rūpa Gosvāmin states in *Laghu-bhāgavatāmṛta* that Goloka is a majestic manifestation (*vaibhava-prakāśa*) of Gokula, which is essentially sweet in appearance and, therefore, greater in excellence.[1] As an instance of the majesty (*vaibhava*) of Goloka he cites the *Vārāha-purāṇa*, which says that the Kadaṁba trees of Goloka spread out majestically with their hundred branches, which is just in keeping with its Aiśvarya, while the Kadaṁba trees of Gokula are medium-sized, which is in keeping with its Mādhurya. A special reason why Gokula excels in Mādhurya is that in Goloka Kṛṣṇa is present eternally without birth, on account of which his Līlā in Goloka differs in certain respects from its sweet human aspect in which it reveals itself in the phenomenal Gokula. *Brahma-saṁhitā* describes the Līlā of Vṛndāvana as Nara-līlā or man-like Līlā and the Līlā of Goloka as Deva-līlā or God-like Līlā. The theory is supported by the *Rāsa* dance in Goloka, which Kṛṣṇa is said to have performed on the head of Kāliyā Nāga, the thousand headed cobra, in *Bṛhad-bhāgavatāmṛta* and of which there is no mention in the *Bhāgavata*.

According to Jīva Gosvāmin also Goloka is the Vaibhava Prakāśa of Vṛndāvanya.[2] He describes Vṛndāvana as the inner side (*antarmaṇḍala*) of Goloka and Goloka as the outer side (*bahirmaṇḍala*) of Vṛndāvana. But they are not the outer and inner side of each other in the physical sense. For it is possible to see Goloka in Vṛndāvana,[3] but it is not possible to see Vṛndāvana in Goloka.[4]

Goloka, according to Rūpa and Jīva, can be attained by Vaidhī or ritualistic Bhakti, but Vṛndāvana can be attained only by Rāgānugā-bhakti or Bhakti, which flows spontaneously like a current, disregarding the rules and regulations of ritualistic Bhakti.[5] This is a further indication of the difference between the two Dhāmans.

Sanātana seems to differ from Rūpa and Jīva both in regard to the relation between Goloka and Vṛndāvana and the means of their realisation. According to him Goloka (or rather the part of Goloka called Gokula) and the phenomenal Gokula or Vṛndāvana are identical.[6] In his *Bṛhad-bhāgavatāmṛta* Gopa Kumāra sometimes stays in Goloka and sometimes in Vṛndāvana without being able to make out any difference between them.[7] Both the Dhāmans, according so him can be attained only by Rāgānugā-bhakti and not by any other means.[8]

[1] *Laghu-bhāgavatāmṛta*, 1, 277, 78.

[2] *Gopāla-campū*, Pūrva Khanda, 19.

[3] This is so because Goloka is the Vaibhava Prakāśa of Vṛndāvana.

[4] *Kṛṣṇa-saṁdarbha*, 116.

[5] *Bhakti-rasāmṛta-sindhu*, *Ṭīkā*, 1, 4.

[6] *yathā krīṇāti tadbhūmau goloke'pi tathaiva saḥ|*
atha ūrdhvatayā bhedo' nayoh kalpyeta kevalam|| —*Br. Bh.*, 2, 5, 168.

[7] ibid, 2, 6, 374.

[8] ibid, 2, 5, 172.

The difference between the two points of view, however, will seem to become negligible, if we take into consideration the following points:

1. Although Sanātana Gosvāmin regards Goloka and Vṛndāvana as identical, it is clear from his *Tīkā* on *Bṛhad-bhāgavatāmṛta*, 2, 5, 78-79, that Vṛndāvanā is the *marmatarāṁśa* of Goloka or that part of Goloka, which supersedes the whole in excellence.
2. Sanātana also admits that the excellence of the phenomenal Vraja exceeds the excellence of Goloka at the time of the manifest Līlā (*Prakaṭa-līlā*) of Kṛṣṇa.[1]
3. Although Rūpa and Jīva regard Goloka as the Vaibhava-prakāśa of Vṛndāvana, Jīva seems to regard them as essentially identical. He establishes their identity by referring to the *goloka eva nivasti* text of *Brahma-saṁhitā* and the *tattraiva ramaṇārtha hi nitya kāla sa gacchati* text of the *Ādi-purāṇa*, one of which says that Kṛṣṇa always stays in Goloka and the other that he always stays in the phenomenal Vṛndāvana, and by saying that the contradiction between them can be resolved only if the two are regarded as actually one and the same. In answer to a question regarding the mention in *Harivaṁśa* of the lifting of the Govardhana hill by Śrī Kṛṣṇa in Goloka he clearly states that since Goloka and Gokula are identical, a Līlā, which took place in Gokula can always be mentioned in reference to Goloka.[2]
4. As regards the means of realisation of the two Dhāmans, although Sanātana holds that it is Rāgānugā-bhakti in the case of both, he maintains that if a Sādhaka adopts any other means, he has a vision of Goloka, but he is not able to see Kṛṣṇa perform his Līlā with his Parikaras, and if He is able to do so, he cannot himself participate in the Līlā.[3]
5. Viśvanātha Cakravartī states that those, who wish to realize the Mādhurya of Rādhā-Kṛṣṇa but practise Vaidhī-bhakti, cannot attain Rādhā-Kṛṣṇa in Vṛndāvana, because their Bhakti is not Rāgānuga, and they cannot attain Kṛṣṇa in Dvāraka, because they do not desire to do so. Therefore they attain Rādha-Kṛṣṇa in Goloka, the Vaibhava-prakāśa of Vṛndāvana.[4]

We may conclude from the above that there is essntially no difference between Goloka and Gokula or Vṛndāvana. Goloka is particular manifestation of Vṛndāvana in which Mādhurya predominates, but not to the extent to which it predominates in Vṛndāvana. It is, therefore, called

[1] *Br. Bh* , 2, 5, 196, *Tīkā*.
[2] For a fuller discussion on the subject *see* Śrī Manīndra Nāth Guhā's *Śrī Mādhava Mādhurya Manjūṣā*, pp. 165-66.
[3] *Bṛhad.*, 2, 51, *Tīkā, Bhāgavatāmṛta*, 72
[4] *Bhakti-rasāmṛta-sindhu, Sādhana-bhakti-laharī*, 1, 2, 303, *Tīkā*.

the Vaibhava-prakāśa of Vṛndāvana. Vṛndāvana is attained by Rāgānugā-bhakti, while Goloka is attained by Vaidhī-bhakti. The greater the dominance of Rāgānugā-bhakti the fuller is the realization of the Mādhurya of Goloka.[1] But when Rāgānugā-bhakti is pure Goloka is realized in the highest aspect, in which Mādhurya is fully displayed. This aspect of Goloka is called the Antarmaṁḍala of Goloka. In this aspect Goloka is identical with the phenomenal Vṛndāvana and the Mādhurya displayed here is the same as in the phenomenal Vṛndāvana, except for such difference as is caused by the fact that Śrī Kṛṣṇa is always present in Goloka as a young boy of tender age (*nitya-kiśora*) while in the phenomenal Vṛndāvana He takes birth and gradually attains boyhood.

The veracity of the claim that the phenomenal Vṛndāvana, which looks so much like any other part of the material world to our material eyes, is itself the spiritual Vṛndāvana, the highest abode of Bhagavān, surpassing even Goloka in its excellence, may be questioned. But Śrī Caitanya and his followers are ever so emphatic in their statements about its transcendental character. Śrī Rūpa Gosvāmin says that the devotees, who have ardent love for Kṛṣṇa, are even today blessed with a vision of His divine Līlā in this very Vṛndāvana. Sanātana Gosvāmin says that Vṛndāvana is here on earth and Kṛṣṇa's unmanifest Līlā is going on in it even now, but none except those to whom he or his devotees are kind, can see it. Prabodhānanda Sarasvatī describes how he actually sees this Vṛndāvana in its real form with all its transcendent beauty and excellence:

> *aho sarvoparyati vimala-vistīrṇa-mādhurya-sphurac-candra-prāyaṁ*
> *sphurati mama vṛndāvanaṁ idaṁ*. *Vṛndāvana-mahimāmṛta*, 4, 83.

"Oh! this Vṛndāvana of mine, stationed above every other Dhāman! How it shines near me like a big moon in all its resplendent beauty!"

The Parikaras (*Retinue*) *of Kṛṣṇa*

Whatever the form in which Bhagavān manifests himself, he has his *Parikaras* or retinue, with whom he is eternally engaged in his divine Līlā. The *Parikaras* have a spiritual body like him and resemble him in divine qualities, temperament and dress etc. The *Parikaras* of Śrī Kṛṣṇa are the Yādavas in Dvārakā and Mathurā and the Gopas and Gopīs in Gokula or Vṛndāvana.

Parikaras are either Nitya-siddha or Sādhana-siddha. The Nitya-siddha *Parikaras* are the manifestations of the Svarūpa-śakti of Bhagavān and their presence in His Dhāman is Anādi or beginningless. The Sādhana-siddha *Parikaras* are the Jīvas, who have attained *Pārṣadattva* (the state of being a *Parikara*) by practising devotion. There are also some *Nitya-mukta* (eternally free) Jīvas, who are eternally engaged in the service of

[1]This is in accordance with the principle: *yādṛśī bhāvanā yasya siddhirbhavati tādṛśī*.

Bhagavān, but whose Pārṣadatva, instead of being inherent like the Pāraṣadatva of the *Nitya-siddha Parikaras,* is the gift of the Svarūpa-śakti. Pārṣadatva is inherent in the *Nitya-siddha Parikaras,* because they are the integral parts of the Svarūpa-śakti.

The Parikaras serve Bhagavān according to the particular bond of relationship like parenthood or wifehood, which obtains between them and Bhagavān. The relationship is neither due to birth nor an external ceremony like adoption or marriage, but it is due to the particular kind of Bhāva or devotional love a *Parikara* has for Bhagavan. Vasudeva-Devakī and Nanda-yaśodā are not the parents of Kṛṣṇa in the worldly sense, because Kṛṣṇa, really has no birth. He is eternally the son of Yaśodā and Devakī without ever entering into their womb. In the Prakaṭa-līlā He makes His appearence not by actual birth but by entering into the minds of Vasudeva and Devakī.[1] The theory of His appearence is thus not one of immaculate conception like the conception of Virgin Mary, but of immaculate birth. Śrī Jīva Gosvāmin says that just as Nārāyaṇa and Lakṣmı are husband and wife without ceremonially entering into wedlock, on account of their Bhāva or natural loving disposition towards each other, Nanda—Yaśodā and Kṛṣṇa are related as parents and son, not on account of birth, but on account of their Vātsalya Bhāva or natural affectionate disposition towards each other such as exists between parents and son.[2]

We have stated earlier that Vasudeva is Viśuddha-sattva or the principle of pure existence. One aspect of Viśuddha-sattva is the Ādhāra-śakti, which is the ground and source of all existence, including the existence of Bhagavān Himself. It is, therefore, natural that Śrī Kṛṣṇa should appear as the son of Vasudeva-Devakī and Nanda-Yaśodā, who are the personified forms of Ādhāra-śakti.[3] Other *Parikaras* of Kṛṣṇa, who have Vātsalya Bhāva towards him are also the manifestations of the Ādhāra-śakti. Similarly the Gopas of Vraja and the Yādavas of Dvārakā and Mathurā are the manifestations of Kṛṣṇa, while the Gopīs of Vraja and the Mahiṣīs of Dvārakā, who have Kāntā-bhāva or the loving attitude of a wife towards Kṛṣṇa, are the personified forms of His Svarūpa-śakti. In Paravyoma Lakṣmī and the wives of the other partial manifestations of Bhagavān are the manifestations of the Svarūpa-śakti, while the other *Parikaras* are the manifestations of Kṛṣṇa.

The theory that the *Parikaras* are the manifestations of Kṛṣṇa or His Svarūpa-śakti seems to be cotradicted by some incidents in Kṛṣṇa-līlā like the Gopa's losing consciousness from the effect of the poison of the

[1] *saccidānanda vigrahasya tasya tan-manasyavesa eva. Kr. S.*
[2] *anādito vātsalya-rasa-siddha-pitṛ-putra-bhāvo vidyate|*
[3] *Kr. S.*, 150.

Kāliyā lake, the destruction of the Yādavas and the leaving of the physical body (*guṇamaya-deha*) by the Gopīs. Śrī Jīva Gosvāmin explains that such occurrences are illusory (*māyika*) and are brought about by the will of Bhagavān so that the character of the Līlā as human (*nara-līlā*) and the Madhura-rasa generated by it are secured. The Yādavas were not destroyed but they disappeared and went to their Loka alongwith their bodies (*sa-śarīram*). The *guṇamaya-deha* in the case of the Gopīs refers to the illusory body, which they left behind to join the *Rāsa-līlā* so that their husbands might think that their wives were with them, or it refers to the physical body in the case of the Sādhaka-carī Gopīs, who became the Gopīs of Vraja on the completion of their Sādhanā and whose phenomenal bodies (*asiddha-deha*), unlike the eternal bodies of the Nitya-siddha Gopīs, are not fit for entrance into the *Rāsa-līlā*.

The Līlā (Beatific Sports) of Kṛṣṇa

Since Kṛṣṇa is all perfection, he has no wants and his activities are without any motive or conscious effort. They spring from exuberance of intrinsic bliss or Ānanda. They are, therefore, called Līlā, which is imperfectly rendered into English by the word 'sport.'

Līlā is either manifest (*prakaṭa*) or unmanifest (*aprakaṭa*). But this does not mean that there are two different kinds of Līlā. It is the same Līlā, which is called Manifest, when it is visible to the phenomenal beings and Unmanifest, when it is not visible to them.[1] There are, however, some important points of difference between them. Aprakaṭa-līlā is wholly transcendent. It has no contact with the phenomenal world. But Prakaṭa-līlā is a mixture of the phenomenal and the non-phenomenal. In the Prakaṭa-līlā a particular manifestation of the transcendental Kṛṣṇa-loka descends on earth, so that there is a mixing of the phenomenal and the non-phenomenal. But it is not mixing in the ordinary sense, for the touch of the non-phenomenal world makes the particular part of the phenomenal world, where it descends, also non-phenomenal.

In the Prakaṭa-līlā there is an appearence of Kṛṣṇa's birth and death and He grows from infancy to tender youth (*kiśorāvasthā*), while in the Aprakaṭa-līlā He is eternally young and there is neither birth nor death. Nitya-kiśore or the eternal state of budding youth is intrinsic to Kṛṣṇa, while the different stages leading from infancy to early youth, namely Śaiśava, Bālya, Kaumāra and Pogaṇḍa are superimpositions brought about by the Svarūpa śakti, so that Kṛṣṇa and His devotees may have a taste of different kinds of bliss (*Rasa*) generated by them (*CC*, Madhya, xx, 215, 313).

Aprakaṭa-līlā is a continuous flow. It goes on unimpeded like the continuous flow of time. It is eternal in the sense that it has neither

[1]*Kr. S.* 153.

beginning, nor middle, nor end. But though eternal and continuous as a whole it is not changeless. Each day different Līlās are performed at different periods of time, for example, breakfast in the morning, pasturing the cows (*go-cāraṇa*) during the day, and the Rāsa-dance at night. But these Līlās also go on repeating themselves like the different parts of a wheel in motion and are in this sense eternal. On the other hand the Prakaṭa-līlā has its beginning, middle and end. It begins in a particular universe (*brahmāṇḍa*) when it becomes manifest in that universe and ends when it becomes unmanifest in it. Each of the different Līlās constituting the Prakaṭa-līlā is also not continuous and eternal in the sense in which the different Līlās in the Aprakaṭa-līlā are continuous and eternal. For example, the Go-cāraṇa Līlā ceases when Kṛṣṇa goes to Mathura.[1]

The Aprakṭa-līlā we have described above is called Svārasikī, because it is unrestricted in flow and continues to be performed at different times and places in different forms. But the Aprakaṭa-līlā, which is realised in a limited way through Mantras and Upāsanā is called Mantropāsanāmayī. It is limited by the particular time and place necessary for the particular Līlā to which the Mantra relates and is characterised by such form and activity of the deity as are the object of meditation according to the Mantra. All the different Līlās constituting the Svārasikī stream of Līlā have beginning, middle and end, but the Mantropāsanāmayī-līlā does not have beginning and end. It goes on eternally at the same time and place and in the same form. The Svārasikī stream of Līlā is compared to the continuous flow of the Ganges, while the Mantropāsanāmayī-līlā is compared to a stagnant lake circumscribed out of it. Mantropāsanāmayī-līlā can lead to Svārasikī, because the stream of Svārasikī, when it passes through the lake of the Mantropāsanāmayī, can carry the mind of the Sādhaka with it in its onward course, as soon as the particular part of the Svārasikī, which is identical with the Mantropāsanāmayī, is over.[2]

There are different kinds of *Mantropasnāmayī-līlā*, such as *Gocāraṇa-līlā*, *Rāsa-līlā* and *Kuñja-krīḍa-līlā*.[3] Each of these Līlās takes place in a particular Prakāśa of Vṛndāvana, and each one of the participants in the Līlā, including Kṛṣṇa, appears in it in a particular manifestation of his

[1]Intrinsically the *Prakaṭa-līlā* is also eternal though it appears to have a beginning and end from the point of view of a particular Brhmānda. Just as the sun never actually disappears, and while it sets in one country it rises in another, the *Prakaṭa-līlā* never ends, and while it seems to end in one country it begins in another. Just as all the different parts of the day, caused by the different positions of the sun, are present in some country or the other, all the different parts of the *Prakaṭa-līlā* are present and visible in some Brahmānda or the other. Thus each of the Līlās, like the Līlā of the birth of Kṛṣṇa, or the killing of Pūtanā, is eternal.

[2]Rādhā Govinda Nāth, *Gaudiya Vaiṣnava Darśana*, I, 1, 119.

[3]The Mantropāsanāmayī Kunja-krīṇā-līlā finds a mention in *CC: rātri din kuñja-krīṇā kare Rādhā sange]* Madhya, VIII, 148.

self, which is unaware of its other manifestations and their activities. Thus it is possible that while Kṛṣṇa and *Rādhā* are separate from each other in the Prakaṭa-līlā they are in eternal union in the Aprakaṭa-līlā.[1] This is contradictory from our mundane point of view, but since it relates to the All-perfect Being, it only gives a higher meaning to his perfection.

Kṛṣṇa as Rasa

The scriptures describe Para-brahman Śrī Kṛṣṇa as the highest bliss and the highest bliss as Śrī Kṛṣṇa. Kṛṣṇa is bliss in its concentrated form (*ānanda-ghana*). But the bliss or *brahmānanda* of which Kṛṣṇa is the embodiment is different from ordinary happiness. Ordinary happiness is material while *brahmānanda* is spiritual; ordinary happiness is transient and limited while *brahmānanda* is eternal and unlimited (*bhūmā*).

Taittirīya-upaniṣad mentiones various grades of material happiness.[2] It says that the material happiness enjoyed by Brahmā is the highest of all material happiness and describes *brahmānanda* as infinitely superior to the happiness of Brahmā.[3] The superiority of *brahmānanda* is not only quantitative but qualitative. Even the highest material happiness is both quantitatively and qualitatively inferior to an infinitesimal part of *brahmānanda. Brahmānanda* is unique and indescribable. It is transcendental.

Kṛṣṇa is not only the embodiment of bliss but of Rasa.[4] The word '*rasa*' is usually translated as 'relish.' It implies both the object that is relished (*āsvādya-vastu*) and the person who relishes (*āsvādaka*). Kṛṣṇa is both the object that is relished and the person who relishes, in other words, He is both Rasa and Rasika. As Rasa He is the highest thing to be relished (*parama-āsvādya*); as Rasika He is the greatest enjoyer of relish.

Both *ananda* or bliss and *rasa* are relished. But the relish of Rasa has two distinctive qualities. Firstly it is characterised by delicious astonishment. Astonishment is the essence of Rasa. Therefore Rasa is always wonderful (*adbhuta*);

raso sāraścamatkāro yaṁ binā na raso rasaḥ|
taccamatkāra-sāratve sarvatraivādbhuto rasaḥ||

Alaṁkāra-kaustubha, 6, 5, 7.

Secondly, it is characterised by total absorbtion of the mind and the senses. The mind and the senses are so much absorbed in the astonishingly delicious experience of Rasa that they become completely unaware of all other things.

Rasa is transcendental (*aprākṛta*) or phenomenal (*prākṛta*). But pheno-

[1]Rādhā Govinda Nāth, *Gauḍīya Vaiṣnava Darśana*, I, 1, 119.
[2]*Taittiriya*, Brahmānanda Vallī, 8.
[3]ibid.
[4]*raso vai saḥ, rasam hyevāyaṁ labdhvā ānandī bhavati* (*Taittirīya*, Ānanda Vallī, 7).

menal Rasa is not Rasa in the real sense, because astonishment and absorbtion in phenomenal Rasa are momentary. Repeated enjoyment of phenomenal Rasa deprives it of all its charm. It becomes stale and causes neither astonishment nor absorbtion of the mind and the senses. But repeated experience of transcendental Rasa or Rasa pertaining to Para-brahman does not make it less astonishing or less absorbing, because He is full of infinite variety (*ananta-vaicitrīpūrṇa*), which makes Him eternally new. Para-brahman Śrī Kṛṣṇa is new every moment. He is full of infinite variety both as object of relish and as the enjoyer of relish Therefore He is called *akhila-rasāmṛta-mūrti* or the embodiment of all Rasas.[1]

The infinite diversity and novelty of Kṛṣṇa is due to His Svarūpa-śakti. The Svarūpa-śakti is a conscious principle eternally engaged in His service. It serves Kṛṣṇa by diversifying in endless ways His aspect as *āsvādya-rasa* or Rasa as an object of relish and His aspect as *āsvādaka-rasa* or Rasika by implanting in Him an ever growing desire for relishing an infinite variety of Rasa. It also serves Him by manifesting itself in the form of His abode (*dhāman*) and His associates (*parikaras*), by appearing in the hearts of His devotees as Prīti or love for Kṛṣṇa, by enabling the Jīvas engaged in His devotional service as Sādhakas to attain His company (*parikaratva*), by giving *ānanda* to Him and fulfilling His desire to give *ānanda* to His parikaras and devotees, and by doing everything else to enable Kṛṣṇa to enjoy the relish of new sportive activities (*līlā-rasa*) in the company of His *Parikaras* and devotees.

Kṛṣṇa's ever-growing desire for relishing new forms of Rasa is not to be interpreted as a sign of imperfection. It is not the kind of desire that springs from any kind of want. It springs from fulness It is like the spilling of boiling milk from a pot that is full to the brim, or like the spontaneous bursting into laughter and the exercising of limbs of a healthy child free from hunger or thirst. It is the spilling over of perfection. It springs from the very nature of Kṛṣṇa as Rasa. The desire for Rasa is a necessary condition for the enjoyment of Rasa, just as hunger is a necessary condition for the enjoyment of delicious food. The greater the desire the greater the enjoyment. The desire for Rasa is as natural to Kṛṣṇa as the power of burning is natural to fire. Otherwise how could Kṛṣṇa be the supreme enjoyer of Rasa (*rasika-śekhara*) or the embodiment of all Rasas (*akhila-rasāmṛta-mūrti*).

Svarūpa-śakti or, more correctly speaking, Svarūpa-śakti as dominated by its own partial aspect Hlādinī-śakti (*hlādinīpradhāna-svarūpa-śakti*) is the ultimate source of bliss or *ānanda.* Therefore the *ānanda* enjoyed by Kṛṣṇa is also caused by Hlādinī-śakti. There are broadly speaking two categories of *ānanda* which Svarūpa-śakti provides to Kṛṣṇa: Svarū-

[1] *sa eṣa rasānāṁ rasatamaḥ paramaḥ. Chāndogya*, 1, 1, 3.

pānanda and Svarūpa-śaktyānanda. When the Hlādinī-śakti resides in Kṛṣṇa, it enables Him to enjoy Svarūpānanda or the *ānanda* inherent in his own self; when it resides in the heart of a devotee desirous of serving Kṛṣṇa, it assumes the form of Kṛṣṇa-prīti or the love of Kṛṣṇa, which is much more relishing to Kṛṣṇa than Svarūpānanda. The *ānanda* which Hlādinī-śakti enables Kṛṣṇa to derive from the love of His devotee is called Svarūpa-śaktyānanda.[1]

How is it that Kṛṣṇa's own Hlādinī-śakti provides greater happiness to Him when it resides in the heart of a devotee? Śrī Jīva explains this with reference to the example of the flute and the flute-player. The flute-player is capable of producing a whistling sound, which is pleasing to the ear, by blowing air out of his mouth. But when he blows the same air into the flute and makes it pass through its different holes, it produces a melodious sound, which is more pleasing than the whistling sound produced by him without the aid of the flute. Similarly the Hlādinī-śakti has a relish of its own, which is sweet beyond description when it resides in Kṛṣṇa, but its sweetness increases a thousand-fold, when it is implanted in the heart of the devotee. The devotees have a passionate desire to serve Kṛṣṇa according to their different *bhāvas* (sentiment). The Hlādinī-śakti mixes with the different *bhāvas* of the devotees and their passionate desire to serve Kṛṣṇa and aquires a variegation (*vaicitrī*), which makes it so astonishingly sweet that even Kṛṣṇa is charmed by it. Therefore He always implants Hlādinī-śakti in the hearts of His devotees, who desire to serve Him.'[2]

Svarūpa-śaktyānanda is also of two kinds: Aiṣvaryānanda and Mānasānanda. The dominant aspect of a devotee's realisation of Kṛṣṇa may either be his knowledge of the Aiṣvarya (power) of Kṛṣṇa or his knowledge of the Mādhurya (sweetness) of Kṛṣṇa. The Kṛṣṇa-prīti (love of Kṛṣṇa) of devotees in whom the knowledge of His Aiṣvarya predominates is naturally *prīti* mixed with the knowledge of Aiṣvarya (*aiṣvarya-jnāna-misrā-prīti*). The *ānanda* which Kṛṣṇa derives from such Prīti is called Aiṣvaryānanda. Prīti is always shy before Aiṣvaryajnāna. It flows freely where Aiṣvarya-jnāna is absent. The more the Aiṣvarya-jnāna the less is the intensity of Prīti.

Prīti dominated by Aiṣvarya-jnāna is enjoyable, because there is also an element of Mādhurya in it. But it is not as enjoyable as Prīti dominated by Mādhurya-jnāna. There are also devotees, who have no Aiṣvarya-jnāna at all. Kṛṣṇa to them is not the great Lord, the all powerful creater, destroyer, and sustainer of the universe, but only a sweet and loving person having all the ordinary human wants and weaknesses. Their Prīti is relished by Kṛṣṇa more than anything else. The Ānanda, which

[1] *Pr. S*, 62.
[2] ibid, 65.

Kṛṣṇa derives from it is called Mānasānanda.

In Paravyoma Prīti is entirely dominated by Aiṣvarya. In Dvārakā and Mathurā it is governed by Mādhurya more than by Aiṣvarya. But in Gokula and Vṛndāvana it is entirely governed by Mādhurya. This does not mean that in Gokula and Vṛndāvana there is no Aiṣvarya. Both Aiṣvarya and Mādhurya are present here in there most perfect form. But Mādhurya has the natural tendency to cover and conceal Aiṣvarya. Mādhurya in its highest form envelops Aiṣvarya completley. Therefore in Paravyoma, Bhagavān enjoys Aiṣvaryānanda; in Dvārakā and Mathurā He enjoys Aiṣvaryānanda, which is mixed with Mādhurya; but in Gokula and Vṛndāvana He enjoys pure Mānasānanda. In Vṛndāvana Mādhurya is intensified because of the birth and other Līlās of Kṛṣṇa, which are not manifested in Gokula. Therefore the Ānanda of Vṛndāvana is superior to the Ānanda of Gokula.

The highest development of Prīti is possible only when neither Bhagavān nor His devotees are conscious of His Divinity. This is possible only in Vraja, where He has the two-armed human form (*narākṛti*). In Vraja, though in reality Para-brahman, He has the natural conceit of being an ordinary human being; though in reality eternal and without any beginning or birth, He knows Himself as the son of Nanda and Yaśodā and Nanda and Yaśodā as His parents. The style of His dress, which is like that of a cow-herd boy, the peacock feather, which He is fond of wearing as His crown, and His flute are all the emblems of Mādhurya, not of Aiṣvarya. Therefore the *prīti-rasa* of Vraja is the highest *rasa* and the *līlā* of Vraja is the highest *līlā.*[1]

How much the Lord enjoys the *prīti*, which is completly free from Aiṣvarya-jnāna and unrestricted by a feeling of reverence towards Him is evident from His exhortation to Prahlāda, as described in *Haribhaktisudhodaya*. The Lord says to Prahlāda, "Because you think of me as the great Lord you have a feeling of fear and reverence towards me. Give up all fear and reverence. For I do not like this kind of attitude. Let your love for me be free from all constraints. Although I am Pūrṇakāma (free from all desires) I have a craving for the love of my devotees, who are wholly free in their talk and behaviour with me. I am attracted by their *prītī*, in which I always find a new relish. Though eternally free I am eternally a captive in their hearts."[2] About such devotees Kṛṣṇa once said to Durvāsā, "The devotees are my heart and I am the heart of my devotees. The devotees do not recognise anyone except me and I do not

[1] *śrī kṛṣṇera jateka khelā sarvottama nara-līlā,*
naravapu tāhāra svarūpa/
gopaveśa veṇukara, nava-kiśora natavara,
nara līlā haya anurūpa// CC, 11, 21, 83.

[2] *Haribhaktisudhodaya*, xiv, 27-30.

recognise anyone except them."[1]

The union of love between Kṛṣṇa and His devotee does not imply a monistic union in which the devotee completely loses his identity. It is, as Śrī Jīva explains, like the union between fire and a piece of iron. A piece of iron when put for a long time in fire becomes red hot like fire. Every part of it is permiated by fire and aquires the characteristics of fire. Still iron remains iron and fire remains fire. Similarly both Kṛṣṇa and the devotee retain their identity. They are so absorbed in each other's love and lost in each other's thought that there is hardly any room in their hearts for the thought of anything else.

The union of love implies that neither Kṛṣṇa nor the devotee has any freedom in respect of each other. Each is a tool in the hands of the other. Each is subservient to the other. Kṛṣṇa's subservience to His devotee is evident from the *Bhāgavata Śloka* in which He says, "Even though free in all respects, I am subservient to my devotee, as if I have no freedom at all."[2]

It is Kṛṣṇa's craving for Mānasānanda that makes him subservient to His devotee. Indeed subservience to the devotee is an essential condition of the generation of Mānasānanda. By His very nature as Rasa He is eternally a slave of His devotees. He is above everything but not above Prema. He controles everything, but is controlled by Prema.

An example will make this clear. Yaśodā chastises the child Kṛṣṇa for swallowing clay. Kṛṣṇa denies having done so, whereupon Yaśodā asks Him to open His mouth. As He opens His mouth she sees in it the entire universe, including herself. This manifestation of Aiśvarya leaves the motherly affection (*vātsalya-prema*) of Yaśodā unaffected. She still regards Kṛṣṇa as her dear child, who stands in need of all her care and protection, and attributes the vision of His unlimited Aiśvarya to some kind of error in her own perception. Kṛṣṇa's Aiśvarya does not make Yaśodā's Prema shrink. It fails to arouse in her a reverential attitude towards Kṛṣṇa. On the other hand it is Yaśodā's Prema that makes Kṛṣṇa's Aiśvarya shrink Kṛṣṇa forgets all about His Divinity and its unlimited Aiśvarya. He is compelled to regard Himself as a child born of Yaśodā, depending entirely upon her care and protection for His welfare and happiness. It is not that He pretends like this to Himself and to others. It is natural for Him to think and act like this under the spell of the Prema of Yaśodā. For such is the controlling power of *prema* in relation to Him.[3]

[1]*sādhvo hṛdayaṁ mahyaṁ sādhunāṁ hṛdayantvaham/*
madanyatte na jānanti nāhaṁ tebhyo manāgapi// *Bh.*, ix, 4, 68.

[2]*ahaṁ bhakta parādhīno hyasvatantra iva dvija/*
sādhubhirgrastahṛdayo bhktairbhaktajanāpriyaḥ// *Bh.*, ix, 4, 63.

[3]*bhaktivaṣaḥ puruṣaḥ; bhaktireva bhūyasīta. Māṭhara Śruti.*

It is important to note that subjugation by *prema-bhakti* is not a defect or shortcoming in Kṛṣṇa but an embellishment.[1] For it is on account of this that He is enabled to enjoy the highest Rasa.

As we have said before Śrī Kṛṣṇa is the embodiment of all the different kinds of Rasa (*akhilā-rasāmṛta-mūrti*). Each one of the infinite partial manifestations of Kṛṣṇa is the embodiment of a particular kind of Rasa. Each manifestation is enjoyable as Rasa and enjoyer as Rasika. Through each manifestation Kṛṣṇa enjoys separately the Svarupānanda and Śaktyānanda of that manifestation. But in the Svarūpānanda and Śaktyānanda of His own personality (*svayaṁ-rūpa*) is included the Svarūpānanda and the Śaktyānanda of all the different partial manifestations. Therefore His own form is so sweet that even Nārāyaṇa, the Lord of Paravyoma and His consort Lakṣmī feel attracted by it.[2]

For the sake of variety in Rasa Kṛṣṇa manifests from His Svarūpa-śakti His infinite retinue (*parikaras*). Each partial manifestation of Kṛṣṇa has its own retinue. Each of the retinue is conditioned by the special kind of Prīti of which that particular manifestation is the embodiment. Each manifestation enjoys through its retinue its Svarūpa-śaktyānanda.

All the divine activities (*līlās*) of Śrī Kṛṣṇa are due to the spontaneous swelling, as it were, of the infinite ocean of Rasa of which He is the embodiment. The activities are caused by Rasa and augment Rasa. Whatever Kṛṣṇa does adds to His enjoyment of bliss as well as to the enjoyment of bliss by His devotees.

Kṛṣṇa himself says, "All the different activities I perform are intended to cause happiness to my devotees."[3] This is natural in love. Kṛṣṇa loves His devotees as much as they love Him. Just as the devotees always aim at the happiness of Kṛṣṇa, Kṛṣṇa always aims at the happiness of His devotees. His manifestation of Himself in various different forms is also for the sake of the happiness of His devotees. The devotees have different kinds of relish (*ruci*). Each devotee worships Him according to his own relish. Therefore Kṛṣṇa has to appear before His devotees in different forms according to their different kinds of relish.[4]

Kṛṣṇa causes happiness to His devotees in two ways: by passing into their hearts His Hlādinī-śakti, which takes the form of Prīti and enables them to enjoy Prīti-rasa; and by Himself residing in their hearts in the particular form, which they meditate upon, and enabling them to enjoy His Svarūpānanda. The devotees enjoy His Svarūpānanda in His proximity in the same way in which we enjoy the warmth of fire in its proximity.

[1] Kṛṣṇa's subjugation by *bhakti* does not imply His loss of freedom, because *bhakti* is a function of His own Hlādinī-śakti.

[2] *CC*, II, 21, 88.

[3] *madbhaktānāṁ vinodārthaṁ karomi vividhāḥ kriyāh. Padma-purāṇa.*

[4] *ye yathā māṁ prapadyante tāṁstathaiva bhajāmyahaṁ. Gītā.*

in winter.

But as we have said above Kṛṣṇa Himself experiences the highest bliss in causing happiness to His devotees. Therefore the different forms in which He appears in the hearts of His devotees to enable them to enjoy the different kinds of Rasa are also the forms through which He Himself enjoys the different kinds of Rasa.

The person, who enjoys Rasa is either the *Viṣaya* or the *Āśraya* of *Rasa.* The person in whom *Prīti* inheres or the person who loves is called *Āśraya* of *Prīti* and the person towards whom *Prīti* is directed or the person, who is loved, is called the *Viṣaya* of *Prīti.* Kṛṣṇa is both the *Viṣaya* and *Āśraya* of *Prīti,* since according to the *Gītā* text "*ye yathā māṁ prapadyante tāṁstathaiva bhajāmyahaṁ*" Kṛṣṇa loves his devotees in the same manner in which they love Him.[1] But He is only the Viṣaya and not the *Āśraya*[2] of the highest kind of *Prīti* called Mādana of which Śrīmatī Rādhā is the only Viṣaya.[3] Therefore Kṛṣṇa is known primarily as *Viṣaya* and not as *Āśraya.*

The Mādhurya (Sweetness) of Śrī Kṛṣṇa

Anything that is relishable or enjoyable is Madhura. Kṛṣṇa as Rasa is supremely enjoyable. Therefore He is Madhura. Mādhurya or sweetness is the very essence of his nature.[4] But the Śrutis describe both *Mādhurya* (sweetness) and *Aiśvarya* (power) as equally qualifying the Svarūpa-śakti of Para-brahman Śrī Kṛṣṇa. How is it then that Mādhurya alone is regarded as the essence of His perfection?

It is because Kṛṣṇa's Mādhurya is due to His Hlādinī-śakti. The function of Hlādinī-śakti is Prema, which governs Kṛṣṇa. Therefore Hlādinī-śakti governs all other Śaktis of Kṛṣṇa, including His Aiśvarya-śakti. We have seen how, in the case of Yaśodā, Aiśvarya is governed by Mādhurya. Even in ordinary life we find that Aiśvarya does not have as much power to govern as Mādhurya. A king can make a man captive by his power, but he can win his heart and soul only by his sweet behaviour.

Mādhurya is the intrinsic quality (*svarūpa-lakṣaṇa*) of Bhagvān; Aiśvarya is His accidental quality (*taṭastha-lakṣaṇa*). There is no Aiśvarya in the impersonal form of Bhagavān, because it is wholly devoid of Śakti. But it is not without any Mādhurya. Its Mādhurya manifests itself in the form of Brahmānanda, which is so attractive and intoxicating that it

[1] *nānā bhaktera rasāmṛta nānā vidha haya/*
sei saba rasāmṛtera viṣaya āśraya// *CC*, II, 8, 111.

[2] U.N., Sthāyī, 155.

[3] *sei premāra śrī rādhikā parama āśraya/*
sei premāra āmi hai kevala viṣaya// *CC*, I, 4, 114.

[4] *CC*, II, 21, 92.

makes the Jīvas, who attain Sāyujya Mukti (state of union with Brahman) forget their very existence.

Aiśvarya seems to predominate in Paravyoma. But that is not because it overpowers Mādhurya. It is because Mādhurya does not fully manifest itself in Paravyoma. It does not manifest itself in order that Bhagavān, Who is the repository of all the different types of Rasas in their highest form, may enjoy Aiśvaryānanda or the happiness that is experienced in the manifestation and exercise of power. If it is believed that Mādhurya in Paravyoma is dominated by Aiśvarya, the Śruti text '*bhaktireva bhūyasī*' would have no meaning.

Similarly the dominance of Mādhurya in Vraja does not imply the absence of Aiśvarya. Since Kṛṣṇa of Vraja is the Divine in His most perfect form, all the divine Śaktis are fully realised in Him. Aiśvarya is, therefore, also present in Him in its highest form. But it is completely dominated by Mādhurya. It manifests itself only when it must for the unfoldment of the divine Līlā, and its manner of manifestation is such that Mādhurya is not only preserved but hightened and Kṛṣṇa's conceit as the fond child of Nanda and Yaśodā or an ordinary cowherd-boy remains unchanged. For example, when Pūtanā, the female demon, comes to Vraja in the guise of a beautiful lady to kill the child Kṛṣṇa by making Him suck at her breast smeared with poison, the Aiśvarya-śakti of Kṛṣṇa comes to know of her evil intention and manifests itself through Viṣṇu, a part and *parcel* of His Divine Personality. The result is that Kṛṣṇa sucks her life through her breast without even being aware of it. For it is actually Viṣṇu and not Kṛṣṇa, who kills Pūtanā. He only uses Kṛṣṇa's organs to do this. It is like the king's officials using his power and authority to punish a wrong doer, while he is enjoying a meal in his palace and is not aware of what is going on outside. When Pūtanā dies and lies on the ground with her develish form thoroughly exposed, He is still seen playing joyfully with her breasts as if nothing has happened.[1] The functioning of the Aiśvarya-śakti does not minimise His Mādhurya. Nor does it change the attitude of Yaśodā and the other Gopīs, who still regard Him as their fond child standing so much in need of their care and protection. They regard this episode as a bad omen for the child and take immediate steps to ward off its evil effects.[2]

Everything pertaining to Kṛṣṇa is sweet. But Śrī Rūpa Gosvāmin has specially described the sweetness of (a) His Līlā, (b) His Prema, (c) His Veṇu (flute) and (d) His Rūpa (beauty)[3]:

Līlā-Mādhurya: Bhagavān performs different kinds of Līlā in different *dhāmas*. But His Līlā in Vraja excels all other Līlās in Mādhurya, be-

[1] *Bh.*, X, 6, 18.
[2] *See* Sanātana Gosvāmin's *Tīkā* on *Bh.*, X, 13, 18 and X, 14, 42.
[3] *Bh. R. S.*, 1, 17-18.

cause His subjugation by love (*prema-vaśyatā*) is the highest in Vraja. Of the Līlās of Vraja the Rāsa-Līlā excels all others, because it provides an excellent combination of all the different kind of Rasa. Kṛṣṇa Himself says in connection with Rāsa-līlā, "There is no end to my Madhura-līlās. But the Mādhurya and the charm of Rāsa-līla is unique. Not to speak of the bliss I experience in my actual participation in it, the very idea of the Rāsa-līlā puts me in a blissful state of mind, which I cannot describe."[1]

Prema-mādhurya: Reference here is mainly to the Prema-mādhurya of the *Parikaras* (retinue) of Śrī Kṛṣṇa. The Mdāhurya of Kṛṣṇa is relative to the Prema of His Parikaras. In the soothing and enchanting light of their Prema the Aiśvarya of Kṛṣṇa shrinks and His Mādhurya bursts and blooms, in the same manner in which in the light of the full moon the ocean swells and the tides flow. The Prema of Yaśodā makes the all powerful and all-pervading Kṛṣṇa allow Himself to be tied by her; the Prema of Nanda makes Him carry his shoes over His head; the Prema of His companions makes Him carry them on His shoulders; the Prema of the wives of the ṛṣis makes Him beg for food at their door step; the Prema of the Gopīs of Vraja makes Him roll at their feet. The Prema of the Gopīs is so powerful that it makes Kṛṣṇa dance to their tune like a straw cast to and fro by the waves of an ocean in strom.[2] And the *ānanda* He experiences in dancing to their tune is even superior to the most concentrated form of *ānanda*, which He enjoys in His own self.

Veṇu-mādhurya: The Mādhurya of Śrī Kṛṣṇa's flute is uniqe and indescribable. *Laghubhāgavatāmṛta* tries to give an inkling of it by saying that even an iota of the sweetness of Kṛṣṇa's flute is superior to the sweetness of all the sweet sounds of the world put together. The bliss caused by the sound of the flute is so intense and penetrating that it reverses the functions of the animate and the inanimate objects. The animate objects become steady and motionless like the inanimate objects and the inanimate objects become dynamic and mobile like the animate objects.[3] The *Bhāgavata* says that on hearing the sound of the flute the mountains begin to shake, the rivers become still, the trees develop signs of spiritual emotions (*sāttvika bhāvas*)[4] and the milk-maids of Vraja begin to run in the direction of the sound, forgetting all about their body and mind, their pride and prestige and the ordinary norms and duties of their family and society.[5]

[1] *santi yadyapi me prājyā līlāstāstā manoharāḥ/*
nahi jāne smṛte rāse mano me kīdṛśaṁ bhaveta// *Bṛhadvāmana-purāṇa* text cited in *Bh. R. S.* II, 1, 111.

[2] *kṛṣṇere nacāya prema, bhaktere nācāya/* *CC*, III, 18. 17.

[3] *L. Bh.*., *Kṛṣṇāmṛta*, 812-13.

[4] *Bh.*, X, 35, 8-9.

[5] ibid, x, 29, 40.

Rūpa-mādhurya: The Mādhurya of Śrī Kṛṣṇa's beauty is also indescribable.[1] Rādhā describes Kṛṣṇa as an ocean of beauty. Even her mind, which is as unshakable as a mountain, is easily swept away by the powerful waves of that ocean and remains submerged in it.[2] Kṛṣṇa Himself feels so much attracted by it that He longs very much to enjoy it.[3]

But a special feature of the Mādhurya of Śrī Kṛṣṇa's beauty is that it increases concomitantly with the Mādhurya of the Prema of His devotee. Since the Prema of Śrīmati Rādhikā is the highest, the beauty of Śrī Kṛṣṇa comes to a climax when He is in her company. Kṛṣṇa in the company of Rādhā is, therefore, called Madanamohana or One, Who has the capacity to charm even Cupid, who charms every one else:

rādhāsaṅge yathā bhāti tadā madanamohanaḥ/ *Govinda-līlāmṛta*, viii, 32.

The Manner and Purpose of Kṛṣṇa's appearance on Earth

Kṛṣṇa was not born of Devakī or Yaśodā like an ordinary person under the influence of Prakṛti or the law of Karma to reap the fruits of His past deeds. His birth, like all His other activities is supernatural.[4] His body is not material. It is made of *sat* (existence), *cit* (consciousness) and *ānanda* (bliss) and is eternal. Therefore, truly speaking, the question of His birth does not arise. He does not actually take birth, but *appears* to do so under the influence His Yogamāyā-śakti (creative power) for the sake of Līlā. He does not actually enter the womb of Devakī but her heart. But Yogamāyā makes all the signs of a pregnant lady, giving birth to a child, appear on her body so that she thinks that she actually gives birth to a child.[5]

Viṣṇupurāṇa argues that Kṛṣṇa was not born but He appeared, because there was no change in Him after His appearance. Before and after His appearance He was the same—the ground and support (*āśraya*) of the whole universe. Due to His inconceivable power (*acintya-śakti*). He appeared in the heart of Devakī in a limited form, still He was the same unlimited (*aparicchinna*) being as before.[6]

Devakī herself was not a manifestation of the Jīva-tattva. She was a concrete manifestation of Śuddha-sattva (pure existence) or rather of Svarūpa-śakti as dominated by Saṁdhinī-śakti, the energy which upholds all existence.

The whole story of Kṛṣṇa's birth is supernatural. He was born of

[1] *Kṛṣṇakarṇāmṛta*, 92.

[2] *Govinda-līlāmṛta*, VIII, 3.

[3] *rūpa dekhi āpanāra kṛṣnera haya camatkāra, āsvādite mane uṭhe kāma*/ *CC*, 11, 21, 86.

[4] *Bh.*, III, 2, 12.

[5] *janma nityasiddhasya eva mama saccidānandaghanasya līlayā tathānukaraṇaṁ.* Śrīdhara's commentary on *Gītā*, IV, 9.

[6] *Viṣṇupurāṇa*, V, 2, 12-20.

both Yaśodā and Devakī at the same time on an Aśtamī day (the eighth day of a lunar fortnight)—of Yaśodā as the two-armed Yaśodānandana (son of Yaśodā) and of Devakī as the four-armed Devakīnandana (son of Devakī). Shortly after, the same night but on the Navamī *tithi* (the ninth day of lunar fortnight) Yaśodā gave birth to Yogamāyā, the younger sister of Kṛṣṇa. Thus Yaśodā gave birth to two children on the same night. But, surprisingly enough, she was not at all aware of the birth of the second child. For she was asleep when the second child was born. But when Vasudeva came to the bedroom of Yaśodā, he saw only Yogamāyā. He did not see Kṛṣṇa. He left his son Devakīnandana on her bed and carried Yogamāyā with him. When, however, Yaśodā woke up, she saw neither Yogamāyā nor Devakīnandana. She saw only Kṛṣṇa. No one in Gokula came to know of the birth of Yogamāyā or her replacement by Devakinandana, since every one was asleep[1] when this happened and Devakīnandana got merged in Yaśodānandana as soon as Vasudeva placed Him on Yaśodā's bed or as soon as he entered her room.[2]

It is true that *Ṣrīmad-bhāgavata* does not make any direct mention of Kṛṣṇa's having been born of Yaśodā, but the fact is clearly indicated by it by use of such terms as '*nandātmaja*'[3] (the real son of Nanda) and Nanda's '*angaja*'[4] (born from the body of Nanda) for Kṛṣṇa and '*anuja*'[5] (the younger sister of Kṛṣṇa) for Yogamāyā.

As regards the purpose of His appearance Śrī Kṛṣṇa says in *Gītā* that He appears in every age to protect the good and punish the wicked.[6] But *Caitanya-caritāmṛta* says that this is not the function of Kṛṣṇa; it is the function of His partial manifest Viṣṇu, the sustainer (*pālana-kartā*) of the universe.[7] *Śrīmad-bhāgavata* also says that it is not Kṛṣṇa, but His partial manifestations, the Yugāvatāras, who appear from age to age to relieve the world from sin. Kṛṣṇa appears only in the Dvāpara Yuga of the twenty-eighth Caturyuga of the Vaivasvata Manavantara.[8] The Yugāvatāra does not appear independently in the Yuga in which Kṛṣṇa appears. For He is already present in Kṛṣṇa as a part of His infinite personality and performs the function of the Yugāvatara through the medium of the body of Kṛṣṇa.[9]

[1] *Viṣṣnupurāna*, V, 3, 20.
[2] *Vaiṣnavatoṣaṇī Tīkā* of Sanātana Gosvāmin on *Bh.*, X, 5, 1.
[3] ibid, X, 8, 14. [4] ibid, X, 14, 1. [5] ibid, X, 5, 1.
[6] *paritrānāya sādhunāṁ vināśāya ca duṣkratāṁ|*
dharma saṁsthāpanārthāya saṁbhavāmi yuge yuge|| *Gītā*, IV, 8.
[7] *svayaṁ bhagavānera karma nahe bhāra haraṇa|*
sthiti-kartā viṣṇu kare jagata-pālana|| *CC*, 1, 4, 7.
[8] *See* p.
[9] *ataeva viṣṇu takhana kṛṣṅera śarīre|*
viṣṇu dvāre kare kṛṣna asura saṁhāre|| *CC*, I, 4, 12.

Therefore the *Gītā* Śloka referred to above should be understood in the sense that it is not Kṛṣṇa Himself but Kṛṣṇa in the form of His partial manifestations who comes down from age to age to relieve the suffering of the world. The purpose of Kṛṣṇa's own appearance in the Vaivasvata Manavantara must be different. It must be something which is beyond the capacity of His partial manifestations.

Bhāgavata says that the purpose of His appearance is to impart Bhakti to the fallen souls (*bhaktiyoga vidhānārtha*)[1]; not the ordinary type of Bhakti, which aims at Mukti, but Rāgānugā-bhakti, which consists in intense loving attachment to Kṛṣṇa called Prema. Mukti can be given by any of the partial manifestations of Bhagavān including the Yugāvatāras, but Prema can be given only by Śrī Kṛṣṇa:

santvatārā bahavaḥ puṣkaranābhasya sarvatobhadrāḥ|
Kṛṣṇādanyaḥ ko vā latātvapi premado bhavati||
L. Bh., *Pūrvakhaṁda*,V, 37.

Kṛṣṇa is naturally anxious to impart Rāgānugā-bhakti, because He is so merciful and He knows that unless He comes down on earth to impart it there is no other means by which the Jīvas may attain it and enjoy His unlimited Mādhurya.[2]

Brahmā said to Kṛṣṇa in his *Stuti* (hymn of praise) after the Brahmamohana-līlā, "My Lord, You are beyond *prapañca* or the phenomenal world. Yet you come down on earth and perform activities like the phenomenal activities of those bound by *prapañca* in order that the persons, who have taken refuge in You may enjoy the unlimited *ānanda* of Your Līlā's."[3] Kṛṣṇa Himself says that whatever He does is to cause happiness to his devotees:

"*madbhaktānāṁ vinodārthaṁ karomi vividhāḥ kriyāḥ*" *Padma-purāṇa*.

But it is not only for the sake of His devotees that He comes down. He also comes for the sake of the people who are averse (*bahirmukha*) to Him. The object of His Madhura-līlā on the phenomenal plane is that even those who are averse to Him may feel attracted to Him by reading or hearing them:

anugrahāya bhaktānāṁ mānuṣaṁdehamāsṛitāh
bhajate tādṛśīḥ krīṇā yāḥ srutvā tatparo bhavet| *Bh.* X, 33, 37.

But there is a deeper reason for Kṛṣṇa's appearance on earth. He appears not only to give but also to gain. But is there anything that He

[1] *Bh.*, I, 8, 30.
[2] *kṛṣṇa-kṛpādi hetu haite svabhāva udaya|*
kṛṣṇaguṇākṛṣṭa haiyā tahāre bhajaya|| *CC*, II, 24, 135.
brahmānda bhramite kona bhāgyavāna jīva|
guru-kṛṣṇa prasāde pāya bhakti-latā-bīja|| *CC*, II, 19, 133.
[3] *prapañcaṁ niṣprapañco'pi vidambayasi bhūtale|*
prapannajanatānanda sandohaṁ prathituṁ prabho|| *Bh.*, X, 14, 37.

may gain? Is He not already perfect? He is undoubtedly perfect in knowledge, perfect in power, perfect in goodness, perfect in love. But the very nature of His perfection in love imposes a strange kind of limitation upon Him. Truly speaking, love can never be perfect though it may be limitless.[1] By its very nature it is imperfect. It is never satisfied with itself. The more love one has the more one longs for it. Love is essentially dynamic. It is ever growing, ever trying to overreach itself. This, at any rate, is spiritual love or Prema. Because Kṛṣṇa's love is limitless, His hunger for love is also limitless. To satisfy His limitless hunger His effort is limitless. His descent on earth, time and again, to impart Bhakti is a result of this effort. He descends to impart Bhakti in order that He may have more persons to love and to be loved by.

As we have said before, the love of His devotees has a special charm for Him. He relishes it more than He relishes anything else, than even the Ānanda natural to Him as the concentrated from of Ānanda (*ānanda-ghana*) itself. It provides Him with higher bliss or Rasa. He does not enjoy His lording it over the infinite universes of which He is the master as much as He enjoys being lorded over in love by His devotees. He does not enjoy His omnipresence as much as He enjoys His presence as an infant in the lap of mother Yaśodā. He does not enjoy embracing the universe as much as He enjoys to be lost in the loving embrace of the milkmaids of Vraja. He is not pleased so much when the Vedas and the gods sing His praises as He is pleased when His playmates in Vraja—Śrīdāma, Sudāma, Madhumangala and others find fault with him and even scold and reprimand Him in pastimes of love. He does not relish it so much when the gods bow down to Him as when He bows down at the feet of Rādhā on account of her all-absorbing love for Him.

This reason of Kṛṣṇa's appearance is indicated by Kuntī in her Stava to Kṛṣṇa, when she says, "All the sins are easily expiated if only one calls to mind Your Name, yet You consider Yourself a sinner for breaking mother Yaśodā's earthen pot full of curd. You cut asunder at Your will the difficult tie which binds the Jīvas to the world of Māyā yet You, Who are feared by Fear itself, fear mother Yaśodā to see her bent upon tieing You with a cord for breaking her pot, and You stand before her like a culprit with Your head bent low and tears trickling from Your eyes. I cannot but be fascinated when I call to mind Your beautiful figure in that plight." Kuntī obviously indicates that the compulsion which puts Kṛṣṇa in such a plight is nothing except His own strong desire to enjoy the relish of Yaśodā's motherly affection (*vātsalya-rasa*). The strong current of Yaśodā's love for Kṛṣṇa makes Him forget completely His infinite greatness, power and perfection and enables Him to relish her

[1]Śrī Jīva: *Śrī Premasamputaḥ*, 51.
[2]*Bh.*, 1, 8, 31.

vātsalya prema by compelling Him to behave like her child.

Thus the purpose of Kṛṣṇa's appearance is two-fold. He appears in order that He may propagate Rāgānugā-bhakti and His devotees may enjoy *prema-rasa* as well as His *mādhurya*, and in order that He may Himself enjoy the Prema-rasa of His devotees.

prema-rasa niryāsa bhaktera karite āsvādana|
rāga-mārga-bhakti loke karite pracāraṇa|| *CC*, I, 4, 14.

Accordingly the causes of His appearance are two: His *rasikaśekharatva* (nature as the Supreme enjoyer of Rasa) and His *parama-karuṇatva* (nature as the most Merciful Being):

rasika śekhara kṛṣṇa parama-karuṇa|
ei dui hetu haite icchāra udgama|| *CC*, 1, 4, 15.

These two reasons of Kṛṣṇa's appearance may outwardly seem to be incompatible. The reason must either be His benevolent attitude towards the souls in bondage or it must be His desire to enjoy the Rasa, the supreme bliss caused by the loving service of His devotees. He must either aim at His own happiness or the happiness of the souls in bondage. He cannot be both self-seeking and self-sacrificing or merciful, in one and the same act. Therefore one of these reasons must be primary and the other secondary.

It may be supposed that because Kṛṣṇa is both *rasa* (bliss) and *rasikaśekhara* (the supreme enjoyer of bliss) the primary reason of His appearance is His desire to enjoy the highest of all *rasas*, the *prema-rasa* of His devotees. His mercy towards the Jīvas in imparting Bhakti is, therefore, motivated by His own desire to enjoy their Prema.

But the idea of Kṛṣṇa's *rasikaśekharatva* being the primary cause of His appearance is neither compatible with His mercy towards the Jīvas, which the scriptures describe as causeless, nor with His Prema for His devotees. Prema by its very nature is other-regarding, not self-regarding. Premika or the person who loves, aims always at the happiness of the *premāspada*, the person who is loved.[1]

Kṛṣṇa as Premika does not desire anything except the happiness of His devotees. Just as devotees care only for His happiness, Kṛṣṇa cares only for the happiness of His devotees. Kṛṣṇa's concern for the happiness of His devotees is an expression of His mercifulness, which, thus, seems to acquire greater importance in His character than His *rasikaśekharatva*.

But the opposition between these two aspects of Kṛṣṇa's nature is only apparent. Kṛṣṇa's mercy is not like the ordinary act of mercy, which involves some costraint or sacrifice. His mercy is natural and spontaneous. By being merciful He does not lose but gains. His mercy is like the mercy

[1] *prīti viṣayānande āśrayānanda|*
tahan nahi nijasukhavāñchāra sambandha|| *CC*, I, 4, 169.

of the mother, who feeds the child with the milk of her breast. The feed gives satisfaction to both the mother and the child. Similarly Kṛṣṇa experiences bliss in the very act of mercy, which prompts Him to come down to the world to impart Bhakti.

The mother feeds the child, because she cannot help doing it. She feeds him, because she would be unhappy if she did not do it. Similarly Kṛṣṇa is merciful, because He cannot help being merciful. He would be unhappy if He was not merciful. His mercy is the kind of mercy that blesses the person, who gives, as well as the person, who receives.

Kṛṣṇa as Rasa is essentially dynamic. Though perfect in all respects, He is always growing and changing in Rasa. Mercy is an essential part of His dynamic nature. In every act of mercy He realises Himself as a better, a higher and a happier self. Every act of mercy for Him is, therefore, also an act of self-fulfilment and of self-transcedence in bliss.

CHAPTER IX

Jīva—The Finite Self

The *Avatāras*, we have described above, are the non-differentiated manifestation (*svāṁśa-rūpa*) of Kṛṣṇa. But the Jīvas are His differentiated partial manifestation (*vibhinnāṁśa-rūpa*) (*CC*, Madhya, XXII, 6). The *Avatāras* are the manifestation of His own self while the Jīvas are the manifestation of His Jīva-śakti or Taṭasthā-śakti.[1] The Taṭasthā-śakti is distinct from both Svarūpa-śakti and Māyā-śakti, but is closely connected with them both, just as the Taṭa or bank is distinct from both land and sea, but is connected with them both (*CC*, Madhya, XX, 101). The *Avatāras* share the perfection and power of Kṛṣṇa and are beyond the influence of *Māyā*. But the *Jīvas*, like the bank which may form a part of the sea or the land, according as there is a rise or fall in the sea, are subject to the influence of both the Svarūpa-śakti and the Māyā-śakti. As parts of the Taṭasthā-śakti they are themselves described as Śakti in relation to which Kṛṣṇa is described as Śaktimān. The following verses from *Gītā* and *Viṣṇupurāṇa* are cited in support of this:

apareyamitastvanyāṁ prakṛtiṁ viddhi me parāṁ|
Jīvabhūtāṁ mahābāho yayedaṁ dhāryate jagat||

Gītā, 7, 5, cited in *CC*, Ādi, vii, Ś 6.

viṣṇuḥ śakti parāproktā kṣetrajnyākhvā tathāparā|
avidyākarmasaṁjnāñyā tṛtīyā śaktiriṣyate||

Viṣṇupurāṇa, 6, 7, 61, cited in *CC*, Ādi, vii, Ś 7.

The Jīva is not simply intelligence or attributeless self-shining consciousness (*svaprakāśa caitanya*) identical with Brahman, which is neither knower, nor doer, nor enjoyer, as maintained by the Advaitavādins. Though a manifestation of the Śakti of Brahman, it has a distinct metaphysical reality of its own, and has knowledge, action, and enjoyment (*jnātṛtva-kartṛtva-bhoktṛtva*) as its attributes.

Śrī Jīva Gosvāmin describes the attributes of Jīva somewhat in detail.[2]

[1]S.N. Das Gupta translates *taṭasthā* as 'neutral,' which signifies that the *Jīva-Śakti* stands equally apart from both *Svarūpa-śakti* and *Māyā-śakti*. But this is not very accurate. For though the *Jīva* is free to surrender either to *Svarūpa-śakti* or to *Māyā-śakti*, and may choose to serve *Māyā* under ignorance, its intrinsic nature is to serve Kṛṣṇa under the guidence of *Svarūpa-śakti*.

[2]*Par. S.* 19.

In his description of the attributes of *Jīva* Śrī Jīva follows Jāmatra Muni of the Viśiṣṭādvaita school, who lived before Rāmānuja.

According to him, the Jīva is self-luminous (*svayaṁ-prakāśa*). Like the light of a lamp, it reveals itself as well as the objects falling within the focus of its consciousness. Its luminosity, however, is derived from Paramātman, who alone is self-luminous in the real sense. It is called self-luminous only in contrast with the material objects (*jaṇa-pratiyogitvena*),[1] which neither reveal themselves nor anything else.

It is atomic (*aṇu*) in size. It is so infinitesimally small that it is described as the one-thousandth part of the thickness of a hair:

bālāgraśatabhāgasya śatadhā kalpitasya ca/
bhāgo jīvaḥ sa vijneya iti cāhāparā śrutiḥ//

Śvetāsvatara, cited in *CC*, Madhya, XIX, Ś 16.

But though atomic it has the quality of pervading (*vyāpti-śīlaḥ*) the physical body in which it is temporarily encased.

It is the subject of ego-consciousness (*ahamarthaḥ*). But its ego or *ahaṁ* should not be identified with the *ahaṁ* of the empirical ego, which is the product of *prakrti* and its modifications—the body and the senses. Being the product of *Prakṛti*, the empirical ego is impermanent, impure and liable to suffering. But the pure ego, which is unaffected by Prakṛti is eternal, uniform (*eka-rūpaḥ*), identical with itself (*svarūpa-bhātt*), spiritual, blissful (*cidānandātmakaḥ*) and enternally pure (*nitya-nirmalaḥ*). Birth and death, development and decay, refer to the body in which the Jīva is encased under the influence of Māyā and not to its intrinsic nature, which is eternally the same. The consciousness of bliss is explicit in the case of the released Jīvas, but implicit in the case of the bound Jīvas.

The relation between the Jīvas and Paramātman is described as that of inconceivable identity-in-difference (*acintya-bhedābheda*). It is neither the relation of bare or exclusive identity in which the Jīvas lose their separate existence on the attainment of Mokṣa, nor of complete or exclusive difference, but of both identity and difference. It is identity, because *Paramātman* is the very source and ground of existence of the *Jīvas* and they derive their nature as existence (*sat*), consciousness (*cit*) and bliss (*ānanda*) from him. It is difference, because the *Jīvas* share the nature of *Paramātman* in a very small measure. Existence, knowledge and bliss, in their case, are limited, while in the case of *Paramātman*, they are unlimited. This is natural, because *Jīva* is atomic consciousness (*aṇu caitanya*) while Paramātman is infinite consciousness (*vibhu caitanya*).

The Jīvas are infinite in number (*CC*, Madhya, XIV, 138), and their intrinsic nature is always the same. But there are differences among them according to their past and present deeds and the different positions occupied by them on the mundane or the spiritual plane. Jīvas on the mundane plane are divided into *Sthāvara*, those who cannot move, e.g.,

[1]*Par, S.*, 28.

the trees and *Jaṅgama,* those who can move. The *Jaṅgama* or the moving ones are of three kinds—*Jalacara,* who live and move in water, *Sthalacara,* who live and move on land, and *Tiryak,* who move in the air. Among the *Sthalacara,* the class of human beings is the smallest in number. Very few of the human beings are *Veda-niṣṭha,* or such as profess to follow the Vedas. The rest are Mlekṣa (the untouchables), *Pulinda* (savages), Bauddha and Savara (barbarians). Among the *Veda-niṣṭha* there are those, who follow the vedas in words only (*adharmācārī*) and those who follow them in thought, word, and deed (*dharmācāri*). The latter are mostly Karma-niṣṭha or those who believe in action. Among the Karmaniṣṭha the Jnānī is very rare; among the Jnānīs the *Mukta-puruṣa* or the released soul is rare; and among the *Mukta-puruṣas* the devotee of Kṛṣṇa is rare. The devotee of Kṛṣṇa alone is happy, because he is without any desire. All the rest are unhappy, because they desire either enjoyment (*Bhukti*) or release (*Mukti*) (*CC,* Madhya, XIX, 127-32).

The eternal function of Jīva is to serve Bhagavān (*C. Bh.*, Antya, III, 32). But it has the freedom to serve him or not. On account of the peculiar *Taṭastha* or marginal position occupied by it, between the Svarūpa-śakti and the Māyā-śakti, it is free either to serve Bhagavān by submitting to His Svarūpa-śakti or to enjoy *Prakṛti.* This gives rise to the distinction between the Jīvas, who are released (*Nitya-mukta*) and the Jīvas, who are eternally bound (*Nitya-baddha*) (*CC,* Madhya, XXII, 8). The Jīvas, who choose to serve Kṛṣṇa, the Lord of Māyā (*Māyādhīśa*), are placed eternally beyond the influence of Māyā and are known as *Nityamukta* (*CC,* Madhya, XXII, 9). Those, who do not choose to serve Kṛṣṇa (*bahirmukha*) are eternally under the influence of Māyā and are known as *Nitya-baddha.* The *Nitya-muktas* dwell with Kṛṣṇa as his Pārṣadas or companions in his Dhāman and enjoy the bliss of devotion. The *Nitya-baddhas* are confined within the world, the product of Māyā, and undergo all sorts of suffering and pain (*CC,* Madhya, XXII, 10).

The Baddha-jīva, on account of its aversensess to Kṛṣṇa forgets its real nature as a spiritual being and a servant of Kṛṣṇa. This forgetfulness is brought about by *Māyā,* which is said to have two aspects (*vṛttis*)—*Vidyā* and *Avidyā.* The former makes the Māyā-śakti mercifully inclined towards the *Jīva,* while the latter enables it to give punishment to it for the offence committed in not serving the divine feet of Kṛṣṇa. *Avidyā* also has two Vṛttis—Āvaraṇātmikā, which prevents Jīva's knowledge of it's real nature, and Vikṣepātmikā, which gives rise to a wrong type of knowledge in it—the knowledge that it is the physical body and not the soul (*Dehātma-buddhi*).[1]

Avidyā-māyā draws a two-fold curtain over the *Jīvas.* One is the Liṅga-śarīra or the subtle body and the other is the Sthūla-śarīra or the gross

[1] *Par. S.*, 58.

body. The Liṅga-śarīra consists of the ingredients of *Mana* (mind), *Buddhi* (intelligence), *Cit* (consciousness) and *Ahaṁkāra* (egoism), which are conditioned by Māyā in the case of the Baddha-jīva, but exist in their pure form in the Mukta-jīva. When the veil of the Liṅga-śarīra is cast upon the Jīva, it, for the time being, identifies itself with it. But the Liṅga-śarīra is incapable of action (*karma*) and enjoyment (*bhoga*). Therefore, the Sthūla-śarīra is further imposed on it, which has the effect of intensifying its material consciousness (*Jaṇābhimāna*). Then begins the eternal cycle of births and deaths and the long history of its untold sufferings. According to the good or bad deeds performed by it, it is sometimes raised to heaven and sometimes consigned to hell (*CC*, Madhya, XX, 105). It has to pass, again and again, through eighty-four lacs of cycles of birth and death and, during its sojourn in the world, has to suffer the three pains—*Ādhidaivika* (which proceeds from the gods, e.g., famine and epidemics), *Ādhibhautika* (which proceeds from material causes) and *Ādhyātmika* (which pertains to the mind) (*CC*, Madhya, XXII, II).

But we have seen that the *Jīva*, being a part of Brahman, is essentially of the same nature as Brahman and perfect and eternal happiness belongs to it as one of its intrinsic qualities. Therefore, even while under the influence of *Māyā*, which hides its essential nature from itself, it naturally shuns pain and desires eternal and perfect happiness. But it does not find real and perfect happiness in the objects of the senses; whatever pleasure it derives from them is short-lived and not altogether unmixed with pain. It only has the effect of further strengthening the bond of Māyā. It is only when, as a result of its past good deeds, it finds the company of a saint that its fortune turns. The saint helps it turn away from Māyā by imparting right knowledge and initiating it into Bhakti (*CC*, Madhya, XII, 28-29). In due course it finds the Lord, and as it finds Him it also finds itself reestablished in its eternal nature as the enjoyer of perfect happiness, since the cover of Māyā is removed with the appearance of the Lord, just as the cover of darkness is removed with the rising of the sun. Attainment of the Lord is, therefore, the end (*puruṣārtha*) which every individual must seek. There is no real happiness without it.

The Śāstras, however, mention, besides the attainment of the Lord, four other ends: *Dharma* (virtue), *Artha* (wealth), *Kāma* (sensuous enjoyment), and *Mokṣa* (freedom from bondage). The question naturally arises, if attainment of the Lord is the only true end, why do the Śāstras speak of these? The answer is that the Śāstras do not actually prescribe them as ends. But these are the ends which people actually seek. They are so attached to them that they would not listen to any advice directed against them. The Śāstras say that these ends can be realised if one leads a life according to *Dharma*. The object is not to ask people to seek these ends, but to lead them to the path of *Dharma* by providing these natural incentives (*C. Bh.*, Madhya, XIX, 65-67). But even *Dharma* is not an end in itself. It is desirable and necessary, because unless the natural propensities for *Artha* and *Kāma* are regulated by *Dharma*, the heart is not purified, and, unless the heart is purified, *Mokṣa* cannot be attained. The Advaitins also regard disinterested performance of duties not as an end in itself, but as a means to the attainment of *Mokṣa*. The Śāstras enjoin the renunciation of *Dharma*, which means duties relating to Varṇāśrama, etc., for the sake of *Mokṣa*:

varṇāśramācārayutā vimūḍhaḥ karmānusāreṇa phalaṁ labhante|
varṇādidharmaṁ hi parityajantaḥ svānandatṛptāh puruṣā bhavanti||

Maitreyī-sruti, I, 13.

"The ignorant practise Varṇāśrama Dharma and obtain the fruits of their deeds. But it is only by renouncing Varṇāśrama and the other Dharmas that one can realise one's intrinsic self and enjoy eternal happiness."

In *Gītā* Śrī Kṛṣṇa asks Arjuna to renounce all *Dharmas* and take refuge under him and promises, on his so doing, to absolve him of all sins (and grant *Mokṣa*).[1]

But the Śāstras lay down that one must not renounce *Dharma* until the heart is purified and one develops faith in the Lord and interest in the discourses relating to His divine attributes and Līlā.[6] If *Dharma* is renounced before this state is reached, it will give rise to libertarianism and spell disaster for the individual and the society.

Mokṣa is an end in itself, because it really means the attainment of Bhagavān in some form or other. If, however, *Mokṣa* is taken in the negative sense of mere cessation of suffering or freedom from bondage, it is not regarded as the Ultimate End by Śrī Caitanya, but only as a means to it.

We shall do well to consider the nature of *Mokṣa* or *Mukti* in some detail.

Mukti—Freedom from Bondage

Mukti, according to Nyāya-vaiśeṣika and Sāṁkhya, means cessation of suffering, while according to the Advaitins it means absorption in Brahman. But Śrī Caitanya defines *Mukti* as the attainment of the Jīva's natural state: *Muktirhatvānyathārūpaṁ svarūpeṇa vyavasthitiḥ| Bh.*, 2, 10, 6, cited in *CC*, Madhya, XXIV, 43.

In its natural state the Jīva is a part (*aṁśa*) of Bhagavān and its natural function is to serve Him. The attainment of this state implies (*a*) the attainment of Bhagavān, (*b*) the attainment of bliss, (*c*) the removal

[1]*Gītā*, XVIII, 66.
[2]*Bh.*, I, 20, 9.

of the fetters of *Māyā* and *Karma*, (*d*) the attainment of a state from where there is no possibility of returning to this world, and (*e*) the cessation of all pain and suffering. Bhagavān may be attained in his least-developed form as the impersonal Brahman or in one of his more developed personal forms. The higher the form of Bhagavān attained, the higher is the bliss experienced by the *Jīva*. *Mukti* is thus a positive state of bliss and not simply cessation of suffering. When Bhagavān is attained in his impersonal form as Brahman, the *Jīva* has an experience of absorption in it. But the absorption is not complete or real. The separate identity of the *Jīva* is always maintained because of the essential nature of the relationship between it and Bhagavān, which, we have seen, is that of identity in difference. But the *Jīva* is so immersed in the bliss of Brahman that it becomes unaware of its identity.

The Advaitin's view that on attaining *Mukti* the *Jīva* becomes one with Brahman is based on such scriptural texts as *brahma veda brahmaiva bhavati* (*Mund.*, III, 2, 9). But these texts actually mean that the *Jīva* becomes similar to Brahman and not identical with it. The similarity is in respect of the attributes of bliss and knowledge, which are inherent in the *Jīva*, but are obscured under the influence of *Māyā*. This is confirmed by a number of texts, such as *nirañjanaḥ paramaṁ samyamupaiti* (*Mund.*, III, 1, 3), *idaṁ jnānamupāsritya sadharmyamagataḥ* (*Gītā*, XIV, 2).

The Advaitins maintain that since the *Jīva* loses its identity in the state of absorption in Brahman and no subject of experience is left, there is in the state of Mukti bliss without any feeling or experience of it. The *Jīva* becomes bliss, though it cannot experience it. But such a state of *Mukti* cannot be prescribed as the Highest End, because it is totally uninspiring.[1] Nobody would like to be *Mukta*, if *Mukti* is devoid of any experience. That there is an experience of bliss even on the attainment of Brahman cannot be denied on the basis of the Śāstras, though, it is true, it is very inferior in comparison to the varied and wonderful experience of bliss experienced by the devotee who attains Bhagavān in His personal aspect, in which there is a fuller manifestation of the Svarūpa-śakti. The text *rasaṁ hyevāyaṁ labdhvānandī bhavati* (*Chand.* VII, 25, 2) clearly states that the *Jīva*, on the attainment of Mukti, becomes blissful and not bliss, which means that it continues to be the subject of the experience of bliss.

The attainment of Bhagavān in *Mukti* means a direct experience (*sākṣātkāra*) of him, which may be either an inward experience (*antaḥ sākṣātkāra*) in contemplation or an outward experience (*bahiḥ-*

[1] Śrī Ramakrishna Paramahaṁsa was once asked why he chose to remain in the state of a devotee, though he had attained the state of *Nirvikalpa-samādhi*, or union with Brahman. He replied that instead of becoming sugarcandy he found it more enjoyable to relish it.

sākṣātkāra) involving the mind and the senses.[1] The latter experience is higher because it is more vivid and perspicacious.[2] It should, however, be noted that the mind and the senses involved in this experience are different from the ordinary. The ordinary mind and senses are transformed and spiritualised by the ingress of Svarūpa-śakti and made fit for the experience, which is essentially super-sensuous. In fact, the whole self is transformed and purified and the soul regains its original composure and tranquility. It is thus that the stage is set for the appearance of the divine being, which otherwise would appear but not be apprehended. In the *Prakaṭa-līlā*, Indra and Śiśupāla did not have a revelation of the divine personality of Kṛṣṇa, although they saw him directly, because they did not possess the purity and tranquility of mind necessary for the revelation. But Kṛṣṇa revealed himself to the Gopīs and Gopās, because their minds were purified by Bhakti.

Mukti may be attained while the *Jīva* is in the physical body or after death when both the physical and the sublte bodies are destroyed. The latter kind of *Mukti* is the real end, as it implies complete transcendence of the phenomenal plane, and the elimination of all the extraneous factors that block the Jīva's inherent capacity to realise the highest kind of bliss.

Since *Mukti* primarily means the attainment of Bhagavān, there are five different kinds of it, according to the five different forms in which Bhagavān may be attained. They are (*a*) *Sāyujya*, absorption in the divine self, (*b*) *Sālokya*, attainment of the Loka or *Dhāman* of the deity, (*c*) *Sārūpya*, attainment of the form similar to that of the deity worshipped and a place in His Dhāman, (*d*) *Sārṣṭī*, attainment of the Aiśvarya or power similar to that of the deity,[3] (*e*) *Sāmīpya*, attainment of proximity to the deity.

Sāyujya-mukti is the absorption into any non-phenomenal manifestation of Bhagavān. It is of two kinds—*Brahman-sāyujya* and *Īśvara-sāyujya.* Brahman-*sāyujya* is the absorption in the impersonal Brahman and *Īśvara-sāyujya* is the absorption in any non-phenomenal manifestation of *Iśvara*, the Personal Brahman.

We have already said that absorption in Brahman in *Sāyujya-mukti* is not real but apparent, and the bliss experienced in it is of a very inferior kind as compared to the bliss experienced by the Jīvas, who have a revelation of the Personal Brahman or the *Para-brahman*. It is said that the bliss experienced in the revelation of Brahman (*brahmānanda*) is not even a drop in comparison to the bliss of loving communion

[1]*Pr. S.*, p. 119.

[2]ibid, p. 165.

[3]Though the *Aiśvarya* of the *Jīva* in *Sārṣṭi-mukti* is in many respects similar to that of the deity, it is not in every respect similar to it. The *Jīva*, for example, does not have the power to create or destroy the universe. *Prī. S.*, p. 188.

(*premānanda*) with the Personal Brahman, which is like an ocean (*CC*, Ādi, VII, 85). Not to speak of the bliss of loving communion with or the direct perception of the Personal Brahman, even the bliss caused by the partial experience of any object associated with him is by far superior to *Brahmānanda*. As stated in the Bhāgavata, Sanaka, Sanandana, Sanātana and Sanata Kumāra, who were immersed in *Brahmānanda* since their very birth, were dislodged from Brahman consciousness as soon as they got the smell of the Tulasī leaves offered to Bhagavān.[1]

The bliss of *Īśvara-sāyujya* is superior to the bliss of *brahman-sāyujya*, for though the *Jīva* does not have its own spiritual body and senses, it sees and hears through the senses of the deity into whose body it has entered and thus enjoys the variety of transcendental bliss which in *Brahman-sāyujya* is absolutely changeless and colourless.

The bliss enjoyed in *Sālokya*, *Sārṣṭi* and *Sārūpya-muktis* is superior to the bliss of *Sāyujya-mukti*, because the *Jīva*, who attains any of these has his own transcendental body as a Pārṣada and is capable of having a more varied experience of the transcendental world by participating in its activities. But the bliss of *Sāmīpya-mukti* is even higher, because the *Jīva* attains proximity to the deity and enjoys seeing him and his Līlā directly. This is not possible in *Sālokya*, *Sārūpya* and *Sārṣṭi-muktis*, because in them the *Jīva* has only an inward experience of the deity. In *Sāmīpya-mukti* the experience is outward. Outward experience, as we have stated before, is more vivid and enjoyable. As stated in the *Bhāgavata*, Nārada Muni went about from place to place singing the praises of the Lord and as he sang Bhagavān appeared in his heart, but still he went to Dvārakā repeatedly to see Kṛṣṇa, because he found an outward experience of Him much more attractive and pleasing.[2]

The Ultimate End

We have seen that *Mokṣa* implies the attainment of Bhagavān in some form or the other and that *Sāmīpya-mukti* is the highest kind of *Mukti*, because it implies proximity to Bhagavān. But even though the devotee, in *Sāmīpya-mukti*, enjoys proximity to Bhagavān, he deos not fulfil all the conditions necessary for His fullest realisation and, therefore, the bliss enjoyed by him is also not of the highest order. The reason is that though outwardly he is near Bhagavān there is something that keeps him at a distance from the core of his heart. That is lack of *Prīti* or loving devotion, without which real proximity with Bhagavān, which means loving intimacy with Him is not possible.

Prīti is the highest function of the highest *Śakti* of Bhagavān, namely the *Hlādinī-śakti*. It implies both the quality of loving and being loved.

[1] *Bh.*, 3, 15, 43.
[2] ibid, 1, 6, 34.

To realise Bhagavān fully one must realise Prīti, which means that one must realise Bhagavān both as object of love and as capable of love Himself. This, in other words, means that one must realise Him in His Madhura aspect. In His Madhura aspect Bhagavān loves His deveotees just as He is loved by them. Kṛṣṇa says in *Bhāgavata*:

sādhavo hṛdayaṁ mahyaṁ sādhūnāṁ hṛdayaṁ tvahaṁ|
madanyatte na jānanti nāhaṁ tebhyo manāgapi|| Bh., 9, 4, 68.

"My devotees are my heart and soul and I am the heart and soul of my devotees, my mind is wholly occupied by them and their mind is wholly occupied by me."

Bhagavān, in His highest Madhura aspect is not so much the object of worship as the object of love; not so much the bestower of gifts as One, Who Himself hungers for the offerings of His devotees; not so much the protector of those, who take shelter under Him, as One who Himself stands in need of the loving protection and care of His devotees; not so much the controller and the ruler of the universe as One, Who is Himself subservient to the will of His devotees:

ahaṁ bhakta parādhīno hyasvatantra iva dvija|
sādhubhirgrastahṛdayo bhaktairbhaktajanapriyaḥ|| Bh., 9, 4, 63.

"I have no freedom. My heart is in the grip of my devotees. I depend wholly upon them; for they love me and I love them."

The *Jīvas* who attain *Mukti*, cannot realise Bhagavān in his *Madhura* aspect, because their view of Bhagavān is dominated by His Aiśvarya and they are not capable of cultivating personal emotional relationship with him. Aiśvarya causes fear and confusion and produces respect rather than intimate personnel attachment called Mamatā, which is essential for the loving service or *Prema-sevā* of Bhagavān. The Muktas of the above categories are, therefore, called *Śānta-bhaktas* and there *Bhakti* is called *Taṭastha-bhakti*, to be distinguished from the *Mamatā-bhakti* of the devotees, who cultivate personnel emotional relationship with Bhagavān. The difference between the two is also described by their general attitude towards Bhagavān. The *Śānta-bhakta* has what may be called the "I am thine" attitude (*tadīyatāmaya bhāva*), while the devotees, who cultivate personal emotional relationship with Bhagavān, have what may be called the "Thou-art-mine" attitude (*madīyatāmaya bhāva*).

Śrī Rūpa mentions two kinds of *Śānta-bhaktas*: those, who have a predominating desire for enjoying the Aiśvarya and the happines of Vaikuntha (*sukhaiśvaryottarā*) and those, who have a predominating desire for the loving service of Bhagavān (*prema-sevottarā*). The Śānta Bhaktas of the latter category have some experience of the Mādhurya of Bhagavān, but their experience of Mādhurya is of the lowest order, because they are lacking in the Madīyatāmaya-bhāva. Mādhurya in the real sense, implying the ever growing and ever fresh charm and grace of the Divine

Personality, is enjoyed by the devotees, who have realised *Prīti.*[1]

Prīti or *Prema* is, therefore, the fifth end (*pañcama-puruṣārtha*), and the highest end (*Parama-puruṣārtha*) (*CC*, Madhya, IX, 261). *Prema* is passion to serve Kṛṣṇa for His happiness alone. The person desirous of *Prema-sevā* or the loving service of Kṛṣṇa does not desire anything for himself. He does not even desire *Mokṣa.* Even if Kṛṣṇa offers him *Mokṣa* without *Prema-sevā*, he does not accept it.[2] This does not, however, mean that he does not attain *Mokṣa. Mokṣa* is a natural concomitant of *Prema.* Just as darkness is automatically dispelled with the rising of the sun, the fetters of Māyā are automatically removed with the attainment of Prema (*C. Bh.*, Antya, V, 59). *Prema* is not desired as a means to *Mokṣa.* It is an end in itself. It is the highest bliss of which *Mokṣa* is the natural accompaniment (*CC*, Madhya, XX, 140).

[1]*āmāra mādhurya nitya nava nava haya/*
sva-sva prema anarūpe bhakte āsvādaya// *CC*, Ādi, 4, 115.

[2]*Bh.*, 6, 29, 13.

CHAPTER X

The Phenomenal World

The Doctrine of Māyā

The world, as already indicated, is the manifestation of *Māyā.* But Śrī Caitanya's interpretation of *Māyā* is essentially different from its Advaitic interpretation by the school of Śaṁkara, According to Śaṁkara Māyā is illusion, and the world as the product of *Māyā* is unreal. But according to Śrī Caitanya *Māyā* is a potency of Bhagavān, and the world, as a product of the potency of Bhagavān, is real.

The real nature of Māyā is defined in the following *Śloka* cited in *Caitanya-caritāmṛta* from *Srīmad-bhāgavata*:

ṛte'rthaṁ yat pratīyeta na pratīyeta cātmani|
tadvidyādātmano māyāṁ yathābhāso yathā tamaḥ||

Bh., 2, 9, 33. cited in *CC*, Madhya, XXV, 21.

Māyā is here described as that which appears outside the real self of Bhagavān, but which cannot appear without him. Bhagavān in his intrinsic selfhood transcends *Māyā* (*CC*, Madhya, XXV, 96), but *Māyā* as a potency of Bhagavān depends for its existence on Him (*CC*, Madhya, XXV, 97).

Māyā has a twofold aspect as (1) *Nimitta-māyā* or *Jīva-māyā* and (2) *Upādāna-māyā* or *Guṇa-māyā* (*CC*, Madhya, XX, 232). *Nimitta-māyā* is the efficient cause of the world, while *Upādāna-māyā* is its material cause (*CC*, Madhya, XX, 232).[1] *Nimitta-māyā* is compared in the *Śloka*, cited above, to the reflection of the sun, as it appears to the eye in the beginning, and *Guṇa-māyā* to the reflection, as it appears after some time. In the beginning the reflection looks bright and splendid, but later it looks like a patch of darkness. In both cases the reflection exists apart from the sun but not independent of it. In the same manner *Jiva-māyā* and *Guṇa-māyā* exist apart from the intrinsic selfhood of Bhagavān, but not independent of him. Just as the bright reflection of the sun is due to the rays of the sun and shares the nature of the sun as brightness, *Jīva*, even when under the influence of *Māyā*, is a particle of the *Taṭasthā* or *Jīva-śakti* of Bhagavān and shares His nature as a conscious being; and just as the reflection of the sun as a patch of darkness is devoid of brightness

[1]*māyāra tin vṛtti—māyā āra pradhāna|*
māyā nimitta hetu prakṛti viśvera upādhāna||

the *Guṇa-māyā*, as a manifestation of the external or Bahirangā potency of Bhagavān is devoid of consciousness. Again, just as the patch of darkness does not exist in the sun but depends on it, in the sense that it cannot be perceived without its light in the eye, the *Guṇa-māyā* does not exist in Bhagavān, but depends on Him, in the sense that it cannot exist without Him.

Nimitta-māyā has an obvious reference to Jīva. It has no relation with the eternally free or the *Nitya-mukta Jīvas*. But in the case of the *Jīvas*, who allow themselves to be influenced by it, it has a two-fold function, as Science (*vidyā*) and Nescience (*avidyā*). As Vidyā it is mercifully inclined towards them and leads them to deliverance by creating an opening for the inflow of *Svarūpa-śakti*, or the transcendental consciousness, though it cannot by itself reveal that consciousness. As *Avidyā* it helps the process of creation by concealing the true nature of the self from itself and by generating empirical consciousness, with its attachment to the body and the objects of the senses. In respect of its former function the *Avidyā-māyā* is called *Āvaraṇātmikā*, because it puts an *Āvaraṇa* or covering on the self and makes it forget its real nature as eternally self-conscious servant of Bhagavān, while in respect of its latter function it is called *Vikṣepātmikā*, because it causes *Vikṣepa* or distraction by creating empirical consciousness of the body.[1]

As the efficient cause of the world *Nimitta-māyā* consists of *Kāla*, *Karma*, *Daiva* and *Svabhāva* (*Bh.*, 10, 63, 26). Each of these concepts is thoroughly explained by Jīva Gosvāmin in his *Paramātma-saṁdarbha*. *Kāla*, as defined by him, is a *vṛtti* or mode of *Paramātman* by which the equilibrium of the three *Guṇas* in *Prakṛti* is disturbed. It is, therefore, called Kṣobhaka, or the source of provocation. *Karma* is the series of actions performed by the empirical ego, which serve as the efficient cause of the disturbance. *Daiva* means the essential nature of these acts to produce effects. Svabhāva means the tendency formed in the ego as a result of the impressions left by the Karmas.

The *Upādāna-māyā* or *Pradhāna* is the state of equilibrium of the three *Guṇas*[2]—*Śattva*, *Rajas* and *Tamas*, and the source of the material world. It consists of the ingredients of *Drvya*, *Kṣetra*, *Prāṇa*, *Ātmān* and *Vikāra* (*Bh.*, 10, 63, 26). *Drvya* means the five elements in their subtle state. Kṣetra means *Prākṛti*. *Prāṇā* is the vital principle in the human body. *Ātmān* indicates the empirical ego. *Vikāra* implies the five senses, the five gross elements or the *Pañca-mahābhūtāni* and the *Manasa* or the mind. *Deha* or the physical body is the collective effect of all these. The primal matter is the state of equilibrium of all these ingredients and the Guṇas. It cannot start the process of creation because it is unintelligent. It is the Ikṣaṇa or the look of *Paramātman* that makes it active.

[1] *Par. S.*, 59.

[2] *Guṇa* here means a constituent element or a strand and not an attribute.

The Process of Creation

A detailed account of the process of creation appears in Śrī Caitanya's discourse to Prakāśananda Sarasvatī, according to which before the beginning of creation there exists Bhagavān with his six-fold lordliness, and there is nothing that exists besides him (*CC*, Madhya, XXV, 91). At the time of creation the infinite Jīvas and universes are projected out of him, and at the time of dissolution they are again resolved into him (*CC*, Madhya, 92-94).

The ultimate source of creation is Bhagavān in His partial aspect Mahāviṣṇu, who appears as soon as Bhagavān desires to create (*CC*, Ādi, VI, 4). The whole process of creation proceeds from him as a result of his will. The Sāṁkhya view that *Prakṛti* is the ultimate cause of creation is rejected, because *Prakṛti* is inert and powerless to produce anything without the aid of the Śakti of Bhagavān (*CC*, Ādi, VI, 15; Madhya, XX, 214). It becomes active only when energised by Bhagavān (*CC*, Adi, VI, 16). *Prakṛti* derives its power of creation from Bhagavān, just as iron derives its power of burning from fire (*CC*, Madhya, XX, 226). Bhagavān is the primary cause of creation and *Prakṛti* is the secondry cause (*CC*, Ādi, V, 51-53).

Mahāviṣṇu or Kāraṇārṇvaśāyī Saṁkarṣaṇa, who is a partial manifest of the Saṁkarṣaṇa of Paravyoma and rests in the Kārṇa-samudra, the spiritual causal ocean outside the Brahman-loka, moves *Māyā* to action by casting his glance at it (*CC*, Madhya, XX, 227-230). By his glance two kinds of effects are produced. From his spiritual body emanate infinite Jīvas, like the rays from the sun, and from *Prakṛti* emanate infinite *Brahmāndas*. His glance at *Prakṛti* is described in erotically figurative imagery as the intercourse of his partial manifest śambhū with Prakṛti (*CC*, Ādi, V, 57; Madhya, XX, 232-33; *Brahma Saṁhitā* V, 10).

First of all in the process of creation is created the principle of Mahat, and then in gradual succession are manifested the mundane ego (*ahaṁkāra*), the five elements (*Pañcamahābhūta*), their attributes (*tanmātrā*) and the senses (*indriyāṇī*), which together from the basis of the evolution of infinite universes (*CC*, Madhya, XX, 236).

Since *Mahat* is the product of *Prakṛti* it is constituted of Sattva, Rajas and Tamas, but predominated by Sattva and Rajas. The attributte of Sattva is knowledge and the attribute of Rajas is action. So *Mahat* is a subtle principle underlieing the phenomenal world which is both intelligent and active (*Bh.*, 2, 5, 23). As present in the individual self, it is called *buddhi* or intellect. Since it is the product of *Prakṛti* as energised by Mahāviṣṇu, the cosmic consciousness, it is not wholly unconscious. It is a unique mixture of the conscious and the unconscious (*cidacit misrita*). It is similar to the priciple of Mahat in Sāṁkhya, which reflects the consciousness of *Puruṣa* and is, therefore, apparently conscious.

Ahaṁkāra arises directly from *Mahat* and is the mixture of the conscious and the unconscious like *Mahat*. It is the 'I' (*ahaṁ*) and 'Mine' (*mama*) consciousness on account of which the self considers itself the doer of actions and the owner of properties. *Ahaṁkāra* is *Sāttvika*, *Rajas* or *Tamas*, in accordance with the predominance in it of one *Guṇa* or the other. From the Sāttvika Ahaṁkāra arise the eleven organs, namely the mind (*manas*), the five organs of perception (*jnānendriya*) and the five organs of action (*karmendriya*). From the Tamas *Ahamkāra* arise the five subtle elements (*tanmātras*) or the potential elements of sound, touch, colour, taste and smell. The gross physical elements (*pañca-mahābhūta*) of ākāśa, air, light, water and earth, having respectively the qualities of sound, touch, colour, taste and smell, arise from the Tanmātras.

Śrī Caitanya's view of the evolution of the world, thus, bears a close resemblance to the Sāṁkhya theory of evolution in its terminology and method. The essential defference, however, is that while in Sāṁkhya Prakṛti is an independent Tattva, according to Śrī Caitanya it is the result of the external potency of Bhagavān. In Sāṁkhya-prakṛti is both the material and efficient cause of the world, because *Puruṣa* is essentially inactive and unchanging. But according to Śrī Caitanya Paramātman, in His partial aspect Mahāviṣṇu is the initiator and regulator of the entire process of creation. It is stated that the seeds of infinite universes (*brahmāndas*) reside in each pore of the spiritual body of Mahāviṣṇu and these are exhaled or inhaled by him with his breath (*CC*, Madhya, XX, 237-41). His partial manifest Garbhodaśāyī Puruṣa enters each one of the millions of Brahmāndas exhaled by him. On entering each Brahmānda the Garbhodasāyī-puruṣa finds it pervaded by darkness and without a place for him to rest. He then fills half of the Brahmānda with the sweat of his body, and in the ocean thus formed he rests on the thousand-headed cobra called Śeṣa. From the navel pit of his body springs a golden lotous, out of which is born the four-faced Brahmā, who finally creates the entire universe with the fourteen Lokās (*CC*, Madhya, XX, 241-48).[1]

Śakti-Pariṇāmavāda

Śrī Caitanya, thus, believes in Pariṇāmavāda, or the theory of creation, according to which the world is a Pariṇāma or transformation of Brahman and not in Vivartavāda, according to which the world is a Vivarta or illusory appearance of Brahman. Upon the latter theory is based the Advaitavāda of Śaṁkara, according to which Brahman alone is real and everything else is illusion. The world is an illusory production from Brah-

[1]This is said only of the manifestation of the *Māyā-śakti*, which is inactive before the process of creation starts and not of the manifestations of the *Svarūpa-śakti*, which is eternally active. The Dhāman and the Parikaraṣ as the manifestation of the *Svarpua-śakti* exist even before the process of creation.

man just as the snake is an illusory production from rope or silver is an illusory production from the conch. Pariṇāmavāda implies the production of an effect, which is of the same nature as the cause. The world, according to it, is real, because it is the effect of Brahman. Śrī Caitanya, however, emphasises that the reality of the world is relative while the reality of Brahman is absolute. Brahman does not depend for its existence on anything else, while the world depends for its existence on Brahman. Brahman is eternal, but the world is non-eternal, in the sense that it ceases to exist after dissolution, though eternal in the sense that even after dissolution it continues to exist in a subtle form in Brahman.

The scriptural texts like '*tadātmānaṁ svayamakurūta*' (*Taittirīya-brahmāna*, 7,1) and '*ātmakṛteh pariṇāmāṭ*' (*Br.*, I, 4, 26) clearly state that Brahman creates the world out of itself, thereby indicating that it is both the efficient and the material cause of the world. The famous texts '*sarvaṁ khalvidaṁ brahman*' and '*etadātmyamidaṁ sarvam*' also support this view.

Śaṁkara accepts the view that Brahman and the world are identical, but, according to him, the world is identical with Brahman in its true nature as Brahman, and not as world, which is an appearance, while according to Śrī Caitanya the world is identical with Brahman as a manifestation of its external potency, and is real, because the potency is real.

Both Śaṁkara and Śrī Caitanya believe in Satkāryavāda,[1] or the theory of causation, according to which the cause and the the effect are identical, and the effect exists implicitly in the cause prior to its production. But while according to Śrī Caitanya the effect is real, according to Śaṁkara it is illusory.

It is insisted by the philosophers of the school of Śrī Caitanya that since the material cause and the effect are identical, the effect cannot be substantially different from the cause. The world being an effect of the Māyā-śakti of Brahman cannot be substantially different from the Māyā-śakti. Existence is an essential attribute of Māyā-śakti. It must, therefore be an essential attribute of the world. In other words, the world cannot be illusory. The theory that the world is illusory violates the theory of identity of cause and effect, which Śaṁkara himself upholds.

The analogy of rope-snake or the analogy of silver-in-conch, on which Śaṁkara's theory of the world-illusion is based, is false, because Brahman, as Śaṁkara accepts, is both the efficient and the material cause of the

[1]Satkāryavāda means that the effect is *sat* and existent in the material cause before its production. It is opposed to Asatkāryavāda, which means that the effect is *asat* and non-existent in the material cause before its production. Pariṇāmavāda and Vivartavāda are the two different kinds of Satkāryavāda. According to Prināmavāda there is a real transformation of the cause into the effect, while according to Vivartavāda the transformation is only apparent.

world, but neither the rope is the efficient or material cause of the snake nor the conch is the efficient or material cause of silver. Śrī Jīva Gosvāmin in his *Sarvasamvādinī* cites a number of Śruti and *Brhma-sūtra* texts to prove that the Śāstras insist on the reality of the world by emphasising the fact of their production from Brahman. The analogies, therefore, would be appropriate if the snake or silver were the products of the rope or the conch. But they are only superimpositions.[1]

Śrī Jīva subjects Śaṁkara's doctrine of *Māyā* to a detailed and scathing criticism, which we shall discuss later in connection with the specific problem of relation between Brahman and the world.[2] But we may, here, make a brief reference to Ajnāna, which is the central feature of the doctrine of Māyā in Advaitism. Everything in Advaitic cosmology is explained as a mode of Ajnāna, just as everything in Sāṁkhya is explained as a mode of *Prakṛti*. What, we may ask, is the ultimate status of Ajnāna in Advaitism? Is Ajnāna something subjective or objective? At least some of the Advaitins regard it as objective. In Advaitic literature it is described as beginningless (*anādi*) and as something positive (*bhāvarūpa*), which has the power of veiling (*āvaraṇātmikā*) and producing things (*vikṣepātmikā*) and which constitutes the material cause of the world. It is maintained, besides, that if Ajnāna were a subjective fancy it would not be possible to explain the objects of the world, which are not like fancied things, and since there is no fancy in the state of deep sleep, everybody would realise Mokṣa in sleep. According to this theory Brahman is the support of Ajnāna and the basis of all that is perceived as a part of the world appearance. But Brahman does not appear into the actual form or content of an appearance, in the same way in which a real object, which is mistaken for an illusory one, does not enter into its content. It is Ajnāna that determines the content of all appearances. Brahman, under the cover of Ajnāna, appears in the form of the different objects of the world.

The objective view of Ajnāna, however, does not fit into the Advaitic system, because it undermines the absolute unity of Brahman. The main purpose of Advaitism is to reduce the empirical facts to non-facts and to remove Ajnāna by means of right knowledge. But if Ajnāna is made something objective, then however unlike Brahman it may be, it is difficult to understand how this purpose may be acheived. Knowledge may reveal the nature of things, but it cannot destroy them. This difficulty does not arise if Ajnāna is considered as mere ignorance. This is, therefore, the actual position adopted by many Advaitins.

But, if Ajnāna is mere ignorance, to whom does it belong? It cannot belong to the individual self, because it is itself the result of ignorance.

[1] *SS*, p. 147.
[2] *See* Chapter XI.

It cannot belong to Brahman, because it is pure consciousness. It is, therefore, maintained that ignorance does not really exist. The world is no doubt the result of ignorance, but it is sheer ignorance to suppose that this ignorance is real. If this ignorance were real another ignorance would be required to account for it, and there would, thus, be an infinite regress. But if ignorance is not real, how can the world come into existence? The reply is that the world is, in fact, not there. Because it appears without being there, it is called *Māyā,* which is described as Anirvacanīya or indescribable.

One of the main arguments on which the theory of illusion is based is that we all have the experience of illusion, and since there is no essential difference in the manner of presentation of the illusory object and the object of ordinary experience, all objects are in their essence illusory. But the argument itself is founded on the distiction between illusory experience and valid experience, and if all experiences are equally illusory, it automatically falls to the ground. The most that we can infer from our experience of illusory objects is that the other objects, which are similarly presented, may also be illusory, but we can never definitely conclude that they are actually so. But even if this carelessness in the Advaitin's mode of reasoning is allowed and it is admitted, for the sake of argument, that there are no external objects, it would still remain to be proved that there are no subjective states of mind, which is not possible. We may deny objective existence to an object that we see, but how can we deny our seeing of it? If the perception itself is regarded as non-existent, there would be no object of perception and nothing at all to be described as illusory.

Thus the world may be described as illusory but the illusion itself cannot be denied. Bare negation is a myth, since every negation is significant and is grounded on something positive.[1] The world may, therefore, be denied existence, but the fact of its appearance cannot be denied, and if the appearance cannot be denied its seat must be found. It is on this point that the boat if the Advaitin seems to capsize. "It is true," he says, "that no explanation is possible of the rise of the bewildering force of Avidyā, creator of false values, which has somehow come into phenomenal being in spite of the eternal and inalienable purity of the original self-existent Brahman.[2]

Śrī Caitanya's *Pariṇāmavāda,* as applied to the problem of creation, differs in an important respect from *Pariṇāmavāda* in the ordinary sense. In the ordinary sense it means the modification of the material cause from which the world is produced. In Sāṁkhya it means the modification of *Prakṛti,* while in the Viśiṣṭādvaitavāda of Rāmānuja it means the

[1]*See* Bergson's analysis of the idea of 'Nothing' in the last chapter of his 'Creative Evolution,' and the chapter on 'Negation' in Bernard Bosanquet's *Logic,* I.

[2]Dr. S. Radhakrishnan, *History of Indian Philosophy,* III, p. 578.

modification of the matter in Brahman, and therefore of Brahman itself. But, according to Śrī Caitanya, though Brahman creates the world out of itself, it does not undergo any modification. Even a part of it does not undergo modification, because it does not consist of parts, and the part, in its case, is actually the whole.

Another respect in which the *Pariṇāmavāda* of Śrī Caitanya differs from the *Pariṇāmavāda* of *Rāmānuja* is the fact that according to Śrī Caitanya Brahman in its intrinsic selfhood has nothing to do with the creation and destruction of the world, which proceeds from the external potency inhering in its partial manifest Paramātman. The *Pariṇāmavāda* of Śrī Caitanya is, therefore, called *Śakti-pariṇāmavāda.*

But even though the world is the result of the external potency of Brahman, it is strictly speaking, *Pariṇāma* or effect of Brahman, and the question as to how it remains unchanged (*avikṛta*) even though it produces the world out of itself, remains a mystery. But that this is actually so we have to accept on the basis of the scriptures. The Śakti of Brahman is Acintya or inconceivable and the only source of knowledge about it is Śabda (*CC*, Ādi, VII, 117; Madhya, VI, 155).[1] But even so the belief in Acintya-śakti is based not on blind faith, but on a logical necessity, which we shall strive to bring out in our discussion of the doctrine of Acintya-bhedābheda.[2]

Pariṇāmavāda, in the above sense, is the real meaning of the Sūtras of Śrī Vyāsa (*CC*, Madhya, VI, 170), but it is concealed by the imaginary interpretation of Śaṁkara (*CC*, Madhya, XXV, 34-36),[3] The Śāstras invariably speak of the production of the world from Brahman. There is not a single instance in which they have said that the world is a Vivarta or superimposition on Brahman.[4]

[1]*avicintya śakti-yukta śrī bhagavān|*
icchāye jagat-rūpe pāya pariṇāma||
maṇi jeche avikṛta prasave hemabhāra|
jagadrūpa haya īsvara tabu avikāra||

[2]*See* Chapter XI.

[3]*ei ta kalpita artha mane nāhi bhāya|*
śāstra chāṇi kukalpanā pāṣaṁde bujhāya|
vyāsa sūtrera artha ācārya kariyāche ācchādana|
eī haya satya srīkṛṣṇacaitanya bacana||

[4]Rādhā Govinda Nāth, *Gauḍīya Vaiṣṇava-darśana*, III, Sec. 50.

CHAPTER XI

The Doctrine of Acintya-bhedābheda

Philosophical thinking in regard to the problem of relation between God and man, the Absolute and the world of finite experience, the noumena and the phenomena, is directed along two main lines. Some, emphasising the essential distinction between the infinite and the finite, accept the absolute transcendence of the one over the other, while others, emphasising the identity between them regard God as immanent in the human spirit and the phenomenal world.

The view of God as transcendent gained prominence in Europe with the rise of individualism in the eighteenth century. Locke was chiefly responsible for shaping the thought of this century in England and France, and Leibnitz in Germany. To Locke God was an extra-mundance deity, having no connection with man and the finite world; to Leibnitz He was the monad of monads, the supreme monad, absolutely self-sufficient and eternally shut up from other beings and monads. Both Locke and Leibnitz denied any kind of relation between God and man.

The difficulties of this kind of philosophy are obvious. Too much stress upon the transcendence of God gives rise to a kind of mechanical deism; God is reduced to a great first cause. Like a watch-maker, he creates the machinery of the world once for all, and, without interfering with it any more, merely contents himself by 'seeing it go.' Apart from the fact that such a God hardly suits the religious conscience, the deistic position involves an unbridgeable gulf between God and man and undermines the notion of the essential unity of all beings. Thus, Leibnitz finds himself at a loss to explain the unity or the harmony of things, and is led, in the end, to account for the same by his belief in the pre-established harmony of the universe. Besides, dualism and pluralism are the necessary outcome of the philosophy of transcendence, and these imply limitation on the absolute freedom and infinite perfection of God. Insistence on transcendence leads to an incurable agnosticism in Kant: the universe is bifurcated into noumena and phenomena, the world within experience and the world beyond it; God is regarded as a reality that belongs to the noumenal world as the unknowable thing-in-itself, in all its pristine purity, which human reason dare not touch and contaminate.

Immanence is emphasised by Hegel. He revolts against the agnosticism of Kant and insists on the immanence of divine reason in the world. But, undue emphasis on immanence in Hegel leads to the identification of

God with the world of experience. The world is regarded as the thought of God and the different finite thinkers as functions or modes of one universal self-consciousness. The finite souls are deprived of their independent existence and made the shadows of God.

From another point of view, by identifying the process of human experience with divine experience, Hegel virtually denies any actuality of God for himself. He regards the history of humanity as a necessary process, through which God becomes self-conscious. His doctrine of evolution is undoubtedly one of his most important contributions to philosophy, but his identification of the divine sources and the goal of evolution with its highest human manifestations, brings him down to the level of the materialistic position. God is no more self-subsistent, but depends for his existence on the appearance of man: the appearance of man is identical with the creation of God.

Bradley tries to extricate the Hegelian absolute from this difficulty by insisting on its independent existence and its absolute transcendence of our categories of thought and 'being.' This leads to pantheism, or acosmism, which is to admit an undifferentiated, all-pervading substance as the only reality and to reject the finite existence as a species of illusion.

In western philosophy pantheism finds expression chiefly in the philosophy of Spinoza and Neo-Platonism, while in Indian philosophy it finds its chief exponent in Śaṁkara. Both Spinoza and Śaṁkara, instead of explaining the relation between the finite and the infinite, explain it away by cancelling one of the terms in the relation. Spinoza describes the finite as the manifestation of the attributes of the undifferentiated substance, which do not really belong to it, but are superimposed upon it. Śaṁkara describes it as the result of *upādhis*. Since the nature of a falsehood, illusion, or *upādhi* is that it does not exist, there can be no problem of relation between that which exists and that which does not exist. But the problem, which the pantheist tries thus to dismiss, returns for him in another and a more difficult form. For, though the finite is sought to be eliminated as non-existent, it persists in the form of its appearance, which cannot be denied, and the problem of relation between the finite and the infinite reappears in the form of the problem of relation between appearance and reality, which Spinoza and Śaṁkara fail to solve.

The history of philosophy bears evidence that neither immanence nor transcendence can solve the problem of relation between God and the world. The concepts of identity and difference are both inadequate to describe the nature of being. Exclusive emphasis on the one leads to a virtual denial of the world as illusion, while exclusive emphasis upon the other bifurcates the reality into two and creates an unbridgeable gulf between God and the world. Both the concepts, however, seem to be equally necessary. Identity is a necessary demand of reason and difference is an undeniable fact of experience. An ideal synthesis of identity and difference must be the cherished goal of philosophy. But the synthesis, though necessary, is not possible or conceivable.

This is the final test of human logic. It fails. But the logic of the infinite succeeds where our human logic fails. In the perfect being there is no conflict between necessity and possibility. Here, what is necessary actually is.

The clue to the solution of the problem, according to the school of Śrī Caitanya, therefore, lies in the inconceivable power (*acintya-śakti*) of God, by which the concepts of identity and difference are transcended and reconciled in a higher synthesis. Transcendence and immanence are made the associated aspects of an abiding unity in God, or, in other words, in the doctrine of *Acintya-bhedābheda*, which is the distinguishing feature of the school of Śrī Caitanya.[1] The immanent aspect of God is called *Paramātman*, while God, with all His spendour of infinite perfection, infinite potencies, and infinite attributes, transcending all the finite things, is called Bhagavān. As *Paramātman* he is the immanent regulator and observer of the actions of the finite souls, and the unifier of all existing things; as Bhagavān he is the Blissful Personal Absolute, beyond and above the world of sense. Śrī Kṛṣṇa Dās Kavirāja cites the *Gītā* text IX, 4-5, to support this view of transcendence and immanence of God and the concept of Acintya-śakti, which makes simultaneous existence of transcendence and immanence possible.[2]

The transcendence and immanence of Brahman may be explained without reference to his Śakti by saying that Brahman is immanent by one part and transcendent by another, but this would be introducing internal difference (*svagata-bheda*) in Brahman, who is *advaya*. The very idea of part and whole, according to which one part excludes another, is repugnant to the nature of Brahman as *advaya*.

Śrī Rūpa Gosvāmin illustrates the simultaneous presence of identity and difference in Brahman by referring to the fact that Kṛṣṇa lived with his sixteen thousand wives in their separate houses simultaneously.[3]

That nothing is impossible for Brahman on account of his *Acintya-śakti* is implied by *Brahman-sūtra*: *ātmani caivaṁ vicitraśca*.[4] But the following *Śloka* of *Mahābhārata* states it clearly:

acintyaḥ khalu ye bhāvā na taṅstarkena yojayeta|
prakṛtibhyāḥ paraṁ yattu tadacintyasya lakṣṇaṃ||

[1]*SS*, p. 149; *CC*, Madhya, VI, 170-71.

[2]*ei mata Gītā te punaḥ punaḥ kaya|*
sarvadā īśvara tattva acintya śakti haya||
āmī ta jagate basi jagat āmāte|
na āmī jagate basi na amā jagate|| *CC*, Ādi, V, 88-89.

[3]*Saṁkṣepa-bhāgavatāmṛtaṁ*, I, 365-66, 370-71.

[4]*Br. S.*, 1, 4, 26.

Therefore, it is possible for Brahman to be both different from the world and identical with it, to create the world out of himself and remain out of it. This cannot be explained by reasoning. But Śrī Caitanya tries, in *Caitanya-caritāmṛta*, to make it comprehensible to Sārvabhauma Bhattācārya by using the example of *Cintāmaṇi* (the philosopher's stone), which produces gold out of itself and yet remains unchanged.[1] In course of his discussion with Prakāśānanda also he uses this example and says that if a worldly object can have such *Acintya-śakti*, why should anyone be surprised at the *Acintya-śakti* of God.[2]

In his *Bhagavat-saṁdarbha*, Śrī Jīva defines Acintya as the power which can reconcile the impossible (*durghata ghatakatvaṁ hyacintyatvaṁ*.[3] Again, commenting on *Viṣṇu-purāṇa* verses I, VI, 1-3, he interprets the word Acintya as that which, though incomprehensible on account of the contradictory notions of identity and difference it involves, can be realised by *arthāpatti* (logical implication).[4]

Therefore, he proceeds to prove the doctrine of Acintya-bhedābheda by *arthāpatti*. He shows how it is implied in the concept of Śakti, inherent in the philosophy of the school. Śakti is different from the object in which it inheres, because it cannot be conceived as identical with it; it is identical with the object, because it cannot be conceived as different from it. Simultaneous existence of identity and difference is *acintya*, or inconceivable, because it is contradictory.[5]

Śrī Jīva illustrates the relation of inconceivable identity-in-difference by referring to fire and its power. We cannot think of fire without the power of burning; similarly, we cannot think of the power of burning without fire. Both are identical. Fire is nothing except that which burns; the power of burning is nothing except fire in action. At the same time, fire and its power of burning are not absolutely the same. If they were absolutely the same, there would be no sense in warning the child of its power to burn by saying 'fire burns.' It would be enough to say 'fire.' 'Fire burns' would involve needless repetition, for 'fire' would mean the same thing as 'burns.' Besides, if there were no difference between fire and its power, it would not be possible to neutralise the power of burning in fire by means of medicines or *mantra*, without making fire disappear altogether.[6]

[1]*acintya śakti īśvara jagadrūpa pariṇata||*
maṇi jaiche avikṛte prasave hema bhāra|
jagadrūpa haya īśvara tabu avikāra| *CC*, Madhya, VI, 170-71.

[2]*prākṛta vastu te jadi acintya śakti haya|*
īśvarera acintya śakti ithe ki vismaya?|| *CC*, Ādi, VII, 120.

[3]*Bh. S.*, XVI.

[4]*bhinnābhinnatv-ādi-vikalpaiścintayitum akṣyāḥ kevalam arthāpatti-jnāna-gocarāḥ.*

[5]vide *SS*, pp. 36-37.

[6]*SS*, pp. 36-37.

Just as there is neither absolute identity nor absolute difference between fire and its power, there is neither absolute identity nor absolute difference between Brahman and his Śakti. If there were absolute identity between Brahman and his Śakti, there would be absolute identity between Brahman and his different forms, which are the result of his Śakti, and the statements of the scriptures, describing the different forms of Brahman, like the *Jnātaścaturvidho rāśih* Śloka of *Viṣṇu-purāṇa*,[1] mentioning *Parabrahman*, *Īśvara*, *Viśvarūpa* and *Līlā-murti* as the four forms of Brahman, would be tautological. Absolute identity would mean absolute identity between Brahman and the individual souls or between Brahman and the world. The faults of the Jīvas and the world would then be the faults of Brahman. To keep Brahman free from these faults, it would be necessary to regard the Jīvas and the world as illusory. But, in the absence of any other real thing, Brahman will have to be regarded as the seat of illusion. Thus, Brahman would still not be faultless. Besides, the belief in absolute identity will falsify the *Śruti* texts which clearly distinguish the Jīvas and the world from Brahman.

If Brahman and his Śakti are regarded as absolutely different, that would give rise to dualism and the principle of oneness of all things (*advayatva*) stressed by the Śastras and implied in logical thinking, would be contradicted. It would also not be possible for Brahman to appear in the four different forms mentioned above by his own power or Śakti. If he appears in these forms as a result of the Śakti of other things, his freedom would be compromised. Absolute difference would also contradict the Ŝruti text *parāsya śaktirvividhaiva srūyate svabhāvikī jnāna bala kriyā ca*,[2] because in this text *jnāna*, *bala* and *kriyā* have been described as *svabhāvikī* or internal Śaktis of Brahman.[3]

Śrī Jīva has explained, with reference to the Bhāgavata text *Jnānavijnānanidhaye brahmaṇeananta-śaktaye*,[4] that the view relating to absolute identity is as illogical as the one relating to absolute difference. In the former case the word 'Brahman' would signify both Śakti and Śaktimān, and it would be tautological to describe Brahman as *Jnāna-vijnānanidhi* or *ananta-śakti sampanna.* In the latter it would not be possible to ascribe these predicates to Brahman at all.

Similarly, there are other statements of Śrutis which cannot be adequately explained without postulating *Acintya-bhedābheda. Vijnānaṁ ānandaṁ Brahman*[5] is one such statement. Śrī Jīva asks: Are *vijnāna* and *ānanda* synonymous? If they are synonymous, the statement would be tautolo-

[1] *VP*, 6, 7.
[2] vide *Svetāśvatara*, 6, 8.
[3] vide *SS*, p. 35.
[4] *Bh.*, 10, 16, 40.
[5] *Bṛhadāraṇyaka*, III, 9,28.

gical; if they have different meanings, it would introduce internal difference (*svagata-bheda*) in Brahman, which would contradict its oneness or *advayatva*.[1]

But it may be asked if the relation of *bhedābheda* between God and the world can be thus explained, why should it be called *acintya*? The answer is that the relation itself is not thus explained. What is explained is that it involves both *bheda* and *abheda*. How exactly the two are reconciled is beyond our comprehension. The analogies of material objects, like the sun and its rays, fire and its heat, and musk and its smell, are employed to explain the *acintyatva* (inconceivability) and not the relation. What is intended to be emphasised by means of these examples is that both *bheda* and *abheda* are actually present, though logical thinking precludes their co-presence in the same object, and that the relation of *acintya bhedābheda* is unlimited in scope. It applies not only to God and His *śaktis*, but also to the material objects and their *śaktis*.[2] Jīva states this clearly in his commentary on *Śrīmad-bhāgavata*.[3]

The inconceivability of the relation is evident from the contradiction it involves. But there is also another reason for calling it inconceivable in the case of God and His Śaktis. It is so called because the relation cannot be adequately described in terms of the relation between the part and the whole, or substance and attribute, or even in terms of the relation between an ordinary object and its Śakti. For, in the case of God, the part is not merely a part and the *śakti* is not merely a *śakti*. The part and the whole, the *śakti* and the *śaktimān* (the possessor of Śakti), interpenetrate and form an undivided whole.[4] God is essentially *advaya jnāna-tattva*, though not a pure identity. He appears in many forms and yet he is One; His *līlā*, name and form are at once different and non-different. Even the different parts of His body are different yet non-different, for each part can perform the functions of the other parts and of the whole. The part is, thus, actually identical with the whole, though still a part, and as such different from the whole.

The concept of *acintya* is found in numerous *Śruti* texts. The *Māṅdūkya-upaniṣad*,[5] *Kaivalya-upaniṣad*,[6] and *Subāla-upaniṣad*[7] describe Brahman as *acintya*. The *Gītā* also describes him as *acintyarūpa*.[8]

[1] *SS*, p. 38.

[2] *Viṣṇu-purāṇa*, 1, 3, 2.

[3] Jīva on *Srīmad-bhāgavata*, 11.3.37.

[4] vide *Par. Saṁ.*, 34: Jīva on the *Bhāgavata* text *parasparānu-praveśāt tattvānāṁ puruṣarṣabha*, XI, 22, 7.

[5] vide *Māṅdūkya-upaniṣad*, 1.

[6] vide *Kaivalya-upaniṣad*, 1, 6.

[7] vide *Subāla-upaniṣad*, Khaṅda VIII.

[8] vide *Gītā*, VIII, 9.

The *Brahma-sūtra* texts *srutestu śabdamūlatvāt*[1] and *ātmini caivaṁ vicitrāśca hi*[2] have a similar meaning. Śaṁkara, commenting upon the former, says, "Even certain ordinary things, such as gems, spells, herbs and the like, possess powers, which, owing to difference of time, place, occasion, and so on, produce various opposite effects, and nobody, unaided by instruction, is able to find out by mere reflection the number of these powers, their favouring conditions, their objects, their purposes, etc.; how much more impossible is it to conceive, without the aid of scripture, the true nature of Brahman, with its powers unfathomable by thought! As the *Purāṇa* says, 'Do not apply reasoning to what is unthinkable! The mark of the unthinkable is that it is above all material causes.'[3] Therefore, the cognition of what is supersensuous is based on the holy texts only."

We must, however, distinguish the concept of *acintya*, as understood in the Caitanya school, from the concept of *anirvacaniya* (indescribable) in the Advaita-vedānta of Śaṁkara. *Brahman* and his Śakti, according to the former, are *acintya*, but not *anirvacanīya*. The *acintya* is that which is illogical, but which we have to accept on the basis of the holy texts. This meaning of *acintya* is supported by Śaṁkara's own commentary on the *Brahman-sūtra* quoted above. Śrīdhara, in his commentary on the *Gītā* text quoted above explains the *Acintya-rūpa* (Inconceivable form) as that which cannot be conceived because it is infinite and immeasurable.[4] This does not imply that the *acintya* cannot be described, as the concept of *anirvacanīya* does, but that its infinitude, which implies the inclusion of contradictory qualities in it, cannot be properly understood. The scriptures describe Brahman as 'the greatest of the great' and 'the smallest of the small,'[5] as 'one who moves and yet moves not,'[6] as 'one who is far as well as near, immanent as well as transcendent,' and as one who does not have the mind or sense organs like ours and yet performs all the functions of these.[7] These are descriptions of the *acintya-rūpa* of Brahman, which we cannot comprehend.

Śaṁkara's category of '*anirvacanīya*' is applicable to *Māyā* and its products, which can neither be described as real nor as unreal; it does not apply to Brahman, who is described as real. But the category of *acintya*, in the school of Śrī Caitanya, applies to the relation between Śakti and Śaktimān everywhere, irrespective of the consideration whether it pertains to things in the phenomenal world or the transcendental world. It applies

[1] *Br. S.*, II, 1, 27.
[2] ibid., II, 1, 28.
[3] vide *Mahābhārata*, Bhīṣma Parva, V, 12.
[4] *aparimita-mahimatvādacintyarūpaṁ.*
[5] *aṇoraṇīyāna mahato mahīyāna. Svet. Up.*, III, 20.
[6] vide *Iśāvāsya*, 5.
[7] vide *Svet. Up.*, III, 19.

to Brahman, His associates (*parikaras*), and abodes (*dhāmans*), as much as it applies to the Jīvas and the objects of the physical world. *Anirva-anīya* is a negative concept, while *acintya* is a positive concept. *Anirvac-anīya* signifies the coming together of the opposite concepts of 'reality' and 'unreality' which cancel each other to produce illusion. *Acintya* signifies the marriage of the opposite concepts of 'difference' and 'non-difference' leading to a higher and a fuller unity. The concept of *Anirvacanīya* is born out of respect for the Law of Contradiction. We refuse to describe an object and call it *Anirvacanīya* when it seems to violate this law. The concept of *acintya* is born out of respect for scriptural authority, which ignores the law of contradiction. The former is based on logic, the latter on Srutārthāpatti.

Acintya should also be distinguished from the category of *avaktavyaṁ* (indiscribable) in the *Saptabhaṅgī-naya* of the Jains. The third form of judgement in the *Saptabhangī-naya* 'somehow *S* is *P* and also is not *P*' (*syāt asti ca nāsti ca*), predicates incompatible characters of the subject *successively*, from different points of view. The fourth form 'somehow *S* is indescribable' (*syāt avaktavyam*), represents the predication of incompatible characters of the subject in general, that is, without making any distinction of standpoints, on account of which the subject is regarded as indescribable. The third form says that incompatible characters can be predicated of the same thing successively, from different standpoints, or in different aspects. The fourth form says that incompatible characters cannot be predicated of the same thing simultaneously from the same standpoint and in the same aspect. But, according to the doctrine of *Acintya-bhedābheda*, incompatible characters can sometimes be predicated of the same subject from the same standpoint and in the same aspect. Avaktavyaṁ conforms to the Law of Contradiction, while *Acintya* transcends it.

Dr. Radha Govind Nath has raised the question as to whether the word '*acintya*' in '*acintya-bhedābheda*' has been used by Śrī Jīva to qualify the relation of *bhedābheda* or the Śakti of Brahman? He believes that '*acintya*' relates to the relation of *bhedābheda*, because Śrī Jīva has not specifically mentioned 'Brahman' in this connection[1] and has cited the *Viṣṇu-purāṇa* text '*śaktyaḥ sarvabhāvānāma-cintyajnānagocaraḥ*' which makes a mention of the Acintya-śakti of all the objects and not only Brahman.[2] We agree with Dr. Radha Govind Nath that the doctrine of *Acintya bhebāheda* relates to Śakti and *Śaktimat* (the possessor of Śakti) in general, but we hold that it relates primarily to the Acintya-śakti of Brahman and only secondarily to the Acintya-śakti of objects in general. There are two special reasons for this:

[1] *svamatetv acintya-bhedābhedaveva acintyaśaktimayatvāditi. SS*, p. 149.
[2] ibid, pp. 36-37.

Firstly, Śrī Jīva Gosvāmin has expounded the doctrine of *Acintya bhedābheda* in the context of the problem of relation between God and the world, and not in the context of the problem of relation between objects and their powers in general. Śrī Caitanya has also made a mention of the Acintya-śakti of Bhagavān in the same connection, and used the example of Cintāmaṇi and its power, only to say that if a worldly object can have Acintya-śakti, Acintya-śakti of God can be easily taken for granted.

Secondly, if the doctrine of *Acintya-bhedābheda* was taken to imply the Acintya-śakti of objects in general, the relation of difference and non-difference between God and the world would no doubt proceed as a deduction from the general rule. But the problem of preserving God's purity in spite of His relation with the world would still remain unsolved, there being nothing in the general rule to help solve it. On the other hand under the general rule, God cannot remain unaffected by the power of the individual souls, emanating from His Jīva-śakti, to perform good or bad deeds. It is only the *acintya-śakti* of God that can reconcile transcendence with immanence in such a manner that his purity remains unaffected by His relation with the phenomenal world.

Acintya-bhedābheda and the Advaita Vedānta of Śaṁkara

Śaṁkara's philosophy, usually known as *Kevalādvaita*, is summed-up in the trite phrase *brhaman satyaṁ jaganmithyā*, which means that Brahman is real and the world is an illusion. Brahman is *advaya*, one without a second; nothing at all exists besides Brahman, whether inside it, as its part or attribute, or outside it. It is a pure unity, absolutely homogenous in nature (*kūtastha*); it is pure existence and pure consciousness. Consciousness or thought is not its attribute, it is thought or intelligence itself (*Jnāna-svarūpa*).

But, if nothing else exists, whence the appearance of the physical world and the individual beings like ourselves? To answer this question, Śaṁkara introduces in his philosophy the theory of *Māyā* and the distinction between the esoteric (*pāramārthika*) and exoteric (*vyāvaharika*) points of view. Brahman is without any attributes (*nirguṇa*) from the esoteric or transcendental point of view, but from the exoteric or worldly point of view, it is qualified (*saguṇa*) and possesses the magical creative power called *Māyā*. The Saguṇa Brahman or Īśvara conjures up the world-show through His magical power, just as the magician produces illusory appearances of physical objects and living beings by his incomprehensible magical power. *Māyā* is thus the material cause (*upādānā kāraṇa*) of the world.

Thibaut thus describes the evolution of the world from *Māyā* and the illusory nature of its manifold objects; "Māyā, under the guidance of the Lord, modifies itself by a progressive evolution into all the individual existences distinguished by special names and forms, of which the world consists; from it there spring in due succession the different material elements and the whole bodily apparatus belonging to sentient beings. In all these apparently individual forms of existence the one individual Brahman is present, but owing to the particular adjuncts into which *Māyā* has specialised itself, it appears to be broken up, as it were, into a multiplicity of intellectual or sentient principles, the so-called *jīvas* (individual or personal souls). What is real in each *jīva* is only the universal Brahman itself; the whole aggregate of individualising bodily organs and mental functions, which, in our ordinary experience separate and distinguish one *jīva* from another, is the offspring of *Māyā* and as such unreal."[1]

Śaṁkara's doctrine is called Vivartavāda as against the doctrine of Pariṇāmavāda. According to Pariṇāmavāda, Brahman is the material cause of the world, while according to Vivartavāda, the world is a superimposition upon Brahman, due to *ajnāna* or ignorance. According to Vivartavāda, Brahman does not undergo any change in creation, as the world-appearance is merely a projection (*adhyāsa*). But according to Pariṇāmavāda, Brahman undergoes real change.[2]

Māyā is not real, because Brahman is the only thing real; it is not unreal, because it produces the world appearance. It is both real (*sat*) and unreal (*asat*). It is indeterminate or indescribable (*anirvacanīya*). It is beginningless (*anādi*) but not endless (*ananta*), since it is cancelled in deliverance or *Mukti*.

As regards the problem of relation between Brahman and the world, it is supposed that it simply does not arise, since Brahman is real and the world, including the individual souls, is unreal.

Śrī Jīva has levelled a number of charges against Advaitavāda, some of which are as follows:

What, he asks, is the support (*āśraya*) of *ajnāna*, which causes the illusion of the world? The *Jīva* cannot be the support, because it is itself the product of *ajnāna*. There is nothing else that can be its support except Brahman. But, if Brahman is the support, what happens to its purity and its essential nature as *jnāna* (*Jnānasvarūpa*)?[3]

In an illusory experience, the illusion is due to projection or superimposition. Superimposition involves separate existence of the object superimposed, its past experience, the present revival in the mind of the image of the past experience, and the consciousness of identity between the image and the object now actually experienced. The world-illusion, therefore, presupposes, besides the existence of Brahman, the actual

[1]Thibaut, *Vedānta-sūtras with Śaṁkara's Commentary*, p. XXV.

[2]According to the Sakti-pariṇāmavāda of Śrī Caitanya Brahman does not undergo any change although it is the material cause of the world.

[3]*SS*, p. 137.

existence of a world, whose image is projected on it.[1]

It may be argued that the actual existence of a world and its past experience is not necessary for projection, because each successive illusion of the world may be due to a previous illusion. This is illogical. The cause which produces an effect cannot itself be caused by the same effect, The position does not improve even if this chain of one illusion causing another is regarded as timeless,[2] which is clear from Śaṁkara's own reasoning in another connection.[3]

In fact, no illusion of any kind is possible in Brahman. It is clear from the example of illusion of silver in a conch, that the illusion is due to the quality of whiteness in the conch, which is similar to the quality of whiteness in silver. Therefore, in the case of the world-illusion, or any other illusion projected on Brahman, it is necessary that there should be some quality in Brahman which bears similarity to the quality of the illusory image projected on it. But Brahman is *nirguṇa* and does not possess any quality.[4]

The advaitins compare the world-illusion to a dream. The dream objects appear to be real in sleep, but on waking they disappear. Similarly, the world appears to be real under the spell of *Māyā* or *ajnāna* and disappears as *ajnāna* is removed on the attainment of Mokṣa. Śrī Jīva turns this argument against the Advaitins themselves by saying that, according to the Śāstras[5] the dream objects are real, since they are also created by *Īśvara*, who endows the Jīva in his dream state with another body similar to the physical body, and creates objects needed for his enjoyment or suffering according to the good or bad deeds performed by him. If the objects of daily life are like the objects of the dream-world, they must also be real like them.[6]

Śrī Jīva has not repeated most of the arguments commonly used by Rāmānujācārya and others against the Advaitins. The purpose of those arguments is to show in different ways how the theory of *Māyā* is inconsistent with the belief in Brahman, who is self-luminous (*svayaṁprakāśa*), without any second (*advaita*), and without any attributes (*nirguṇa*). The Advaitins are, therefore, compelled, in their own interest, ultimately to deny the existence of *Māyā*. They say that actually there is no *Māyā*, and no world-appearance; *Māyā* exists only as long as there is ignorance. The questions: 'What is the cause of *Māyā*? and 'How can *Māyā* conceal Brahman?' are easily set aside by saying that they simply do not arise, because, in the last analysis, *Māyā* does not exist.

[1] *SS*, p. 137.
[2] ibid, pp. 137-38.
[3] *See* Śaṁkara-bhāṣya on *Brahma-sūtra*, 1, 1, 4.
[4] *SS*, pp. 137-38.
[5] *See Brahma-Sūtra*, 3, 2, 1-2.
[6] *SS*, 138-41.

But if *Māyā* is regarded as non-existent, the logical implication is that the world is real. A.E. Taylor has, therefore, aptly described Śaṁkara's philosophy as 'illusion of illusion.'

To avoid the logical implications of both the positions, the Advaitins hold that *Māyā* is both real and unreal; real from the exoteric point of view and unreal from the esoteric point of view. But is not the exoteric point of view itself unreal? What then is the meaning of *Māyā* being real from the exoteric point of view?

The distinction between the esoteric and exoteric points of view is, for the Advaitins, the magical key for the solution of all their problems. If a problem arises in relation to the world, they say it does not exist from the point of view of Brahman, or the esoteric point of view; if there is a problem in relation to Brahman, they say it is due to the worldly or exoteric point of view. If, for example, the question is, 'Why does *jīva* who is identical with Brahman, suffer pain?,' the answer is 'Pain is due to bondage and bondage is due to *ajnāna*. There is no bondage and no pain from the point of view of Brahman.' If the question is, 'How can there be *ajnāna* when self-luminous Brahman is the only reality?,' the answer is, truly speaking, there is no *ajnāna*. *Ajnāna* is only from the worldly point 'of view and for the *jīva* in bondage.' This is actually no solution of the problem, but running away from it. To tell the *jīva*, suffering pain and death, hunger and disease, that he is actually not in bondage and there is actually no suffering *from the point of view of Brahman*, is no solution of the problem *for him*. The Advaitin, obviously, commits the fallacy of shifting the ground.

We have seen that the Advaitin also tries to solve the problem of dualism of Brahman and the world, or Brahman and *Māyā* by saying that the dualism is only apparent and from the exoteric point of view. But the dualism does not thus disappear. It only gives place to a new kind of dualism—the dualism of points of view. Though the Advaitin explains away the world, he is at a loss to explain the existence of two contradictory points of view in one and the same conscious principle. He will, of course, argue that no contradiction is involved, since the seats of the two points of view are different. But the seat is really the same, since *jīva*, who is regarded as the seat of the exoteric point of view, is also Brahman.

When thus cornered, the Advaitin says that there is, truly speaking, only one point of view, and that is the esoteric point of view. From that point of view, there is neither the world nor anything like the worldly point of view. If the Advaitin really means what he says, he should stop at this. Any other assertion by him would be meaningless, for it would involve the exoteric point of view. But he continues to talk of the necessity of the Guru and Upāsanā (worship) for the actual realisation of the esoteric point of view, and quotes the Śrutis, in support of what he says, even though he knows that from the esoteric point of view the Guru, the

God of worship, and the Śrutis, are all illusory.

It is, therefore, evident that the Advaitins cannot completely deny the existence of the world. Śaṁkara himself describes *ajnāna* as something positive or *bhāvarūpa*. His commentary on *Bṛahma-sūtra* also seems to confirm the view that he does not regard the world as completely unreal. Commenting on '*sattvāccāvarasya*' Sūtra, he says that if an effect does not already exist in the cause, the cause cannot produce that effect,[1] just as sand cannot produce oil. Since the world is caused by Brahman, it must exist in Brahman as Brahman, before its production; and since Brahman is eternal, the world must exist eternally.[2] Elsewhere, he says that before its production, the world lies concealed by positive ignorance (*bhāvarūpa tama*), just as water lies concealed in milk.[3]

If the world must exist in some form, the monism (*advaita*) of the Advaitins cannot be pure or unqualified. It must be qualified by the world, by *Māyā*, or by just a point of view that creates the appearance of the world. Thus qualified, it must involve both identity and difference, which means that it must be some kind of *bhedābheda*. This view is confirmed by Dr. Dasgupta, who thinks that Śaṁkara's commentary on Brhman-sūtra is convincingly in favour of some kind of *bhedābheda*.[4]

The concept of *Māyā* as both real and unreal itself seems to lead to *acintya-bhedābheda*. It implies that all the individual existences are both real and unreal, real as existence, unreal as particulars. It follows that the individual existences are atonce different and non-different from Brahman—different as particulars and non-different as existence. Being both real and unreal, they are described as *anirvacanīya* or indescribable. Therefore, the relation of difference in non-difference, which follows from their contradictory nature as real and unreal, must also be *anirvacanīya*.

The *anirvacanīya* of Śaṁkara, however, is not truly *anirvacanīya*. If it were so, *Māyā* would not be described as both real and unreal, and as beginningless but not endless. Śaṁkara knows it for certain that *Māyā* is both real and unreal, and describes it as such, but he cannot hold the two concepts together in thought. Therefore, *Māyā* is not *anirvacanīya* but *acintya* and the relation of *bhedābheda* between Brahman and the world, which follows from the nature of *Māyā* as both real and unreal, is also *acintya* and not *anirvacanīya*.

Śaṁkara's description of the transcendental reality also seems to imply the concept of *acintya-bhedābheda*. It is said to be a unity, which is neither identity nor difference, nor identity-in-difference. It is an inconceivable

[1]'*yacca yadātmana yatra na vartate, na tat tata utpadyate.*'—*Śaṁkara-bhāṣya* on *Br. S.*, 2, 1, 16.

[2]*yathā ca kāranaṁ brahman tṛṣu kāleṣu sattvaṁ ṇa vyabhiçarati, evaṁ kāryamapi jagat tṛṣu kāleṣu sattvaṁ na vyabhicarati.* ibid.

[3]*Vedāntakesarī*, 25.

[4]Dasgupta, *A History of Indian Philosophy*, II, p. 42.

unity (*acintya-abheda*). What is important in this description is not the unity but its inconceivability. Once it is granted that the nature of transcendental reality is inconceivable, it does not seem to make much difference whether we call it inconceivable unity, or inconceivable difference, or inconceivable identity-in-difference. Both inconceivable identity and inconceivable difference should mean inconceivable identity-in-difference. For neither is identity inconceivable without difference, nor is difference inconceivable without identity. That by *acintya-abheda* Śaṁkara actually means *acintya-bhedābheda* or inconceivable identity-in-difference is clear from some of his own statements. Śrī Sanātana Gosvāmin in his *Bṛhad-bhāgavatāmṛta* quotes Śaṁkara to explain the relation between the individual who has attained transcendental consciousness and the transcendental reality as that between a wave and the sea, in which the latter predominates.[1] In his commentary on *Śrī Nṛsinha-pūrvatāpanīya-ūpaniṣad*, Śaṁkara says, 'Even the liberated taking form worship God,'[2] which clearly implies that on the attainment of transcendental consciousness the identity of the Jīva is not completely merged; there is still a trace of difference left.

Also, from the epistemological point of view, the relation of *acintya-bhedābheda* between *jīva* and Brahman, which follows from Śaṁkara's characterisation of *Māyā* as both real and unreal, bears a strong resemblance to the doctrine of *acintya-bhedābheda* in the philosophy of Śrī Caitanya. Dr. M. Sircar, commenting on Śaṁkara's conception of *Māyā*, says, 'Though logically such nebulous character of *Māyā* cannot be denied still Vedantism here follows the affirmation of psychological experience and accepts such a category because its affirmation and denial are facts of psychological experience. Psychological revelations have in Śaṁkara's Vedāntism greater weight than logical determination. In fact, the logic of Vedāntism has followed the lead of psychic experience." The concept of *acintya-bhedābheda* in the philosophy of Śrī Caitanya is similarly based on experience, which eludes categorical determination. The Śakti is seen to be both different and non-different from its possessor and the relation of *bhedābheda* between the two is accepted as an instance of *arthāpatti*, though it is beyond logical understanding.

Acintya-bhedābheda and Viśiṣṭādvaita of Rāmānuja

Rāmānuja recognises three categories: *cit*, *acit*, and *Īśvara*. These are real and distinct from each other, yet together they form a unity. The 'unity' of Rāmānuja is, thus, not blank, but qualified. Although *cit*, *acit*, and *Īśvara* are equally real, ultimately, Īśvara alone is independent,

[1] *Bṛhad-bhāgavatāmṛta*, II, 2, 196.

[2] *muktāśca līlayā vigrahṁ parigṛhyanamantityanusaṅgah. Śrī Nṛsinha-pūrvatāpaniya-upaniṣad*, 2, 4. 6.

while *cit*, and *acit*, are dependent upon him. They are the body and modes, or attributes of *Īśvara*. Though essentially different in themselves, they cannot, as modes and attributes of *Īśvara*, exist by themselves. Just as the body is controlled, supported and utilised by the soul for its own end, matter and the souls are governed and sustained by *Īśvara*, and used by Him for the realisation of his ends.[1]

Rāmānuja's conception of the Absolute has been described as 'an organic unity in which, as in a living organism, one element predominates over and controls the rest. The subordinate elements are termed *viśeṣaṇas* and the predominant one *viśeṣya*.' 'Because the *viśeṣaṇas* cannot by hypothesis exist by themselves separately, the complex whole (*viśiṣṭa*) in which they are included is described as unity. Hence, the name '*Viśiṣṭādvaita*.'[2] The quality is not the same as substance, but, at the same time, it cannot exist outside the complex whole which it forms with the substance. The blueness of lotus is distinct from the lotus, yet it necessarily forms a part of the complex whole which the lotus is. For this reason, *Īśvara* is sometimes regarded by Rāmānuja as the absolute reality having two integral parts—matter and the souls. He is free from external distinction (*sajātīya* and *vijātīya bheda*), but not free from internal distinction (*svagata bheda*).

To explain this, Rāmānuja formulates a special kind of relation, which he calls *apṛthak-siddhi*, or inseparability. This relation subsists between substance and attribute and may also be found between two substances. *Apṛthak-siddhi* is an internal relation. As such, it differs from the *Nyāya-Vaiśeṣika* relation of *samavāya*, which is an external relation. It is a relation between members which are quite distinct and real, and in this respect it differs from the *Vedānta* view, in which all distinctions are unreal. It is not a bare identity which excludes all differences, but an identity which includes differences; it is the differences which lead to the affirmation of the identity. It should be noted carefully that Rāmānuja does not admit any kind of identity between the relata which the relation of *apṛthak-siddhi* brings together. The unity which is affirmed implies only the unity of a complex whole.

Rāmānuja accepts the *pariṇāma* doctrine, or *sat-kārya-vāda*. Thus, he speaks of two kinds of Brahman—*kārāṇa-brahman* and *kārya-brahman*. In the former state, pure matter and bodiless souls remain in Brahman in an unmanifested (*avyakta*) form; in the latter state, they become manifest. Creation and dissolution are the appearance and disappearance of the manifested form of pure matter and the souls, which, as modes and attributes, are coeternal with God. In the process of creation and dissolution, God, regarded as *viśeṣya*, does not change. The attributes (*viśeṣaṇa*),

[1] vide *Śrībhāṣya*, II, 1, 9.
[2] Hiriyanna, *Outlines of Indian Philosophy*, p. 399.

alone, change. But since the attributes are a part of the complex whole (*viśiṣṭa*), the whole is said to change.

Rāmānuja's system may be described as concrete monism. His Absolute is not a homogenous mass of abstract being, which denies the world of matter and the finite souls, but a concrete universal, which includes them as elements of its own being. It is not static, but a dynamic and growing reality called Brahman, because it *grows* or bursts forth into the cosmic variety. It is the self-conscious effort of self-realisation through self-revelation. The self-revelation is both transcendent and immanent, transcendent in *nitya-vibhūti* and immanent in *līlā-vibhūti*.

Rāmānuja's doctrine of adjectival predication is criticised by philosophers of the school of Śaṁkara and Mādhva as involving an infinite regress. A predicate must be either different from the subject or identical with it. If it is identical, predication is not possible. If it is different, the difference, if it has any meaning, must be real and absolute in which case also predication is not possible. If another predicate is instituted to bring about a relation that predicate, being different from the original subject and predicate, must again require another predicate to bring about a relation and so on *ad infinitum*.

Another difficulty with Rāmānuja is that although he recognises only one Being, *i.e.* the *viśeṣya*, he admits several entities which are regarded as ultimate. All the entities derive their being from the *viśeṣya*, as the attributes derive their being from the substance. It is not possible to reconcile their existential oneness with the differences between them, which are ultimate. It is also not possible to explain how God Himself remains changeless and free from the imperfection of the attributive elements which undergo change. His anxiety to maintain the oneness of being leads Rāmānuja to accentuate the inwardness of *jīva* and *prakṛti* by making them inhere in God as His attributes, but in so doing he also makes God responsible for their imperfections.

Rāmānuja is fully aware of this difficulty. To avoid the same, it appears, he adopts the analogy of the body and the soul. The analogy accentuates the outwardness of the relation between God and the world. The relation between the body and the soul is not essentially like the relation between the substance and the attributes. The soul remains unaffected by changes in the body and may exist without it. God, in the form of the *Antaryāmin*, regulates the universe, just as the soul regulates the body. But even this analogy does not seem to help very much, for the body is inert and its movements are entirely regulated by the soul. The responsibility for all its actions must, therefore, rest upon the soul. God, as the inward regulator, must be responsible for all the changes in the world and the actions of the Jīvas, who have no freedom of their own. Besides, so long as the soul identifies itself with the body it also suffers from its pains. If the relation between the *Antaryāmin* and the world be so close, how can the *Antaryāmin* remain unaffected by the sorrows and miseries of the world? Sometimes, therefore, Rāmānuja uses the analogy of the ruler and his subjects, which further accentuates the outwardness of the relation. The ruler frames the laws to be followed by his subjects, but the subjects have the freedom to obey or not to obey. He rewards or punishes them according to their deeds, but is not affected by their joys and sorrows.

From this we may conclude that Rāmānuja finds it difficult to describe the relation, which is essentially indescribable, but he accepts both identity and difference. This is clear from his commentary on *Brahma-sūtras*. In his commentary on *Sūtra*, II, 1, 22, he states that 'Just as the material world, or *acit* can never be absolutely identical with *Paramātman*, the *jīva*, or *cit* can never be absolutely identical with *Paramātman*' while in his commentary on *Sūtra*, II, 1.14. he emphasises that the world cannot be absolutely different from Brahman. Again, in his commentary on *Sūtra*, II, 3. 42. he advocates identity-in-difference, which means identity of one substance existing in two different forms (*prakāryādvaita*).[1] At the same time, however, Rāmānuja criticises the relations of identity, difference, and identity-in-difference as inadequate, and formulates the relation of *apṛthak-siddhi* to represent his special point of view. But this makes confusion worse confounded. For *apṛthak-siddhi* is not strictly a relation,[2] though it is sometimes spoken of as such.[3] As Datta and Chatterjee remark, "This is merely giving up the game of logical understanding. For, inseparability of existence is itself a vague relation admitting of various formulations. Even Śaṁkara's conception of the relation between the effect and the cause (*ananyatva*) can come under this."[4]

It is, therefore, evident that Rāmānuja accepts both difference and non-difference, but he cannot bring the relation under any logical category, which necessarily leads to the doctrine of *Acintya-bhedābheda*.

Acintya-bhedābheda and Svābhāvika-bhedābheda of Nimbārka

Nimbārkācārya recognises three entities, *cit*, *acit*, and *Brahman*, also called *bhoktṛ* (the enjoyer *Jīva*), *bhojya* (enjoyable matter), and *niyantṛ* (the controller, the Lord).

Acit is of three kinds—*prākṛta*, *aprākṛta*, and *kāla*. Prākṛta is the product of *prakṛti*. Aprākṛta is defined negatively as that which is not the product of *prakṛti*, but its real nature is not clearly brought out. Puruśottamācārya of the Nimbārka school has, in his *Vedāntaratna-mañjūṣā*, described *acitaprākṛta* as the material cause of the *dhāman* (celestial

[1] *ekama eva vastu dvirūpama pratīyate.*
[2] *Śrībhāṣya*, II, 2. 12.
[3] cf. *Sarvārtha-siddhi* with *Tattva-muktā-kalāpa*, by Vedanta Desika, p. 590.
[4] *An Introduction to Indian Philosophy*, p. 484.

abode) of Brahman and the bodies and ornaments etc. of Brahman and his associates.[1] It does not appear, however, that Nimbārkācārya also regards the body of Brahman as *aprākṛta-acit.* According to Śrī Caitanya, the *dhāman* and body of *Para-brahman* and all other things pertaining to the *dhāman* are *aprākṛta-cit.*

Śrī Nimbārkācārya has called his doctrine *Svābhāvika-bhedābheda* to distinguish it from the *bhedābheda* of Bhāskarācārya and others. Bhāskara's *bhedābheda* is called '*aupādhika-bhedābheda,*' because, according to him, *abheda* is real and eternal, while *bheda* is unreal and accidental. *Bheda* is due to accidental predicates (*upādhis*), like the body and the senses, and disappears on the attainment of *mokṣa.* According to Nimbārka, both *bheda* and *abheda* are equally real, because they characterise the very nature (*svabhāva*) of Brahman.

Thus, the special contribution of Nimbārka to the problem of relation between God and the world is his emphasis on the necessity of reconciling both the points of view of identity and difference. He has reconciled the apparently contradictory statements of the *Śrutis,* which sometimes seem to support identity and sometimes difference. His interpretation of the *Brahma-sūtras* is also, for this reason, more faithful to the Sūtras than the interpretations of Śaṁkara, Rāmānuja, Mādhva, and Vallabha. It is free from any effort to distort their real meaning.[2]

The philosophy of Śrī Caitanya, therefore, bears great resemblance to the doctrine of Nimbārka. Both Śrī Caitanya and Śrī Nimbārka give equal importance to identity and difference; both regard the individual souls and the world as the result of the Śakti of Brahman; both regard Brahman as the material cause of the world and the individual souls; both regard Śrī Kṛṣṇa as the ultimate reality.

The philosophers of the school of Śrī Caitanya did not term their doctrine of *bhedābheda* as *svābhavika* (natural or internal) *bhedābheda,* but this does not mean that they did not regard *bhedābheda* as *svābhāvika.* For, if both difference and identity are real, they must necessarily be *svābhāvika.*

Similarly, it may be surmised that, although Nimbārkācārya did not call his doctrine *acintya bhedābheda,* he must have regarded the simultaneous presence of identity and difference as due to the *acintya-śakti* of

[1] *The Cultural Heritage of India,* article by Dr. Roma Chowdury on 'The Nimbārka School of Vedānta,' p. 339.

[2] Dr. V. S. Ghāte, who has made a comparative study of the *bhāṣyas* of the five Acāryas, remarks 'If at all we insist on seeing in the *sūtras* one of the five systems under discussion, it can be at the most the *bhedābheda* system of Nimbārka, according to which both *bheda* and *abheda* are equally real, without the idea of any subordination of one to the other (*see* in this connection especially *sūtras,* III, 2. 27-29, which fit in with the doctrine of Nimbārka better than with any other—*The Vedānta* by V. S. Ghāte, p. 183.

Brahman. This is plausible, particularly in view of Nimbārka's commentary on *Brahma-sūtras*, *ātmani caivaṁ vicitrāśca*[1] and *srutetsu śabda mūlatvāt*,[2] which indicate his belief in the *acintya-śakti* of Brahman. However, there is nothing in the writings of Śrī Nimbārkācārya to lend support to this view.

On the other hand, it is evident that he tries to prove the relation of *bhedābheda* with the help of his doctrine of causation, according to which, cause and effect involve both identity and difference. The cause, though different from the effect, functionally and qualitatively, is identical with it by its nature and essence. The cause is also identical with the effect in the sense that the latter depends wholly upon the former. The cause is both transcendent and immanent in relation to the effect. Nimbārka also, tries to prove the relation of indentity-in-difference between Brahman and the world on the analogy of the relation between a whole and its parts.

Śri Jīva Gosvāmin says that the relation of identity-in-difference between Brahman and the world, or between Brahman and *Jīva*, cannot be proved by means of the relation of cause and effect, for the cause and the effect can never be one. The cause does not appear as effect in the state of cause and the effect does not appear as cause in the state of effect. The cause is identical with each effect individually, but not with all the effects collectively. If that were so, the distinction between the different forms of effect of a cause would be obliterated. The earth as cause is identical with each form of earthen pot severally, but if it were identical with all the pot forms collectively, there would be no difference between the different forms of earthen pots. It cannot be said that all the different pots are one as class, and different as particulars, for the same thing cannot have two different forms. To remove this difficulty, a third 'thing' will have to be postulated, to unite the two forms, and this will lead to infinite regress.[3]

The relation between part and whole also does not adequately describe the relation between Brahman and the world, for, in the case of Brahman, the identity between part and whole is not of the same type as the identity between part and whole of an ordinary object. In the case of an ordinary object, though the part is identical with the whole, in the sense that it has no existence apart from the whole, it actually is not the whole. But, in the case of Brahman, the part actually *is* the whole and has the same qualities and powers as the whole. This is a peculiar kind of relation, which eludes logical understanding. It is *bhedābheda* of a different kind. It is *acintya-bhedābheda*.

An important charge that Śrī Jīva brings against *Svābhāvika-bhedābheda* is that Brahman is by nature pure and perfect. But, if there is *svābhāvika*

[1]*VPS*, 2. 1. 28.
[2]ibid, 2. 1. 27.
[3]*SS*, pp. 148-49.

abheda between Brahman and *Jīva*, the impurities and imperfections of the latter must also belong to the former. Similarly, the qualities of omniscience and omnipotence, found in Brahman, must be shared by the *Jīvas*, who are by nature limited in their knowledge and power. If the relation of identity between Brahman and *Jīva* is such that Brahman is not in the least affected by the impurities and imperfections of the *jīvas*, it means that the relation is not only *svābhāvika*, but *acintya*. This is the reason why Śrī Caitanya has called his doctrine *acintya-bhedābheda* rather than simply *bhedābheda* or *svābhāvika-bhedābheda*.

It may be urged that the concept of *acintya* is so inextricably connected with the doctrine of *bhedābheda* that the acceptance of the latter necessarily implies the acceptance of the former. Therefore, Nimbāraka could not have accepted *bhedābheda* without, at the same time, recognising its essential nature as *acintya*, even though he tried to make it acceptable to the logical mind by means of reasoning, as far as that was possible. But, even then, *acintya-bhedābheda* would differ from *svābhāvika bhedābheda* in two important respects: Nimbārkācārya can, at the most, be said to have recognised *acintya-bhedābheda* (by implication) in the case of Brahman and his *śaktis*, or parts. But, Śrī Caitanya and his followers have adopted *acintya-bhedābheda* as an universal principle, applicable to *śakti* and its possessor everywhere, and have tried to establish it as such by reasoning. Further, in the case of Brahman, they have developed the idea of Divine Śakti, in its three aspects, as Antaraṅgā, Bahiraṅgā, and Taṭasthā, and have so accentuated difference, in the case of Bahiraṅgā and Taṭasthā Śaktis, that any transformation of them leaves Brahman entirely unaffetcted.

Acintya-bhedābheda and Bhedavāda of Mādhva

Mādhvācārya insists on five absolute and eternal distinctions between *Brahman*, *Jīva* and *Jada*, or the inanimate world: the distinction between *Brahman* and *Jīva*, between *Brahman* and the inanimate world, between one *Jīva* and another, between *Jīva* and the inanimate world, and between one inanimate object and another.

Brahman is Viṣṇu, who creates the world from *Prakṛti*, which is absolutely and eternally distinct from him. He is the efficient cause, but not the material cause, of the world. The Jīvas are the reflected counterparts (*pratibiṁbāṁśa*) of Viṣṇu. The bodies of the *Jīvas*, eternally present in Vaikuṇṭha, the celestial abode of Viṣṇu, are transcendental (*aprākṛta*). Hence, they are called unconditioned-reflected-counterparts (*nirupādhika-pratibiṁbāṁśa*) of Viṣṇu. The bodies of the *Jīvas* of the material world are material; therefore, they are called conditioned-reflected-counterparts (*sopādhika-pratibiṁbāṁśa*) of Viṣṇu.

The fivefold distinction between Brahman, *Jīva* and the inanimate world is not a mere appearance (*māyāmātra*): it is real and beginningless.

The world and the *Jīvas*, however, are wholly dependent on Brahman, who is their immanent ruler and regulator.

A special feature of Mādhva's philosophy is the category of *viśeṣa*, which he introduces to explain the appearance of *bheda*, where there is none. The category distinguishes a quality from a substance and apart from the whole. Between a substance and its quality or between a whole and its parts there is no difference. The difference appears on account of *viśeṣa*. We do not perceive any difference between the cloth and its whiteness, but we do perceive the *viśeṣa* (particularity) of the cloth. If there were difference between the cloth and its whiteness, then there would be difference between the difference and the cloth, and between the difference and the whiteness, and so on *ad infinitum*.[1] Unlike the *viśeṣa* of the *Nyāya-vaiśeṣika*, which characterises the eternal individual substances only, the *viśeṣa* of Mādhva characterises eternal as well as non-eternal substances. In the case of God, the principle of *viśeṣa* is employed to reconcile his unity with the plurality of his qualities and powers, and the plurality of His divine body, divine dress, divine abode, and the like.

The concept of *viśeṣa*, seems to be akin to the concept of *acintya-bhedābheda*. For Mādhvācārya hints that the identity-in-difference between the whole and the part, the substance and the attribute, the *śakti* and *śaktimān*, the agent and the action, in the case of Brahman as well as *Jīva* and *prakṛti*, is due to the *acintya-śakti* of Brahman.[2] *Viśeṣa*, thus, seems to be only another name for the *acintyā-śakti* of Brahman, which underlies the doctrine of *acintya-bhedābheda*. Dāsguptā, in fact, traces the supra-logical concept of *acintya* in the philosophy of Caitanya to the concept of viśesa in the philosophy of Mādhvā-cārya. He says, 'The idea of introducing a concept of the supra-logical in order to reconcile the different scriptural texts, which describe reality as characterless (*nirviśeṣa*), qualified (*viśiṣṭa*), and many, can be traced to the introduction of the concept of *viśeṣa* in the philosophy of Mādhva, by which Mādhva tried to reconcile the concept of monism with that of plurality.'[3] The view gains further support from the fact that Baladeva, the last of the important thinkers of the school of Śrī Caitanya, reverts to Mādhva's doctrine of *viśeṣa* in reconciling monism and pluralism, and characterises the concept of *viśeṣa* as being identical with the concept of *acintya*. He says that Brahman is spoken of as possessing the qualities of *sat*, *cit*, and *ānanda*, although these qualities constitute the essence of Brahman. This is due to the supra-logical functions of *viśeṣa* (*acintya-viśeṣa-mahimā*), because *viśeṣa* does not imply that Brahman is, from one point of view, identical with its qualities, and from another point of view different.[4]

[1] *Tattvapradīpa*, edited by B. N. Krishnamūrti Sharmā, p. 11.
[2] *Madhva-bhāṣya* on *Bhāgavata*, *Śloka*, 11. 7. 51.
[3] *A History of Indian Philosophy*, Vol. IV, p. 18.
[4] *Siddhānta-ratna*, Banaras, 1924, pp. 17-22.

We may, however, state that even though Mādhvācārya has used *viśeṣa* in the sense of *acintya-śakti* of Brahman, the *acintya* of Mādhvācārya is not the same as the *acintya* of the school of Śrī Caitanya. Mādhvācārya has used the concept of *acintya* to explain the relation of *bhedābheda* between part and whole, substance and attribute, and *śakti* and its possessor, in the case of Brahman, *Jīva* or *prakṛti*, but not between Brahman and *Jīva* or *prakṛti*.[1] The relation of *acintya-bhedābheda*, according to Śrī Caitanya, is a relation that obtains universally between *śakti* and its possessor, and since *Jīva* and *prakṛti* are the manifestations of the *śakti* of Brahman, it obtains between Brahman and *Jīva* or *prakṛti* as well.

Mādhvācārya's concept of *acintya* is not so *acintya*, or inconceivable, as the *acintya* of Śrī Caitanya. Mādhvācārya's *acintya* is related to *viśeṣa*, which reconciles the *appearance* of difference with identity, while Śrī Caitanya's *acintya* reconciles *real* difference with *real* identity.

It will not be proper, in this connection, to attach much importance to the expressions like '*acintya-viśeṣa-mahimā*' used by Baladeva, because he does not represent the true spirit of the philosophy of Śrī Caitanya and, in certain respects, his views are influenced by Mādhvācārya. His view on the doctrine of *acintya-bhedābheda*, also, does not seem to be free from this influence. For, like Mādhvācārya, he has also not made any mention of *acintya-bhedābheda* in connection with the problem of relation between God and *Jīva* or the world.

But, even though Mādhvācārya does not show any inclination for the doctrine of *acintya-bhedābheda*, his philosophy appears to lead to it, when pressed to its logical conclusion. His exclusive preference for *bheda*, or pluralism, is in direct contrast with Śaṁkara's exclusive preference for *abheda*, or monism. Just as pluralism, as an essential aspect of the absolute whole of reality, asserts itself time after time in the monistic philosophy of Śaṁkara, monism repeatedly asserts itself in the pluralistic philosophy of Mādhvācārya.

There is an aspect of identity in each of the five distinctions held by Mādhvācārya as absolute. God and the individual soul are identical, since both are conscious and related to each other as a whole is to its parts. God and the inanimate world are identical in as much as the latter is wholly dependent for its creation and maintenance on the former; one individual soul is identical with another, in as much as both are conscious in nature, both are parts of God, and both are dependent upon Him; the individual soul and the inanimate world are identical, in as much as both have a relative existence and are dependent on God; one inanimate object is identical with another, in as much as both are inanimate and wholly dependent upon God, who binds them together in a systematic whole.

[1] *Madhva-bhāṣya*, 2, 3, 28-9.

Having recognised the distinction between God, *Jīva* and the world, as absolute, Mādhvācārya cannot regard God as the immanent regulator of the Jīvas and the world, nor the Jīvas and the world as wholly dependent upon Him. It is only the *acintya-śakti* of God which can make this kind of dependence or immanent regulation, implying identity-in-difference, possible.

Mādhvācārya makes the category of Viśeṣa applicable to the whole and its parts in the case of God, *Jīva*, and the world. But he makes it inapplicable to God in relation to *Jīva*, although he recognises the latter as part of God. Obviously, this is due to his insistence on absolute difference between God and *Jīva*. But, if the difference is absolute, he should not regard the *Jīva* as part of God, which he does, probably to safeguard the infinitude and omnipresence of God. To hide the inconsistency involved in this, he introduces the concept of *pratibiṁbāṁśa*. The *pratibiṁbāṁśa*, or the reflected-counter-part of an object, is supposed to be different from the object as *pratibiṁba*, and identical as *aṁśa*.

Pratibiṁbāṁśa, however, is not a logical concept, for the part of the *pratibiṁba* (or the *pratibiṁba* of a part) of an object cannot be a part of the object itself. In case it is insisted that *pratibiṁbāṁśa* of an object means a reflected counterpart of the object, which is both different and non-different from it, *pratibiṁbāṁśa* must be a supra-logical concept, similar to the concept of *acintya-bhedābheda*.

The role of the concept of *pratibiṁbāṁśa* in the philosophy of Mādhvācārya is very much the same as that of the concept of *apṛthak-siddhi* in the philosophy of Rāmānuja. Both the Ācāryas propound their respective doctrines, but when forced by logic to adopt a position similar to *acintya-bhedābheda*, they use these concepts to conceal their helplessness.

Acintya-bhedābheda and Śuddhādvaita of Vallabhācārya

According to Śrī Vallabhācārya's doctrine of *śuddhādvaita*, Brahman is a pure unity, free from *Māyā*. It is also free from the three kinds of difference known as *svajātīya-bheda*, *vijātīya-bheda* and *svagata-bheda*. It is omniscient and omnipotent and possesses an infinite number of attributes. It has marvellous powers (*aiśvarya*) by virtue of which it can even hold together things or attributes which are mutually opposed.[1] Thus, it is both qualified (*saguṇa*) and unqualified (*nirguṇa*).[2] It is essentially of the nature of *sat* (existence), *cit* (intelligence) and *ānanda* (bliss).

Jīva and the world are identical with Brahman. *Jīva* is Brahman with the quality of bilss obscured and the physical world is Brahman with the qualities of bliss and intelligence obscured. Creation and destruction in their case mean the appearance (*āvirbhāva*) and disappearance (*tirobhāva*) of Brahman in these forms. Brahman is both the material and the efficient

[1]*Anubhāṣya*, 1, 1, 4.
[2]ibid, III, 2, 27.

cause of *Jīva* and the world, manifesting itself in these forms simply for the purpose of sport (*līlā*). In doing so, it does not undergo any change in essence. It is just like snake forming itself into coils.[1]

Jīva is an atomic part of Brahman, produced from its *cit* (intelligence) part, just as sparks are produced from fire. It is not an adjective of Brahman but Brahman under a limit.[2] That thou art implies pure identity between Brahman and *Jīva*.

There are three categories of Jīvas: *śuddha* (pure), *samsārin*, and *mukta*. *Jīva* is *śuddha* when its divine qualities, such as *aiśvaryā*, are not obscured by *avidyā* (ignorance); *saṁsārin* when, by the will of Brahman, its divine qualities are obscured and it comes in contact with *avidyā*, indentifying itself with the gross and subtle bodies; and *mukta* when, again by the will of Brahman, it is freed from bondage by *vidyā*.

The inanimate world (*jaḍa*) is created from the *sat* (existence) part of Brahman. It is, therefore, as real as Brahman. But the *Jīva*, under the influence of *avidyā*, endows it with illusory forms. The world is real, but its appearance (*pratīti*) to the *Jīva* under the spell of *avidyā*, is erroneous. It is like a man sitting on a moving boat perceiving a tree on the bank, to whom the tree appears to be in motion. The tree is real, but the perception of the motion of the tree is illusory. Similarly, the world, which is essentially of the nature of Brahman and, therefore, purely subjective and free from difference, is real, but the objectivity and multiplicity, which the *Jīva* in ignorance perceives in it, are unreal.

As already explained, the manifestation of Brahman as many does not involve any change. Brahman pervades the world in its fulness as existence, knowledge and bliss, but it manifests its three characters in different proportions in different objects of the world. For this reason, Vallabha regards Brahman as the *samavāyī kāraṇa* of the world, and uses the term *samavāya* in a sense different from that in which it is used by the Naiyāyikas. According to the Naiyāyikas, *samavāya* is the relation of inherence which exists between pairs like cause and effect, and substance and quality. But, according to Vallabha, it means identity (*tādātmya*), since, according to him, the substance itself appears in qualities and in cause and effect; there is no separate relation of inherence to combine these pairs. Between Brahman, *Jīva*, and *Jaḍa*, the relation is that of pure identity.

Both Śaṁkarācārya and Vallabha are *advaitins*, but while Śaṁkara's *advaita* implies complete denial of the world, Vallabha's *advaita* implies complete identification of Brahman with the world. By thus completely identifying Brahman with the world, however, Vallabha creates a number of difficulties, for, in this way, it is possible neither to maintain the purity of Brahman nor the independence of *Jīva*.

[1] *Anubhāsya*, III, 2, 27.
[2] ibid, II, 3, 29.

Jīva, being identical with Brahman, is endowed with all the divine powers (*aiśvarya*). It is bound by *avidyā* when, by the will of Brahman, its divine powers are obscured. It is not possible to understand how all the divine powers, including *Jnāna*, can be obscured. For *Jīva* is produced from the *cit* part of Brahman and *Jnāna* is the very essence of it. If *Jnāna* is obscured, the *Jīva* must cease to exist.

Since, according to Vallabha, the *Jīva's* association with *avidyā*, as well as his bondage and freedom, are brought about by the free will of Brahman for the purpose of sport, Brahman must be responsible for all the good and bad deeds of *Jīva*. This not only deprives *Jīva* of its freedom, but makes Brahman the *bhoktā* (enjoyer) of the fruits of its actions, which is contrary both to the nature of Brahman and the teachings of the *Śastras*.

Vallabha identifies the world with the *sat-aṁśa* (existence part) of Brahman. He is, therefore, compelled to regard the *sataṁśa* of Brahman as *Jaḍa*[1] (material), which is against the nature of Brahman as *sat-cit-ānanda. Sat*, *cit* and *ānanda* are, in fact, not three different things in Brahman. *Sat* actually means the *sattā*, or existence of *cit* and *ānanda.*

Vallabha holds that the manifestation of Brahman as many does not involve any change in the nature of Brahman, just as the conversion of gold into ornaments does not involve any change in the nature of gold. But the conversion of gold into ornaments does mean a change in form. Similarly, the manifestation of Brahman as many involves a change, in as much as it means the taking over by Brahman of new forms and it is difficult to see how it can escape the imperfections of these.

Although Vallabha affirms the relation of pure identity between Brahman, *Jīva* and the world, he says that identity is like the identity between part and whole. The relation between part and whole clearly implies identity-in-difference, for the part, though identical with the whole, is not the whole, and one part is different from another.

The relation of *samavāya*, even in the sense in which Vallabha uses it, also implies difference, for how can there be any relation at all without the different terms to be related? Vallabha himself admits difference in Brahman, for the sake of sport. But he is unable to explain how identity and difference are themselves related. The special sense in which the term *samavāya* is used accentuates identity but does not obliterate difference and seems to emphasise the concept of *acintya*, by somehow holding together identity and difference. To say that Brahman, by his own will, manifests himself as many, and to hold, at the same time, that multiplication does not cause any change in Brahman, without explaining how this is possible, amounts to the acceptance of a position similar to the doctrine of *acintya-bhedābheda*. Indeed, Vallabhācārya seems to come very near it when he says, at

[1]*Anubhāṣya*, II, 3, 43.

one place, that creation is possible on account of the unfathomable greatness and the incomprehensible powers (*aiśvarya*) of Brahman, which can hold together all sorts of opposites.[1] But his commitment to the principle of pure unity of Brahman prevents him from openly adopting it as the basic principle of his philosophy.

[1] *Anubhāṣya*, 2, 1, 26-31.

CHAPTER XII

Bhakti, the Means

Bhakti cannot, strictly speaking, be defined, because it is transcendental or *Nirguṇa* and beyond the three *Guṇas—Sattva*, *Rajas* and *Tamas*. Śāṇḍilya, however, defines it as *parānuraktirīṣvare*,[1] which means exclusive and intense loving attachment to the Lord.

Bhakti is recognised in *Śrīmad-bhāgavata* as *parama dharma* or the highest and the most satisfying function of the soul.[2] In *Skandha-purāṇa* Śrī Kṛṣṇa says in reply to a question by Uddhava "Devotion to me is the highest end (*lābho madbhaktiruttamaḥ*)."[3] Nārada describes *Bhakti* as indescribable love (*anirvacanīyaṁ prema svarūpaṁ*) and the grandest and sublimest of all human experiences. Even Madhusūdana Sarasvatī, the writer of *Advaita-siddhi*,[4] according to whom non-duality is the highest truth, regards Bhakti as hundred times superior to liberation.[5] He says that one realises at the dawn of true knowledge that duality is even more beautiful than non-duality.[6]

Śrī Caitanya recognises Bhakti as the only means for the attainment of the supreme Lord. He cites in this connection the following *Ślokas* from *Śrimad-bhāgavata* (*CC*, Madhya, XX, 121):

na sādhayati māṁ yogo na sāṁkhyaṁ dhrama Uddhava|
na svādhyāyastapastyāgo yathā bhaktirmamorjitā|| *Bh.*, II, 14, 21.

"It is not possible to attain me through *Jnāna*, *Yoga*, renunciation, penance, study of the scriptures or the performance of duty in the same manner in which it is possible to attain me through *Bhakti*."

bhaktyāhmekayā grāhyaḥ sraddhyā'tman priyaḥ satāṁ|

"I can be attaimed only through *Bhakti*, not through any other means."

[1]*Śāṇḍilya, Sūtra*, 2.

[2]*sa vai puṁsāṁ paro dharmo yato bhaktiradhokṣje|*
ahaitukyapratihatā yayā'tman samprasīdati|| —*Bh.*, I, 2, 6.

[3]*Skandha-purāṇa*, II, 9, 40.

[4]He has also written *Bhagavadbhakti-rasāyana*, *Bhāgavata-purāṇaprathama-śloka-vyākhyā*, *Bhagvat-gītā-gūḍhārtha-dīpikā*, *Veda-stuti-ṭīkā* and *Śāṇḍilya-sūtra-ṭīkā*, all of which promulgate Bhakti.

[5]*paramārthikam advaitaṁ dvaitaṁ bhajanahetave|*
tādṛsī yadi bhaktiḥ syāt sā tu muktiśatādhikā||

[6]*dvaitaṁ mohāya bodhāt prāk jāte bodhe manīṣayā|*
bhaktyarthaṁ kalpitaṁ dvaitaṁ advaitād api sundaram||

Bhakti, Jnāna, Karman and Yoga

Śrī Caitanya deprecates *Karman*, the way of action, *Jnānā*, the way of Knowledge and *Yoga*, because they do not lead to the same goal as *Bhakti* (*CC*, Madhya, XX, 121). *Jnāna*, which consists in discrimination and contemplation leads to the realisation of *Nirviśeṣa-brahaman* and the soul's immersion in it. *Yoga*, which consists of its eight fold ancillaries namely, *Yama* (restraint), *Niyama* (culture), *Āsana* (posture), *Prāṇāyāma* (breath-control), *Pratyāhāra* (withdrawl of the senses), *Dhāraṇā* (attention), *Dhyāna* (meditation) and *Samādhi* (concentration), leads to the realisation of *Paramātman*. *Karman*, which consists in the performance of *Nitya* (compulsory) and *Naimittika* (occasional) duties, as enjoined by the scriptures, leads to the attainment of heaven for as long as the effect of the good deeds performed by the *Jīva* does not get exhausted. But none of these leads to the attainment of Bhagavān.

Śrī Viśvanātha Chakravartin proves the superiority of *Bhakti* over *Karman*, *Jnāna* and *Yoga* by *anvayavyatireka*, that is, by the methods of agreement in presence and agreement in absence. Realisation of the supreme end as Bhagavān is present where *Bhakti* is present and absent where *Bhakti* is absent. *Jnāna* and *Yoga* do not lead to the realisation of Bhagavān, but only to the realisation of the partial aspects of Bhagavān accompanied by *Mukti*,[1] while *Karman* as such leads neither to Bhagavān nor to *Mukti*. *Karman* leads to *Mukti* only indirectly by preparing the way for it. All actions are not even preparatory to release. It is only actions preformed without any attachment that prepare the ground for ultimate release by producing a tranquil state of mind suitable for enquiry about the real nature of self. Therefore *Gītā* advises the resignation of all acts to Bhagavān.

But, it may be asked, if only disinterested actions are useful from the point of view of liberation, how shall we explain the Vedic injunctions regarding the preformance of ceremonial rites apparently aimed at acquiring facilities for worldly enjoyment? The answer is that the real object of Vedic injunctions is not to produce attachment to worldly objects but gradually to wean us out of them by permitting only restricted use of them and by offering counter-attractions. The ceremonial rites enjoined in the Vedas are, therefore, called *Parokṣa-kṛpā* and the *Karma-vāda* is called *Parokṣa-vāda*.

Jnāna and *Yoga* are not meant for all persons and all times and are not possible under all circumstances. Yoga is not possible for a man, who has not acquired complete control over his mind.[2] It can be practised

[1]The realisation of Saviśeṣa Paramātman to which Yoga leads is regarded as a stage higher than the realisation of Nirviśeṣa Brahman. If the Sādhaka is a Bhakta, Yoga is supposed ultimately to lead to the realisation of Bhagavān.

[2]*Gītā*, V, 6.

only in a sacred place and in a special posture of the body.[1] It enjoins the preformance of exercises, which are not within the capacity of everyone, specially in the age of *Kali*. *Jnāna* is not possible for persons, who have not developed aversion to the objects of the senses and do not possess philosophical acumen, self-restraint and tranquility of mind.[2] But *Bhakti* is possible for everyone—even for the lowliest and the most sinful[3]—and can be practised at all times and under all circumstances. Prahlāda is said to have practised *Bhakti* in his mother's womb, Dhruva in childhood, Ambarīśa in youth, Yayāti in old age, Ajāmila at the time of death, and Citraketu in heaven, after death. Even those consigned to hell[4] or those, who have attained liberation,[5] have practised devotion and attained the supreme end. *Bhakti* is meant alike for those who desire liberation and those who have attained it.

The paths of *Jnāna* and *Yoga* are not eternal. They cease as soon as the goal is attained. But *Bhakti* is the eternal and the supreme function of the soul (*parama dharma*). It is both the means and the end.

Bhakti is independent (*nirpekṣa*) of *Jnāna*, *Yoga* and *Karman*, but *Jnāna*, *Yoga* and *Karman* are dependent on *Bhakti* (*bhakti sāpekṣa*). They cannot lead to liberation or bliss without the aid of *Bhakti* (*CC*, Madhya, XXII, 14-15).[6] *Yoga* cannot even begin without *Bhakti*, because it implies faith in Bhagavān, whom the *Yogin* aims at realising in His partial aspect as *Paramātman*. No matter how long the *Yogin* performs the Yogic exercises and practises austerities, all his efforts will be useless, if he lacks in *Bhakti*.[7] But if he is sincerely devoted and perceives *Paramātman* in everything, he would realise Him and, as the *Gītā* says, the realisation would be lasting.[8] Because *Paramātman* is *Saviśeṣa* or qualified and we cannot realise him through *Yoga* without *Bhakti*, *Yoga* is sometimes regarded as a kind of *Bhakti* and is styled as *Yoga-misra bhakti* (*Bhakti* mixed with *Yoga*) or *Śānta-bhakti*.

The necessity of *Bhakti* for *Jnāna* is recognised even by Śaṁkara, who says in his commentary on *Gītā* that Jnānaniṣṭhā or fidelity to knowledge without which liberation is not possible, is itself the result of *Arcana-bhakti* or *Bhakti*, which consists in the ceremonial worship of the deities.[9]

[1] *Gītā*, VI, 36.
[2] *S. Bh.*, I, I, I.
[3] *bhaktiḥ punāti manniṣṭhā śvapākānapi sambhavāt*/ *Bh.*, II, 14, 21. Also *Gītā*, IX, 30.
[4] *yathā yathā hareranāma kīrtayanti ca nārkāḥ*/
tathā tathā harau bhaktimudbahantau divyaṁ yayuḥ// —*Haribhakti-vilāsa*.
[5] *muktā api līlayā vigrahaṁ kṛtvā bhagavantaṁ bhajante*/ *Nṛsiṁha-tāpanī*, 2, 5, 16.
[6] *kṛṣṇā bhakti haya abhidheya pradhāna*/
bhakti mukha nirīkṣaka karman joga jnāna//
[7] *Bh.*, II, 14, 21.
[8] *Gītā*, VI, 30-31.
[9] *Śaṁkara Bhāṣyā* on *Gītā*; VIII, 56.

Again in his commentary on *Brahma-sūtra*, he says that though liberation is the result of higher knowledge (*vidyā*), *Bhakti* prepares the ground for higher knowledge by bringing the grace of God.[1]

The realisation of *Nirviśeṣa-brahman* through *Jnāna* is also not permanent without *Bhakti*. Śrī Caitanya speaks of two kinds of men who follow the *Jnānamarga*, those, who do not have faith in Bhagavān and seek to realise Nirviśeṣa Brahman independently and those, who have faith in Him, but deisre to attain *Mukti* (*CC*, Madhya, XXIV, 16). The former attain liberation and the state of immersion in Brahman after a great deal of effort,[2] but there is every possibility of their again falling a prey to *Māyā*.[3] The latter attain the state of immersion in Brahman more easily due to the grace of Bhagavān. Bhagavān lets them enjoy this state for some time, but ultimately lifts them up to his own *Dhāman* so that they may enjoy the state of contiguity with him, which entails much higher pleasure than the state of immersion in Brahman. This is natural, because *Bhakti* which conditions their *Jnāna*, is, after all, a potency of Bhagavān himself.

There is no fruit of *Jnāna*, *Karman* and *Yoga* that cannot be attained by *Bhakti* without the aid of any other means. *Mukti*, the ultimate end of *Jnāna*, which the *Jnānin* attains after a long and arduous course of Sādhanā comes to the devotee of itself as a necessary accompaniment of *Bhakti* (*CC*, Madhya, XXII, 16).[4] *Jnāna* and *Vairāgya* are themselves natural concomitants of *Bhakti*.

Brahman being only a partial aspect of Bhagavān the Brahman-*jnāna* of the *Jnānin* is only a part of the knowledge of Bhagavān, which the Bhakta attains through devotion. *Vairāgya*, which is a forced affair in *Jnāna*, is a natural consequence of exclusive devotion to Bhagavān. The more intense is the love for Bhagavān, the less is the attachment to the objects of the world. The desire for worldly enjoyment, which is difficult to suppress and which results in so many complexes, if suppressed forcibly, automatically becomes weak as the desire for the loving service of Bhagavān becomes strong, and ultimately disappears.[5] Thus *Jnāna* and *Vairāgya* as independent means of realisation are redundant to *Bhakti*.

Similarly the tranquil state of mind (*citta-vṛtti-nirodha*), which *Yoga*

[1]*Śārīraka-bhāṣya* on *Brahma-sūtra*, 3, 2, 5 Śaṁkara, however, maintains that liberation is not directly the result of grace.

[2]*Gītā*. xii, 5,

[3]*Jīvanmuktā api punarvandhanaṁ yānti karmabhiḥ|*
yadyacintyamahāśaktyau bhagavatyaparādhīnaḥ||
—*Vāsanā-bhāśya* cited in *Bhakti-Sandarbha*.

[4]*kevala jnāna mukti dite nāre bhakti binā|*
kṛṣṇonmukhe śei mukti haya jnāna binā||

[5]Modern psychology also emphasises the need of sublimation of impulses rather than their suppression. It holds that total suppression of desires and impulses is not possible.

tries to reach through its eight fold (*aṣṭāṅga*) path and the *Asaṁprajnāta samādhi*, the soul's realisation of its real nature as the infinitesimal part of divine consciousness (*cit-kaṇa*), to which it ultimately leads, come to the devotee as the natural result of *Bhakti*.

The superiority of *Bhakti* over the other paths of realisation is thus apparent. Those, who prefer *Jnāna* to *Bhakti* are, therefore, likened to the people, who run after the chaff and leave out the grain. The *Gītā* texts VI, 46-47 state unequivocally that *Yoga* is superior to *Jnāna* and *Karman* and *Bhakti* is superior to them all.

Jnāna, *Yoga* and *Karman*, however, must not be underrated. They are useful as providing alternative ways for realising bliss for people, who are not by nature and temperament inclined towards *Bhakti*. They are also useful as aids to *Bhakti* in as much as they are free from all desires for worldly enjoyment. But since they aim at *Mukti* or a certain blissful state of self, they are not wholly disinterested or selfless in their approach (*CC*, Madhya, XIX, 132).[1] Therefore they may serve as aids to *Bhakti* only in the earlier stages, but must be given up later for the sake of Śuddha-bhakti or pure devotion, which is devotion without any selfish desire and without any cause (*ahaitukī*). But even in the earlier stages *Jnāna*, *Karman* and *Vairāgya* cannot be regarded as essential parts of *Bhakti*. Other virtues like continence, kindness and cleanliness also cannot be treated as parts of *Bhakti*, although they are its natural concomitants (*CC*, Madhya, XXII, 82).[2]

The Nature (*Svarūpa-lakṣaṇa*) *of Bhakti*

Rūpa Gosvāmin defines *Uttamā-bhakt* or the highest devotion as harmonious pursuit of Kṛṣṇa (*ānukūlyena kṛṣṇānuśīlana*), unenveloped by *Jnāna* and *Karman* (*jnānakarmādyanāvṛtam*)[3] and uninterrupted by the desire for anything. The pursuit is not harmonious if the devotee harbours in his heart any desire other than the desire for the service of Kṛṣṇa. Like the Kantian doctrine of the Categorical Imperative of Duty the doctrine of *Bhakti* implies the Categorical Imperative of service to Kṛṣṇa. The devotee serves Kṛṣṇa for the pleasure of Kṛṣṇa and not for anything else.[4] But unlike the Kantian Imperative, which is dry and exacting and an imposition from without, the Categorical Imperative of service to Kṛṣṇa is the natural function of the soul and therefore pleasant and satisfying in itself. Though the devotee serves Kṛṣṇa for the pleasure of Kṛṣṇa pleasure comes to him automatically. Such is the very nature of

[1]*kṛṣṇa bhakta niṣkāma ataeva śānta|*
bhukti mukti siddhi kāmī sakali aśānta||

[2]*jnāna vairāgyādi bhaktir kabhu nahe aṁga|*
ahiṁsā yama niyama ādi bule kṛṣṇa bhakta saṁga||

[3]This is in opposition to Rāmānuja, who defines it as *jnānakarmānugṛhitam.*

[4]*svanuṣṭhitasya dharmasya saṁsiddhiḥ hariṭoṣaṇam|* —*Bh.*, 1, 2, 6.

Bhakti. But if the devotee's attitude of service is tainted in the slightest degree with a concealed desire for his own pleasure, he is deprived to that extent from the supreme delight that comes from Śuddha-bhakti. Even the pleasure that automatically comes to the devotee from an act of service is condemned by a pure devotee, if it is in any manner an obstruction to service.

It is regretable that the idea of service is not properly understood and appreciated by those, who find it difficult to reconcile it with their egoism. They think that the path of *Bhakti* is meant exclusively for persons, who are intellectually weak and temperamently submissive. They cannot understand that in the spiritual world, where love reigns supreme, to serve is to love and to love is to rule. In love self-sacrifice is self-realisation and self-effacement is self-fulfilment. In love there is receprocity. Each member of the loving relation depends on the other; each feels deficient without the other; each wants to draw close to the other and to win the other by love and service. The Lord being the other member in the loving relation of *Bhakti*. He wants to realise Himself more fully through the loving service of His devotees. He derives greater pleasure in being controlled by His devotees than in lording it over them.[1]

But though *Śuddha-bhakti* has no place for *Jnāna*, *Karman* and *Vairāgya* as such, *Jnāna*, *Karman* and *Vairāgya* as directed to Bhagavān are necessarily implied in it. It presupposes a certain knowledge of the object of devotion, His form and attributes and the relationship that obtains between Him and the rest of the world. *Caitanya-caritāmṛta* warns against any indifference towards knowledge of this kind, which is necessary for firm faith in Kṛṣṇa and exclusive devotion to Him (*CC*, Ādi, II, 99).[2] *Bhakti* also implies acts like hearing the praises of the Lord (*sravaṇa*), and chanting his name or singing his praises (*Kīrtana*). It implies *Vairāgya*, not in the sense of renunciation of the objects of the world, but in the sense of their dedication to the service of Kṛṣṇa. It does not imply complete eradication of cravings and impulses, but complete transformation or purification of them under the subordination of the central impulse of service to Kṛṣṇa. In *Bhakti* the natural conflict between life and spirit is saught to be resolved not by denying life but by making it conform to spirit. The infusion of spirit into life changes the very character of our instincts. The instincts are nature's urges. The infusion of spirit turns them into spiritual urges. The manifestations of natural urges are gross and painful, while the manifestations of spiritual urges are fine and delightful. Caitanyism thus introduces a new outlook in life.

[1]*bhaktivaśaḥ puruśo bhaktireva bhūyasī/ —Māṭhara-śruti.*
ahaṁ bhakta parādhīno hyasvatantra iva dvija/ —Bh., 9, 4, 64.

[2]*siddhānta baliyā citte na kara ālasa/*
ihā haite Kṛṣṇa lāge sudṛḍha mānasa//

It promises a new joy by rejuvenating and reforming life on a spiritual pattern. Vairāgya for its own sake or *Vairāgya* consisting in the renunciations of all objects of the world, as a means to the realisation of *Mukti* is, therefore, termed *Phalgu vairāgya*, while *Vairāgya*, which is dedicated to the service of Kṛṣṇa, is called *Yukta-vairāgya*.

Bhakti is not inconsistent with either *Bhoga*, (enjoyment) or *Vairāgya* (indifference to the objects of the world) or *Mukti* (liberation). But neither *Bhoga*, nor *Vairāgya*, nor *Mukti* is the end of *Bhakti* or a part of it (*CC*, Madhya, XXII, 83).[1] True *Vairāgya* is that in which the worldly objects are enjoyed without any attachment (*āsakti*) and with the ultimate aim of realising Kṛṣṇa. Describing the qualification necessary for *Bhakti* Rūpa Gosvāmin says that only those persons are fit for *Bhakti*, who havefaith in Kṛṣṇa (*Jātasraddhā*) and, who are neither too much attached (*nātisakta*) nor too indifferent (*na nirviṇna*) to the world. Kṛṣṇa says to Uddhava '*Jnāna* and *Vairāgya*, as such, usually do not promote the spiritual welfare of persons, who are sincerely devoted to me.'[2]

But *Jnāna*, *Karman* and *Yoga*, as directed to *Bhagavān*, are not only useful but the very channels through which *Bhakti* functions. For *Bhakti* 'works on our entire personality. It takes different shapes in knowledge, devotion, and service. In knowledge it is the divine curiosity; in devotion it is the integrating force; in service it is the will taking the shape of a cosmic force and fulfilling the divine ends in creation.'[3]

Jnāna and *Karman*, therefore, cannot be treated in isolation from devotion. Devotion presupposes a certain knowledge of the object of devotion. This is indicated by the very nature of the Hlādinī-śakti, which includes the Samvit-śakti or the Śakti, which is the seat of knowledge. But as an integrating force it brings us closer to the object of devotion and leads to greater intimacy with it. Greater intimacy results in higher knowledge, which again is followed by active expression in love and service. The knowledge of the devotee is not like the abstract and passive knowledge of the *Advaitin*, which makes him stand as a witness or an independent onlooker of the movement of life in triple *Guṇas*. "To him knowledge and life are eternally associated. To know is to act. Every fresh acquisition of knowledge makes the movement of life more graceful, for it reveals the love that is at the heart of existence; and the two axes of love are knowledge and service."[4]

The path of realisation is but one and that is the integral path of *Bhakti*. This is the real teaching of the scriptures. Śrī Caitanya regards

[1] *jnāna vairagyādi bhaktira kabhu nahen aṁga/*
yama niyamādi bule kṛṣṇa bhakti sāṁga//
[2] *tasmānmadbhaktiyuktasya yoginovaimadātmanaḥ/*
na jnānaṁ ca vairāgyaṁ prāyaḥ sreyo bhavediha// —*Bh*., 11, 20, 31.
[3] M.N. Sircar, *Hindu Mysticism*, pp. 118-19.
[4] *ibid*, p. 115.

it as the very essence of the Vedas (*C. Bh.*, Madhya, I, 148, IV, 33). If the people speak of many paths of realisation, they do so because their intelligence is clouded by *Māyā*.[1] The intelligence of different persons is differently conditioned by the three *Guṇas* of *Prakṛti*. Therefore, they interpret the Vedas differently and speak of the paths of realisation as more than one.[2]

It is not possible to look at *Jnāna*, *Karman* and *Bhakti* as means of realisation in their proper perspective without reference to the nature of Bhagavān and *Jīva* and the nature of relationship that obtains between them. *Jīva* is only an infinitesimal part of Bhagavān, who has strayed away from Him under the influence of *Māyā*. His own power is limited, while the power of *Māyā*, as the Śakti of Bhagavān, is unlimited. He cannot, therefore cross the bounds of *Māyā* without the help of Bhagavān. *Jñāna*, *Karman* and Yoga, in their abstract form, in which they involve independent efforts on his part are of no avail. The very nature of *Jīva*, as an independent being, precludes him from realising the perfect by his own effort (*Bṛhad*, I, 4). The only course open to him is the way of *Bhakti*. Śrī Kṛṣṇa Himself says "It is difficult, indeed, to overcome My *Māyā* independently of Me. Only they can overcome it, who are sincerely devoted to Me" (*Gītā*, VII, 14). Only *Jnāna*, which proceeds from the higher intelligence granted by Śrī Kṛṣṇa to one, who is sincerely devoted to Him, or *Jnāna*, which is the product of *Bhakti*, the Hlādinī-śakti of Bhagavān, can dispel the clouds of ignorance and enable the *Jīva* to attain Bhagavān and not *Jnāna*, based on his own limited understanding (*Gītā* X, 10-11).

Bhakti is a spiritually gravitating force that takes us to the centre. It is a force that works at two ends. In our own hearts it roots out all egoistic impulses that carry us away from the centre and releases the integrating forces leading to complete surrender of all our faculties, so that knowledge love and will may act in complete harmony with the divine rhythm. In God it energises His mercy and releases the forces of redemption, which lead to the final integration of our being with Divine Will. This is confirmed by Kṛṣṇa's exhortation to Arjuna, in which he asks him to surrender himself completely to his will and promises, on his so doing, to free him from all bondage and sin (*CC*, Madhya, XXII, 50, S 44). This is the principle of divine grace necessarily implied in *Bhakti*.

It may be asked as to how the principle of divine grace can be reconciled with the transcendent and self-sufficient character of the Divine Being, Who remains unaffected by *Prakṛti* and is without any desire or motive. The answer lies in the nature of *Bhakti* as a function of the Hlādinī-śakti, which, as we have already seen, energises both Bhagavān

[1]*Bh.*, 11, 14, 9.
[2]*Bh.*, 11, 14, 5-7.

and the *Bhakta*. Like the lamp, which reveals itself as well as the other objects, the Hlādinī-śakti of Bhagavān placed (*nikṣiptam*) in the hearts of His devotees causes bliss to Him as well as to His devotees. In fact, Bhagavān, the supreme relisher of bliss (*rasika-śekhara*) relishes the bliss, flowing from His Hlādinī-śakti, placed in the hearts of His devotees (*śaktyānanda*), even more than He relishes bliss, which flows from the nature of His own self (*svarūpānanda*). On account of the gravitational force of the Hlādinī-śakti the Bhakta is drawn towards Bhagavān and Bhagavān is drawn towards the Bhakta. The Bhakta surrenders himself to Bhagavān and Bhagavān surrenders Himself to the Bhakta. Grace is nothing but the surrender of Bhagavān to the Bhakta.[1]

The whole of spiritual life is governed by the Law of Harmony. Love is the Law of Harmony in its highest form. Self-surrender on our part and Mercy on the part of God are the manifestations of the Law of Harmony.[2] In the Yoga of self-surrender the soul strikes a divine chord and realises an inner harmony, which is of the highest order, and a poise and equilibrium, which is much more than intellectual.

The Effects of Bhakti

What we have said above describes the essential nature (*svarūpa-lakṣaṇa*) of *Bhakti* as a function of the Svarūpa Śakti of Bhagavān. Śrī Jīva shows the supreme efficacy of *Bhakti* by mentioning its non-essential characteristics (*taṭastha lakṣaṇa*) or effects, which naturally flow from it and which further establish the superiority of *Bhakti* over *Jnāna*, *Karman* and *Yoga*. Some of the more important of these are as follows:

1. *Bhakti* leads to the fulfilment of all desires (*sarva-kāmaprada*). It is infinitely more fruitful, in this respect, than any other religious exercise like Yajna, Tapa or Homa.
2. It destroys all evil (*aśubha-hāriṇī*). The Lord Himself says in the *Skandha Purāṇa, Dvārakā Mahātmya*, "Not only do I see that my Bhaktas do not suffer from any evil in this world or the next, I carry millions of their generations to the highest Vaikuṇṭha." Śrīdhara Svāmin says in his commentary on the *Bhāgavata Śloka* 6, 1,15 that the person following the path of *Bhakti* does not feel that he is without any protection, as does a man traversing the path of knowledge.

[1]Grace is not extended to the suffering souls directly, but through the saintly persons, who are themselves the recepients of grace, because God is of the nature of pure bliss and it is not possible for Him to have an experience of their suffering. It is true that the saintly persons are also beyond the phenomenal world and its sufferings, but, it is said, they have the memory of past sufferings, which fill their hearts with sympathy for them.

[2]"God energises as Mercy at the summit and perfection of his activity."—Meister Eckheart, cited by S.C. Chakravarti in *Philosophical Foundations of Bengal Vaisnavism.*

3. It removes all impediments (*sarva-vighna-nāśinī*). Even the liberated souls fall and are reborn, if they commit some offence at the feet of the Lord, but the devotees, even if they are not liberated, they do not fall or slip from the path of Bhakti.[1] Being eternally tied to the feet of the Lord by the bond of love (*baddhasauhṛdāh*) they are always protected by Him, and march ahead fearlessly, crushing all impediments.[2]

4. It instantly removes all fears and anxieties (*sarva-bhaya-kleśa-nāśinī*) just as the sun instantly removes darkness. In *Vṛhannāradīya* Nārada says to Yudhiśṭhira "Where reside the devotees of the Lord neither the king, nor robbers, nor gods, nor demons, nor ghosts, nor disease can do any harm."[3]

5. It counteracts sinful acts (*pāpa-hāriṇī*), whether they have begun to produce effects or not, that is, whether they are *prārabdha* or *aprārabdha*. *Padma-purāṇa* says that just as the flaming fire (*susamiddhārcciḥ*) consumes a heap of wood atonce, devotion to the Lord destroys sins immediately (*tatkṣaṇāt*):

yathāgniḥ susamiddhārcciḥ karotyedhāṁsi bhasmāt/
pāpānibhagavadbhaktistathā dahati tatkṣaṇāt//

The words '*susamiddhārcciḥ*' and '*tatkṣṇāt*' are meaningful. They indicate that *Bhakti* is not dependent even on the rules and regulations (*vidhi sāpekṣa*) of devotional practices like Sravaṇa and Kīrtana. If there be lapses in observing these rules, they do not prevent *Bhakti* from yielding results quickly, just as the demerits of the objects, which fall into the blazing fire, do not prevent it from consuming them quickly. Śrī Jīva takes the word '*tatkṣaṇāt*' to imply that *Bhakti* does not wait for *Karman* or *Jnāna* or anything else to produce results, since it is independent of them and self-sufficient (*nirpekṣa*).

Śrīdhar Svāmin, similarly interprets the *Bhāgavata Śloka* 6, 1, 16, which says that nothing purifies the sinner like total surrender to the feet of Kṛṣṇa through sincere and selfless service of his devotees. Śrī Jīva cites the *Bhāgavata Ślokas* 3, 33,6-7, highlighting the changes Bhakti quickly brings about in the lowliest of persons, to show how it completely and quickly destroys the *Prārabdha* sins.

6. It conquers even the desire for sinful acts (*pāpa-vāsanā-tāriṇī*). Penance (*tapa*), alms-giving (*dāna*) and fasting (*vrata*) etcetra can destroy sin, but not the subtle tendency to perform sinful acts. This can be uprooted only by the practise of devotion to the feet of the Lord.[4]

7. It removes ignorance (*avidyā-nāsīni*). It has been said in the *Bhāgavata*

[1] *BS*, 120.
[2] *tathā na te mādhava tāvakāḥ kvacidbhraśyanti mārgātvayi baddha sauhṛdāḥ/ tvayabhiguptā vicaranti nirbhayā vināyakānīkapa-mūrdhasu prabho// —Bh.*, 10, 2, 27
[3] *Vṛhannāradīya*, 7, 5.
[4] *Bh.*, 6, 2, 17.

that devotion to Bhagavān slowly cuts asunder the knot of ignorance, which arises from the 'I' and 'My' consciousness.[1]

8. It satisfies everyone (*sarvatoṣiṇī*). Just as by watering the roots of a tree we feed its branches and leaves, by practising devotion to the Lord we satisfy the whole of creation. Just as water naturally takes the downward course, all the creatures naturally bow down to the devotee when the Lord is pleased with him.[2]

9. It is the breeding ground of all good qualities (*sarvaguṇa-dāyinī*). The gods themselves are said to reside in the heart of a devotee along with *Dharma*, *Jnāna*. *Vairāgya* and all other auspicious qualities.[3]

10. It is transcendental or beyond the three *Guṇas—Satva*, *Rajas* and *Tamaṣ* (*nirguṇa*). *Jnāna* and *Karman* and all other forms of worship are qualified by the Guṇas (*saguṇa*). All *Jnāna*, except that which is related to Bhagavān, is born of Sattva. It is possible for a person, in whom Sattva predominates, to attain Brahman-jnāna, but it is not possible for him to attain knowledge of Bhagavān without Bhakti. Even the gods and saints, whose hearts are pure and wholly qualified by Sattva, cannot realise Bhagavān without Bhakti.[4] But even a demon like Vṛtrāsura, in whom there isn ot the least trace of Sattva, may attain the knowledge of Bhagavān[5] on account of his association with a devotee like Nārada (whom he had met in his previous birth as Citraketu.)[6] Similarly all karmans, except those performed in the service of Bhagavān, like listening (*sravaṇa*) or singing (*kīrtana*) the praises of the Lord are Nirguṇa, while all other actions are Saguṇa. Actions performed without attachment are qualified by Sattva; actions performed with a view to enjoy the objects of the material worlds are qualified by Rajas; while actions performed blindly, without thinking of their good or bad results, are qualified by Tamas.[7]

11. It is self-manifest (*svaprakāśa*). It is not conditioned by caste, any particular condition of the body, any particular time, or anything else. Thus, it manifested itself in the elephant, who did not have any qualification whatever, when, attacked by crocodile, he was in the mouth of death.[8]

12. It is identical with supreme bliss (*parama-sukha-svarūpa*).[9] It is not

[1]ibid, 4, 11, 29. cited in *BS*, Sec. 130.
[2]ibid, 4, 31, 16. cited in *BS*, Sec. 131.
[3]ibid, 5, 18, 12. cited in *BS*, Sec. 132.
[4]ibid, 14, 2, 5. cited in *BS*, Sec. 134.
[5]ibid, 6, 14, 1. cited in *BS*, Sec. 134.
[6]ibid, 7, 5, 25. cited in *BS*, Sec. 134.
[7]*BS*, Sec. 136.
[8]*BS*, 139.
[9]Śrī Rūpa describes this as a particular kind of compact happiness, which is infinitely superior to the bliss of Brahma-sāksātkāra and which he calls *sāndrānanda-viśeṣātmatā.*

only extremly delightful as an end but also as a means (*sādhana*) and therefore it makes the devotees indifferent towards *Mukti*.
13. It subjugates the Lord (*bhagavadvaśakārṇī*). If there is anything that may vanquish the Lord, the vanquisher of all, it is *Bhakti*.[1]

Sādhana-bhakti

Bhakti is either Sādhana-bhakti or Sādhya-bhakti. Sādhana-bhakti is the means; Sādhya-bhakti is the end. Truly speaking Sādhya-bhakti is not the result of any Sādhanā or effort. It is the eternally realised but non-manifest function of the soul. Sādhana-bhakti consists in the attempt to make this function manifest. Any method or means by which a person can successfully divert his mind towards Kṛṣṇa is, therefore, commonly reckoned under Sādhana-bhakti.

Śrī Caitanya classifies the Aṁgas or elements of Sādhana-bhakti under sixty-four general heads. (*CC*., Madhya, XXII, 61-71). Śrī Jīva reduces them to eleven: *śaranāpattīḥ, guru-sevā, sravaṇa, kīrtana, smaraṇa,pāda-sevā, arcanā, vandana, dāsya, sakhya, ātma-nivedana*.

Śaraṇāpattiḥ consists in resorting to Bhagavān as the only refuge. It is analysed into (*a*) *anukūlasya saṁkalpaḥ pratikūlyavivarjanaṁ*, meaning the attitude that accepts what is congenial and rejects what is not congenial to devotion, (*b*) *rakṣisyatīti viśvāśaḥ* or the belief that Bhagavān will protect against all ills, (*c*) *goptṛtve varaṇam* or choosing Bhagavān as one's protector, (*d*) *ātma-nikṣepaḥ*, or resignation of self and (*e*) *kārpaṇyam*, or humility. Choosing Bhagavān as protector is the central element in the state of Śaraṇāpattiḥ, other elements being auxilaries. Next in importance is the attitude of resignation, which implies the conviction on the part of the devotee that he is not the actual doer and that an invisible power moves him and makes him do what it wills. Kārpaṇya is a state altogether free from self-conceit (*ahaṁkāra*), a state in which the devotee says from the core of his heart "Oh Lord! There is none so Merciful as Ye and none so low and deserving of Thy Mercy as me." God is not so close to anyone as He is to a person, free from self-conceit, while He is not so far away from anyone as He is from a man, who is full of conceit.[3]

Guru-sevā or devotion to the spiritual guide is an essential part of *Bhakti*. The Guru must not be regarded as an ordinary person, but as

[1]Śrī Rūpa calls this *srikṛṣṇākarṣaṇatva*.

[2]*bhaktirevainaṁ navati, bhaktirevainaṁ darśayati, bhaktivaśaḥ puruṣo bhaktireva bhūyasi.* —*Māthara-sruti*

ahaṁ bhakta parādhīno hyasvatantra iva dvija/
sādhubhirgrastahṛdayo bhaktir-bhaktajanapriyaḥ//—*Bh*., 9. 4. 64.

[3]*BS*., Sec. 236.

one, who is identical with Kṛṣṇa, and should be worshipped as such.[1] The Guru is also spoken of as the mediator between the Bhakta and Bhagavān. It is not possible for the earth bound *Jīva* to cross the ocean of *Māyā* and attain Bhagavān without his help. Devotion to the Guru is capable of rescuing the *Jīva* from evil (*anartha*) in all its various forms, lust, anger, greed etc., each of which is difficult to overcome and requires a different kind of effort to be uprooted.[2] Devotion to the Guru is even more important than devotion to Kṛṣṇa. For the Guru can save a devotee if he incurs the displeasure of Kṛṣṇa, but Kṛṣṇa cannot save him if he incurs the displeasure of the Guru.[3] The worship of the Guru should, therefore, always precede the worship of Kṛṣṇa. Kṛṣna Himself says, "I am not pleased by the performance of one's duty as a householder (*ijyā*), Brahmacārī (*prajāti*) Vānaprastha (*tapasyā*), or Saṁnyāsin (*upaśama*) as I am pleased by the worship of the Guru."[4] This does not mean that the Guru should be worshipped to the exclusion of Kṛṣṇa, but that both the Guru and Kṛṣṇa should be worshipped (*CC*, Madhya. XXII, 18). The Guru, however, must fulfil all the reqirements of a Guru as laid down in the scriptures. If he deviates from the path of a Vaiṣṇava, if he cannot discriminate between right and wrong, or if he is full of self-conceit, he should be abandoned.[5]

Sravaṇa is listening to the accounts of the name, form, qualities and sports of Kṛṣṇa. Sravaṇa is particularly efficacious if the person presenting these accounts is a real devotee. There is no rule as to whether one should listen to one or more of these different kinds of accounts. One can realise the end by listening only to the name, or form, or qualities, or sports of Kṛṣṇa. There is also no rule regarding the order to which one must adhere in listening to these accounts. But the order generally recommended is that one should first listen to the account of the name and then to the accounts of the form, qualities and the sports of Kṛṣṇa. Listening to the name purifies the heart and prepares the ground for the gradual appearance of the divine form, qualities, and sports.

Kīrtana consists in chanting the name of Bhagavān, singing His praises, and relating what one has heard in Sravaṇa about His name form, qualities, and sports to others. According to Śrī Caitanya *Kīrtana* is the most important and the most efficacious of all devotional practises. *Kīrtana* in any form is important. But the chanting of the name of the Lord has a special significance for the age of Kali. It is the only means of God-

[1] *ācāryam māṁ vijānīyannāvamanyetakarhicit/*
na martyabuddhyāsuyeta sarvadevamayoguruḥ//—*Bh.*, 11, 17, 27.

[2] *Bh.*, 7, 15, 22-25.

[3] *harau ruṣṭe guruṣtrātā gurau ruṣṭe na kaścana/* —cited in *BS*, sec. 237.

[4] *nahamijyā-prajatibhyam tapaso paśamena vā/*
tṣeyaṁ sarvabhūtātman guruśusruṣayā yathā// —*Bh.*, 10, 8, 34.

[5] *BS*, Sec, 238.

realisation in this age. One can easily attain through it the results, which, in other ages, could be attained through meditation. sacrifice or worship (*CC*, Madhya, XX, 287).[1] Meditation etcetra require the fulfilment of certain conditions, which cannot be easily fulfilled in this age. But the chanting of the name is free from all such conditions. No restrictions of time, place, person, or states of body and mind apply to it. It can be chanted by any one, in any condition, and at any time or place.[2] No wonder, therefore, that the chanting of the Name is glorified in the *Ṛgveda*[3] and is described in the *Caitanya-caritāmṛta* as the very essence of the scriptures (*CC*, Ādi, VII, 72).

Saintly persons of all climes and ages have attached great importance to the Name.[4] But Śrī Caitanya has a philosophy of it, which is unique. The Name, according to him, is not a mundane word or sound. Its similarity with the mundane word is only apparent. It is in essence spiritual.[5] Unlike the mundane word it is one with the person to whom it refers. The relation between it and the object of its reference is that of inconceivable identity-in-difference.[6] It is the Lord Himself, who graciously appears on the tongue of the devotee in the form of the Name. The devotee may not realise this in the beginning on account of the accumulated effect of the sins committed by him in the past, which blurs his vision.[7] But constant repetition of the Name purifies his heart. Then appears the Śuddha Nāma or the name in all its purity and splendour. The clouds of ignorance are then dispelled and the curtain that hides from him the Divine Līlā of Śrī Kṛṣṇa is also removed.

The Name should not be regarded as mundane because it is uttered through the medium of the tongue. Though the Name is uttered through the tongue, like any other word, it is not mechanically manipulated by it. Being identical with Bhagavān, it is independent and incapable of being mechanically manipulated.[8] It appears on the tongue of its own

[1]Also
kṛte yadhyāto viṣṇuṁ tretāyāṁ yajato makhaiḥ|
dvāpare paricaryāyāṁ kalau tadharikīrtanāt||
—*Bh.*, 12, 3, 55. cited in *CC*, Madhya, XX, S55.

[2]*khāite śuite jathā tathā nāma laya|*
deśa-kāla-niyama nāhi sarvasiddhi haya|| *CC*, Antya, XX, 14.

[3]*Ṛgveda* 1, 159, 3.

[4]R. D. Ranade, *Mysticism in Maharashtra*, p. 14.

[5]*etahyevakṣaraṁ brahman—Kaṭhaśruti.*

[6]*nāmacintāmaniḥ kṛṣṇascaitanya-rasavigraḥ|*
pūrṇaḥ śuddhā nityamukto' abhinnatvānnamanāminoḥ||
—*Bhaktirasāmṛtasindhu*, 1, 2, 233.

[7]*hena kṛṣṇa nāma jadi laya bahubāra|*
tabu jadi prema nahe, nahe asrudhāra||
tabe jāni aparādha tāhāte pracura|
kṛṣṇanāma bīja tāhe na kare aṅkura|| —*C. Bh.*, Ādi, VIII, 25.

[8]*aprākṛt vastu nahe prākṛtendriyera gocara|* *CC*, Madhya, IX, 179.

when we desire to utter it,[1] because the Merciful Bhagavān is committed to respond to us in the manner in which we approach Him.[2] Its spiritual character is not lost by its contact with the tongue, just as the character of fire as heat is not lost when it comes in contact with the object it burns. On the other hand, the tongue itself is spiritualised by constant repitition of the Name, just as the object that comes in contact with fire is itself converted into fire.

Śrī Caitanya is particularly known for his contribution to this age in the form of Saṁkīrtana, which Śrī Jīva defines as *Kīrtana* in which a number of persons join in chanting the name or singing the praises of the Lord.[3] *Saṁkīrtana* has been in vogue throughout the length and breadth of the Indian sub-continent since the time of Śrī Caitanya, and is now spreading all over the world through the Hare Kṛṣṇa movement led by the International Society for Kṛṣṇa Consciousness. Śrī Caitanya himself led *Saṁkīrtana* parties consisting of lacs of devotees in the streets of Nadiyā and made the whole town resound with vociferous chantings. He commanded his disciples to go from door to door and teach this unique method of worship to one and all, without any distiction of caste or creed, sex or age, and piety or impiety (*C.Bh*, Madhya, XXII, 78-80 XIII, 6, 7).[4]

This kind of *Kīrtana* is the most efficicacious. Śrī Caitanya thus speaks of its sevenfold efficacy in the first *Śloka* of *Śikṣāṣṭakam*:

"May the congregational chanting of the Holy Name be glorified, which (*1*) sweeps off the dirt from the mirror of our heart, (*2*) extinguishes the great forest-fire of the suffering world, (*3*) and sheds moonlight upon the lily of eternal good, (*4*) which is the very life of the bride of learning, and which (*5*) tastes like nectar at every step, (*6*) swells the ocean of divine bliss, and (*7*) makes the whole self (including the soul, body, mind, and the senses) feel like being engulfed in it.[5]

Any name of Bhagavān is good for *Kīrtana*, because it is endowed with

[1] *ataḥ srīkṛṣṇanāmādi na bhaved grāhyamindriyaiḥ/*
sevonmukhe hi jihvādau svayameva sphuratyadaḥ//—
Padma-purāṇa text cited in *Bhaktirasāmṛtasindhu*, 1, 2, 234.

[2] *Gītā*, 4, 11.

[3] *saṁkīrtanaṁ bahubhirmilitvā tadgānasukhaṁ srīkṛṣṇagānaṁ*
—*Krama-sandarbha, Tīkā*

[4] *dasa pānca mili nija dvāre te basiyā/*
kīrtana karah sabe hāte tālī diyā//
saṁkīrtana kahila e toma sabākāre/
strī putra bāpe milī kara giyā ghare//

[5] *cetodarpaṇamārjanaṁ bhavamahādāvāgni nirvāpanaṁ*
sreyaḥ kairavacandrikāvitaraṇaṁ vidyābadhūjīvanaṁ/
ānandāmbudhivardhanaṁ prtipadaṁ pūrṇāmṛtāsvādanaṁ
sarvātmasvapanaṁ paraṁ vijayate śrīkṛṣṇasaṁkīrtanaṁ// —*Śikṣāṣṭaka*, I.

infinite power to deliver the soul from bondage.[1] But the name 'Kṛṣṇa' excels all other names. *Hari-bhakti-vilāsa* quotes the *Brahmānda-purāṇa* to say that if one chants the name of Kṛṣṇa only once that is equal to chanting the whole of *Viṣṇu-sahastranāma*, consisting of a thousand names of Bhagavān, three times. While any name of Bhagavān can deliver the soul from bondage, the name 'Kṛṣṇa' alone can impart Kṛṣṇa-prema or the divine love of Śrī Kṛṣṇa (*CC*, Madhya, XV, 110).[2] The name 'Kṛṣṇa' is Svayaṁ-nāma or the Name itself, because it is the name of Svayaṁ-bhagavān or Bhagavān Himself, while the other names are the names of different partial manifestations of Bhagavān. Just as all the partial manifestations of Bhagavān are included in Svayaṁ-bhagavān, all the different names of Bhagavān are included in *Svayaṁ-nāma.*

Particular significance is attached by the scriptures to the following combination of names, called the *Mahāmantra*:

hare kṛṣṇa hare kṛṣṇa kṛṣṇa kṛṣṇa hare hare/
hare rāma hare rāma rāma rāma hare hare//
Brahmāṅda-purāṇa, Uttara-khaṅda, 6, 55.

It is called *Mahārmantra*, because of all the Mantras it is the most efficacious. It is described in the *Kalisantaraṇopaniṣad* as the only successful means of deliverance from bondage in this age.[3] Śrī Caitanya enjoins that it should be repeated a definite number of times every day. Recital of the Mantra according to him is more fruitful than silent repetition of it. When the Mantra is repeated silently, only the person repeating it is benifited. But when it is repeated aloud, other persons—even the birds and animals, who cannot themselves recite the name—are benifited by hearing it (*C. Bh.*, Ādī, XI, 275-77).

In order that the chanting of the name may have the desired effect, it is insisted that the qualities of humility and forbearance must be cultivated. Śrī Caitanya says in *Śloka* 3 of *Śikṣāṣṭaka*:

"He, who is humbler than a blade of grass and forbearing more than a tree, and who gives honour to others, without seeking it for himself, is ever worthy of chanting the name of the Lord."

The person chanting the Name must also guard himself against the following ten offences (*dasa-vidha nāmāparādha*):

(1) He must not speak ill of the holy persons.

[1]*nāmnāmakārī bahudhā nijasarvaśakti-*
statrārpitā niyamitaḥ smaraṇe na kālaḥ/
etādṛśī tava kṛpā bhagavan mamāpi
durdaivamīdṛśamihājani nānurāgaḥ// —*Śikṣāṣṭaka*, 2.

[2]*ānuṣaṁgika phale kare saṁsārera kṣaya/*
citta ākarṣiyā karaye kṛṣṇe premodaya//

[3]*iti ṣoṇaṣakaṁ nāmnāṁ kalikalmaṣanāśanam/*
nātaḥ paratаropāyaḥ sarvavedeṣu dṛśyate//

(2) He must not regard Śiva and the other gods as existing independently of Kṛṣṇa.
(3) He must not disobey the Guru or regard him as an ordinary mortal.
(4) He must not find fault with the scriptures.
(5) He must not be lacking in faith in the power (*māhātmya*) of the Mantra and must not try to explain it from the materialistic point of view.
(6) He must not commit sin on the strength of the belief that it can be expatiated through the chanting of the Name.
(7) He must not equate the chanting of the Name with the other good deeds.
(8) He must not give instruction regarding the Name to the non-believers.
(9) He must not be indifferent to the chanting of the Name.
(10) He must not place the interests of the ego before the Name.

If, however an offence is committed against the Name, the only way of expatiating it is to chant the Name.

Smaraṇa is fixing the mind on the name, form, or sports of Bhagavān. There are five stages of Smaraṇa: Smaraṇa-sāmānya, Dhāraṇā, Dhyāna, Dhruvānusmṛti, and Samādhi. In Smaraṇa-sāmānya the mind is fixed slightly on the object of concentration; in Dhāraṇā it is withdrawn from all other objects and fixed on the object of thought in a general way (*sāmānyākāreṇa-dhāraṇam*); in Dhyāna it is specially concentrated on the name, form, qualities or sports of Bhagavān (*viṣesato rupādi-cintanam*). in ***Dhruvānusmṛti*** the special concentration is uninterrupted like a stream of nectar (*amṛta-dhārāvad*); in Samādhi it is aware exclusively of the object of concentration and of nothing else (*dhyeyamātra-sphurṇam*).

Pada-sevā consists of such devotional activities as seeing or circumambulating the deity, following the procession of the deity, bathing in the holy rivers like the Gaṅgā and the Yamunā, and residing in holy places like Mathurā and Vṛndāvāna.

Arcanā is ceremonial worship of the deity, or worship according to the rites as laid down in the scriptures. It is not idolatry or the worship of the image, but the worship of the Lord Himself, Who, out of His infinite mercy descends to the mundane level in the form of the Śrī Mūrti, so that the fallen souls may be provided with an objective basis for spiritual reorientation of their lives. It is a divine dispensation under which it is possible for them to detach their mind and senses from the objects of the world and engage them in the service of the Lord. The installation of the deity at home and the performance of ritualistic service at regular intervals helps the devotee focus his mind constantly on the Divine and fosters an attitude, which gradually turns into Divine love.

The principle of Śrī Mūrti is the central principle underliying all worship, though it is manifested differently in different religions. The Semetic idea of a patriarchal god, the Christian idea of the cross and even the idea of the formless Brahman of the Advaitins or the formless Energy of the Śāktas, are but distant reflections of the idea of Śrī Mūrti. All such ideas, in so far as they have a meaning and a transcendental reference, perform the function of the Śrī Murtī by helping us fix our mind on the Divine. Even if these ideas are regarded as phenomenal representations or imaginary symbols of the Divine, there is nothing wrong with them. "If the divine compassion, love and justice could be portrayed by the pencil and expressed by the chisel, why should not the personal beauty of the Deity, embracing all other attributes, be portrayed in poetry or in picture, or expressed by the chisel for the benefit of man? If words could impress thoughts, the watch could indicate time, and sign could tell us a history, why should not the picture or figure bring associations of higher thoughts and feelings with regard to the transcendental beauty of the Divine Personage?"[1] But, as we have already said, according to Śrī Caitanya and the Vaiṣṇava belief in general, the Śrī Mūrti is not simply a visible symbol of the Divine, but the Divinity itself, and to regard it as otherwise is an offence.

Bandana is act of homage, which includes salutation by prostrating at full length (*daṇḍavat praṇāmah*). This is, truly speaking, a part of Pada-sevā or Arcanā, but is mentioned separately to indicate that it can be employed independently as an Aṅga of *Bhakti.*

Dāsya consists of acts of service accompanied by the feeling that one is the servant of the Lord, which, in fact, underlies all acts of *Bhakti.*

Sakhya is the feeling of fellowship with the Lord. Both Dāsya and Sakhya follow from the very nature of the relation between *Jīva* and Bhagavān.

Ātmanivedana means complete dedication of the self. including the body, mind, senses, and the soul to the service of the Lord. It implies the absence of all efforts for the self (*ātmārtha-ceṣṭa-śūnyatva*) and the presence only of efforts for the Lord (*tad-arthaika-ceṣṭāmayatva*).

All these elements of *Bhakti* are interrelated. One may practise one or more of these exclusively, or one may practise all. The Śāstras extol sometimes one element and sometimes another, because persons differ in their aptitudes and capacities and the particular element that suits a particular individual is the best for him, just as there are different medicines for a particular disease, but the particular medicine that suits a particular patient is the best for him. We find each of these elements of *Bhakti* typified in the scriptures in some great devotee, whom we may adopt as our ideal. Thus Sravaṇa is typified in Parīkṣit, Kīrtana in Śukadeva, Smaraṇa in Prahlāda, Pada-sevā in Śrī Lakṣmi Devī, Arcanā in Mahārāja Pṛthu, Vandana in Akrūra, Dāsya in Hanumāna, Sakhya in Arjuna, and Ātma-

[1]Thakur Bhaktivinod, *Śrī Caitanya Mahāprabhu*, pp. 34-35.

nivedana in king Bali, while Amvarīṣa is the noble example of the devotee who practises all these (*CC*, Madhya, XXII, 77).

Ritualistic (*Vaidhī*) *and Spontaneous* (*Rāgānuga*) *Bhakti*

There are two stages of *Bhakti*—Vaidhī and Rāgānugā. Vaidhī-bhakti is injunctory and ritualistic. It consists in the observance of the rules and regulations or the rituals as laid down in the Śāstras. It is conditioned by the fear of transgression of the rules and is, therefore, more formal and mechanical than spontaneous.[1] The rules are of two kinds, those which create an inclination for *Bhakti* (*pravṛti-hetuḥ*) and those, which tell us what to do and what not to do to steady that inclination. Rāgānugā-bhakti is spontaneous and unconditioned by fear of transgression of the injuctions of the Śāstrās. In Rāgānugā-bhakti there is a continuous flow of Rāga or attachment to the Lord, which makes it impossible for the devotee to follow the rules and regulations of Vaidhī-bhakti. Vaidhī-bhakti may be described, after Martineau, as the Life of Law and Rāgānugā-bhakti as the Life of Love. Love is blind. It seeks the object of love regardless of the norms that usually guide the conduct of an individual in society. So the devotee, who has reached the Rāgānugā stage, has a deep and natural feeling of attachment towards the Lord and the current of devotion that flows from his heart, spontaneously and ceaselessly, overruns, on its course, all barriers of scriptural forms and injunctions,[2] that guide and restrict the course of Vaidhī-bhakti. Rāgānugā-bhakti is ,therefore, described as Prabalā or strong and Vaidhī-bhakti as Nirbalā or weak.[3]

Theologians have differed regarding the actual place of Vidhi or the injunctions and prohibitions in religion. Many in the West consider the sacrament and the church as essential and permanent elements in the life of a devotee. According to Jaimini's dictum "*codanā-laksaṇo'rtho dharmaḥ*" Dharma consists in following the injunctions of the scriptures. Bhāgavata also says that the injunctions of Śruti and Smṛti are the commandments of Bhagavān and one, who violates them cannot be regarded as a true devotee.[4] Jīva Gosvāmin refers to these statements and reconciles the apparent contradiction between them and Rāgānugā-bhakti by saying that *Bhakti* is intrinsically different from ordinary Dharma, since the devotional attitude is spontaneous and indedendent of the injunctions of the Śāstrās. It springs directly from the intrinsic potency of the name and attributes of the divine being. The devotee is automatically drawn towards

[1] *rāgahīna jana bhaje śāstrera ājnāya|*

[2] *je karaye prabhu ājnā pālana tomāra|*
śeī jana haya vidhi niṣedhera pāra|| —*C. Bh* , Antya, VII, 68.

[3] *BS*, Sec. 310.

[4] *sruti-smṛti mamaivājne yaste ullaṅgha'vartate|*
ājnācchedī mama dveṣī madbhakto'pi na vaiṣṇava||

the Lord just as the senses are automatically drawn towards their objects. Devotion may be attained even without the knowledge of scriptural injunctions, though compliance with scriptural injunctions is, in most cases, necessary in the earlier stages, when the mind is distracted and the natural state of composure that characterises Rāgānugā-bhakti does not exist. External observances like the worship of Śrī Murti, the partaking of Mahāprasādam, and the chanting of the Holy Name, are intended gradually to bring about that state of composure by diverting the mind from the objects of the senses to the lotus feet of Kṛṣṇa and lighting the spark of devotion that lies concealed in our heart. Once this spark is lighted the necessity of external observances ceases. For devotion is the function of the soul, not of the body to which the external observances relate. When the function of the soul is roused, the activities of the body and its senses are regulated by the spontaneous activity of the soul. The transgression of the scriptural injunctions at this stage is not voluntary but due to the natural state of *Bhakti*, which is an aspect of the Svarūpa-śakti of Bhagavān.

In Rāgānugā-bhakti the hazards and conflicts of moral life and the strain and stress caused by the imperatives of moral sense are completely overcome. It is a life complete in spirit. It enjoys complete freedom from the sense of 'ought,' which has necessary reference to an unaccomplished process and calls for striving and accomplishing. It is life fulfilled in love—love, that is released from all fetters and sanctions. Sanctioned love is not true love. It is only training in love. It is love that is conditioned by will and intellect. It is love without the zest of love.

Rāgānugā-bhakti is emotional sublimation of intimate human sentiments. Our love towards our children or a lady's love towards her husband or paramour is natural and intense. In Rāgānugā-bhakti the same love in all its intensity and spontaneity, is directed towards Bhagavān. Rāgānugā-bhakti is said to be superior to Vaidhī-bhakti, even if it be adverse or imitative. Its supreme efficacy is vindicated by the examples of Pūtanā and Śiśupāla. Pūtanā merely imitated parental affection for Kṛṣṇa with a sinister motive, and yet she was graciously awarded by the Lord the status of his wet nurse (Dhātri). Śiśupāla had a fervent feeling of life-long enmity towards Kṛṣṇa, yet he was rewarded with Sāyujya-mukti, because the fervency of his feeling made constant concentration of his mind on Kṛṣṇa so easy and spontaneous. But even though Rāgānugā-bhakti is so natural and spontaneous, it is still a means or Sādhana-bhakti like Vaidhī-bhakti.

Rāgānugā-bhakti is so called because it follows (*anugā*) the line of devotion and attachment (*rāgātmikā-bhakti*) of the Śaktis in the form of the Parikaras or divine associates towards the Śaktimat (*CC*, Madhya, XXII, 85). The Parikaras of Bhagavān in Vraja are the embodiments of the different aspects of the divine energy of bliss, which reflects itself in them in the form of different personal relationships, classified in terms of human sentiments into five broad categories of devotional sentiments or Rasas, namely, *Śānta* (quietistic devotion), *Dāsya* (devotion as servitude or faithfulness), *Sakhya* (devotion as friendship), *Vātsalya* (devotion as parentsentiment), *Mādhurya* (devotion as the sweet sentiment of pure love as between husband and wife or between lover and beloved). The Divine Energy of bliss or the Hlādinī-śakti itself is a harmonious combination of all these Rāsas, but it is reflected differently in different Parikaras of Vraja according to the differences in their loving attitude towards Kṛṣṇa, just as the same rain-water tastes differently when it mixes with the different terrestrial objects. In milk it tastes as sweet, in Āmalakī as sour, in some of the vegetables as salty, in pepper as pungent, in Gulañcā as bitter, and in Harītakī as astringent. The varieties of Rasa reflected in the Parikaras become the different types of Rāgātmikā-bhakti, which the devotees, following the path of Rāgānugā-bhakti adopt as their ideals. Thus the types or ideals of Śānta-rasa are Sanaka, Sanātana, Sananda, and Sanatkumāra, the types of Dāsya rasa are Raktaka, Patraka, Madhukantha and others; the types of Sakhya Rasa are Śrīdāma, Sudāma, Subala and others, who have a feeling of friendship towards Kṛṣṇa; the types of Vātsalya-rasa are Nanda, Yaśodā, Vasudeva, and Devakī, who have parental affection for Kṛṣṇa; the types of Mādhurya-rasa are the Gopīs of Vṛndāvana, who regard Kṛṣṇa as their husband or beloved.

Rāgānugā-bhakti is only an imitation of Rāgātmikā-bhakti. In Rāgānugā-bhakti the devotee does not establish a direct personal relationship with Bhagavān. He only imitates the particular mode of Rāgātmikā-bhakti that suits his natural inclination. It is not possible for an ordinary person in physical body to attain the Rāgātmikā-bhakti of the Parikaras of Bhagavān, whose bodies are made of divine bliss. But Rāgānugā-bhakti prepares him for attaining it ultimately in a transcendental body, (*siddha deha*). So long as the devotee stays in the physical body, he performs Sravaṇa and Kīrtana and observes the other rules of Vaidhī-bhakti outwardly, but inwardly he imagines himself to be in the transcendental body, appropriate for the type of *Bhakti* to which he is naturally inclined and to be serving Kṛṣṇa day and night through that body, (*CC*, Madhya, XXII, 89-90).[1] By constant meditation or Smaraṇa he makes the whole of Vraja-līlā live before him. He enters into that Līlā in his imagination and by serving Kṛṣṇa, according to the particular Bhāva or mode of *Bhakti* adopted by him, lives in the ecstasy of that vicarious enjoyment. The imaginary transcendental body (*antaścintita siddha deha*),

[1] *'bāhya' 'antara' ihāra duī ta sādhana|*
bāhya—sādhaka dehe kare sravaṇa-kīrtana||
mane nija siddha dehe kariyā bhāvanā||
rātri dine kare vraje kṛṣṇera sevana||

however, is not wholly imaginary. It is a mental reflection of the transcendental body, which Bhagavān, out of His infinite kindness, imparts to the devotee. That the transcendental body is a gift of Bhagavān is corroborated by the second line of *Śloka* 3.9.11 of *Śrīmad-bhāgavata*, which runs as follows:

yadyad dhiyā ta urugāya vibhāvayanti tattadvapuḥ praṇayase sadanugrahāya|

Śrī Viśvanātha Cakravartī, in his commentary, interprets the text to mean that Bhagavān imparts to the devotee a transcendental body exactly like the one which he imagines himself to possess and which is essential for the particular mode of *Bhakti* practised by him, because He is bound to do so on account of His always being subservient to the devotees.

The idea of the transcendental body may not be acceptable to science. But the scope of scientific enquiry is restricted by its unscientific assumptions. Science must explain everything in terms of matter and energy. The vital, the psychical, and the spiritual revelations of finer forms of energy must always remain sealed to it. For they are the expressions of Primal Energy, not the expressions or radiations of cruder forms of energy, working on the lower levels. Even matter is an expression of Primal Energy. Indeed Śrī Caitanya does not believe in the existence of matter in the ordinary sense. He accepts a kind of dualistic hypothesis in which both matter and finite spirit are related to the Divine, matter indirectly and spirit directly. Matter is not an entity. It may be described as the restricted movement of the Primal Will, very much similar to Bergson's matter, which is described as an inversion of movement of the 'Elan Vital.'

The *Taitrīya-upaniṣad* speaks of the five Koṣas, by which the Ātman is enfolded, the blissful body, the intelligence-body, the vital body, and the physical body. Beyond all these bodies is the spiritual body or the Bhāva-deha. When the devotee is sufficiently advanced in devotion, he becomes free from the Koṣas and realises the spiritual body. The spiritual body is made of Śuddha-sattva, the luminous, expressive and unfettered substance of the spiritual order. The imaginary spiritual body (*antaścintita siddha deha*), which the devotee contemplates in Rāgānugā-bhakti, is an imperfect replica of the spiritual body (*siddha deha*), he attains on the fruition of his devotion. Narottama Thākura says in *Prema-bhakti-candrikā* that what the devotee desires and meditates upon in the stage of Sādhanā, he actually attains on the completion of Sādhanā. The imaginary or contemplated transcendental body, therefore, is just the transcendental body proper in the making (*pakvāpakva mātra vicāra*).[1]

[1] *sadhane bhāviba jāhā, siddha dehe pāba tāhā,*
rāga pathera eī je upāya|
sādhane je dhana cāī siddha, dehe tāhā pāī,
pakvāpakva mātra śe bicāra||—Narottama Thakura's *Prema-bhakti-candrikā*, 54-55.

This does not, however, mean that the devotee can realise himself as Kṛṣṇa by identifying himself with him in contemplation. This does not also mean that he can become Nanda or Yaśodā or any of the other Parikaras of Vraja through contemplation. The *Jīva* is intrinsically a manifestation of the Taṭasthā-śakti of Bhagavān, while the Parikaras are the manifestation of His Svarūpa-śakti. Even on the attainment of realisation (*siddhāvasthā*) the intrinsic nature of the *Jīva* must remain the same. He can imitate and realise the Bhāva of a Parikara, but cannot become the Parikara himself.

Smaraṇa or contemplation and the service of Kṛṣṇa through the medium of the imaginary transcendental body (*antaścintita deha*) is the very essence of Rāgānugā-bhakti. But, as we have already said, Śrī Caitanya emphasises that this should not be done to the exclusion of the external observances of Vaidhī-bhakti through the physical body because they are also helpful in Rāgānugā-bhakti.

CHAPTER XIII

Priti, the End

The concept of *Prīti* implies two things: *Priyatā*, the feeling of attachment or affection (*bhāva*) for the beloved and *Sukha* or happiness. But *Priyatā* is not synonimous with happiness.[1] Indeed, it is opposed to happiness in the ordinary sense. Happiness, in the ordinary sense, means some kind of personal satisfaction. But *Priyatā* is impersonal. It does not seek anything for itself. It implies a longing (*sprihā*) to contribute to the happiness (*ānukūlya*) of the beloved, even if it be at the cost of one's own happiness. It does not desire even the object of love, if such a desire hinders, in any way, the happiness of the beloved.[2]

Priyatā has both a ground (*āśrya*) and an object (*viṣaya*), while *Sukha* has only a ground and no object. The ground of *Priyatā* is, no doubt, the self, but *Priyatā* is meaningless without the object towards which it is directed. Sukha has its ground in the self, like *Priyatā,* but it is not directed towards anyone else. It is self-centred (*CC*, Ādi, IV, 169-170).[3]

But though *Priyatā* is opposed to happiness in the sense of satisfaction sought consciously for the self, it involves happiness, which follow as a natural concomitant of the happiness of the beloved.[4] Whatever contributes to the happiness of the beloved contributes to the happiness of the person loving. Therefore *Prīti* involves happiness both in union and separation.

Since the basic element in *Prīti* is selfless service of the beloved, it is called *Sevā*. *Sevā-sukha* or the happiness that results from the service of the beloved is different from the happiness consciously sought for the self. It is a higher kind of happiness.

Prīti as the *summumbonum* is *Prīti* directed towards Bhagavān. It is an expression of the Svarūpa-śakti of Bhagavān. As an expression of the

[1]*Pr. S.*, 61.

[2]*nija-premānande Kṛṣṇa-sevānanda bādhe|*
se ānandera prati bhaktera haya mahākrodhe|| *CC*, Ād, IV, 171.

[3]*prīti-viṣāyanande tadāsrayānanda|*
tāhā nāhi nija-sukha-bānchāra sambandha||
nirupādhi prema jāhā, tāhā eī rīti|
prīti-viṣayasukhe āsrayera prīti|| *CC*, Ādi, IV, 169-70

[4]*gopīgaṇa karena jabe Kṛṣṇa darśana|*
sukha-bānchā nāhi, sukha haya kotiguṇa|| *CC*, Ādi, IV, 157

Svarūpa-śakti it is transcendental. It is not something that springs from the heart of the devotee himself, but something that is placed (*nikṣipta*) in it by the Svarūpa-śakti, when it is duly purified and is raised to the transcendental level by the ingress of Śuddha-sattva. As an expression of Svarūpa-śakti or as something springing from the intrinsic quality of the Object of Desire it is natural or Svābhāvikī. Bhagavān realises through it His own intrinsic nature (*svabhāva*) as blissful love.[1]

The difference between the bliss caused by Prīti as directed towards Bhagavān or Bhāgavat-prīti and Sukha, in the sense of ordinary happiness, is, therefore, basic. While the bliss caused by *Prīti* is a function of the Svarūpa-śakti, Sukha is a function of Māyā-śakti. While the latter is caused by Sattva-guṇa, the former is Nirguṇa or beyond the three Guṇas of Prakṛti[2] There is difference also between the bliss arising from the Svarūpa or intrinsic self of Bhagavān (*svarūpānanda* or *brahmānanda*) and the bliss caused by Bhāgavat-prīti, which arises from Svarūpa-śakti.[3] The bliss of Bhagavat-prīti intoxicates (*mādayati*) both the Bhakta and Bhagavān and results in their complete engrossment (*parasparāveśatva*) in each other. It is no wonder, therefore that *Prītī* is described in *Bhāgavata* as having the quality of completely subjugating the Lord. We must not, however, take the state of *parasparāveśatva* to imply a state of complete identity between the devotee and the Lord. It is union in love, not identity in substance. It is like the union between iron and fire. When iron is heated it becomes fiery, but it retains its character as iron.

The presence of *Prīti* in a person cannot be known directly. But it can be known indirectly through its outward manifestations. The outward manifestations are the eight Sāttvika-bhāvas and the thirteen Anubhāvas or ensuants. The Sāttvika-bhāvas are *Stambha* (stupor), *Sveda* (perspiration), *Romāñca* (thrilling of body), *Svara-bhaṅga* (break of voice), *Kampa* (trembling), *Vaivarṇya* (change of colour), *Aśru* (tears), and *Pralaya* (loss of consciousness). The Sāttvika-bhāvas are not Bhāvas or emotions but merely the external signs of internal emotion. They are due to the discharge of intense psychic energy, which goes with spiritual intuitions in *Prīti.* Spiritual expressions are vibrations, which do not disturb the inner calm of spirit, but which distrub the equilibrium of the psychic and the vital being, because they are not accustomed to such high pressure. In *Prīti* our psychological constitution is worked up to such an extent that it brings into play some parts of our nervous system, which do not ordinarily function. It is these that bring about such extra-ordinary changes in the physiological apparatus.[4]

[1] *Pr. S.*, 67.
[2] ibid, 62.
[3] ibid, 63.
[4] In Śrī Caitanya himself the Sāttvika Bhāvas manifested themselves in an extreme and unprecedented form.

The Anubhāvas are such outward manifestations of an internal emotion as *Nṛtya* (dancing), *Viluṭhita* (rolling on the ground), *Gītā* (singing), *Krośana* (loud crying), *Tanu-moṭana* (twisting of the body), *Huṁkāra* (shouting), *Jṛmbhā* (yawning), *Śvāsa-bhūman* (profusion of sighs), *Lokānapekṣitā* (disregard of popular opinion), *Lālā-srava* (foaming at the mouth), *Attahāsa* (loud laughter), *Ghūrṇā* (giddiness) and *Hikkā* (hiccough). The Anubhāvas follow and strengthen an emotion. Śrī Jīva includes Sāttvika-bhāvas also under Anubhāvas.

Prīti in itself is one and indivisible just as Bhagavān, to whom it relates, is one and indivisible. But just as Bhagavān manifests Himself perfectly or imperfectly according to the various degrees of the capacity of the devotee, *Prīti* also manifests itself perfectly or imperfectly, according to the various modes of *Bhakti* adopted by the devotee and according to the different degrees of perfection of the deity to whom it relates. Since Kṛṣṇa is the most perfect manifestation of Bhagavān, *Prīti* finds its most perfect manifestation only in relation to Kṛṣṇa. Kṛṣṇa, according to the different degrees of manifestation of the Mādhurya aspect of His personality, is *Pūrṇa* (perfect) in Dvārakā, *Purṇatara* (more perfect) in Mathurā, and *Pūrṇatama* (most perfect) in Vṛndāvana. Therefore *Prīti* relating to Kṛṣṇa also assumes the most perfect form only in Vṛndāvana.

Stages in the Development of Prīti

Prīti is eternally self-established *and self-manifested* in the Parikaras of Bhagavān, who are the ideal devotees. It is also the natural function of an ordinary *Jīva*. But in his case it lies dormant under the influence of *Māyā* and has to be awakened and developed in stages. *Bhaktirasāmṛtasindhu* describes the sequence of its development thus: *Śraddhā* (faith)—*Sādhusaṅga* (company of saintly persons)—*Bhajana-kriyā* (acts of worship)—*Anartha-nivṛtti* (elimination of all evils)—*Niṣṭhā* (reliance)—*Ruci* (natural liking or taste)—*Āsakti* (attachment)—*Bhāva* (emotion)—*Preman* (love).[1] The first stage is that of *Śraddhā*, which means that one must have faith in Kṛṣṇa, the Śāstrās and the *Sādhus* (saintly persons). This is followed by the company of the Sādhus (*sādhusaṅga*). The company of the Sādhus presents an opportunity for *Sravaṇa* and *Kīrtana*. *Sādhusaṅga*, *Sravaṇa* and *Kīrtana* purge the mind of all evil thoughts (*anartha-nivṛtti*). When the devottee is thus freed from all anti-devotional thoughts his reliance on Kṛṣṇa becomes firm (*niṣṭhā*). The firmness of reliance creates a taste or natural liking for devotional activities (*ruci*), which further develops into a strong inclination (*āsakti*) for them. Then sprouts up the seed of

[1]*ādau sradhā tataḥ sadhusango'tha bhajanakriyā/*
tato'narthanivṛttih syāttato niṣthā rucistathaḥ//
athāsaktistato bhāvastataḥ premābhyudañati/
sādhakānāmayaṁ premṇaḥ prādurbhāve bhavet kramaḥ//
Bhaktirasāmṛta-sindhu, 1. 4, 15, 19

unalloyed devotion in the heart of the devotee in the form of spiritual emotion, called *Bhāva* or *Rati*, which ultimately ripens into *Prīti* or *Preman, CC.*, Madhya, XXIII, 5-9).[1]

The emotion called *Rati* is not like the ordinary emotions known to psychology. It is a trans-psychological concept. It is not something that grows out of the phenomenal frame-work, but a manifestation of the Svarūpa-śakti of Bhagavān Himself. It is the first ray of the dawning sun of transcendental love *(premasūryāṁśu sāmyabhāk)* on the spiritual horizon that penetrates the heart of the devotee.[2] It is known by nine ensuing attendant circumstances (*anubhāvas*), which are enumerated thus: serenity of mind (*kṣānti*), which remains undisturbed, whatever be the circumstances; effort not to let a single moment of one's life pass without rememberance of the Lord (*avyartha-kālatā*) distaste for the objects of sense (*virakti*); lack of pride (*nirabhimānitā*); firm faith that Bhagavān will be attained (*āśābandha*); eagerness to attain Bhagavān (*samutkaṅṭhā*); taste for singing the name of the Lord (*nāma-gāne-ruciḥ*); natural inclination for the recital of the attributes of the Lord (*tad-guṇākhyāne āsaktiḥ*); strong desire to live in the place where the Lord lived, e.g. Mathurā, Vṛndāvana etc. (*tad-vasati-sthale prītiḥ*).

When Bhāva is intensified and the feeling of affectionate regard or attachment (*mamatā*) for Kṛṣṇa increases, it is called *Preman. Ujjvala-nīla-maṇi* describes *Preman* as *bhāva-bandhana* (tie of affection) that does not break even in the face of circumstances, which are sufficient to cause its break. For example Candrāvalī knows that Kṛṣṇa loves Rādhā and loves her more intensely. This should be sufficient to turn her mind from Kṛṣṇa. Still she loves him passionately. The reason why the tie of *Preman* is unbreakable is that *Preman* does not even for a moment seek the happiness of the self and there is no price it is not willing to pay for the happiness of the beloved.

Caitanya-caritāmṛta describes *Preman* as a transcendental state, which even the wise cannot understand. The words, the mental states, and the modes of behaviour of a devotee, who has attained Preman are all be-

[1]*kono bhāgye kono jīvera sraddhā jadi haya|*
tabe śeī jīva sādhu-saṅga je karaya||
sādhu-saṅga haite haya srvaṇa-kīrtana|
sādhana bhaktye haya sarvānarthanivartana||
anarthanivṛtti haite bhaktye niṣṭhā haya|
niṣṭhā haite srvaṇādye ruci upajaya||
ruci haite bhaktye haya āsakti pracura|
āsakti haite citte janme kṛṣṇa prītyānkura||
śei bhāva gāḍha hele dhare prema nāma|
sei prema prayojana......sarvanandadhāma||

[2]*śuddhasatvaviśeṣātmā premasūryāṁśu sāmyabhāk|*
rucibhiścittamāsṛṇyakṛdasau bhāva ucyate||

yond our ordinary understanding (*CC*, Madhya, XXIII, 21). He is the one, who has drunk deep of the wine of divine love, and, like one overtaken by divine madness, now laughs, now weeps, now sings, now dances.

Rati and *Preman* can be realised by a devotee while he remains in the physical body. But there are higher stages of divine love, which can be realised only when the physical body drops and the spiritual body is attained. This is probably the reason why Rūpa Gosvāmin deals in detail with only *Ruci* and *Preman* in his *Bhakti-rasāmṛta-sindhu.* He deals with the other stages separately in *Ujjvala-nīla-maṇi.* We shall also, therefore, describe them separately.

Higher Stages in Prīti

As *Preman* grows more and more intense, it develops into *Sneha*, *Māna*, *Praṇaya*, *Rāga*, *Anurāga*, *Bhāva* or *Mahābhāva.*

Sneha is a sublimated form of *Preman* in which the bond of affection is thicker and the attainment of Kṛṣṇa is of a higher order. It causes greater melting of the mind (*citta-dravatva*). A devotee at this stage cannot bear separation from Kṛṣṇa even for a moment. His thirst for the sight of Śrī Kṛṣṇa is never satiated. It grows ever and ever more.[1] *Sneha* is of two kinds: *Ghṛta-sneha* and *Madhu-sneha. Ghṛta-sneha* is love intensified or solidified like *ghee.* Ghee has its own taste, but it does not taste sweet unless it is combined with sugar. Similarly *Ghṛta-sneha* has a taste, but it becomes sweet only in combination with other Bhāvas. *Madhu-sneha*, on the other hand, is sweet in itself like *Madhu* or honey. Just as honey is a combination of *rasas* (juice) collected from different kinds of flowers, *Madhu-sneha* combines within itself different kinds of *rasa*, which account for its intrinisic sweetness. This difference in relish between *Ghṛta-sneha* and *Madhu-sneha* is due to the fact that the former is characterised by "I am Thine" attitude (*tadīyatāmaya bhāva*) while the latter is characterised by "Thou art mine" attitude (*madīyatāmaya bhāva*) towards Kṛṣṇa.

Ghṛta-sneha is exemplified in Candrāvalī, whose *tadīyatāmaya-bhāva*, implying a subdued feeling of regard for Kṛṣṇa, imposes certain natural restrictions on her behaviour towards him, while *Madhu-sneha* is exemplified in Rādhā, whose *madīyatāmaya-bhāva* and exclusive concern for the happiness of Kṛṣṇa override all considerations of propriety or impropriety and make her behave only in such manner as would contribute to his happiness. For example, Candrāvalī cannot think of her feet touching the body of Kṛṣṇa, but Rādhā will even plant her feet on his head if she thinks that it will give him a new amatory pleasure.

Māna is pretended repulse of endearment. It is even more intensified form of love than *Sneha.* Therefore, it leads to even greater melting of

[1] *Bhakti-rasāmṛta-sindhu*, 3. 2. 43.

the mind. But the excess of emotion in it is concealed and an unfavourable response to the beloved is pretended. This kind of curvedness is natural to *Prīti* in its higher stages. But instead of causing any hinderance to the happiness of Kṛṣṇa, it gives him a special kind of pleasure, which surpasses the relish of *Sneha*. *Māna* is either *Udātta* or *Lalita*. *Udātta-māna* is a developed form of *Ghṛta-sneha*, while *Lalita-māna* is a developed form of *Madhu-sneha*.[1]

Praṇaya is *Māna* intensified to such an extent that it develops Viśrambha or confidence.[2] Śrī Jīva describes Viśrambha as the feeling of one's identity with the beloved. This identity,[3] however, is not like the identity of Jīva and Brahman in *Sāyujya-mukti*. This is an identity in which the difference between Āśraya and Viṣaya is not obliterated, for, otherwise *Prīti* itself would not be possible. Viśvanātha Cakravartin describes Viśrambha as the total absence of the feeling of diffidence or hesitation of any kind, which is natural when the beloved is regarded as having an identity, different from one's own, and a general attitude of reverence, howsoever unprominent and undetectable, characterises one's behaviour towards him. This is possible only when the *Prāṇa* (life), *Manaḥ* (mind), *Buddhi* (intelligence) and *Deha* (body) etc. of the lover are regarded as identical with their counterparts in the beloved; in other words, when the lover's concern for the life of the beloved is the same as his concern for his own life, when he feels that what appears as pleasure or pain to him also appears as pleasure or pain to the beloved, and when he thinks that what appears as true or false or as good, bad, or indifferent to him also appears as true or false, or as good, bad or indifferent to the beloved. On account of this feeling of identity the lover does not hesitate to do with the beloved what he does not hesitate to do with himself. For example, he does not hesitate to touch any part of the body of the beloved with his foot, just as he does not hesitate to touch any part of his own body with it.[4] This is why the playmates of Kṛṣṇa do not have any hesitation in riding his shoulders, or offering him to eat things, which they have themselves partly eaten.

Rāga is the state of intensified *Praṇaya*, in which even extreme sorrow is experienced as happiness,[5] if it brings about a meeting with Kṛṣṇa and even extreme happiness is experienced as sorrow if it does not bring about or prevents a meeting with Kṛṣṇa. As an example of Rāga *Ujjvala-nīla-maṇi* cities the case of Rādhā going out of her home on a hot summer day to see Kṛṣṇa, while he is tending cows near the Govardhana hill.

[1]*Ujjvala-nīla-maṇi*, *Sthāyī*, 72-76.
[2]*ibid*, *Sthāyī*, 78.
[3]*visrambhaḥ priyajanena saha svasyābheda mananam*
[4]Viśvanāth Cakravartī's *Ānanda-candrikā Tīkā* on *Ujjvala-nīlamaṇi*, *Sthāyī*, 78.
[5]*duḥkhamapyadhikaṁ citte sukhatvenaiva vyajyate/
yatastta praṇayotkarṣāt sa rāga iti kīrtyate// Ujjvalanīlamaṇi*, *Sthāyī*, 84)

When she learns that Kṛṣṇa is on the other side of the hill, she does not hesitate to climb the top. From the top of the hill she gazes at Kṛṣṇa and is lost in bliss. Though her feet are severly scorched with the heat of the hill-stones and bruised by their sharp edges, she does not feel any pain, because her entire body, from top to bottom, is filled with the supremely soothing and exhilarating calm of divine bliss.[1]

Anurāga is *Rāga* intensified. When *Rāga* is intensified it appears as fresh and makes the beloved also appear as fresh at every step.[2] The form (*rūpa*), attributes (*guṇa*), sweetness (*mādhurya*) and all other things pertaining to Kṛṣṇa appear as always fresh. Though Rādhā always dallies with Kṛṣṇa, he always appears to her as new, as if she had never seen him before.[3] The nature of *Anurāga* and the very special manner in which it functions would be clear if we refer to the following states, which it brings about in the lover and the beloved:

(*a*) *Parasparavaśībhāva* (self-surrender): In *Preman* both the hero and the heroine have a feeling of surrender or subjugation towards each other. But the pequliarity of *Anurāga* is that while in *Preman* the feeling does not become manifest in the heroine on account of *Lajjā* (bashfulness) and *Avahitthā* (dissimulation) in *Anurāga* it becomes manifest in both the hero and the heroine.[4]

(*b*) *Premavaicittya* (loving apprehension of separation): the very intensity of *Preman* in *Anurāga* sometimes makes the lover lose consciousness of the beloved and feel the pangs of separation even in union. This happens for example, when the heroine is so much attracted by a particular aspect of the personality of the hero, or by a particular thing connected with him that her mind is completely lost in it, and she is rendered incapable of apprehending him even though he is present before her.[5] This also happens when the mere apprehension of separation deepens into an actual experience of it.[6]

(*c*) *Aprāṇī-janma-lālasā* (desire for birth as inanimate matter): the thought of greater possibility of enjoying the company of Kṛṣṇa as an inanimate object sometimes makes the milk-maids of Vraja desire to be born as such, *e.g.* they desire to be born as the flute of Kṛṣṇa, which he never likes to part with.[7]

(*d*) *Vipralambha-visphūrti* (vision of the beloved in separation): on account of the intensity of *Preman* in Anurāga the Gopis appear to see Kṛṣṇa in every thing. The vision is so vivid that they do not for a moment doubt its validity.

[1]ibid. [2]ibid, 102.
[3]ibid, 104. [4]ibid, 106.
[5]Rādhāgovinda Nāth, *Gauṇiya Vaiṣṇava Darśana*, IV, p. 2565.
[6]*Ujjvala-nīla-maṇi*, *Prema-vaicittya*, 57.
[7]*Dāna-keli-kaumudī* text cited in *Ujjvala-nīla-maṇi*, *Sthāyī*, 107.

Bhāva or *Mahābhāva* is sublimated *Anurāga*. It is characterised by the following states:

(*a*) *Svasamvedya-daśā*: a particular state of *Anurāga*, which experiences itself. *Anurāga* is the only means for experiencing the Mādhurya of Śrī Kṛṣṇa, The more the intensity of *Anurāga* the more the sweetness of the Mādhurya experienced (*CC*, Ādi, IV, 44). At the same time the higher the experience of *Mādhurya* the greater the intensity of *Anurāga*. *Anurāga* sublimates *Mādhurya* and *Mādhurya* sublimates *Anurāga*. There is, as it were, a race between the two (*CC*, Ādi, IV, 124).[1] The race continues until both *Anurāga* and *Mādhurya* reach the highest stage. At this stage the highest type of bliss is experienced. The bliss is so sweet and intense that it obliterates the subject-object consciousness. The subject loses all consciousness of himself as well as the consciusness of the *Mādhurya* that causes the experience of bliss. Only the bliss-consciousness remains, as if the bliss experiences itself. Śrī Jīva says that in this state *Anurāga* melts the minds of Rādhā and Kṛṣṇa to such an extent that they virtually become one and the perception of difference is not possible. Therefore the question of subject-object relationship does not arise. It is a unique experience of *Anurāga*, which is free from all other elements normally present in an experience. There is neither any scope in it for any other experience, nor is any other experience necessary for it. It is self-sufficient. It is just *Anurāga*, causing and enjoying its own experience.[2]

(*b*) *Prakāśita*: a state, which automatically manifests itself through certain external signs. All the Sāttvika-bhāvas referred to above, or at least five or six of them, appear at a time in their most extreme form to indicate the presence of this state.

(*c*) *Yāvadāśrayavṛtti*: a state, which does not remain confined to the person concerned, but exercises its influence on the other *Āśrayas* of *Bhakti*, the Siddha or Sādhaka-bhaktas present by his side. It also signifies a state, in which Rāga, which is the ground or *Āśraya* of *Anurāga* reaches the highest stage. The chief characteristic of this stage is that it converts even the greatest of sufferings into sources of pleasure. This is exemplified by the Gopīs of Vraja. There could hardly be a more painful circumstance for them than the one under which they would be compelled to disregard the injunctions of the Śāstras and violate the categorical imperatives of duty, which constitute the very breath of their life. They would lay down their lives rather than undergo the suffering caused by the violation of the injunctions of the Śāstras regarding their duty towards their husbands and others. But they do not hesitate for a moment to defy the Śāstras and

[1] *manmādhurya rādhāprema—dohe hoṇa kari/*
kṣaṇe kṣaṇe bāḍhe dohe keho nahi hāri//

[2] *yuñjan ekībhāvena citralekhāya atra parasparamabhinnacittatvāttatrānyasyā apraveśāt svasaṁvedyadaśā darśitā.* (*Ujjvala-nīla-maṇi*, *Sthāyī*, 110, *Locanarocanī Ṭīkā*)

the society for Kṛṣṇa. Their *Rāga* or intense love for Kṛṣṇa converted this extremely painful act into a source of supreme delight for them.

Anurāga can reach the stage of Mahabhāva only in the case of the milk-maids of Vraja, whose only concern is the pleasure of Kṛṣṇa, and for whom there is no sacrifice, they would not happily make, if it contributes even slightly to his pleasure. The queens of Kṛṣṇa in Dvārakā are depriv-ed of the supreme delight of Mahābhāva, because their *Anurāga* is not of this order. It is not altogether unconditioned by a concealed or subdued interest in their own pleasure. Their *Anurāga* is, therefore, called Samañjasā-rati and is regarded as distinct in character and intensity from the *Anurāga* of the milk-maids of Vraja, which is called Samarthārati.

We have already said that the bliss (*ānanda*) and sweetness (*mādhurya*) of Mahābhāva are of the highest order. But the supreme excellence (*mahimā*) of Mahābhava consists in the fact that its bliss and sweetness belong to it intrinsically, even as the sweetness of sugar belongs to it intrinsically. Its sweetness and bliss do not depend on any external factor. Another important characteristic of Mahābhāva is that the mind of the Gopī, who has attained the state of Mahābhāva is itself dissolved into Mahābhāva, and ceases to have a separate existence of its own.[1] The result is that the activities of the sense organs, which are all controlled by the mind, issue directly from Mahābhāva and are its various expressions. They are, therefore, equally pleasing to Kṛṣṇa, whatever be their out ward form.[2] Even the words of reproach uttered by the Gopīs are more pleasing to him than all the praises sung by the Vedas (*CC*, Ādi, IV 23).

Mahābhāva appears in two stages. The first stage is called Rūḍha and the second stage is called Adhirūḍha. The characteristics of Rūḍha-mahā-bhāva are classified into those pertaining to the body and those pertain-ing to the mind. The bodily characteristic is the appearance of five or six or all of the Sāttvika-bhāvas in their most excited from (*uddīpta*) at one and the same time. The mental characteristics are:

(*a*) *Nimeṣāsahatā*: incapacity for bearing separation from Kṛṣṇa even for a moment.

(*b*) *Āsanna-janatā-hṛdviloṇana*: capacity to stir the hearts of all present. This is compared to the rising of waves in the sea, which affect every-thing present within their range. As an example *Ujjvala-nīlamaṇi* men-tions the meeting of the Gopīs of Vraja with Kṛṣṇa, after a long time, in Kurukṣetra. At that time the stream of Mahābhāva, gushing forth from their hearts, stirs the hearts of even the queens of Dvārakā and makes the signs of Rūḍha-mahābhāva appear in them.

[1]*mahābhāvāṁ parthakyena manaso na sthitiḥ*. (*Ānanda-candrikā*, cited by Rādhāgovind Nāth in *Gauṇīya Vaiṣṇava Darśana*, IV, p. 2576)

[2]ibid.

(*c*) *Tat-saukhye'pyārti-śaṅkayā khinnatva*: sorrow through apprehension of distress even in the presence of happiness. The extreme concern of the Gopīs for the happiness of Kṛṣṇa sometimes makes them sorrowful, because they apprehend that their behaviour is causing distress to Kṛṣṇa even though it causes the greatest happiness to him.[1]

(*d*) *Kalpa-kṣaṇatva*: capacity to make a whole age appear as a moment. The night in which the *Rāsa*-dance took place was as long as the night of Brahmā. But the supreme bliss, which the Gopīs experienced in the company of Kṛṣṇa made the whole night appear to them as less than a moment.

(*e*) *Kṣaṇa-kalpatva*: capacity to make a moment appear as a whole age. Kṛṣṇa says to Uddhava in *Bhāgavata* "When I was in Vṛndāvana the nights passed like a moment for the Gopīs in my company. But since I have come here a single night appears to them like a whole age."[2]

(*f*) *Mohādyabhave' pyātmādi-sarva-vismaraṇatva*: forgetfulness of self and all other things in the absence of actual fainting. On account of excess of *Anurāga* for Kṛṣṇa, the Gopīs lose consciousness of themselves and everything else except Kṛṣṇa, without actually fainting, even as the saints forget themselves and everything else except Brahmānaṅda on the attainment of Samādhi.[3]

Adhirūḍha-mahābhāva is a special sublimation of Rūḍha-mahābhāva,[4] in which the Śāttvikas are even further excited. *Ujjvalanīlamaṇi* tries to give some idea of the essentially indescribable character of Adhirūḍha by citing a *Śloka*, in which Śiva says to Pāravatī, "If all the joys and sorrows of the transcendental Vaikuṇṭha and the infinite Brahmāndas were collected into two separate heaps, these would not be equal to the shadow of even a drop of the joy and sorrow of Rādhā's love for Kṛṣṇa."[5] The sorrow of Rādhā is, of course, the transcendental sorrow felt in separation from Kṛṣṇa which, as we shall see later, is even more relishable than the joy of union.

Adhirūḍha-bhāva is of two kinds: *Modana* and *Mādana*. It is called *Modana* when the Sāttvikas attain a special hightened charm in both Rādhā and Kṛṣṇa. *Modana* is found only in the Rādhā-group of Gopīs, because it is a development of *Madhu-sneha*, which is not found anywhere outside this group.[6] *Modana* develops into *Mohana* in separation, when the Śāttvikas are even more hightened (*suddīpta*).[7] Rādhā is the only *Āśraya* of *Mohana*, and in her it manifests itself too frequently.[8] The characteristics of *Mohana* are described as follows:

[1] *Bh.*, 10, 31, 19.
[2] *Bh.*, 11, 12, 11.
[3] *Bh.*, 11, 12, 12.
[4] *Ujjvala-nīlamaṇī*, *Sthāyī*, 123.
[5] ibid, 124.
[6] ibid, 128.
[7] ibid, 130.
[8] ibid, 132.

(*a*) *Kāntāśliṣte'pi mūrchana*: Rādhā's *mohana-bhāva* makes Kṛṣṇa faint even in the embrace of his concert. To illustrate this *Ujjvalanīlamaṇi* cites a *Śloka* from *Padyāvalī*, which describes Kṛṣṇa as enjoying the thrill of the loving embrace of Rukmaṇī in his palace at Dvārakā. At the same time Rādhā is gripped with *Mohana-bhāva* in Vraja, which has immediate effect on Kṛṣṇa. He is reminded of his amorous pastimes with Rādhā in the bowers on the bank of the Jamunā in Vraja and the sweet memory of those pastimes makes him faint.[1]

(*b*) *Asahya-duḥkha-svīkārād api tat-sukha-kāmitā*: desire for causing happiness to Kṛṣṇa even by undergoing unbearable suffering. Nothing can be more unbearable to Rādhā than her separation from Kṛṣṇa. Still the only message she sends to Kṛṣṇa at Mathurā through Uddhava is that he need not return to Vraja, if that is likely to cause the least difficulty or embarrassment to him.[2]

(*c*) *Brahmānda-kṣobha-kāritva*: causing sorrow to the whole world. When Rādhā develops *Mohana-bhāva* in her separation from Kṛṣṇa, all the worlds, including the transcendental Vaikuṇṭha, are struck with a unique wave of sorrow.[3] It is unique in the sense that it is essentially delightful, since it arises from Rādhā, the embodiment of Hlādini-śakti, of which the soul function is to cause delight. In mystic language it is the "sweet-bitter chalice of love" or "poisoned nectar." The very intensity of Rādhā's love in separation gives it an edge, which is pleasantly piercing and piercingly pleasant. Therefore, the wave of sorrow, which it sends round the Brahmāndas also has this dual character. Śrī Jīva, however, says that although *Mohana-bhāva* is more or less a permanent feature of the love of Rādhā, it is only seldom that it acquires this characteristic of engulfing the Brahmāndas with the sweet sorrow or 'the ecstacy of deprivation' she herself experiences.

(*d*) *Tirścām api rodanam*: the weeping of the animals. *Ujjvalanīlamaṇi* cites a *Śloka* from *Padyāvalī*, in which even the animals living in the water of the river Jamunā are said to have wept to hear Rādhā cry in the deep anguish of her separation from Kṛṣṇa.[4]

(*e*) *Mṛtyu-svīkārāt sva-bhutair api tat-saṅga-tṛṣṇā*: craving death to serve Kṛṣṇa with the elements of her body. *Ujjvalanīlamaṇi* cites a *Śloka* from *Padyāvalī*, which describes Rādhā craving for her death so that the five elements composing her body may disintegrate and mix with things that serve Kṛṣṇa in various ways. She desires that the water element of her body may mix with the pool in which he swims, the fire or light element with the mirror he uses, the *ākāśa* element with the *ākāśa* of his court-yard, the earth element with the land on which he moves, and the air element with the air of his fan.

[1]ibid, *Ujjvala-nīlamaṇi, Sthayī*, 133. [2]ibid, 134.
[3]ibid, 135. [4]ibid, 136.

(*f*) *Divyonmāda*: divine frenzy, which expresses itself in some helpless acts and movements (*udghūrṇā*) as, for example, the acts and movements of a Vāsa-sajjāyitā or a Khaṅditā heroine. As Vāsa-sajjāyitā Rādhā forgets that Kṛṣṇa is in Mathurā. She imagines him to be in Vṛndāvana and to have promised to come to her at a particular time of night. In that expectation she adorns herself and her surroundings. But when he does not turn up, she sighs deeply and frets and fumes like a Khaṅditā heroine. Divyonmāda also takes the form of Citra-jalpa, which consists in Rādhā's uttering deeply anxious and resentful words on her meeting a friend of Kṛṣṇa. Of Citra-jalpa also there are several forms, e.g., Saṁjalpa, which consists in regretfully and ironically declaring the hero's ingratitude, or Avajalpa, which consists in declaring the unworthiness of the hero's love on account of his hard-heartedness.

When *Modana* is sublimated it is called *Mādana*. *Mādana* is the highest state, which *Anurāga* can attain. It is the very essence of Hlādinī-śakti. Therefore it includes all the different Bhāvas or stages of *Prema*: *Rati, Sneha, Māna, Praṇaya, Rāga, Anurāga, Mahābhāva*. It excels *Mahābhāva*, because it is *Mahābhāva* intensified. Its only *Āśraya* is Rādhā, in whom it is always present, though not always manifest. It is manifest in union and unmanifest in separation.[1]

As the root '*mad*,' from which the word '*mādana*' is derived, indicates, the pleasure derived from *Mādana* has an intoxicating quality which is not found in *Modana*, despite its extreme blissfulness. But the uniqueness and super-excellence of *Mādana* consists in a special quality, which it is not possible to describe or comprehend. It is the quality of eternally combining a thousand different and even contradictory Bhāvas associated with a thousand different and contradictory experiences (*yadvilāsa virājante nityalīlā sahasradhā*) in relation to Kṛṣṇa. *Mādana* has the unique capacity of directly experiencing a thousand different kinds of enjoyment of union with Kṛṣṇa on only seeing him or recalling his memory. Yet these experiences are not imaginary (*sphūrti*). The capacity to experience Kṛṣṇa in a thousand different ways involves the capacity to bring about his direct appearance (*āvirbhāva*) in these experiences. What, however, makes *Mādana* even more inconceivable is the fact that it presents these multifarious experiences of union simultaneously with multifarious experiences of separation (*viyoga*) involving craving (*utkaṅthā*) for union. The grounds (*āśraya*) of these contradictory experiences are not different *Prakāśas* (manifestations) of Rādhā, which enjoy them separately at the same time. But it is the same *Prakāśa* that enjoys these experiences, howsoever contradictory in nature, simultaneously. Therefore *Mādana* is appropriately called the fountain-head of all the various types of Bhāva and bliss (*sarva-bhāvodgamollāsī*).[2]

[1] *Ujjvala-nīlamaṇi, Sthāyī* 155. [2] ibid.

Sthāyī-bhāva (*Basic Emotion*)

We have described the different grades of devotional feeling one may realise as one advances in *Bhakti*. But the particular grade upto which a devotee may advance depends upon his Sthāyi-bhāva or basic emotion. The Sthāyī-bhāva is determined by the particular character (*svabhāva*) of the deity by which he is inspired and which produces a particular kind of conceit (*abhimāna*) in him. The conceit may take the form of (a) *Anugrāhyābhimāna* (the conceit of being favoured by the deity), (b) *Anugrāhakābhimāna* (the conceit of being one, who favours the deity), (c) *Mitrābhimāna* (the conceit of being a friend of the deity), and (d) *Priyābhimāna* (the conceit of being a beloved of the deity). The conceit of being favoured by the deity may be with or without the feeling of *Mamatā* or affectionate attachment. Those, who are without such feeling are called Śānta-bhaktas. In the absence of the feeling of *Mamatā*, which draws the deity nearer, the Śānta-bhakta has to be content with merely contemplating or looking at him as Brahman or Paramātman from a distance.[1] The examples of Śānta-bhakta are Sanaka, Sanātana and others. They are called Jnānin-bhaktas, because their attitude of devotion is mixed with Jnāna. Their devotion cannot go beyond the state of Rati and their proper place is Vaikuṇṭha. Those who have the feeling of *Mamatā* regard the deity as their *Pālaka* (protector), *Prabhu* (master) or *Lālaka* (superior) and themselves as his *Pālya* (subject), *Dāsa* (servant) or *Lālya* (inferior in relation). They can go up to the state of Rāga.

The devotees, who have the conceit of favouring the deity, have Vātsalya-bhāva or parental affection towards him. They regard the deity as their son and themselves as his father or mother. In their case devotion reaches the state of *Anurāga* (*CC*, Madhya, XXIII, 35). The devotees, who have the conceit of being a friend of the deity, regard him as their friend. Their devotion also is of the nature of *Anurāga* (*CC*, Madhya, XXIII, 35). It is called *Maitrya* or *Sakhya*. But if both *Vātsalya* and *Sakhya* types of devotion are characterised by *Anurāga*, what, one may ask, is the difference between them? The answer is provided by the *Caitanya-caritāmṛta* text Madhya, XXIV, 26, which indicates that the devotional feeling in the case of Vātsalya-bhāva goes up to the last stage of *Anurāga*, while in the case of Sakhya-bhāva it goes up to its first stage only.

The devotees, who have the conceit of being the beloved of the deity, regard him as their lover. Their Bhāva is called *Kānta-bhava* or *Madhurā-rati*. In the case of the queens of Dvārakā, Madhurā-rati goes up to the last stage of *Anurāga* or the first stage of Mahābhāva, while, in the case of the Gopīs of Vraja, as we have stated before, it goes up to an advanced

[1]*śāntera svabhāva kṛṣṇe mamatā gandhahīna|*
parabrahman-paramātman-jnāna pravīṇa||

stage of Mahābhāva called *Modana*, and, in the case of Rādhā herself, it goes up to the last stage of Mahābhāva called Mādana.

Thus there are five kinds of basic emotion or Sthāyi-bhāva: Śānta, Dāsya, Sakhya, Vātsalya and Mādhurya, corresponding to the five different kinds of conceit a devotee may have in relation to Kṛṣṇa. They are also known as the five kinds of Rati (*CC*, Madhya, XXIII, 25).

CHAPTER XIV

Rasa or Transcendental Relish

The Sthāyī-bhāvas, when combined with the four *Sāmagrīs* (ingredients), called Vibhāva, Anubhāva, Sāttvika-bhāva and Vyabhicāri-bhāva are raised to their corresponding states of transcendental relish, called Rasa, in the same manner in which curd, when mixed with sugar, camphor and pepper becomes *rasāla,* which has a unique taste of its own (*CC*, Mahya, XXIII, 26-29).

Vibhāvas are the exciting conditions, which make the basic or dominant emotion (*sthāyi-bhāva*) capable of being relished (*ratyāsvāda-hetavaḥ*). They are of two kinds: *Ālambana* (substantial excitants) and *Uddīpana* (enhancing excitants). Ālambana is further divided into Āśraya and Viśaya. Āśraya is the person in whom Rati originates and Viśaya the person towards whom it is directed. Thus the devotee of Kṛṣṇa is Āśraya and Kṛṣṇa is Viṣaya. But in relation to the Rati of Kṛṣṇa himself Kṛṣṇa is Āśraya and the devotee towards whom his Rati is directed is Viṣaya. Uddīpana Vibhāva of Kṛṣṇa-rati consists of the attributes, the dress, the ornaments, the flute, the smile etc. of Kṛṣṇa, which excite the devotional sentiment (*CC*, Madhya, XXIII, 30). The Anubhāvas or the ensuants like dancing and singing, which follow an emotion and strengthen it and the Sāttvika-bhāvas have already been explained. The Vyabhicāri-bhāvas, also called Saṁcārī-bhāvas are auxiliary feelings of transitory character, which appear and disappear like waves in the sea, but leave the dominant emotion unaffected. Thirty-three Vyabhicāri-bhāvas are usually mentioned, e.g. *Nirveda* (self-disparagement), *Viṣāda* (despondency), *Harṣa* (joy), *Vitarka* (doubt), *Asūyā* (envy,) *Nidrā* (drowsiness), *Bodha* (awakening) (*CC*, Madhya, XXIII, 32). Corresponding to the five Sthāyī-bhāvas there are five principal Rasas, namely, Śānta, Dāsya, Sakhya, Vātsalya and Madhura (*CC*, Madhya, XXIII, 33). Seven other Rasas of the orthodox poetics, namely, *Hāsya* (the comic), *Adbhuta* (the marvellous), *Vīra* (the heroic), *Karuṇa* (the pathetic), *Raudra* (the furious), *Bhayānaka* (the terrible), *Vibhatsa* (the abhorrent) are regarded as secondary, because they are only indirectly related to Kṛṣṇa-rati.

Each succeeding one of the principal Rasas is superior to the preceding.[1] The superiority of a Rasa consists in greater intimacy with Kṛṣṇa,

[1]*Bhakti-rasāmṛta-sindhu*, 2, 5, 115-17.

lesser feeling of regard for his power and majesty as God (*aiśvarya*) and higher bliss. Each succeeding Rasa also has all the qualities of the preceding besides a distinguishing quality of its own. The distinguishing feature of Śānta-rasa is relinquishment of all worldly desires (*tṛṣṇā-tyāga*) and faith in Kṛṣṇa (*Kṛṣṇa-niṣṭhā*) (*CC*, Madhya, XIX, 176-77).[1] As already stated the Śānta-bhakta knows Kṛṣṇa as Brahman or Paramātman and in his case the question of conceiving a personal relationship with him does not arise. Dāsya-rasa implies personal relationship as between a master and servant. The only desire that animates the devotee, who has the conceit of a servant is the desire to give comfort to Kṛṣṇa and contribute, in whatever way possible, to his happiness. But his devotional attitude is characterised by a feeling of respect towards the master, which prevents him from coming too close to him (*CC*, Ādi, III, 14; IV, 17).[2]

In Sakhya the feeling of regard for Kṛṣṇa as a superior person is transcended. The devotee treats him as his equal. He serves him, but also allows himself to be served by him (*CC*, Ādi, IV, 22).[3] In Vātsalya the conceit that the devotee is equal to Kṛṣṇa is also transcended. He regards himself as superior in power and intelligence and Kṛṣṇa as wholly dependant upon him for his care and protection. The Aiśvarya aspect of Kṛṣṇa is further eclipsed by his Mādhurya aspect and the feeling of 'mineness' (*madīyatā-bhāva*) in the devotee is particularly hightened (*CC*, Ādi, IV, 21). Mother Yaśodā refuses to regard Kṛṣṇa as the creater or destroyer of the universe, even when she sees the entire universe, including herself and the child Kṛṣṇa, in his mouth. On the other hand she regards it as her privilege to scold and beat him when he does not behave properly. This Bhāva completely subjugates Kṛṣṇa (*CC*, Ādi, IV, 20).[4] In Madhura-rasa the feeling of mineness reaches its climax and the relationship is much more intimate than even in Vātsalya, since the lordship of Kṛṣṇa is almost completely overcome. The love of the milk-maids of Vraja is unrestricted by any kind of fear, hesitation, delicacy, convention, or feeling of reverence. This is evidenced by the narrative in *Bhāgavata*, according to which they do not feel at all attracted by Kṛṣṇa in his majestic form having four hands. But even the milk-maids of Vraja are not capable of fully subjugating the lordship of Kṛṣṇa, which is possible only in the case of Śrīmatī Rādhikā. Kṛṣṇa finds it impossible to retain

[1] *kṛṣṇaniṣṭhā, tṛṣṇātyāga—śāntera dui guṇe||*

[2] *aiśvarya śithila preme nāhi mora prīti||*
āmāre īśvara māne āpanā ke hīna|
tāra preme vaśa āmi na haī adhīna||

[3] *sakhā śuddha sakhye kare skandhe ārohaṇa|*
"tumi kona baṇa loka?—tumi āmi sama||

[4] *āpanā ke baṇa māne āmāre sama hīna|*
sarva bhāve āmi haī tāhāra adhīna||

his four-armed form before her.

Madhura-rasa expresses itself in two forms—Vipralambha and Sambhoga. Vipralambha signifies separation in love, and Sambhoga signifies union or consumation in love. Vipralambha, according to Śrī Caitanya, represents the highest form of spiritual realisation. It increases the intensity of *Preman* and embellishes the joy of Sambhoga. The bitterness caused by Vipralambha is only apparent, because it does not, like the state of separation between the lovers on the phenomenal plane, imply interposition of time and space. In the transcendental world, where union and separation can exist simultaneously, there is no substantive experience except that of unmixed joy and inseparable union.

A special characteristic of the Rasas is that, although, speaking objectively, they are higher and lower in relish and Madhura-rasa is the highest of them all, the devotee of each type of Rasa has the feeling that his own Rasa is the highest (*CC*, Ādi, IV, 38-42). The Rasas are sometimes mixed up. For example, in Yudhiṣṭhira we find a mixture of Sakhya and Dāsya, in Baladeva a mixture of Sakhya, Dāsya and Vātsalya and in Paṭṭa-mahiṣis a mixture of Dāsya and Madhura-bhāva. The *Prīti* in which all the five types of Bhāva are absent is called *Sāmānya* (general) *Prīti*. The devotees of the Sāmānya and Śānta type are called Taṭastha, because they lack in the feeling of intimate personal attachment to the deity. The devotees of the remaining type, who have the feeling of intimate personal attachment to the deity are called the Parikaras of the deity.

Since the outer structure of the theory of Rasa in Bengal Vaiṣṇavism is based on the secular theory of Rasa in orthodox poetics, the question is often asked as to whether *Bhakti* can at all be regarded as a Rasa. While some of the theorists like Bhoja and Sudeva regard *Bhakti* as Rasa, expressly or by implication, others hold that it cannot be regarded as Rasa, because it is lacking in the ingredients of Rasa, and because it involves unequal relationship between the *Bhakta* and the deity, while Rasa is possible only in affectionate relationship between equals. Śrī Jīva replies to this objection by showing that all the ingredients of Rasa, the Sthāyī-bhāva, Vibhāva etc. are fully present in *Bhakti*, and by stating that the relationship between the Bhakta and the deity is unequal only in the case of devotion to ordinary deities (*prākṛta-devādi-viṣaya*) and not in the case of devotion to Kṛṣṇa, in whom Mādhurya operates to remove all inequalities. He also points out that Rasa, in the real sense, is possible only in Kṛṣṇa-rati, which is a modification of Aprākṛta-sattva and not in Laukika-rati (mundane love) between the ordinary hero and heroine, which is a modification of Prākṛta-sattva-guṇa. In Laukika-rati the Sthāyī-bhāva, Vibhāva and Vyabhicārī bhāva etc. are all Prākṛta, while in Kṛṣṇa-rati they are all Aprākṛta. Therefore the pleasure in Laukika-rati is slight, short-lived and painful at the end, while the pleasure in Kṛṣṇa-rati is permanent, transcendental and higher than even the relish of Brahman, to which the pleasure of Laukika-rati is said to resemble to some extent by the rhetoricians.[1] The only Rasa, which, according to Śrī Jīva, Laukika-rati is capable of awakening is Vibhatsa or Disgustful, The *Śruti* text *raso vai saḥ* also identifies Rasa with Bhagavān and not with anything Laukika.

Madhura-rasa and Eroticism

It should be clear from what has been said above that the theory of Rasa in Bengal Vaiṣṇavism is basically different from the theory of Rasa in orthodox poetics. It has borrowed from the latter only its outer structure, with necessary modifications to suit its convenience, while in actual content it is based on the Rasa-vijnāna of *Śrīmad-bhāgavata*, in which the five-fold principle of Kṛṣṇa-rati (Śānta, Dāsya etc.) is clearly laid down[2] and which speaks of *Bhakti* as *rasa*.[3]

This outward resemblance of the theory of Rasa in Bengal Vaiṣṇavism with the theory of Rasa in poetics, and the outward resemblance of Kṛṣṇa-līlā with the general behaviour of human beings on earth, have given rise to serious misunderstanding among scholars, particularly in regard to the divine sports of Kṛṣṇa with the Gopīs. These are sweepingly described as vulgar[4] or immoral,[5] and the emotionalism of the devotee, who contemplates them is deprecated as sensual delirium.[6] "The mystic experience of the divine sports," says S.K. De, "is almost entirely governed by the erotic feeling and wholly steeped in it, the other sentiments only touching its fringe. The highest object of religious adoration and worship is conceived and moulded, after the *Paurāṇic* legend, in a frankly erotic cast, and there is nowhere any suggestion of allegory in the circumstantial working out of its minute sensuous details. The glorification of the sex impulse is supreme."[7]

If the charge of sensuality is directed against the post-Caitanya Sahajiyā cult of Bengal, whose followers also claim allegiance to Śrī Caitanya, it is justified. There is no doubt that ugly facts can be pointed out in support of it. The almost open debaucheries of these so-called followers of Śrī Caitanya have more than once been brought to our notice by the critics, and they are so painfully true that it would be absurd to play the role of an apologist for them. But it should be clearly understood that the

[1]Rasa in poetics is said to be like the *Pratinidhi* (representative) or *Sahodara* (brother) of Brahmānanda, but not Brahmānanda itself. But Bhakti-rasa is infinitely more relishable than even Brahmānanda. *Haribhaktisudhodaya*, 14, 36.

[2]*Bh.*, 3, 25, 38.

[3]ibid, 1, 1, 3.

[4]E. W. Hopkins, *Ethics of India*, Yale University Press, New Haven, 1924, p. 200.

[5]John Mckenzie, *Hindu Ethics*, pp. 177-78.

[6]Barth, *Religions of India*, p. 228.

[7]S. K. De, *Early History of Vaiṣṇava Faith and Movement in Bengal*, p. 418.

Sahajiyas have not the remotest connection with Śrī Caitanya or the *Bhakti* movement initiated by him. They are the dregs of the most degenerated and perverted form of Vaiṣṇavism, which the Caitanyaites have not only always disclaimed but condemned in the most emphatic terms.

Śrī Caitanya's views on sex and sensuality are too well known. Even critics like S.K. De have freely admitted that "he held an ascetic type of morality and expressed strict views regarding sexual relationship."[1] He is even criticised for over-strictness in his insistence that an ascetic must under all circumstances avoid the company of a woman. In this connection the punishment he gave to his disciple Choṭā Haridāsa for begging rice of Mādhvī, an old woman, who was also one of his foremost devotees, is usually pointed out. Choṭā Haridāsa had gone to Mādhvī to beg for good quality of rice at the instance of Bhagavān Ācārya, who had invited Śrī Caitanya to have his meal at his house. When Śrī Caitanya came to know of this he ordered that Choṭā Haridāsa must never be admitted to his presence. Damodara Svarūpa and other intimate companions of Śrī Caitanya felt that the punishment was too severe for Choṭā Haridāsa to bear. They, therefore, begged the Master to forgive him. The Master replied "I cannot bear the sight of a Vairāgin, who has conversed with a woman. Better you attend to your business and stop idle talks. If you again plead with me for Choṭā Haridāsa, you will not find me here." The pleadings of Paramānanda Purī, a brother disciple of Śrī Caitanya's Guru Īśvara Purī, whom he respected greatly, also failed to soften him. Choṭā Haridāsa waited for a year, hoping that the Master may yet show mercy on him. But finding him still inexorable, he went to Prayāg and gave up his life in the holy waters of the Trivenī, so that he may serve him in the next life. When his end was related to Śrī Caitanya he commented with a light heart, "this is the penalty for looking at a woman" (*CC*, Antya, II, 163). The example of Choṭā Haridāsa was not lost on the other disciples of Śrī Caitanya. *Caitanya-caritāmṛta* says: "They stopped talking with women even in their dreams" (Antya, II, 140). It is, therefore, universally recognised that even the followers of Śrī Caitanya, in their actual life, upheld the highest standard of morality.[2]

But, Dr. De has held that though in actual life the devout saints of Bengal Vaiṣṇavism have been 'morally irreproachable' and though Bengal Vaiṣṇavism condemns direct erotic practice, it encourages 'vicarious erotic contemplation.' It emphasises the inward realisation of the divine sports in all their erotic implications as the ultimate felicitous state, and thereby promotes the abnormal satisfaction of a highly refined erotico-religious sensibility.'[3]

This sadly betrays an attitude of mind, which is either wholly biased or

[1]S.K. De, *Early History* of *Vaiṣṇava Faith and Movement in Bengal*, p. 419.
[2]ibid. [3]ibid.

utterly ignorant of the basic principles of human psychology. The view that Bengāl Vaiṣṇavism condemns direct erotic practice, but encourages vicarious erotic contemplation is obviously based on the assumption that our mind consists of isolated processes, that our willing is independent of our thinking and feeling, and that the general pattern of our thoughts and feelings may be entirely different from the general pattern of our manifest behaviour. This is altogether a false assumption. Psychology does not bear witness to a mind that is an aggregate or a mechanical whole of isolated parts. It says that our thoughts, feelings and volitions are phases in the life history of the same conscious individual and the inner and outer expressions of the same complex whole. It is, therefore, preposterous to presume that they can run in opposite directions. It is impossible that a devotee may indulge in vicarious erotic contemplation and be pure in life, or that he may be pure in life and indulge in vicarious erotic contemplation. The spotlessly pure outward life of Śrī Caitanya and his followers and the highest ideals of morality, which they preached and practised, wholly preclude any possibility of their indulging inwardly in imaginative experience of erotic sentiment. They had not renounced power and pelf and spurned extensive opportunities of sense enjoyment only to indulge in imaginative and vicarious experience of sensual pleasure.

Śrī Caitanya and his followers do not miss any opportunity to emphasise that the amours of Kṛṣṇa with the Gopīs of Vraja, which they recommend as the highest object of religious contemplation, must not be viewed as similar to the love affairs of the ordinary heroes and heroines of this world (*prākṛta-kāma*). They are the spiritual pastimes of Kṛṣṇa with the bodily manifestations of his own highest energy of bliss (Hlādinī śakti) and as such the natural expression of the divine self. They are designated as *Kāma*, not because they have anything to do with *Kāma* or lust, in the ordinary sense, but because the outward movements (*ceṣṭā*) in them are similar to those in the love affairs of the ordinary heroes and heroines. Basically the two are opposed to each other as light is opposed to darkness.[1] *Kāma* in transcendental Vṛndāvana is not actually *Kāma*, in the ordinary sense, but *Kāma*, in the transcendental sense, or *Aprākṛta-kāma*, which actually means *Preman* or transcendental love. The fundamental difference between *Kāma* and *Preman* is that while the former is self-regarding and aims at one's own pleasure, the latter is other-regarding and aims entirely at contributing to the pleasure of the divine object.

Preman is not simply the idealised form of mundane love. The Bengal school of Vaiṣṇavism is not an advocate of the ethics of Perfectionism, which believes in the highest development of all our faculties, including

[1] *ataeva kāme preme bahuta antara/*
kāma andha-tamaḥ, prema-nirmala bhāskara// CC, Ādi, IV, 147.

the faculty of sex, under the control of reason. It believes in the complete transcendence of everything mundane. The transcendental love of Vṛndāvana has no scope for the sensuous and self-seeking love of the mundane world.

The question of sex simply does not arise with the denizens of Vṛndāvana because they do not have physical body and senses. Their body and senses are all spiritual. Therefore their movements and activities are also spiritual, even though the language generally used to describe them and the imagery which these descriptions arouse may make them appear as little different from the physical movements and activities of the lovers on earth. The difficulty pertaining to language is unavoidable, and it has been experienced by all the religions of the world in describing the highest truths of religious experience. The only thing one may do in this connection is to use necessary safeguards and take necessary precautions. Śrī Jīva has, therefore, cautioned that so long as our mind and senses are not purified and there is any possibility of our deriving vicarious erotic pleasure from the contemplation of the amorous pastimes of Kṛṣṇa with the Gopīs, we must not contemplate them.[1]

The outward similarity between the amours of Kṛṣṇa and the love affairs of the worldly people is but natural, because the latter, according to Bengal Vaiṣṇavism, are the perverted reflection of the former. But to interpret the former in terms of the latter is to interpret the higher in terms of the lower, the substance in terms of the shadow. The fallacy, however, is involved in the epistemological situation itself. The critic, whose own mind is perverted and who has not been able to rise above the shadowy world of senses cannot think of amorous activities, which are categorically different from sensuousness. The Sṛngāra-rasa of Vṛndāvana is altogether of a higher dimension and involves a higher plane of existence to which he must rise before he can comprehend and appreciate it. Until then he must accept the account given by the saints and the sages, who have themselves risen to that plane and realised the ultra-sensory character of the Rasa. The sage Śuka has said in *Bhāgavata* that the Madhura-līlā of Kṛṣṇa with the Gopīs, far from being a sport in sexsuality provides an excellent remedy for the malady of sex, if we listen to its narrative with faith and devotion.[2] The fact that even a Jnānī-bhakta like Uddhava who had gone to Vṛndāvana with the sole purpose of communicating right knowledge to the Gopīs so that they might not feel the pangs of separation from Kṛṣṇa, returned converted and longed to be a Gopī himself so that he might taste the pleasure of the conjugal love of the Gopīs, shows that their love was not worldly or sensual. The *Padma-purāṇa* says that even the *Śrutis* incarnated as Gopīs

[1] *pauruṣa vikāravat indriyaih rahasyalīlā tu na upāsyā. BS*, Sec. 338.
[2] *Bh.*, 10, 33, 39.

to relish their transcendental love.

According to *Vedānta-sūtra*, II, i. 33 (*lokavat tu līlā kaivalyam*) the Lord's intrinsic self consists of the spontaneous sports of his bliss, and in his amorous sports with the Gopīs he realises his own nature as bliss in its perfection. His sports are similar in form to those of the phenomenal beings (*lokvat*), but not phenomenal (*laukika*). In the phenomenal world the pleasure derived from conjugal love is regarded as the highest kind of sensuous pleasure. Similarly in the non-phenomenal world the sports of Kṛṣṇa taking the form of his conjugal love with the Gopīs are the highest expression of divine bliss. This does not mean as Dr. De thinks, that "the sex instinct is thus acknowledged in this theology as one of the highest human instincts which finds a transfigured counterpart or ideal in the highest sportive instinct of the divine being"[1] but that the sex instinct and its expressions in the phenomenal world are a disfigured and distorted counter-reflection of the Lord's eternal urge to sport with his own Śaktis. It only suggests that the sex instinct is rooted in reality as the shadow is rooted in the very object of which it is the shadow, and explains why it is psychologically impossible to eliminate it completely, unless one rises above the shadowy existence of the world of senses and the link with Reality, temporarily lost or forgotten under the influence of *Māyā*, is revived. As soon as this is done the way is opened for the inflow of Śuddhasattva, the divine light that makes the shadow disappear, leaving no scope for the morbid growth of sensuality that flourishes under it.

There is, however, an aspect of Madhura-rasa, which is not even outwardly similar to the Laukika-śṛngāra-rasa. Kavikarṇapūra calls it Prema-rasa and regards it as distinct from Śṛngāra-rasa.[2] Aṅgasaṅga or bodily contact is possible in Śṛngāra-rasa but not in Prema-rasa. As an instance of Prema-rasa can be cited the following lines of Śrī Rūpa in which Rādhā and Kṛṣṇa are seated together in the *Yoga-pīṭha*, calm as the deep sea, with tears of love incessantly trickling down their eyes and the Sakhīs, standing on either side, wiping them out with the hem of their garments:

taraṅgadangayā kila rangadevyā, savye sudevyā ca lanairasavye|
slaksā abhimarśena vimṛjyamānasvedāśru-dhārau siciyāñcalena||

The depth of their love seems to make their bodies incapable of movement. The same sentiment seems to be expressed in the following line of Candīdāsa in which the lover yearns for the company of the beloved but vouchsafes not to touch her body:

ekatra thākiba nāhi paraśiba, bhāvinī bhāvera dehā|

It has been suggested that Prema-rasa belongs to a *Prakāśa* (manifestation) of Rādhā-Kṛṣṇa, which is different from the *Prakāśa* to which Śṛn-

[1]S. K. De, op. cit., p. 287.
[2]*Alaṁkāra Kaustubha*, 5, 34.

gāra-rasa belongs,[1] as if the two are antagonistic to each other. But in our view Prema-rasa is like the sea to which Śṛngāra-rasa belongs as its waves, and the essential character of both is the same. Therefore, they can co-exist. In the Rāsa-līlā of Śrī Kṛṣṇa, perhaps, the dominant Rasa is Śṛngāra-rasa, while in the Vastra-haraṇa-līlā the dominant Rasa is Prema-rasa, as Śrī Jīva also seems to think.[2]

Parakīyā-rasa

The most important contribution of Śrī Caitanya to the Rasa-śāstra is his doctrine of Parakīyā-rasa. Śrī Rūpa defines a Parakīyā heroine as one, who offers herself to Kṛṣṇa on account of her Rāga or natural attachment towards him, without entering into a formal wedlock, and without caring for the propriety or impropriety of the act according to the Śāstras. The very intensity of her love makes her oblivious of all other considerations. This kind of love for Kṛṣṇa is eulogised in *Bhāgavata*, but no one before Śrī Caitanya recognised it as the highest devotional sentiment. There is no doubt that authorities like Bharata Muni have recognised the superiority of Parakīyā-rasa in secular Rasa-śāstra. Bharata Muni holds that the natural impediments and inaccessibility in the case of a Parakīyā heroine highten the erotic sensibility to the highest degree and make her love much more enjoyable than the legitimate love of a Svakīyā heroine or a duly married woman. But it is doubtful whether he recognises Parakīyā-rasa as a devotional sentiment.

According to Śrī Caitanya the Kāntas of Kṛṣṇa may be classified as (a) Laksmīs in Paravyoma, (b) Mahiṣīs in Dvārakā and Mathurā, and (c) Gopīs in Vraja (*CC*, Ādi, IV, 63-65). The Lakṣmīs and the Mahiṣīs are Svakīyās while the Gopīs are Parakīyās. Of the Gopīs some are Paroḍhās or women married to other persons, and some are Kanyakās, or maidens. Both Paroḍhās and Kanyakās regard Kṛṣṇa as their real husband, although he is, from the worldly (*laukika*) point of view, only their *Upapati* or paramour. Their love is so natural, so pure, so deep and substantial that it does not stand in need of being solemnised or strengthened by an external ceremony or vow in the presence of the holy priest.

Śrī Caitanya's preference for the Parakīyā-rasa is indicated by his recitation, at the time of Ratha-yātrā at Purī, of the *yaḥ kaumāraharaḥ Śloka,* ascribed to Śīlā-bhaṭṭārikā (Padyāvalī, 382), which describes the superiority of the Parakīyā-rasa over Svakīyā-rasa, and by his appreciation of the *priyaḥ-so'yaṁ Śloka* of Śrī Rūpa (Padyāvalī, 383), composed by him as a variation of the above *Śloka*, which, Śrī Caitanya said, indicated that Rūpa had correctly understood his mind, and which

[1]Dīnaśaraṇadās, *Prema-rasa o Ananta Prakāśa.*

[2]*vidagdhānām yathā vanitānurāgāsvādane vāñchā na tathā tatsparśādoṣāvapi.* (*Pr. S.*, Sec. 377)

established, in his eyes, his eligibility for delineating the secrets of Rasa-śāstra (*CC*, Madhya, 1, 63). He, therefore, enjoined Svarūpa Dāmodara to describe them to him fully (*CC*, Madhya, 1, 68).

Some Vaiṣṇavas do not subscribe to the view that the Gopīs were the Parakīyās of Kṛṣṇa. As an argument against the Parakīyā-vāda they point out that the maidens, who had tried to appease the goddess Kātyāyanī by observing Kātyāyanī-vrata with the object of obtaining Kṛṣṇa as their husband, were married by him secretly on the day of the Vastra-haraṇa-līlā, as described in the *Bhāgavata*. But marriage is primarily a social function. It has no significance unless it is generally recognised. The very fact that the marriage was secretly performed and neither the parents nor anyone else knew anything about it shows that for all practical purposes even those maidens were the Parakīyās of Kṛṣṇa.

The indications of Parakīyā-vāda in *Bhāgavata* are so clear and convincing that it is futile to argue against it. After Śukadeva had described the Rāsa-līlā of Kṛṣṇa with the Gopīs, the king Parīkṣita asked: "Why did Kṛṣṇa, who had incarnated with the special purpose of re-establishing *Dharma* and destroying *Adharma*, himself commit adultery?" (*Bh.*, 10, 33, 26-28). Śukadeva replied, "Fire burns everything, whether pure or impure, and still remains untouched by the impurity of things it burns. Similarly, the acts performed by the all-powerful gods do not cause any blemish to them, even if they are wrong (*Bh.*, 10, 33, 29)." Both the question and the answer indicate that Kṛṣṇa's dalliance with the Gopīs was immoral from the worldly point of view, and suggest that the Gopīs were his Parakīyās.

The point is brought out more clearly in the dialogue between Kṛṣṇa and the Gopīs before the commencement of the Rāsa-līlā. Kṛṣṇa pretends not to be pleased with them, because they had gone to him in the forest at night to entertain him with the Rāsa dance against the wishes of the elderly members of their families and says "Go home, you respectable ladies to serve your husbands and their relatives. That is your first and foremost duty (*Bh.*, 10, 29, 24). For ladies of high descent like you the service of a paramour is condemnable (*jugupsitam ca sarvatra aupapatyam kulastriyaḥ*). It brings sorrow in this life and leads to hell after death (*Bh.*, 10, 29, 26)." The Gopīs reply: "What you say is correct. But according to your own advice we should serve no one except you. For, are you not our own, our heart and soul and our Lord for all times? What have we to do with our husbands and other kith and kin of this world with whom our relationship is temporary and painful? (*Bh.*, 10, 29, 32, 33)." This makes it clear beyond doubt that the Gopīs had their husbands and their relationship with Kṛṣṇa was non-marital, based simply on Rāga or most intense loving attachment. The specific use of the words *jāra* (paramour) (*Bh.*, 10, 29, 11) and *aupapatya* (*Bh.*, 10, 29, 26), in this connection, seems to put the final seal on it.

At the same time, however, there are scriptural texts, which state with equal emphasis and clarity that the Gopīs are the Svīyās or Kāntas of Kṛṣṇa. *Brahma-saṁhitā* says: *priyaḥ kāntaḥ kāntaḥ parapuruṣaḥ|* (5, 56) (The Gopīs are the consorts of Kṛṣṇa and Kṛṣṅa is their husband). In *Gopālottara-tāpanī Śruti,* Durvāsā Ṛṣi says to the Gopis: *sa vohi svāmin bhavati* ('He [Krṣṇa] is your husband'). Śukadeva himself describes the Gopīs as *Kṛṣṇa vadhvaḥ* or 'wives of Kṛṣṇa' in the context of the Rāsa-lilā in the *Bhāgavata* (10, 33, 8).

The two points of view seem to be irreconcilable. But the Parakīyā-vāda of the Caitanya school provides the right solution. It implies that although the Gopīs are Kṛṣṇa's own consorts (*svakīyās*), they appear as belonging to others (*parakīyamānāḥ*) in the Prakaṭa-līlā, on account of the illusion created by the divine *Yogamāyā.* The Gopas are not the real husbands of the Gopīs. Their relationship with the Gopīs is that of Pat-yābhasa, that is, they only appear to be their husbands, just as Kṛṣṇa only appears to be their paramour or *Upapati* (*CC*, Ādi, IV, 26). The Gopīs were never actually married to the Gopās. They were also never bodily touched by them. At the time of their marriage their illusory forms were substituted by *Yogamāyā*, which created the illusion of their marriage with them and their living with them as their wives. This is clearly indicated by the following *Śloka* of *Bhāgavata* which says that the Gopas did not have any jealousy towards Kṛṣṇa for sporting with their wives, because through the *Māyā* of Kṛṣṇa each had an apparent wife with him:

nāsūyān khalu kṛṣṇāya mohitastasya māyayā|
manyamānāḥ svapārśvasthān svān svān dārān vrajaukasaḥ||

The Gopīs are the special manifestations of the highest Hlādini-śakti of Kṛṣṇa. As such they are his eternal Svakīyās and his real and only favourites. His marriage with the princesses at Dvārakā does not disprove this, because according to *Padma-purāṇa,* they are identical with the Gopīs (*tābhir gopa-kumāribir ekātmatvāt*), as different manifestations of the same divine Śakti. Śrī Jīva calls them *Parama-svīyās* to distinguish them from both the Svakīyās of the phenomenal world and the Svakīyās of Dvārakā. The Svakīyā relationship of this world ends with death, while the Svakīyā relationship of the Gopīs is eternal. He quotes the Gautamīya Tantra to show that in each Kalpa they appear with Kṛṣṇa in the Prakaṭa-līlā and after they have sported with him for some time as his Parakīyās their Parakīyā relationship is converted into Svakīyā. The Svakīyā relationship of the princesses of Dvārakā is also eternal and they also appear with Kṛṣṇa in each Kalpa as his Svakīyās, but they are lacking in Samartha-rati of the Gopīs, which implies total dedication to eternal selfless service of Kṛṣṇa, free from even a moment's thought of pleasure for themselves, whether as Svakīyās or as Parakīyās, which makes them eternally Kṛṣṇa's own in a deeper sense. But Śrī Jīva says that although the Gopīs are really Parama-svīyās of Kṛṣna in the Prakaṭa-līlā they appear as Parakīyās (*vastutaḥ parama svīyā api prakaṭalīlāyāṁ parakīyāyamānāḥ srīvrjadevyaḥ*).[1] Śrī Rūpa says that even in the Prakaṭa-līlā they should be taken as Svīyās, because they were in fact married by Kṛṣṇa according to *Gandharva* rites (self-choice), but they are generally considered (*prāyena visrutaḥ*) as *Parakīyā*, because of the secrecy of their love (*pracchanna-kāmatā*) and the unmanifest character of their marriage.[2]

The Parakīyāvāda of Bengal Vaiṣṇavism, therefore, does not mean that the Gopīs are actually Parakīyās in relation to Kṛṣṇa but that their Bhāva alone is *Parakīyā*. In the words of Kavi Karṇapūra it means that their Svakiyā-bhāva is concealed by *Parakīyā-bhāva* (*parakīyā-bhāva-nigīrṇa-dāmpatyaṁ*). To foster the Parakiya-bhāva in them *Yogamāyā* brings about the illusion of their marriage with the Gopas. The conceit (*abhimāna*) as *Parakīyā* is a temporary superimposition upon the real and eternal conceit as Svakīya. The superimposition is as inexplicable as the Māyā-śakti which brings it about. For Kṛṣṇa as well as the Gopīs forget for the time being the Svakīyā character of their relationship and behave towards each other as each other's paramour:

āmiha nā jānī ihā nā jāne gopī-gaṇa|
dohāra rūpa-guṇe dohāra nitya hare mana||
dharma chāṇi rāge dohe karaye milana|
kabhu mile kabhu na mile daivera ghaṭana|| CC, Ādi, IV, 27-28.

Neither I nor the Gopīs know that we belong to each other eternally. We feel attracted towards each other by each other's form and attributes. We try to meet each other, transgressing the rules of morality, our meeting and separation depending always on luck.

The superimposition is, in fact, self-imposed, because Māyā-śakti, whose function is to serve Kṛṣṇa, cannot bring this about against his own wish. Śri Kṛṣṇa is Para-brahman, whose essential nature, according to *Śruti*, is *Rasa* (*raso vai saḥ*). His divine activities (*līlā*) are the natural outcome of his nature as *Rasa* (*rasa-svarūpa*). Śrī Rūpa says that the real purpose of his incarnation is to taste the essence of Rasa in Vraja (*rasa-niryāsasvādārthamavatāriṇi*). The essence of all Rasas is Sṛṅgāra-rasa and the essence of Sṛṅgāra-rasa is *Parakīyā-rasa*. In Parakīyā-rasa Śṛṅgāra-rasa assumes a new dimension, a new freshness, a new intensity and a new taste, on account of the very impediments which block its way. But Parakīyā-rasa cannot be enjoyed in Goloka, where Kṛṣṇa revels eternally with his Kāntas as his Svīyās. He has, therefore to appear in Vraja along with his Kāntas, under conditions favourable for Parakīyā-rasa, specially contrived by Māyā-śakti in the Prakaṭa-līlā:

parakīyā bhāve ati rasera ullāsa|
vraja binā ihāra anyatra nāhi bāsa|| CC, Ādi, IV, 42.

[1] *Pr. S.*, Sec, 278.
[2] *Ujjvala-nīlamaṇi*, Haripriyā, 10, 12.

But even the Māyā-śakti, which produces conditions favourable for Parakīyā-bhāva cannot bring about actual Parakīyā-relationship, since there is no *para* (other) for Kṛṣṇa, who is one without a second (*advaya*) and everything in the universe belongs to him as the manifestation of his Śakti.

What we have said above regarding the real nature of the Parakīyā doctrine as upheld in Bengal Vaiṣṇavism should set aside all doubts regarding the morality of the Parakīyā Rasa. Since the Gopīs are actually immaculate wives of Kṛṣṇa and only appear as his paramours, there is nothing wrong in their amorous relationship. Śrī Rūpa, however, takes up the question of propriety of Parakīyā-rasa from the point of view of the secular Rasa-śāstra and discusses it in some detail. Rasa-śāstra disapproves of union with the wife of another person, because it is unlawful and disgusting and its vulgarity obstructs Rasa. Śrī Rūpa says that secular Rasa-śāstra deals with Prākṛta (phenomenal) Rasa and Prākṛta heroes and heroines. It is, therefore, not competent to pronounce on the Aprākṛta (transcendental) Rasa and Aprākṛta heroes and heroines such as Kṛṣṇa and the Gopis.[1] Kṛṣṇa and the Gopīs have a human form (*narākṛti*) but a transcendental body, but the ordinary heroes and heroines have a physical body with which they identify themselves on account of ignorance. Sporting in Śṛṅgāra-rasa is the natural function of Kṛṣṇa, just as it is the natural function of fire to burn.[2] But Śṛṅgāra-rasa is not the natural function of the ordinary human beings. In Śṛṅgāra-rasa the former eternally realises himself, while the latter ultimately find their doom in unrestricted indulgence in it.

Since Śṛṅgāra-rasa is the very essence of Kṛṣṇa as Rasa and the Gopīs are the manifestations of his own Śakti, he sports with them amorously in the most natural manner, in Svakīya-bhāva or Parakīyā-bhāva, and the question of piety or impiety simply does not arise, just as it does not arise in the case of a child, who plays innocently with his own shadow (*Bh.*, 10, 33, 17). On the other hand the *Bhāgavata* says that by listening to the account of the divine sports of Kṛṣṇa and the Gopīs one can purify himself and attain *Bhakti* (*Bh.*, 10, 33, 36). If this were not actually so, a person like Śukadeva, who had risen far above the world of senses, would not relate the amorous pastimes of Kṛṣṇa with the Gopīs to Parīkṣita at the time of his death, and in the presence of thousands of Ṛṣis, and Uddhava, the wisest and the most beloved of Kṛṣṇa's companions, would not desire for the dust of the holy feet of the Gopīs (*Bh.*, 10, 47, 61). He realises that the Gopīs have made the highest sacrifice for Kṛṣṇa.

[1] *Ujjvala-nīlamaṇi, Nāyaka-bheda*, 16.

[2] *śṛṅgārarasasarvasvaṁ śikhipiñchavibhūṣam| aṅgikṛtanarākāramāśraye bhuvanāśrayam|| Kṛṣṇakarṇāmṛta Śloka*, cited in *Ujjvala-nīlamaṇi, Nāyakabheda*, 17.

They have renounced their kith and kin and even the traditional path of duty (*dharma*), which is, indeed, very difficult (*dustyajasvajanamāryapathaṁ*) for respectable ladies of high descent to renounce. Even Rukmiṇī, the most beloved of the queens of Kṛṣṇa could not forsake her people and override the considerations of duty to obtain Kṛṣṇa as her husband, against the wishes of her people. She preferred to fast unto death, life after life, to obtain him rather than to renounce her people and relinquish the Vedic path of duty (10, 47, 61). But the Gopīs placed selfless service of Kṛṣṇa above everything else and allowed neither the Vedas nor the thought of heaven or hell to come in their way. Even Kṛṣṇa eulogised them for this (*evaṁ madarthojhitalokavedasvānāṁ, Bh.*, 10, 32, 21) and helplessly acknowledged defeat for not being able to return their love (*napāraye' haṁ niravadyasaṁyujāṁ, Bh.*, 10, 32, 22). Śrī Rūpa emphasises that only the Parakīyā or Samarthā-rati of the Gopīs can develop into the highest Mahābhāva state (*iyameva ratiḥ proḍhā mahābhāvadaśāṁ vrajet—Ujjvalanīlamaṇi*, 74, 57), while the Samañjasā-rati of the queens of Dvārakā can develop only upto the Anurāga stage.

S.K. De, however, thinks that Rūpa and Jīva, the two authoritative Gosvāmins of Caitanyism were "never in favour of Parakīyāvāda" which "assumed importance in the later history of the cult."[1] "During the Prakaṭa-līlā at Vṛndāvana," he says, "there was the semblance and not the reality of the Parakīyā-bhāva of the Gopīs, but as explained in the *Kṛṣṇasaṁdarbha*, even this attitude was short-lived; for at the termination of the Prakaṭa-līlā, they entered into eternal union with Kṛṣṇa as his Svīyās in the Aprakaṭa-līlā, occurring simultaneously. Jīva Gosvāmin holds that this is the view of his own authority Rūpa Gosvāmin, expounded in the latter's *Ujjvalanīlamaṇi* and *Lalita-Mādhava*, where it is clearly indicated that Kṛṣṇa was really the husband (*Pati*), but only appeared for a short time as the paramour (*Upapati*) of the Gopīs during the Prakaṭa-līlā."

Obviously, this is a wrong interpretation of the views of the two Gosvāmins. No doubt they lend themselves to this interpretation to a casual reader on account of their repeated assertions that the Gopīs are really the Svīyās of Kṛṣṇa and their Parakīyā relationship with him is an illusion. But a more careful study of their works will show that they have with equal emphasis asserted the reality of the appearance of the Parakīyā relationship and the reality of the Parakīyā-bhāva. Even though the Parakīyā-relationship is an illusion, it is an illusion that is specially contrived by the Māyā-śakti so that Kṛṣṇa may realise the pleasure of a higher Rasa. Does not this give a special and a higher meaning to the Parakīyā rasa? How can a Rasa, in which Kṛṣṇa himself finds the highest satisfaction be merely an appearance?

The impression that Śrī Rūpa and Śrī Jīva were not in favour of Para-

---

[1] S. K. De, op. cit., p. 312.

kīyāvāda is probably created by their repeated insistence that the Gopīs are really Nitya (eternal) Svakiyās of Kṛṣṇa, that the Parakīyā character of the Gopīs in the Prakaṭa-līlā is an illusion, and that the illusion also is short-lived, since the Gopis are ultimately married to Kṛṣṇa, on his return to Vṛndāvana from Dvārakā, as Śrī Rūpa has shown in *Lalita-mādhava* and Śrī Jīva in *Gopāla-campū.* The point that the illusion is created with a purpose—the purpose of realising Rasa-niryāsa or the essence of the highest Śṛṅgāra-rasa is ignored. The question that is really important is not whether the Parakīyā-relationship is real or apparent, or whether it is permanent or transient, but whether it involves a higher Rasa or not. Both Śrī Rūpa and Śrī Jīva emphasise that Parakīyā-rasa is the highest of all Rasas and Kṛṣṇa specially appears in the Prakaṭa-līlā with the conceit of an *Upapati* and makes the Gopīs appear with the conceit of his paramours, in order that he may realise it.

It is true that in *Lalita Mādhava* and *Gopāla-campū* both Śrī Rūpa and Śrī Jīva make the illusory Parakīyā-relationship come to an end. There are two special reasons for this Firstly, this is necessary because of the illusory character of the relationship, which would otherwise become real, and the objection that it involves Rasābhāsa or a vulgar relationship that obstructs the principal sentiment of Rasa, would seem to be valid. Secondly, it is necessary for *Samṛddhimān-sambhoga*, which is regarded as the highest kind of Sambhoga or love-in-union. *Ujjvala-nīlamaṇi* mentions four kinds of Sambhoga, or rather four stages in Sambhoga, marked in order of intensity: *Saṁkṣipta* or brief such as occurs after *Pūrvarāga* or incipient love, consequent upon first sight, *Saṁkīrṇa* or mixed with contrary feelings, *Saṁpanna* or developed, as, for example, after the return of the hero from near Pravāsa or a place not very distant, and *Samṛdhimān* or complete and excessive, as for example, after the return of the hero from distant Pravāsa. The apparent Parakīyā-relationship prior to Samṛddhimān-sambhoga is necessary as an element in heightening the pleasure of *Samṛddhimān-sambhoga.*

But this neither detracts from the value of the Parakīyā-rasa as the highest Rasa, nor it makes the Parakīyā-bhāva short-lived in the absolute sense. If Kṛṣṇa as Rasa realises himself fully in Parakīyā-bhāva, the Parakīyā-bhāva must not only be real but eternal. It is in fact both short-lived and eternal in the same sense in which any other part of the Prakaṭa-līlā is short-lived yet eternal, short-lived from the point of view of a particular Prakaṭa-prakāśa and eternal from the point of view of all the infinite Prakaṭa-prakāśas taken together, for in one Prakaṭa-prakāśa or the other each Līlā of the Prakaṭa-prakāśa is always going on. Śrī Rūpa and Śrī Jīva could not have been averse to this view originally expressed by Śrī Caitanya himself to Śrī Sanātana (*CC*, Madhya, XX, 315-30). Besides, the *Padma-purāṇa* says that in the Nitya-līlā of the Aprakaṭa (unmanifest) Prakāśa of Bhauma (phenomenal) Vṛndāvana the

Nitya-kāntās (eternal consorts) of Kṛṣṇa eternally have the Parakīyā conceit and serve Kṛṣṇa accordingly:[1]

parakīyābhimāninyastathā tasya priyā janāḥ|
pracchannenaiva bhavena ramayanti nijapriyaṁ||

Padma-purāṇa, Pātāla-khanda 52, 11.

Those writings of Śrī Jīva in which he seems to emphasise the Svakīyā-relationship are sometimes sought to be explained by reference to a *Śloka*, which appears at the end of his commentary on *Śloka* 16 of the *Nāyaka-bheda Prakaraṇa* of *Ujjvala-nīlamaṇi*. The *Śloka* runs as follows:

svecchayā likhitaṁ kincit kiñcidatra parecchayā|
yatpūrvāparasambandhaṁ tatpūrvamaparaṁ param||

Part of what I write is according to my own wish and part according to the wish of others; that which is consistent with my previous writings is according to my own wish, while that which is not consistent with my previous writings is according to the wish of others.

It is suggested that his writings, which are in favour of Parakīyā-bhāva as the highest Bhāva, represent his own views, while those which are in favour of Svakīyā-bhāva represent the views of others, because the former are consistent with his writings in general, and also because his disciples (*śikṣā-śiṣya*) Śrī Śrīnivāsācārya, Śrī Narottam Thākura and Śrī Shyamānanda freely preached the Parakīyā-doctrine.[2]

The fact, however, is that there is no such contradiction in the writings of Śrī Jīva. He clearly and consistently maintains that Parakīyā-bhāva is the highest Bhāva, but at times emphasises the Svakīyā character of the relationship between Kṛṣṇa and the Gopīs, particularly from the ontological point of view, so that their Parakīyā-bhāva may not be misconstrued as actual Parakīyā-relationship.

Viśvanātha Cakravartin, a later theorist of the school, is a more enthusiastic supporter of the Parakīyā doctrine. His views seem to run counter to those of Śrī Jīva. He maintains that, though the Gopīs are the Svakīyās of Kṛṣṇa, as the manifestations of his Hlādinī-śakti, their Parakīyā-bhāva is eternal (*nitya-satya*), because the marriage of the Gopīs with the Gopas, though brought about by the *Bahiraṅgā* (external) Māyā-śakti, is real, in the same sense in which the identification of the Jīva with the body, brought about by Bahiraṅgā-māyā, and the relationships based upon the body, are real. He also maintains that the Parakīyā-bhāva prevails both in the Prakaṭa and the Aprakaṭa-līlās.

The difference between their views will, however, appear to be slight if we scrutinise them carefully. According to both the Svakīyā relationship between Kṛṣṇa and the Gopīs is fundamental and the Parakīyā-relationship is a superimposition, brought about by Māyā for the realisation of

[1]*See* Sundarānanda Vidyāvinoda, *Paratattvasīmā Śrīkṛṣṇacaitanya*, p. 802.
[2]ibid, pp. 298-99.

the highest Rasa; according to both Parakīyā-rasa is the highest Rasa, and the Parakīyā-bhāva is eternal at least in the Prakaṭa-prakāśa in the sense already explained; again, according to both, the Parakīyā-bhāva, in the case of Śrī Kṛṣṇa and the Gopīs, is not only not vulgar, but commenddable, because it is transcendental (*aprākṛta*).

The difference between them seems to be more a matter of emphasis and expression rather than of fundamentals. Śrī Jīva emphasises the temporary and illusory character of the marriage between the Gopas and the Gopīs in the Prakaṭa-līlā, probably to satisfy those, who are not capable of fully appreciating the argument based on the transcendental nature of their Parakīyā-relationship, while Viśvanātha Cakravartīn emphasises the reality of the marriage, because it is the basis, in the Prakaṭa-prakāśa, of Parakīyā-rasa, which cannot be illusory, for the simple reason that it is desired by Kṛṣṇa. But Śrī Jīva, inspite of his emphasis on the transitoriness of the Parakīyā-relationship, is anxious not to divest it of all reality so that the very base of the Parakīyā-bhāva is negated. He, therefore, says that though the marriage is illusory, its appearance is real, because it is created by *Yogamāyā*, who instils in all concerned deep and unshakable faith in its reality. Similarly Viśvanātha Cakravartin, inspite of his emphasis on the reality of the Māyika marriage of the Gopīs with the Gopas, is anxious to maintain the fundamentally Svakīyā character of their relationship with Kṛṣṇa. He ascribes only secondary reality to the former. In his commentary on *Ujjvala-nīlamaṇī*, Nāyakabheda, 16, he says that the Māyika marriage is like a real marriage (*nitya-satyameva jneyaṁ*), which implies that it is not absolutely real. It is precisely to emphasise this point that he describes the marriage as the result of Bahiraṅgā-māyā (the external potency) and not of Yogamāyā (the internal potency) of Kṛṣṇa. Thus, according to both, the marriage seems to have a dual character as both real and unreal and is, truly speaking, *anirvacanīya* (inexplicable), like the Māyā of Śaṁkara, which is *satasat*, or real yet unreal. But each tries to describe it in his own way, emphasising different points on which they basically agree.

In regard to the Aprakaṭa-līlā, while Jiva holds that the relationship of the Gopīs with Kṛṣṇa is Svakīyā, there being not even a semblance of their marriage with others, Viśvanātha Cakravartīn holds that though the actual relationship is Svakīyā, the Bhāva is Parakīyā. Here, again, the difference may seem to relate more to the mode of expression rather than to the character of relationship. Śrī Jīva describes the relation as that of *Svābhavika-dāmpatya*, or natural conjugal relationship without marriage. But if Parakīyā-relationship does not necessarily imply the actual marriage of the paramour with someone else, and if it is based simply on Raga, or natural and intense loving attachment of the lover and the beloved towards each other, the relationship, here also, is Parakīyā, and '*Svābhavika-dāmpatya*' is only another and, perhaps, a more acceptable term for it. The essential point is that the relationship is not based on marriage. The possibility of Parakīyā-bhāva in Goloka, without the marriage of the Gopīs with the Gopas, cannot be questioned. For all relationships, here, are natural and beginningless (*anādi*). Even the Vātsalya-bhāva of Nanda and Yaśodā is not based on the actual birth of Kṛṣṇa from Yaśodā. Besides the Parakīyā-bhāva is implied in the Mahābhāva itself, which characterises the Gopīs in Goloka as much as in the Prakaṭa-līlā in Vṛndāvana.

The correct view with regard to the nature of relationship between Kṛṣṇa and the Gopīs in the Aprakaṭa-līlā seems to be that it is neither Svakīyā nor Parakīyā in the ordinary sense. Svakīyā and Parakīyā are the concepts of the phenomenal world, and they do not, strictly speaking, apply to the unique and transcendental relationships in Goloka. Kedār Nāth Bhaktivinod Thākur has, therefore, rightly described the relationship between Kṛṣṇa and the Gopīs in Goloka, as a kind of inconceivable unity-in-difference (*acintya-bhedābheda*) of Svakīyā and Parakīyā. He thinks that the belief in the absence of the highest Parakīyā-rasa in Goloka is not in conformity with the supreme excellence of the Dhāman and that the superiority of the Prakaṭa-līlā in Vṛndāvana, in comparison to the Aprakaṭa-līlā in Goloka, does not consist in its presentation of Parakīyā-rasa as a new Rasa, but in its presentation of it in greater intensity in the setting of a seemingly actual Parakīyā-relationship, which, with all its natural impediments, provides the necessary background for a fuller expression of the sentiment.[1] Jīva Gosvāmin also holds that the impediments in the Parakīyā-relationship do not account for the origin or growth of the sentiment of the Gopīs, but only for its superior realisation, just as the obstacles in the way of a mad elephant do not account for his strength but for its better inward realisation and outward expression.

[1]*See* Sundarānanda Vidyāvinoda, *Paratattvasīmā Śrī kṛṣṇa caitanya*, p. 802.

Select Bibliorgaphy

Acintya-bhedābheda-vāda by Sunderānand Vidyāvinod, Gaudiya Mission, Calcutta, 1951.

Ānanda-vṛndāvana-campū by Kavikarṇapūra, ed. by Purīdas Gosvāmī, Vṛndāvana, 1952.

Aspects of Early Viṣṇuism by J. Gonda, Utrecht, N. V. A. Oosthoek's Uitgevers Mij, 1954.

Bāṁglār Vaiṣṇava-darma, by Tarkabhūṣaṇa Pramath Nāth, Calcutta, C.U. 1939.

Bāṁglār Vaiṣṇava-dharśana by Tarkabhūṣaṇa Pramath Nāth, Calcutta, Śrī Guru Library, 1963.

Bengal Vaiṣṇavism by Bepin Candra Pal, Calcutta, 1933.

Bhagavad-bhakti-rasāynam by Madhusūdan Sarasvatī, ed. Vārāṇasī, Vikrama, 2018.

Bhagavat-saṁdarbha by Jīva Gosvāmin, ed. Shyāmlāl Gosvāmī, Calcutta, Śaka, 1812 (AD 1890); ed. Satyānanda Gosvāmī, Calcutta, 1926.

Bhakti Cult in Ancient India by Bhāgavata Kumāra Śāstrī, Calcutta, 1922.

Bhakti-rasāmṛta-sindhu by Rūpa Gosvāmin, ed. Purīdās, Vṛndāvana, 1946; ed. with three commentaries by Haridās Dās, Navadvīpa, 1948; ed. with Jīva Gosvāmin's Durgamasaṁginī commentary, Rādhāraman Press, Murshidabad, B.S. 1331, ed. with the same commentary by Dāmodar Gosvamī, Vārāṇasī.

Bhakti-ratnāvali by Viṣṇu Purī, ed. Balāichānd Gosvāmī and Atulkrishṇa Gosvāmī, Caitanya Era 419.

Bhakti-saṁdarbha by Jīva Gosvāmin, ed. Shyāmlal Gosvāmī, Calcutta, Śaka 1812 (AD 1890): ed. Purīdās Gosvāmī, Vṛndāvana, 1951; ed. Bhakti-siddhānta Sarasvatī Gosvāmī, Caitanya era 438 (AD 1924); ed. Rādhāraman Gosvami and Kṛsnagopāl Gosvāmi, with Bengali tr., C.U. 1962.

Bhāgavat Dharmera Prācīn Itihāsa by Svāmī Vidyāraṇya, Calcutta.

Bhāratīya Madhya Yuge Sādhanāra Dhārā by Kṣitimohan Sen. English translation by Manmohan Ghosh, London, Luzac and Co., 1935.

Brahma-Saṁhitā with Jīva Gosvāmin's commentary, ed. Thākur Bhaktivinod, B.S. 1304.

Brahma-sūtra: Śārīraka-bhāṣya by Saṁkarācārya. English translation by (i) George Thibaut, S.B.E., O.U.P., 1904. (ii) S.K. Belvalkar, Poona and (iii) V.M. Apte, Bombay, 1960,

Brahma-sūtra: Śrī-bhāṣya by Rāmānuja. English translation by George

Thibaut, S.B.E., O.U.P., 1904, (ii) R.D. Karmarkar, Poona, University of Poona.

Brahma-sūtra: Vedānta-pārijāta-saurabha of Nimbārka. English translation with the Vedānta-kaustubha commentary of Srīnivāsa by Roma Bose, Calcutta, B.I. 2 Vols., 1940-41.

Brahma-sūtra: *Madhva-bhāṣya*. English translation by S. Subha Rao, Madras, 1904, revised edition of the same under the title *Vedānta-sūtras* with the commentary of Śrī Madhvācārya, Śrī Vyasa Press, Tirupati, 1936.

Brahma-sūtra: Aṇū-bhāṣya by Vallabhācārya, ed., Mulcandra Tulsidās Telivala with *Bhāṣya-prakāśa* commentary of Purusottama and Rasmi, commentary of Gopesvara, Bombay, 15 Vols. V.S. 1925-41.

Brahma-sūtra: *Govinda-bhāṣya* by Baladeva Vidyābhūṣaṇa, ed. by Kṛṣṇa-Gopāl Bhakta with Bengali translation by Shyāmlāl Gosvāmī, B.S. 1301 (AD 1894). English translation by S.C. Basu, Allahabad, S.B.H., 1912; second ed. 1934.

Bṛhad-Bhāgavatāmṛta by Sanātana Gosvāmin, ed. Nityasvarūpa Brahmacārin, Vṛndāvana, 1905; ed. Gosvāmī Purīdās, B.S. 1352.

Bṛhat-Vaiṣṇava-toṣanī by Sanātana Gosvāmin, ed., Nityasvarūpa Brahmacārin, Calcutta, Caitanya era, 425.

Caitanya and His Age, D.C. Sen, C.U., 1922.

Caitanya and His Companions, D.C. Sen, C.U., 1917.

Caitanya-candrāmṛta by Prabodhānanda Sarasvatī, ed. Berhampur, B.S. 1319.

Caitanya-candrodaya nāṭaka by Kavikarṇapūra, ed. Rajendralal Mitra, Calcutta, B.I. 1854; Kāvyamālā series 87, Nirnaya Sagar Press, Bombay, 1917.

Caitanya-śikṣāmṛta by Thakur Bhaktivinod, B.S. 1312.

Caitanya-caritāmṛta by Kavikarṇapūra, ed. Radharaman Press, Murshidabad, 1884.

Caitanya-caritāmṛta by Kṛṣṇadāsa Kavirāja, ed. Rādhā-Govinda Nāth, 7 vols. (4th ed.) with *Gaura-kṛpā-taranginī* commentary, Sādhanā Prakāśanī, Calcutta. ed. Bhaktivinod Thākur; ed. Makhanlal Dās, B.S. 1315. ed. Gaudiya Mission, Caitanyābda 442.

Caitanya-bhāgavata by Vṛndāvana Dāsa, ed. Radha-Govinda Nath with *Nitāi-karuṇā-kallolinī* commentary, Sādhanā Prakāśanī, Calcutta, 1967. ed. Kālīprasanna Vidyāratna, Vasumati Kāryālaya, Calcutta, B.S. 1315 (AD 1908); ed. Bhakti-Siddhānta Sarasvatī Gosvamī, Calcutta, Caitanyābda 442 (AD 1928).

Caitanya Movement by M.T. Kennedy, Oxford University Press, 1925.

(*Śrī*) *Caitanya's Concept of Theistic Vedānta*, Śrī Gaudiya Math, Madras, 1964.

Caitanya's Life and Teachings by Jadunath Sircar, Calcutta, 1922.

Christian Mysticism by Inge, Oxford University, 1899.

Comparative Religion (*Lectures*) by A.A. Macdonell, University of Calcutta.

Comparative Studies in Vedāntism by Mahendranath Sircar, Bombay, 1927.

(*The*) *Cultural Heritage of India*, 2nd ed., Vols III and IV, The Ramakrishna Mission Institute of Culture, 1953, 1956.

Contemporary British Philosophy, edited by J.H. Muirhead.

Development of Religion in South India by K.A. Nīlakānta Śāstrī, 1963.

Early History of the Vaiṣṇava Faith and Movement in Bengal by S.K. De, Calcutta, 1942.

Early History of Vaiṣṇavism in South India by S. Krishnaswamī Aiyanger, Oxford University Press, 1920.

Eastern Religions and Western Thought by S. Radhakrishnan, London, 1950.

Encyclopaedia of Religion and Ethics, ed. James Hastings.

Gauḍīyā-vaiṣṇava-sāhitya by Haridās Dās, Navadvipa, Caitanyābda 462. (AD 1945).

Gauḍīyā-vaiṣṇava-darśana by Radhā-Govinda Nāth, 5 Vols., Prācyavāṅī Mandir, Calcutta, 1957-60.

Gaura-gaṇoddeśadīpikā by Kavikarṇapūra, Radharaman Press, Murshidabad, 2nd ed., B.S. 1300 (AD 1893); ed. Sasibhusan Bandopadhyaya, Ambika Kalna, 2nd ed. Caitanyābda 456 (AD 1942).

Gauḍiyā-vaiṣṇava-rasera Alaukikatva by Uma Ray, Calcutta, Murari Saha, 1951.

Gauḍiyā-darśanera Itihāsa Vaiśiṣtya, Gauḍiyā Mission, Calcutta, 1953.

Hari-bhakti-vilāsa by Gopāla Bhatta Gosvāmin, ed. Purīdās, published by S.N. Roy Chowdhury, Mymensingh (E. Pakistan); ed. with a Bengali translation and notes by Śyāmācaran Kaviratna, Calcutta.

Hindu Mysticism by Mahendranath Sircar, Calcutta, 1943, reprinted, New Delhi, 1974.

History of Bengali Language and Literature by D.C. Sen.

History of Dharma-śāstra by P.V. Kane, 5 vols, B.O.R.I., 1930-62.

History of Indian Philosophy by S.N. Das gupta, Cambridge University Press, 1922-55.

History of Philosophy Eastern and Western, edited by S. Radhakrishnan, George Allen and Unwin, London, 1953.

Idea of the Holy by Otto.

Indian Philosophy by S. Radhakrishnan, George Allen and Unwin, London, 1948.

Jaiva-dharma by Thākur Bhaktivinod, 6th ed. Gaudiya Math, Calcutta.

(Śrī) *Kṛṣṇa-Caitanya-caritāmṛta* by Murari Gupta, ed. Mrinalkanti Ghosh, Calcutta, Caitanyabda 401 (AD 1931); tr. in Bengali by Haridas Das, Calcutta.

(*Śrī-*) *Kṛṣṇa-prasaṁga* by Gopīnāth Kavirāj, Sri Krishna Sangha, Calcutta 1967.

(*Śrī-*) *Kṛṣṇa-saṁdarbha* by Jīva Gosvāmin, ed. Purīdās Gosvāmi, Vṛndāvana, 1950, ed. Shyamalal Gosvami, Śaka 1822; ed. Prangopal Gosvami.
Laghu-bhāgavatāmṛta by Rūpa Gosvāmin, Radharaman Press, Murshidabad, B.S. 1303.
(*The*) *Living Religions of the Hindūs* by N. Macnicol, 2nd ed. revised by M.H. Harison, New Delhi, 1964.
Lord Gaurāṅga by Śiśir Kumār Ghosh, Patrika Office, Calcutta, 1907.
Madhva and Madhvism by C.N. Krishnaswami Iyer and S. Subba Rao.
Mādhurya-kādambinī by Viśvanātha Cakravartin, ed, Shyamalal Gosvamin, B.S. 1311.
Materials for the Study of Early History of the Vaiṣṇava Sect by H.C. Raychaudhuri, Calcutta, 1920, reprinted, New Delhi, 1975.
Nārada-bhakti-sūtra, Gītā Press, Gorakhpur.
Padyāvalī by Rūpa Gosvāmin, ed. Purīdas Gosvamī, 1946; ed. S.K. De, Dacca University, 1934.
Paramātma-saṁdarbha by Jīva Gosvāmin, ed., Purīdās Gosvāmī, Vṛndāvana, 1951; ed. with Bengali translation by Rāmnarāyan Vidyāratna, Berhampur, B.S. 1299; ed. by Radharaman Vidyaratna, B.S. 1348.
Philosophy of Hindū Sādhnā by N.K. Brahma.
(*The*) *Philosophy of Religion* by Galloway.
(*The*) *Philosophy of Śrīmad Bhāgavata*, 2 vols. by Siddhesvara Bhattacarya, Visva-Bharati Research Publication, 1960.
Philosophy of Vaiṣṇava Religion by Girendra Narayan Mallik, Lahore, 1927.
Philosophy of the Viśiṣṭādvaita by P.N. Srīnivāsa Chāri, Madras, 1943.
Post-Caitanya Sahajiyā Cult of Bengal by M.M. Basu, Calcutta University, 1930.
(*A*) *Psychological Study of Religion* by Leuba.
Prameya-ratnāvalī by Baladeva Vidyābhūṣaṇa, ed., Bhaktisiddhānta Sarasvatī Gosvamī, Caitanyābda 439 (AD 1925): ed. Umeshcandra Bhattācārya, Baṁgīya Sāhitya Pariṣat, 1927.
Prīti-saṁdarbha by Jīva Gosvāmin, ed., Purīdās Gosvāmī, Vṛndāvana, 1951, ed. Prāṇgopāl Gosvāmī, Noakhali, B.S. 1336 (AD 1929).
Rāga-vartma-candrikā by Viśvanāth Cakravartin, ed., Bābā Kṛṣṇadās, Vṛndavān.
Reign of Religion in Modern Philosophy by S. Radhakrishnan.
Religions of India by E.W. Hopkins, Boston, 1895, reprinted, New Delhi, 1972.
(*A*) *Review of Philosophy of Hindū Sādhanā* by N.K. Brahma, Kegan Paul, London, 1932.
Saṁkṣepa-vaiṣṇava-toṣanī by Jīva Gosvāmin, ed., Purīdās Gosvāmī, Vṛndāvana.
Sarvasaṁvādinī by Jīva Gosvāmin, ed. Purīdās Gosvāmī, Vṛndāvana, 1953; ed., Rasik Mohan Vidyabhusan, with Translation in Bengali, Cal-

cutta Bangīya Sāhitya Pariṣat, 1921.

Sārārtha-darśinī by Viśvanāth Cakravartin, ed., Bhaktisiddhānta Sarasvatī, Caitanya era 437.

Selections from the Literature of Theism by Caldecott and Mackintosh.

Siddhānta-darpaṇam by Baladeva Vidyābhuṣaṇa, ed., Shyāmlāl Gosvāmī, B.S. 1934; ed. with Bengali tr., Bhakti Vinod Thākur, B.S. 1297 (AD 1890).

Śikṣāṣṭaka by Śrī Caitanya Mahāprabhu, ed. with Hindi translation and Commentary by Rādhāmādhava Sevā-saṁsathāna, Gorakhpur, 1969.

Śrī-Śrī Caitanya Maṁgala by Locana-dāsa, ed. by Mrināl Kānti Ghosh, B.S. 1354 (A.D.I (47);

Śrī-Caitanya-caritera Upādana by B.B. Majumdar, 2nd edition, Calcutta University, 1959.

Stavāvalī by Raghunāthadāsa Gosvāmin, ed., Purīdās Gosvāmi, Vṛndāvana, 1947; ed., Radharaman Press, Murshidabad, Caitanyābda 402 (AD 1888).

Studies in Mystical Religion by Rufus M. Jones.

(*A*) *Study of Vaiṣṇavism* by K.G. Gosvami, Calcutta, Oriental Book Agency, 1956.

Study of Vaiṣṇavism in Ancient and Medieval Bengal—upto the Advent of Caitanya by S.C. Mukherjee, Punthī Pustak, Calcutta, 1966.

Tattva-saṁdarbha by Jīva Gosvāmin, ed., Satyānanda Gosvāmī, B.S. 1318; (AD) ed. Purīdās Gosvāmī, Vṛndāvana, 1951; ed. Sītānāth Gosvāmī, with the commentary of Baladeva Vidyābhuṣaṇa and English notes and extracts from the commentary of Rādhāmohan Gosvāmī, Jādavapur University Sanskrit Series, No. I. 1967.

Tattva-sūtram by Bhakti Vinod Thākur, B.S. 1301.

Theism in Medieval India by J.E. Carpenter, Constable and Co., 1926.

Ujjvala-nīla maṇi by Rūpa Gosvāmin, ed., Durgāprasād and V.L.S. Pansikar with *Locana-rocanī* commentary of Jīva Gosvāmin and *Ānanda-candrikā* commentary of Viśvanātha Cakravartin, Kāvyamālā Series, 95, 2nd ed. 1932; ed. Purīdās Gosvāmī, Vṛndāvana, 1946.

Vaiṣṇavism, Śaivism and other Minor Religious Systems by R.G. Bhandārkar, Strassburg, I (13, Poona, 1928).

Varieties of Religious Experience by James.

Vaiṣṇava-siddhāntamālā by Bhakti Vinod Thākur, B.S. 1295.

Vedānta Syamantaka by Baladeva Vidyābhūṣaṇa, ed., Shyamalāl Gosvāmī, B.S. 1907. The work is sometimes ascribed to Rādhā-Dāmodar Gosvāmī.

(*The*) *Vedāntā* (*A Study of the Brahma-sūtras with the Bhāṣyas of Saṁkara, Rāmānuja, Nimbārka, Madhva and Vallabha*) by V.S. Ghate, Poona, 1926.

INDEX

Abheda, 155
Abhidhā-vṛtti, 71, 84
Acintya, 155
Acintya-bhedābheda, 150-75
Acintya-bhedābheda, *See* Sunderananda
Acintya-rūpa, 156
Acintya-śakti, 85-86, 88, 153, 156
Acit, 163
Acit-aprākṛt, 166
Acit-jagat, 96
Acosmism, 151
Acyuta, 103
Acyutānanda, 33
Acyuta Prakāśa or Puruśottama Tīrtha, 46
Adbhuta (rasa), 213
Adhirūḍha-mahābhāva, 207-8
Adhiṣṭhāna, 78
Adhokṣaja, 94, 103
Adhyāsa, 79, 159
Advaita, 173
Advaita-prakāśa, 39, 53
Advaita-siddhi, 176
Advaita-vāda, Advaitism, 26, 159
Advaitācārya, 22-23, 29, 33, 59
Advaya, 90, 152
Agni, 1
Agnosticism, 150
Ahaṁ, 133
Ahaṁkāra, 135, 145, 187
Aiśvarya, 95, 102, 119
Aitihya, 63
Aitreya Brāhmaṇa, 1*f*
Ajāmila, 188
Ajita, 105
Ajnāna, 79, 147-48
Akhila-rasāmṛta mūrti, 118, 122
Akrūra, 193
Alaṁkāra-kaustubha, 220
Ambarīṣa, 194
Ananta, 107
Ananyatva, 166
Anartha-nivṛtti, 201
Aṅga-saṅga, 220
Aniruddha, 103
Anirvacanīya, 156-57, 162
Antaryāmin, 95
Anthropomorphism, 94
Anubhāṣya, 172-74
Anubhava, 201, 213
Anugrāhakābhimāna, 211
Anumāna, 63
Anupalabdhi, 63
Anupama, 32
Anurāga, 203-4
Anurāgavallī, 39
Antaḥkaraṇa, 32
Antaraṅga-śakti, 96, 99
Antaryāmī, 165
Aprakaṭa-līlā, 115-17
Aprakaṭa-prakāśa, III
Aprākṛta-acit, 167
Aprākṛta Kāma, 218
Aprāṇi-janma-lālasā, 205
Apṛthaka-siddhi, 164, 172
Arcanā, 2, 192
Arjuna, 193
Artha, 135
Arthāpatti, 63, 153
Asamprajnāta-samādhi, 180
Asiddha-deha, 115
Aśru, 200
Attahāsa, 201
Aupādhika-bhedābheda, 167
Aupapattya, 222
Avahittā, 205
Avaiduṣa-pratyakṣa, 65
Avajalpa, 210
Avaktavyaṁ, 157
Avidyā-māyā, 134, 173
Avyakta, 164
Avyarthakālatā, 202
Ābhīras, 10
Ācāryas, 7, 38
Ādhāra-śakti, 114
Ādhibhautika, 135
Ādhidaivika, 135

Ādhyātmika, 135
Ādi-caturvyūha
Ākhyāna, 72
Ālambana, 213
Ālvārs, 6ff
Āmnāya, 71
Ānanda, 82-83, 94, 97
Āṇḍāl, 6
Āraṇyaka, 2
Ārsa, 63
Āśābandha, 202
Āsakti, 201
Āsana, 177
Āsanna-janatā-hṛdviloṇana, 207
Āśraya, 123:—of Ajnāna, 159, 213
Ātman, 143
Ātma-nivedana, 193
Āveśa, 101

Bahiraṅgā-śakti, 96, 99
Balabhadra Bhattācārya, 30
Baladeva, 38-39, 49, 77, 80, 92, 110, 170-71, 215
Balarāma, 102
Bandana, 192
Bali, 193
Bānīnātha, 28
Bārāh-purāṇa, 111
Bergson, 99, 148f, 197
Bhagavadbhakti-rasāyana, 176
Bhagavat-gītā-gūḍhārtha-dīpikā, 176
Bhagavata-saṁdarbha, 54
Bhaktamālā, 88
Bhagavān, 92-96; as Pūrṇa-āvirbhāva, 93; as Līlāmaya, 93; etymological meaning of, 95; qualified in endless ways, 95; Śaktis of, 96-100;—Kṛṣṇa, 101-31
Bhagavān Ācārya, 28
Bhajana-kriyā, 201
Bhakta-avatāra, 105
Bhaktamāla, 39
Bhakti, 174ff; Maryādā—, 13; Puṣṭi—, 13; as Rasa, 115-16; as more relishable than Brahmānanda, 216ff; Yoga-miśra—, 188; Śānta—, 188; Svarūpa-lakṣaṇa of—, 180-84; Śuddhā—, 181; the effects of, 184-87; Sādhana—, 187; Sādhya—, 187; Vaidhī—, 194-98; Rāgānugā—, 194-98; Rāgātmikā—, 195
Bhakti Cult in Ancient India, *See* Shāstri, B.K.G.
Bhakti-rasāmṛta-sindhu, 111, 124, 190, 201, 203, 213
Bhakti-ratnākara, 33-34, 39
Bhakti-sandarbha, 54, 185, 187, 194, 219
Bhaktivinoda, 86f, 193
Bhandārkar, 3-6, 9-10, 22f
Bharata Muni, 221
Bhavānanda Rāya, 28
Bhayānaka-rasa, 213
Bhāgavata, *Bhāgavata-purāna*, 9, 72-75, 88, 91, 96, 101, 110, 121, 124, 127-29, 136,139-44, 178, 180, 183-88, 194, 208
Bhāgavata religion, 4-5; Christian influence on—, 10-11
Bhāgavata-sātvata, 3
Bhāgavatāmṛta, 75
Bhāgavata-sandarbha, 54, 96
Bhāskara, 167
Bhāva, 16, 97, 199
Bhāva-deha, 195
Bheda, 153
Bhedavāda, 169-72
Bhedābheda, 9, 162, 167
Bhīṣma, 10
Bhoga, 182
Bhoja, 215
Bhoktṛ, 166
Bhoktṛtva, 132
Bhrama, 63
Bhū, 9
Bliss, 81-82, 99
Bradley, 157
Brahman, 7, 12, 76-90, 92-95; as asamyaka-āvirbhava of Bhagavān, 93-94; etymological meaning of—, 95, 98-99
Brahma-saṁhitā, 27, 76, 83
Brahma-sampradāya, 7
Brahma-sūtra, 7, 72, 152, 156, 160
Brahman-vaivarta-purāṇa—, 4, 15
Brahmā, 104-5
Brahmānanda, 117, 139
Brahmānda-purāṇa, 191
Bṛhdāraṇyaka-upaniṣad, 77, 81f, 83f, 154f
Bṛhad-bhāgavatāmṛta, 50, 108, 111-12, 163, 183
Buddha, 104
Buddhi, 135, 144

Caitanya, or Śrī Kṛṣṇa Caitanya, also called Gaura, Nimaī or Gaurāṅga, his life, 16ff; his ancestors, 16; his divinity, 16, 106; incarnation of Kṛṣṇa, 16; the purpose of his in carnation, 16; his images, 17ff; his divine forms as revealed to his devotees, 17f; his dances, 18; his boyish frolics, 18; as student, 18; as householder, 19ff; as teacher, 20; his visit to East Bengal, 20; his initiation, 20; his personality, 21; as the leader of Vaiṣṇavas, 22ff; his Saṁkīrtana, 23; his Saṁnyāsa, 23; his Journey to Puri and the conversion of Sārvabhauma, 25; his travels in South India and the meeting with Rāmānanda, 26; his conversion of Pratāparudra, 28-29 his pilgrimage to Vṛndāvana, 29; his conversion of Rūpa and Sanātana; his conversion of Prakāśānanda Sarasvatī, 32; his last days in Purī, 33; his mysterious passing away, 33ff; his affiliation with Mādhva, 36ff; his difference with Mādhva in doctrinal matters, 36; as the presiding deity of his Sampradāya, 37; his scholarship, 53; his works 53; his theory of evolution, 142-45; his views on sex, 217; on Parakīyā-rasa, 221

Caitanya and His Age, *See* Sen D.C.

Caitanya and His Companions, *See* Sen, D.C.

Caitanya-candrodaya, 38

Caitanya-caritera Upādāna, *See* Majumdar, B.B.

Caitanya, His Life and Doctrine, *See Majumdar*

(*Sri*) *Caitanya Mahāprabhu*, *See* Bhaktivinoda, T.

Caitanya Movement, *See* Kennedy

Caitanya-bhāgavata, 17f, 19-26, 33, 48-50, 53, 57, 60, 65, 67, 77, 90-91, 105-6, 141, 183, 189-91, 194

Caitanya-caṅdrodaya, 27, 37, 40, 44

Caitanya-caritāmṛta, 15-17, 19, 25, 28-29, 31-32, 37, 44-47, 49, 51-52, 54-71, 73, 75, 82, 84, 86, 90-110, 115, 116, 120, 122-123, 126-30, 132-36, 141-42, 144, 177-83, 187-98, 191, 194, 196, 199, 202-3, 206-7, 211-15, 217

Caitanya Caritera Upādana, *See* Majumdar, B.B.

(*Sri*) *Caitanya Mahāprabhu*, *See* Bhaktivinoda, T

Caitanya Maṅgala, 158

(*The*) *Caitanya Movement*, *See* Kennedy

Candīdāsa, 13, 220; Ananta Badu—, 13f, Dvija—, 13f

Candraśekhara Ācārya, 30

Candrāvalī, 202

Caste, 24

Catuḥ-sana, 106

Cāṅda Kāzī, 24

Cārvāka, 63

Ceṣtā, 63

Chāndogya-upaniṣad, 11, 86, 118, 137

Cit, 9, 94, 97, 163

Citrajalpa, 210

Citraketu, 188

Cit-śakti, 96

Citta-vṛtti-nirodha, 189

Cognition, mystical, 65

Comparative Studies in Vaiṣṇavism and Christianity, *See* Seal

Contemporary British Philosophy, *See* Muirhead

Concrete monism, 76

Creative Evolution, *See* Bergson

(*The*) *Cultural Heritage of India*, 167

Daiva, 143

Dasaślokī, 9

Dāsgupta, S. N., 162, 170

Das, S., 30

Datta and Chatterji, 166

Dāmodara, 103

Dāsya, 6, 193, 211

Deism, 150

De, S. K., 13-14, 19, 26, 28; on Śrī Caitanya's influence on the followers of Advaita Vedanta, 32, 37-38; on Caitanya's affiliation with Mādhva, 46-47; on Caitanya's formulation of the philosophical tenets of his school, 54-56; on Caitanyism and eroticism, 217

Devakī, 10, 126

Devakīnandana, 39, 126

Devānanda, 74

Dharma, 135

Dharma-setu, 105

Dhāmn, 108ff

Dhāraṇā, 177, 192

Dhruva, 188

Dhruva-smṛti, 8

Dhruvānusmṛti, 192

Dhyāna, 6, 177, 192

Digvijayī, Pandit, 20

Dināra, 10

Divyonmāda, 210
Dikṣā-guru, 40
Dinasaran Das, 220
Dravya, 143
Dualism, 150
Dvaita, 12, 37
Dvaitādvaita, 9
Dvāpara, 105
Dvārakā, 109
Dvita, 10
Dynamism, 99-100

Early History of Vaisnava Faith and Movement in Bengal, *See* De, S. K.
Early History of Vaisṇava Sect, *See* Raychaudhuri
Efficient Cause, 8
Ego, 133
Ekāntika, 30
Ekata, 10
Elan vital, 197
Electron, 89
Empiricism, 69
Eroticism, 216-21
Ethics of India, *See* Hopkins, E. W.

Farquhar, 43-44
Flint, 70

Gadādhara Pandit, 23, 31f, 41, 44, 59
Gangādās, Pandit, 18
Garbhodakaśāyī, 95, 104, 145
Gauḍīya Vaiṣṇava Darśana, *See* Radha Govinda Nath
Gaura-gaṇoddesa-dīpikā, 39, 43
Gauragaṇa-svarūpa-tattva-candrikā, 39
Gautamiya-tantra, 223
Gāthā, 72
Gāyatrī, 73
Ghāte, V.S., 167
Ghṛta-sneha, 203-4
Ghūrṇā, 201
Gīta-govinda, 13
Gītā, Bhagvadgītā, 3, 38, 77, 88, 96, 109, 136, 152, 155, 177-80, 183, 190
God, 21, 23
Gokula, 109-10
Goloka, 111
Gopa, 11
Gopāla Bhatta, 27, 54-55
Gopāla-campū, 60, 111, 227
Gopāla Kṛṣṇa, 8, 12,
Gopāla-tāpanī, 83
Gopī, 97, 99, 221
Gopīnath Ācārya, 28
Govinda, 28, 38, 103
Govinda-bhāṣya, 38, 40, 43, 77
Govinda Karmakāra, 27, 58
Govinda-līlāmṛta, 26, 126
Govindāṣṭaka, 74
Grace, 5, 184
Guṇas, 143
Guṇamaya-deha, 115
Guṇāvatāra, 104
Guru, 70; kinds of, 70, 187-88
Guru-paramparā, 38

Haṁsa, 7
Hanumāna, 193
Haṇāi Pandit, 23
Hari, 105
Hari-bhakti-sudhodaya, 120
Hari-bhakti-vilāsa, 56, 191
Haridāsa, 22-23
Hari-vaṁśa, 10
Harivyāsadeva, 9
Hāsya-rasa, 213
Henotheism, 2
Hegel, his criticism of relativity, 63, 150
Hindu Ethics, *See* Mackenzie, J.
Hindu Mysticism, *See* Sarkar, M.N.
Hinduism, 99
Hikkā, 201
Hinton, 89
Hiriyanna, 399
History of Bengali Language and Literature, *See* Sen
Hopkins, 11, 216
Hṛṣīkeśa, 103
Hume, 63
Huṁkāra, 201
Hussain Shah, 30

Identity-in-difference, 86, 133
Idolatory, 192
Illusion, *See* Māyā and Vivarta
Immaculate birth, 114
Immanence, 150-53
Incarnation, 104

Inconceivable power, 76, 85
Indeterminate Brahman, 93
Indian Antiquary, 6, 10-11
Indra, 1, 4
Inference, 63
Infinity, 89
Introduction to Indian Philosophy, See Datta and Chatterji
Intuition of God, See Watt, T.M.
Itihāsa, 71-72
Īkṣaṇa, 144
Īśāna Nāgara, 39
Iśāvāsya, 156
Īśvara, 9
Īśvara Dās, 33
Īśvara Purī, 14, 20, 23, 45

Jagadānanda, 25, 28, 33
Jagannātha, 104
Jagannātha Vallabha, 29
James, William, 66f
Jana, 12
Janārdana, 103
Jangama, 134
Jayadeva, 13
Jayānanda, 19, 34, 59
Jāmātra Muni, 132f
Jātasraddhā, 182
Jīva, 96, 132-41; freedom of—, 134; the eternal function of—, 134; *Nitya-mukta* and *Nitya-baddha*, 134
Jīva-brahmā, 104, 107
Jīva Gosvāmin, 26, 38; his authorship of *Bhāgavata-saṁdarbha*, 54; on perception, 65; on inseparability of *Purāṇa* and *Itihāsa* from Veda, 72; his commentary on *Bhāgavata*, 75; on etymological meaning of 'bhagavān,' 95; on the relation between Bhagavān and Bahiraṅgā-śakti, 96; on the Māyika character of certain events in Kṛṣṇā-līlā, 15; on Hlādinī-śakti, 119; on union between Kṛṣṇa and his devotee, 121; on the attributes of Jiva, 132-33; on Nimitta-māyā, 143; on the concept of Acintya, 153; on Acintya-bhedābheda, 152-58; on Viśrambha, 204; on Bhakti as Rasa, 215-16; on Prema-rasa, 220; on Parakīyāvāda, 223, 226-30; on Rāgānugā-bhakti, 194-95
Jīva-śakti, 96
Jnāna, 7, 92, 95
Jnāna-niṣṭhā, 186
Jnāna-svarūpa, 158
Jnānendriya, 145
Jnānī-bhakta, 211
Jnātṛtva, 132
Journal of Royal Asiatic Society, 3
Journal of Royal Asiatic Society of Great Britain, 3
Jṛmbhā, 201

Kabir, 11
Kaḍacā of Murari Gupta, 50, 57-58
Kaḍacā of Raghunāth Dāsa, 60
Kaḍacā of Svarūpa Dāmodara, 60
Kaivalya, 79
Kaivalyopaniṣad, 88, 155
Kalisantaranopaniṣad, 191
Kaliyuga, 105
Kalki, 104
Kalpa-śuddhi, 72
Kalpa-kṣaṇatva, 208
Kamalākānt, 18
Kampa, 63, 150, 180
Kantian Imperative, 180
Kanyakā, 221
Karaṇāpātava, 63
Karma, 6, 8, 143, 177-80; Naimittika—, 177; Nitya—, 177
Karmendriya, 145
Kartṛtva, 132
Kaṭhopaniṣad, 71, 83, 88
Kāla, 143
Kali, 24
Kāma, 135, 218
Kānta-bhāva, 114
Kāraṇa-brahman, 164
Kāraṇāravaśāyī, 95, 104
Kāraṇa-samudra, 95
Kārpaṇyam, 187
Kārya-brahman, 164
Kāśī Misra, 28
Kāśīśvara, 28
Kavikarṇapūra, 39, 43, 220
Keith, 3, 5, 11
Kennedy, 31f, 57
Keśava, 103
Keśava Bhāratī, 24, 47, 49-50
Keśava, Bhatta, 19-20f
Kevalādvaita, 158
Kierkegaard, 69
Kīrtana, 188-91

Koṣa, 197
Krama-saṁdarbha, 75
Krishnamūrti Sharmā, B.N., 170
Krishnaswami, 6
Kroṣana, 201
Kṛṣṇa, his Līlā-mādhurya, 124; his Veṇu-mādhurya, 125; his Prema-mādhurya, 125; his Rūpa-mādhurya, 126; his mercy, 130-31; his dynamic nature, 131; as Pūrṇa, Pūrṇatara and Pūrṇatama, 201; on Saṁkīrtana
Kṛṣṇadāsa, a Muslim divine (Pīra), 31
Kṛṣṇadāsa Kavirāja, 30, 60-61, 152
Kṛṣṇa-loka, 109
Kṛṣṇānanda, 18
Ksaṇā-kalpatya, 208
Kṛṣṇā-karṇāmṛta, 27, 126
Kṛṣṇa-saṁdarbha, 54, 111, 114-115
Kṛṣṇa-vāsudeva, 3
Ksānti, 143
Kṣīrodaśāyī, 95, 104
Kulaśekhara Ālvār, 6
Kūrma, 74, 104
Kūṭastha, 158

Laghu-bāgavatāmṛta, 108, 111, 125, 128
Lajjā, 204
Lakṣaṇā, 71, 74, 84
Lakṣmī, 4, 6, 9, 19, 193
Lakṣmī-pati, 40, 43
Lakṣmīs in Paravyoma, 221
Lalita-mādhava, 227
Lalita-māna, 203
Laukika-rati, 215-16
Laukika-sṛṅgāra-rasa, 220
Lāladāsa, 39
Lālā-śrava, 201
Lālya, 211
Leibnitz, 63, 150
Leuba, 65f
Līlā, 9, 115-17;—mādhurya, 25; vibhūti, 8, 165
Līlāvatāra, 104
Liṅga-śarīra, 134-35
Locana Das, 50
Locke, 150
Lokanatha Ācārya, 29
Lokanapekṣitā, 201
Macdonell, 5, 11
Madhurkavi Ālvār, 6
Madhura-rasa, 99, 211, 214-30
Madhura-rasa-upāsanā, 31f
Madhura-rati, 211
Madhu-sneha, 203-4
Madhusūdana, 103
Madhusūdana Sarasvatī, 176
Mādhva, 7, 36, 38, 44
Madīyatā, 1, 40, 203
Mahat, 144-45
Mahābhārata, 3-4, 152, 156
Mahā-bhāva, 16, 97, 203, 205
Mahā-kāvya of Kavikarṇapūra, 50
Mahā-pralaya, 95
Mahā-vākya, 5
Mahā-viṣṇu, 95, 144-45
Mahisī, 221
Maitra, S. K., 56
Majumdar, A. K., 5, 13, 14, 21f, 31f; on the conversion of Prakāśānanda, 32f
Majumdar, B. B., 34f, 39, 59
Malāi Kāzī, 23
Mamatā, 140, 211
Manas, 135, 145
Mansel, 64, 87
Mantropāsanāmayī-līlā, 116
Manohar Das, 40
Manvantara, 105f
Manvantarāvatāra, 105
Material cause, 8
Mathura, 109
Matsya-avatāra, 103
Matsya-purāṇa, 12
Mādana, 123, 208-9
Mādhava, 103
Mādhurya, 6, 120, 125-26
Mādhva-bhāṣya, 170-71
Mādhvendra Puri, 14, 44
Mālinī, 25
Māna, 203
Mānasānanda, 119
Māndukya-upaniṣad, 155f
Martineau, 194
Mātariśvā, 2
Māṭhara-sruti, 187
Māyā-śakti, Māyā, 8, 12, 95, 142-43, 146-48, 159-60
Mckenzie, J., 216
Meditation, 105
Meru, 11
Miśra-sattva, 94

Mitra, 1
Mitrābhimāna, 211
Modana, 208-10
Mohana, 208
Mohādya-bhāve' pyātmādi-sarvavismaraṇatva, 208
Mohenjodaro, 11
Mokṣa, 135-9
Monadism, 64
Monism, 8; Pure—, 11; qualified—, 11
Monotheism, 2-3
Mother goddess, 11
Muirhead, 69f
Mukta, 173
Mukti, 36, 48
Mukunda, 19, 25
Mundaka-upaniṣad, 137
Muralī-vilāsa, 39
Murārī Gupta, 18, 40, 42, 50, 58-59
Mūrti, 192-93
Mysticism, Mystic experience, Mystic intuition, 65-70
Mysticism in Maharashtra, *See* Ranade, R. D.

Naiyāyikas, 173
Namaskāra, 2
Nāmmālvār, 6
Narottama, 40, 45, 56
Narottama Thakura, 195
Nappinnai, 13
Narahari Cakravartin, 32, 39
Nābhā, Ji, 12
Nāma (Divine Name), Nāma saṁkīrtana, 17, 37
Nāma-gāne-rucih, 202
Nāmāparādhas, 191-92
Nārada, 5, 73, 106, 176
Nārāyaṇa, 6, 8, 23, 38, 103, 121
Nārāyaṇi, 58-59
Nātha Muni, 7
Neo-Platonists, 151
Nīlāmbara Cakravartin, 25
Nimbārka, 7-8ff, 166-69
Nimeṣāsahatā, 207
Nimitta-māyā, 142-43
Nirabhimānitā, 202
Nirguṇa, 158, 172
Nirveda, 213
Nirviśeṣa-brahman, 76-89
Niṣṭhā, 201
Nitya-kiśora, 113, 115
Nitya-vibhūti, 165
Nityānanda, 22, 25, 28-29, 41, 59
Niyama, 117
Niyantṛ, 166
Nīlāmbara Cakravartin, 16
Noumena, 150
Nṛsiṁha, 150
Nṛsiṁha-pūrvatāpanī, 163
Nṛtya, 201
Nyāya-tattva, 7
Nyāya-vaiśeṣika, 136, 164, 170

Ocean of Milk, 11
Otto, 66
Outlines of Indian Philosophy, *See* Hiriyanna

(*An*) *Outline of the Religious Literature of India*, *See* Farquhar
Padma-Purāṇa, 39, 74, 84, 223, 227
Padma-nābha, 103
Padmāvatī, 23
Padyāvali, 53
Pañcabheda, 12
Pañcamahābhūta, 144
Pañcarātra, 3
Pañcarātra-saṁhitās, 12
Pantheism, 151
Para-brahman, 101
Parakīyamānah, 223
Parakīyā heroine, 221
Parakīyā-rasa, 221-30
Parakīyāvāda, 222
Parama-svīyās, 223
Param-pada, 1
Paramānanda Purī, 28
Paramātmā, 92, 95, 97
Paramatma-saṁdarbha, 55, 132-34, 143, 155
Paraspara-vaśī-bhāva, 205
Paraśurāma, 106
Paratattva-sīmā-Śrī Kṛṣṇa Caitanya, See Sunderananda
Paravyoma, 109
Parā-śakti, 97
Parikaras, 113-15, 215
Parīkṣit, 193
Pariṇāmavāda, 8-9, 12, 145, 159
Paroḍhā, 221

Parokṣavāda, 177
Pathāna Vaiṣṇavas, 31
Patta-mahiṣi, 275
Pada-sevā, 192
Pālaka, 211
Pālya, 211
Pāṇinī, 5
Paramārthika, 158
Parekh, M. C., 31f, 81
Pātanjali, 3, 5, 11
Pey Ālvār, 6
Perception, 63
Periy Ālvār, 6
Personal Absolute, 76, 88
Pīta-avatāra, 105-6
Pluralism, 12, 150
(*The*) *Poems of Tukaram*, *See* Fraser, G. N.
Polytheism, 2-3
Prabandham, 6-7
Prabodhānanda, 27, 37, 43
Pradhāna, 142-45
Pradumna, 103
Prahlāda, 5, 178, 193
Prakaṭa-līlā, 112, 115-17
Prakaṭa-prakāśa, 111, 127
Prakārādvaita, 166
Prakāśita, 206
Prakāśānanda, 22, 43, 48, 58, 153
Prakṛti, 6, 12
Pralaya, 200
Pramāda, 64
Prameya-ratnāvalī, 39-41, 48-49
Praṇava, 3
Praṇaya, 203-4
Prapatti, 6, 8
Prasthānatraya, 7
Pratāparudra, 28
Pratibimbāṁśa, 169, 172
Pratyakṣa, 63; Vaiduṣa—, 65
Pratyāhāra, 177
Prayojana, 75
Prābhava-prakāśa, 102
Prākṛta, 84, 94
Prākṛta-kāma, 218
Prākṛta-śakti, 94
Pramāṇya, 1
Prāṇa, 143
Pre-established harmony, 150
Prema, 37, 97, 105, 129, 201, —and Kāma, 218
Prema-bhakti-candrikā, 56, 197
Prema-mādhurya, 125
Prema-rasa, 220
Prema-sevā, 140-41
Prema-samputaḥ, 129
Prema-vaicittya, 205
Prema-vilāsa, 29
Primary meaning, 71
Prime Cause, 102
Pringle Pattison, 83
Priyatā, 139-41, 199-212
Priyābhimāna, 211
Prīti, 139-41, 199-212
Prīti-saṁdarbha, 54, 118, 138, 199-200, 221, 224
Pṛthu, 106, 193
Psychology of Religion, 65-70
(*A*) *Psychological Study of Religion*, *See* Leuba
Purāna, 71-75; in relation to Veda, 72; regarded as the fifth Veda, 72
Pure identity, 78, 86
Pure consciousness, 79-80, 85
Pure non-being, 80
Purgation, 67
Purity of heart, 67
Pūrṇa-avatāra, 107
Pūrṇatama-avatāra, 107
Puruṣa, 6
Puruṣa-sūkta, 1
Puruṣārtha, 135, 139-41
Puruṣāvatāra, 104
Puruśottama, 103
Puruśottamācārya, 166
Pūrṇa-kāma, 120
Pūrva-rāga, 227
Pūtanā, 10, 195

Raghunātha Bhatta Gosvāmin, 30, 54
Raghunātha Dās Gosvāmin, 54, 60, 61
Raghupati, 58
Rajas, 143
Raktaka, 196
Rāma, 10-12
Rāmānanda, 11
Rāmabhadra Ācārya, 28
Rasa, 37, 93, 118, 213-30
Rasa-vjnāna, 216
Rasika, 184
Rati, 203, 213
Raudra-rasa, 213
Rādhā, 9, 12, 97-98, 110
Rādhādāmodara, 92

Radha Govind Nath, 40-41, 43-46, 49, 116-17, 149f, 157
Radhakrishnan, 148f
Rādhā Mohan Gosvāmin, 38
Rāga, 203-4
Rāgānugā, 111, 128
Rāgātmikā, 195
Rāghavānanda, 11
Rājasika-purāṇa, 72
Rāma, 8, 104
Rāmānanda, 11
Rāmānanda Rāya, 26, 58
Rāmānuja, 7, 89, 107, 163-66
Rāmānuja-bhāṣya, 81
Rāmkrishna Paramahaṁsa, 137f
Ranade, 189
Rāsa-līlā, 125
Rationalism, 64
Raycaudhuri, H., 2-5, 10, 11
Relativist, 64
(*The*) *Religions of India*, *See* Hopkins
Revelation, *See* Śabda
Ritualistic worship, 105
Ṛgveda, 1-2, 11, 109
Romance, 200
Ṛṣabha, 105-6
Ruci, 201
Rūḍha, 207
Rudra, 7, 104-5
Rukmini, 226
Rūpa, 26
Rūpa Gosvāmin, 25, 32, 37, 55, 58, 74, 111, 152; on Svarūpa-lakṣaṇa of Bhakti, 180-84; on Parakīyā-bhāva, 180-84, 226-27

Śabda, 63, 73-75
Śaktyāveṣa-avatāra, 104, 106
Śaci, 16, 18
Saguṇa Brahman, 158
Sahajiyā cult, 58, 216
Sajātīya-bheda, 78, 91, 164
Sakhya, 6, 193, 214
Śakti, 96-97
Śakti-parināmavāda, 145-49
Śaktyānanda, 184
Samañjasā-rati, 207
Samarthā-rati, 207
Samavāya, 164, 173
Samvāyī Karana, 173
Samādhi, 177, 192
Sambandha, 72, 95
Sambhava, 63
Sambhoga, 215, 227
Saṁcārī-bhāva, 210
Saṁhitā, 5
Saṁjalpa, 210
Saṁkarṣaṇa, 103
Saṁkīrtana, 105-6
Saṁkṣepa-bhāgavatāmṛta, 74, 152f
Saṁkīrṇa-sambhoga, 227
Samṛddhimān-sambhoga, 227
Saṁsarin, 173
Samutkanthā, 202
Saṁvit-sakti, 97
Śaṁkara, *See* Śaṅkara
Sanaka, 198
Sanandana, 211
Sanātana, 211
Sanātana Gosvāmin, 26, 32, 36, 55, 58, 74, 108, 112, 163, 196
Sanat Kumāra, 211
Sanātana Misra, 20
Śaṅkara, 8, 38, 40, 107; his attitude towards *Bhāgavata*, 72, 79, 81, 84, 110, 188-89
Śaṅkara-bhāṣya, 79, 84, 162f, 188
Sanskrit Literature, *See* Macdonell
Saptabhaṅgi Naya, 157
Śaraṇāgati, Śaraṇāpatti, 187; elements of, 187
Sarva-saṁvādinī, 38, 54, 63, 76, 78f, 81, 86f, 147f, 152-55f, 157f, 159f, 160f, 168
Sarvārtha-siddhi, *See* Vedanta Desika
Satpathabrāhmaṇa, 1f
Sattva, 13, 69, 97, 143
Satya-yuga, 105
Satyasena, 105
Saviśeṣa, 82-83
Sādhana, Sādhanā, 46
Sādhana-siddha, 113
Sādhu-saṅga, 201
Sākṣātkāra, 20, 137
Sākṣī, 8
Sālokya, 138-39
Sāmagris, 213
Sāmānya-bhakti, 215
Sāmīpya, 138-39
Sāṁkhya, 6, 136
Sāndilya, 5, 174
Sāndilya-sūtra, 176
Śānta-bhakta, 140, 211
Śānta-rasa, 213-14
Sārṣṭi, 138-39
Sārūpya, 138-39
Sārvabhauma, 105

Sārvabhauma-nirukti, 25
Sāttvikas, Sāttvika-bhāva, 30, 200, 213
Sātvatas, 3
Sāttvika-purāṇa, 72
Sāyujya, 138-39
Scepticism, 63
Schrader, O., 5f
Science, 89
Scientific Romances, See Hinton
Seal, 2, 3f
Selections from the Literature of Theism, See Mansel
Sen, D.C., 25, 31f, 34, 57-59, 61
Sevā, 2, 199
Sevā-sukha, 199
Shastri, B.K.G., 2f, 3
Siddha-deha, 196
Siddha-loka, 109
Siddhānta-ratna, 81, 170
Śikṣāṣṭaka, 55, 190-91
Sirkār, M., 163, 182
Śiśupāla, 10, 195
Sītā, 11
Śiva, 13, 74
Skanda-purāna, 176
Smarana, 192
Smarana-sāmānya, 192
Sneha, 203; Ghṛta—, 203; Madhu—, 203
Spinozā, 151
Sraddhā, 201; —bhakti, 2-3
Sravana, 189
Śrī, 4, 95
Śrī-bhāṣya, 8, 164, 166
Śrīdhara, 103
Śrīdhara Svāmin, 47, 156
Srīman Mahāprabhūra Śikṣā 86f
Srīnivāsācarya, 33
Śrī-sampradāya, 7
Śrī Vallabhācārya, 31f
Śrīvāsa, 22-23, 40
Sṛṅgāra-rasa, 224
Śruti, 70
Śrutārthāpatti, 157
Stambha, 200
Sthāvara, 134
Sthāyi-bhāva, 211-12
Sthūla-śarīra, 134-35
Studies in Philosophy and Religion, See Maitra
Subāla-upaniṣad, 155
Sudarsana Pandit, 18
Śuddha-man, 105
Suddha-jīva, 173
Śuddha-sattva, 94, 114, 200
Sudeva, 215
Suffering, 135
Sugrīva, 5
Śuka, Śukadeva, 193, 222
Sukha, 199
Summum bonum, 199
Sunderānanda Vidyāvinod, 40, 42-43, 45, 216-17, 220, 226, 228
Sūkṣmā-ṭīkā, 39-40, 43
Śūnya-saṁhitā, 33
Śūnyavāda, 80
Svabhāva, 141
Svagata-bheda, 78, 91, 152, 164, 172
Svajātīya-bheda, 78, 91, 152, 164, 172
Svara-bhaṅga, 200
Svarūpa-Dāmodara, 20, 25, 28, 49, 61
Svarūpānanda, 119
Svarūpa-śakti, 96, 114, 118, 199-200
Svarūpa-śaktyānanda, 118
Svarūpānanda, 184
Svasaṁvedya-daśā, 205
Svayaṁ-dhāman, 108
Svayaṁ-rūpa, 101-2
Svārasikī-līlā, 116
Svābhavika-bhedābheda, 166-69
Svābhāvika-dāmpatya, 229-30
Svāṁśa, 103
Svāsabhūman, 201
Sveda, 200
Śvetadvīpa, 10-11
Śvetāśvatara-upaniṣad, 88, 154, 156
Svīyā, 222
Śyāmakuṇḍa, 30

Tadekātma-rūpa, 102-3
Tadguṇākhyāne-āsakti, 202
Tadvasati-sthāne-prītiḥ, 201
Tadīyatā, 203
Taittrīya-upaniṣad, 76, 117, 197
Tamas, 13
Tanmātrā, 144-45
Tanumoṭana, 201
Tapana Misra, 30
Taittirīya Āraṇyaka, 11
Taṭastha-bhakta, 215
Tatasthā-śakti, 96
Tatsaukhye 'pyārti-śaṅkayā khinnatva, 208
Tattva-muktāvali, 71
Tattva-saṁdarbha, 38, 54, 71-73

Tattva-vāda, 36f
Tamas, 143
Taylor, 161
Tāmasika-purāṇa, 72
Tenakalai, 28
Thakura Bhaktivinoda, 86f, 193
Theism, 70
Thibaut, 158, 159f
Tiruppana Ālvar, 6
Transcendence, 150-54
Trans-infinite numbers, 89
Tretā, 105
Trita, 10
Trivikrama, 103
Tukārāma, 26

Ubhaya-vedāntins, 7
Udātta-māna, 203
Uddhava, 110, 225
Uddīpana-vibhāva, 213
Udghūrṇā, 210
Ujjvala-nīla-maṇi, 23, 202-4, 224-27, 229
Upamā, 63
Upaniṣads, 2
Upapati, 226
Upādāna-kāraṇa, 158
Upādāna-māyā, 142-43
Upādhi, 151
Upākhyāna, 72
Upendra, 103

Vadkalai, 8
Vaibhava-prakāśa, 102
Vaidhī-bhakti, 111
Vaiduṣa-pratyakṣa, 65
Vainkata Bhatta, 58
Vaikuṇṭha, 105, 109
Vairāgya, 181; phalgu—, 182; Yukta—, 182
Vaiṣṇava-sampradāyas, 7
Vaiṣṇava Literature of Mediaeval Bengal, See Sen, D.C.
Vaiṣṇavism, early history of, 1-13; Guptan —, 6; Tamilian—, 6-7; Pre-Caitanya— in Bengal, 13-15; —and Hinduism, 99
Vaiṣṇavism, Śaivism and Minor Hindu Religions, See Bhandarkar
Vaivarṇya, 200
Validity, of knowledge, 65-70
Vallabha Ācārya, 20
Vallabhācārya, 7, 31, 41, 172-75
Varieties of Religious Experience, See James William
Varṇāśrama Dharma, 36, 136
Varāha, 103-4
Varuṇa, 1
Vāmana, 103-5
Vāsa-sajjāyitā, 210
Vāsudeva, 3-4, 94, 102, 110
Vāsudeva Sārvabhauma Bhattācārya, 19, 57
Vātsalya, 214, 217
Vāyu-purāṇa, 9
Veda, 71; *Vaiṣṇava*—, 6, 84
Veda-niṣṭha, 134
Veda-stuti-ṭīkā, 176
(*The*) *Vedanta, See* Ghate, V.S.
Vedānta Deśikā, 166
Vedāntakesarī, 162f
Vedānta-pārijāta-saurabha, 9, 168
Vedānta-ratna-manjūṣā, 166
Vedānta-siddhānta-muktāvali, 32
Vedārtha-saṁgraha, 7
(*The*) *Vedic index*, 11
Venkata Bhatta, 27
Veṇu, 125
Vibhatsa-rasa, 213
Vibhāva, 213
Vibhu, 84, 105, 108
Vidagdha-mādhava, 36f
Vidyā, 82, 134
Vidyāpati, 13
Vijātīya-bheda, 78, 91, 164, 172
Vijnāna, 85, —ghana, 83
Vikāra, 143
Vikṣepa, 143
Vilūṭhita, 201
Vilva-maṅgala, 27
Vilāsa, 103
Vipralambha, 215
Vipralambha-visphūrti, 205
Vipralipsā, 64
Virajā, 108
Virakti, 202
Vīrya, 95
Viṣaya, 143, 213
Viṣāda, 213
Viśeṣa, 12, 80, 170; Visesana, 164
Viśeṣya, 164
Viśiṣṭa, 165
Viśiṣṭādvaita, 6, 8, 163-66
Viṣṇu, 1-4, 12, 95, 103
Viṣṇupriyā, 17f, 20
Viṣṇu-purāṇa, 83-84, 95, 126, 132, 153-55

Viṣṇu-sahastranāma, 191
Viṣṇu-sūkta, 1
Viṣṇusvāmin, 7, 12, 42
Viśrambha, 204
Viśvaksena, 105
Viśvanātha Cakravartin, 38-39; on Parakīyā-bhāva, 228-30; on the excellence of bhakti, 177; on Siddha-deha, 197
Viśvarūpa, 16
Vitarka, 213
Vivarta-vāda, 145-48, 159
Vṛhad bhānu, 105
Vṛhad-vaiṣṇava-bandanā, 40
Vṛndāvana, 38, 108ff
Vṛndāvana Dāsa, 23, 49, 58-59, 74
Vṛtrāsura, 186
Vyabhicārī-bhāva, 213
Vyavahārika, 150
Vyāsa, 73, 106
Vyūha, 5, 12

Watt, T.M., 66
Weber, 10f

Yajna, 2, 105
Yama, 2, 177
Yamunācārya, 1
Yaśas, 95
Yaśodā, 88, 121
Yaśodnāandana, 127
Yādava-prakāśa, 7
Yāvadāśraya-vṛtti, 206
Yayāti, 188
Yoga, 6, 12, 92, 177-80
Yogamāyā, 127, 223
Yoga-pītha, 220
Yoga-rahasya, 7
Yudhiṣṭhira, 215
Yugāvatāra, 104, 127